# TO IMPROVE THE ACADEMY

# TO IMPROVE THE ACADEMY

*Resources for Faculty, Instructional, and Organizational Development*

Volume 32

James E. Groccia, Editor

Laura Cruz, Associate Editor

o

JB JOSSEY-BASS™

POD

Professional and Organizational Development
Network in Higher Education

*To Improve the Academy* is published annually by the Professional and Organizational Network in Higher Education (POD) through Jossey-Bass Publishers and is abstracted in ERIC documents and in Higher Education Abstracts.

## Ordering Information

The annual volume of *To Improve the Academy* is distributed to members at the POD conference in the autumn of each year. To order or obtain ordering information, please contact:

> John Wiley & Sons, Inc.
> Customer Care Center
> 10475 Crosspoint Blvd.
> Indianapolis, IN 46256
> Phone: 877-762-2974
> Fax: 800-597-3299
> E-mail: custserv@wiley.com
> Web: www.josseybass.com

## Permission to Copy

The contents of *To Improve the Academy* are copyrighted to protect the authors. Nevertheless, consistent with the networking and resource-sharing functions of POD, readers are encouraged to reproduce articles and cases from *To Improve the Academy* for educational use, as long as the source is identified.

## Instructions to Contributors for the Next Volume

Anyone interested in the issues related to instructional, faculty, and organizational development in higher education may submit manuscripts. Manuscripts are submitted to the current editor early in December of each year and selected through a double-blind peer review process.

Correspondence, including requests for information about guidelines and submission of manuscripts for Volume 33, should be directed to:

> Laura Cruz, PhD
> Director, Coulter Faculty Commons

Western Carolina University
Cullowhee, NC
Phone: 828-227-2093
Fax: 828-227-7340
E-mail: lcruz@wcu.edu

## Mission Statement

As revised and accepted by the POD Core Committee, April 2, 2004

### Statement of Purpose

The Professional and Organizational Development Network in Higher Education is an association of higher education professionals dedicated to enhancing teaching and learning by supporting educational developers and leaders in higher education.

### Mission Statement

The Professional and Organizational Development Network in Higher Education encourages the advocacy of the ongoing enhancement of teaching and learning through faculty and organizational development. To this end, it supports the work of educational developers and champions their importance to the academic enterprise.

### Vision Statement

During the twenty-first century, the Professional and Organizational Development Network in Higher Education will expand guidelines for educational development, build strong alliances with sister organizations, and encourage developer exchanges and research projects to improve teaching and learning.

### Values

The Professional and Organizational Development Network in Higher Education is committed to:

- Personal, faculty, instructional, and organizational development
- Humane and collaborative organizations and administrations

○ Diverse perspectives and a diverse membership

○ Supportive educational development networks on the local, regional, national, and international levels

○ Advocacy for improved teaching and learning in the academy through programs for faculty, administrators, and graduate students

○ The identification and collection of a strong and accessible body of research on development theories and practices

○ The establishment of guidelines for ethical practice

○ The increasingly useful and thorough assessment and evaluation of practice and research

## Programs, Publications, and Activities

The Professional and Organizational Development Network in Higher Education offers members and interested individuals the following benefits:

○ An annual membership conference designed to promote professional and personal growth, nurture innovation and change, stimulate important research projects, and enable participants to exchange ideas and broaden their professional network

○ An annual membership directory and networking guide

○ Publications in print and in electronic form

○ Access to the POD Web site and listserv

## Membership, Conference, and Programs Information

For information, please contact:

Hoag Holmgren, Executive Director
The POD Network
P.O. Box 3318
Nederland, CO 80466
Phone: 303-258-9521
Fax: 303-258-7377
E-mail: podoffice@podnetwork.org
Web: podnetwork.org

# CONTENTS

PART ONE

## New Paradigms for Faculty and Organizational Development

PART TWO

## Faculty Development Audience and Partners

PART SIX
## Enhancing Student Learning

PART SEVEN
## New Pedagogical Concepts

# ABOUT THE AUTHORS

## The Editors

*James E. Groccia* is director of the Biggio Center for the Enhancement of Teaching and Learning and professor of higher education in the Department of Educational Foundations, Leadership, and Technology at Auburn University. He was a Fulbright Scholar in the Institute for Educational Sciences at the University of Tartu in Estonia in 2011. In addition to faculty development work, he teaches graduate courses on teaching and higher education and coordinates the university's graduate certificate in college and university teaching. He is a former POD Network president and received his EdD in educational psychology and guidance from the University of Tennessee. He is the coauthor with Mary Stuart Hunter of *The First-Year Seminar: Designing, Implementing, and Assessing Courses to Support Student Learning And Success: Volume 2—Instructor Training and Development* (2012), and author of *The College Success Book: A Whole-Student Approach to Academic Excellence* (1992). He is coeditor with Mohammed Alsudairi and Bill Buskist of *The Handbook of College and University Teaching: A Global Perspective* (2012); with Bill Buskist of *Evidence-Based Teaching* (2011); with Judy Miller of *On Becoming a Productive University: Strategies for Reducing Costs and Increasing Quality in Higher Education* (2005); *Student Assisted Teaching: A Guide to Faculty-Student Teamwork* (2001); and *Enhancing Productivity: Administrative, Instructional, and Technological Strategies* (1998). He may be reached at groccje@auburn.edu.

o

*Laura Cruz* is associate professor of history and director of the Coulter Faculty Commons at Western Carolina University, a large and productive teaching and learning center that won a national award in 2010 from *Campus Technologies* magazine. In addition to publications in her discipline (European history), she is the author of articles on faculty development, educational technology, history pedagogy, graduate student development, peer review, and (especially) the Boyer model of scholar-ship. She currently serves as editor-in-chief of *MountainRise*, the inter-national journal of the scholarship of teaching and learning. She has won multiple teaching and engagement awards and is the principal organizer of an annual nationwide retreat on the Boyer model of scholarship. She regularly participates in professional organizations including POD, Southern Regional Faculty and Instructional Development, International Scholarship of Teaching and Learning, and those related to her discipline of history. She is frequently invited to present, provide workshops and invited sessions, and consult on the topics of SOTL, the Boyer model of scholarship, and faculty center organizational models. She may be reached at lcruz@email.wcu.edu.

## The Contributors

*Praise Agu,* a Posse Scholar alumna, graduated from Bryn Mawr College in 2012. She majored in economics, was an active member of Bryn Mawr's African and Caribbean Students' Organization and the Student Finance Committee, and served as a mentor and tutor for elementary school students in Philadelphia. Between her sophomore and senior years, she worked through the Andrew W. Mellon Teaching and Learning Institute at Bryn Mawr College as a student consultant with a range of faculty members across disciplines to develop, teach, and assess their courses. She may be reached at praise.agu@gmail.com.

---------- o ----------

*Terre H. Allen* is professor of communication studies and director of the Faculty Center for Professional Development at California State Univer-sity, Long Beach. Her PhD is in interpersonal communication and cogni-tive psychology, and her research includes theoretical and applied work in communication in higher education. She has received several research awards from the National Communication Association, where she has served as a member of the assessment council, general education advisory board, and several journal editorial boards. She has published numerous articles and book chapters on group communication, communication in instruction, interpersonal communication, instructional technology, and faculty development. Her current research is on STEM-specific culturally responsive pedagogy. In addition, she has facilitated meetings and retreats for more than one hundred groups in business, nonprofit, and higher education. She is codeveloper and coauthor of USAFunds Life Skills, a twenty-four-book series on student success and student finance management. She may be reached at Terre.Allen@csulb.edu.

————— o —————

*Roger G. Baldwin* is a professor of higher, adult, and lifelong education at Michigan State University (MSU). His scholarship focuses on academic career issues, faculty professional development, and changing conditions in the academic workplace. His research with colleagues from MSU on midcareer faculty won the Robert J. Menges Award at the 2007 POD conference. Currently he is studying senior professors in a research university context, focusing on their challenges, contributions, and professional development needs. He may be reached at rbaldwin@msu.edu.

————— o —————

*Kathleen M. Brennan* is associate professor of sociology (PhD, Kent State University) at Western Carolina University. Her research focuses on the sociological study of stress processes and mental health. She is studying college student perceptions and experience of mental illness, as well as how the university context may advance the educational experiences of students with mental illness. She has served in administrative positions and been selected for various teaching and engagement awards. She may be reached at kbrennan@wcu.edu.

————— o —————

*Warren E. Christian* is a PhD candidate in the School of Education at the University of North Carolina at Chapel Hill. He teaches in the Preparing International Teaching Assistants Program. He has worked with Latina/o and Burmese employees, international graduate students, and visiting scholars who wish to improve their English and has taught English in Japan and Saudi Arabia. He currently researches the relationships between international teaching assistants and undergraduates in the United States. He may be reached at wechrist@unc.edu.

————— o —————

*Margaret W. Cohen*, PhD, is associate provost for professional development and founding director of the Center for Teaching and Learning, University of Missouri–St. Louis, where she supports the professional success of faculty, graduate assistants, peer tutors, and academic leaders. Her faculty appointment in the Department of Educational Psychology, Research and Evaluation includes teaching a campuswide doctoral seminar, Teaching for Learning in the University. She is a coauthor of *The Course Syllabus: A Learning Centered Approach* (2008). She may be reached at Peggy_Cohen@umsl.edu.

○

*Bob Cole* is the director of the Digital Learning Commons at the Monterey Institute of International Studies in Monterey, California. He has taught English as a second language and trained language teachers to integrate technology. His professional work explores the intersections of emerging technologies, constructivist pedagogy, educational and organizational innovation, and reflective practices. He may be reached at bob.cole@miis.edu.

○

*Alison Cook-Sather* is professor of education and coordinator of the Andrew W. Mellon Teaching and Learning Institute at Bryn Mawr College. She has developed internationally recognized programs that position students as pedagogical consultants to prospective secondary teachers and to practicing college faculty members and has published over sixty articles and book chapters and four books on this work. *Engaging Students as Partners in Teaching and Learning: A Guide for Faculty*, coauthored with Catherine Bovill and Peter Felten, is forthcoming from Jossey-Bass. She may be reached at acooksat@brynmawr.edu.

○

*Mary E. Dankoski,* PhD, is associate dean for faculty affairs and professional development at Indiana University School of Medicine, where she also serves as vice chair for faculty and academic affairs in the Department of Family Medicine and associate professor and Lester D. Bibler Scholar in family medicine. Her scholarly interests include the advancement of women faculty, the study of faculty vitality in the health professions, and the policies that shape faculty life. She may be reached at mdankosk@iupui.edu.

○

*Patricia Marten DiBartolo* is a professor and chair of psychology at Smith College. She teaches courses in child clinical psychology, advanced research methods, and child and adolescent anxiety disorders. Her research investigates the phenomenology of perfectionism and its clinical and learning correlates in both adult and youth samples. Recently her writing has focused on teaching and learning in psychology. She may be reached at pdibarto@smith.edu.

○

*Carolyn L. Dufault* is assistant director of the Teaching Center and lecturer in the Department of Psychology at Washington University in St. Louis. Her work is focused on developing and delivering professional development programs to graduate students and postdoctoral fellows. These programs include workshops on effective teaching, as well as mentoring on the design of educational research projects. She teaches experimental psychology and coteaches Introduction to Teaching as Research. She may be reached at cdufault@wustl.edu.

○

*Glenn W. Ellis* is a professor of engineering at Smith College who teaches courses in engineering science and STEM education. His research focuses on developing idea-centered learning environments in the field of engineering that engage learners' imaginations and help them develop a proficiency in working innovatively with knowledge. In particular, his work is now centered on middle school informal educational settings and undergraduate engineering education. He may be reached at gellis@smith.edu.

○

*Bret Eynon,* a historian and associate dean for academic affairs at LaGuardia Community College (CUNY), oversees LaGuardia's Center for Teaching and Learning and the Making Connections National Resource Center. An AAC&U senior faculty member, he co-led the Visible Knowledge Project (with Randy Bass), a scholarship of teaching project that produced *The Difference That Inquiry Makes: A Collaborative Case Study on Technology and Learning.* Widely published, he was named 2011 Distinguished Humanities Educator of the Year by the Community College Humanities Association. He may be reached at beynon@lagcc.cuny.edu.

○

*Peter Felten* is assistant provost, executive director of the Center for the Advancement of Teaching and Learning, director of the Center for Engaged Learning, and associate professor of history at Elon University.

His research interests and recent publications focus on faculty peer mentoring and student-faculty partnerships in teaching and learning. He may be reached at pfelten@elon.edu.

○

*Beth A. Fisher* is director of academic services at the Teaching Center and lecturer in the women, gender, and sexuality studies program at Washington University in St. Louis. Her work focuses on training and mentoring graduate students in their teaching and on collaborating with faculty to develop effective teaching methods, especially those involved in the teaching of writing. She teaches courses in American literature and gender studies. She may be reached at bfisher@wustl.edu.

○

*Regina F. Frey* is the Florence E. Moog professor of STEM education in the Department of Chemistry, executive director of the Teaching Center, and codirector of the Center for Integrative Research in Cognition, Learning, and Education at Washington University in St. Louis. Her courses include General Chemistry, Women in Science, and Introduction to Teaching as Research. She conducts research on active learning approaches in STEM and works with faculty across the disciplines on developing effective teaching. She may be reached at gfrey@wustl.edu.

○

*Laura M. Gambino* is a founding faculty member of the New Community College (NCC) at City University of New York, which opened in August 2012. As the assessment and e-portfolio leader for NCC, she is responsible for implementing e-portfolio pedagogy throughout the curricular and cocurricular areas of the college, as well as developing, implementing, and evaluating NCC's assessment plan. She also serves as the research coordinator for LaGuardia's Connect to Learning project. She may be reached at laura. gambino@ncc.cuny.edu.

○

*Holly Harbinger* has served as associate vice president for faculty affairs at California State University, Long Beach (CSULB), since March 2008. Prior to that, she was associate dean of the College of the Arts at CSULB, as well as the director of graduate studies and a tenured professor in the

Theatre Arts Department. She received a BA in English from the University of California, Santa Cruz, and an MFA in dance from New York University, Tisch School of the Arts. She has been a performer, choreographer, and fight master in theater, dance, and opera companies in New York and throughout the rest of the United States and Europe. She was a contributing author of a textbook on university actor training, a conference presenter on applications of Laban movement analysis for actor training programs, and a specialist in historical dance and movement. She may be reached at holly.harbinger@csulb.edu.

———— o ————

*Krista Hoffmann-Longtin* is the program and evaluation director in the Indiana University School of Medicine Office of Faculty Affairs and Professional Development, where she develops programs, policies, and research to increase the awareness and effectiveness of faculty. Since 2002, she has served as an associate faculty member in the IUPUI Department of Communication Studies. She is a doctoral candidate in education leadership at IU. Her research interests include organizational change and teaching and learning. She may be reached at klongtin@iu.edu.

———— o ————

*Freya B. Kinner* is an instructional developer (MA in educational psychological studies, University of Colorado at Boulder) in the Coulter Faculty Commons at Western Carolina University. Her research interests include best practices in instructional development and evaluation and assessment strategies for classes and programs in higher education. She may be reached at fkinner@wcu.edu.

———— o ————

*Suzanna Klaf* is the associate director of the Center for Academic Excellence at Fairfield University in Fairfield, Connecticut. She received her BA and MA from Binghamton University and her PhD from Ohio State University. Though trained in the social sciences, she considers herself a generalist. She brings her interdisciplinary interests and eleven years of teaching experience to her faculty development work on course design, active learning strategies, integrative teaching and learning, and assessment of student learning. She may be reached at sklaf@fairfield.edu.

———— o ————

*Murali Krishnamurthi* is professor of industrial and systems engineering and director of the Faculty Development and Instructional Design Center at Northern Illinois University. Along with teaching and pursuing research in database systems and project management in the Department of Industrial and Systems Engineering, he is responsible for planning, budgeting, reporting, and managing personnel at the center. He may be reached at mkrishna@niu.edu.

○

*Sally Kuhlenschmidt* has been director of the Faculty Center for Excellence in Teaching at Western Kentucky University since 1994. She received her PhD in clinical psychology from Purdue University. Her current research interests include assessment of faculty development and using technology to enhance development. She may be reached at sally .kuhlenschmidt@wky.edu.

○

*Thomas F. Nelson Laird*, PhD, is an associate professor of higher education at Indiana University, Bloomington, where he manages the Center for Postsecondary Research's Faculty Survey of Student Engagement. His work focuses on improving collegiate teaching and learning, particularly the design, delivery, and effects of student experiences with diversity. He may be reached at tflaird@indiana.edu.

○

*Paula Kay Lazrus* is assistant professor in the Institute for Core Studies at St. John's University. She has been using the Reacting to the Past pedagogy since 2002 and has been an active member of the Reacting community since then. In order to introduce fellow faculty to Reacting, she has run several on-campus workshops and is currently developing two new game ideas for the Reacting community. She may be reached at lazrusp@stjohns.edu.

○

*Kathryn E. Linder* is the director of the Center for Teaching Excellence at Suffolk University in Boston. She received her PhD from Ohio State University. Her research interests include cultural studies of education, academic writing development, and faculty development. Some of her recent articles may be found in *Discourse: Studies in the Cultural Politics of Education* and the *Journal on Centers for Teaching and Learning*. She may be reached at klinder@suffolk.edu.

○

*Deandra Little* is associate director and an associate professor in the Teaching Resource Center at the University of Virginia, where she also teaches nineteenth- and twentieth-century US literature. Her research interests and publications focus on teaching consultation techniques, navigating the middle ground of educational development work, graduate student professional development, student and faculty writing, and teaching with images across the curriculum. She may be reached at dlittle@virginia.edu.

○

*Gail M. McGuire* is associate professor of sociology at Indiana University South Bend. She teaches courses in research methods, statistics, and gender. Her research focuses on race and gender stratification in the workplace, but she has also has published on faculty mentoring and undergraduate research. She may be reached at gmcguire@iusb.edu.

○

*Gretchen Kreahling McKay* is associate professor of art history and chair of her department at McDaniel College. Since being introduced to Reacting to the Past in 2006, she has helped many faculty adopt it at her institution as director for the Center of Faculty Excellence. She is also a member of the Reacting Consortium board. In addition to using games in many of her classes, she has two games of her own in development on late-nineteenth-century French art and Byzantine iconoclasm. She may be reached at gmckay@mcdaniel.edu.

○

*Gwendolyn Mettetal* is professor of education and of psychology at Indiana University South Bend, where she was the founding director of the University Center for Excellence in Teaching. She teaches courses in developmental psychology, educational psychology, and research methods. Her research focuses on faculty development for K–12 and higher education teachers through action research, mentoring, and leadership development. She may be reached at gmetteta@iusb.edu.

○

*Linda B. Nilson* is founding director of the Office of Teaching Effectiveness and Innovation at Clemson University and a previous editor of *To Improve the Academy* (volumes 25–28). She is also the author of *Teaching at Its Best*, now in its third edition (2010); *The Graphic Syllabus and the Outcomes Map: Communicating Your Course* (2007); and *Creating Self-Regulated Learners: Strategies to Strengthen Students' Self-Awareness and Learning Skills* (2013). She gives keynotes and workshops at conferences, colleges, and universities nationally and internationally. She may be reached at nilson@clemson.edu.

———— o ————

*Leslie Ortquist-Ahrens* is director of the Center for Transformative Learning, associate professor of Comparative Literature at Berea College, and president-elect of POD. Her areas of interest include collaborative learning, programming for new faculty members, professional learning communities, and organizational development for supporting change at small colleges and universities. She may be reached at leslie_ortquist -ahrens@berea.edu.

———— o ————

*Megan M. Palmer*, PhD, is an assistant dean for faculty affairs and professional development at Indiana University School of Medicine, where she also serves as vice chair for education and assistant professor in the Department of Emergency Medicine. Her scholarly interests include the study of faculty vitality, college teaching and learning, and faculty development. She may be reached at mmpalmer@iu.edu.

———— o ————

*Michael S. Palmer* is associate professor and associate director of the University of Virginia's Teaching Resource Center and teaches in the Chemistry Department. His educational development research centers on teaching consultation techniques and graduate student professional development. He was the 2011 POD conference cochair, is a current POD Core Committee member (2013–2016), and has served on the core faculty of the New Faculty Developers Institute since 2009. He may be reached at mpalmer@virginia.edu.

———— o ————

*Donald J. Para* is provost and senior vice president for academic affairs at California State University, Long Beach (CSULB), responsible for undergraduate and graduate education, research and creative activity, international education, service-learning, community engagement, service to the profession, and faculty and academic staff development. He served as dean and associate dean of the College of the Arts and twelve years as chair of the Department of Music at CSULB. He received a BM in music education and an MM in music composition from Western Michigan University, and his PhD in music composition from Michigan State University. He has presented papers and given presentations at numerous meetings of arts education organizations and music theory conferences. He served the National Association of Schools of Music as chair of Region One from 1994 to 1997. He may be reached at Donald.Para@csulb.edu.

o

*Gail A. Rathbun* is director of the Center for the Enhancement of Learning and Teaching at the jointly run regional campus of Indiana University and Purdue University in Fort Wayne, Indiana. She received her PhD in instructional systems technology from Indiana University. Her interests include design consulting, the application of activity theory to the workplace of higher education, and the assessment of academic development programs. She may be reached at rathbun@ipfw.edu.

o

*Michael Reder* is the director of the Joy Shechtman Mankoff Faculty Center for Teaching and Learning at Connecticut College, where he teaches contemporary literature and culture. Among his areas of interest are creating cultures of evidence-informed decision making to improve teaching and learning and the creation of faculty teaching and learning programs at small colleges. He also is a Senior Teagle Scholar working with the Wabash National Study of Liberal Arts Education. He may be reached at reder@conncoll.edu.

o

*Michelle D. Repice* is research and communication specialist at the Teaching Center and the Center for Integrative Research in Cognition, Learning, and Education at Washington University in St. Louis. She collaborates on educational research, develops the Teaching Center's database, and serves as the communications expert for both centers. She teaches courses in American history and American culture studies. She may be reached at mdrepice@wustl.edu.

o

*Jason Rhode* is assistant director of Faculty Development and Instructional Design Center at Northern Illinois University. He is responsible for overseeing the development and delivery of training programs and support on teaching with technology and related topics, providing leadership on technology-related issues, and performing supervisory functions at the center. He may be reached at jrhode@niu.edu.

○

*Amy K. Ribera,* PhD, is an assistant research scientist for the Center for Postsecondary Research at Indiana University, Bloomington. Her primary role at the center is to provide analytical support for the National Survey of Student Engagement and other related survey projects. Her research focuses on student engagement in higher education, deep approaches to learning, first-generation college students, faculty teaching practices, and faculty vitality in academic medicine. She may be reached at agarver@indiana.edu.

○

*Tony Ribera*, PhD, is the director of program evaluation in the Office of Undergraduate Medical Education at the Indiana University School of Medicine. His current research interests focus on faculty and student affairs practitioner engagement in the scholarship of teaching and learning and satisficing in the course and instructor evaluation process. He earned his PhD in higher education and student affairs from Indiana University. He may be reached at aribera@iu.edu.

○

*Al Rudnitsky* is professor of education and child study at Smith College. He teaches courses in the learning sciences and the design of learning environments. His research focuses on the creation of learning environments that support student understanding. His current work is aimed at understanding factors that create high-quality group discourse. His recent publications include "What Happens When a College Teacher Meets the Learning Sciences," *International Journal of University Teaching and Faculty Development* (with P. DiBartolo) and "Applying Knowledge Building in an Engineering Class: A Pilot Study," *International Journal of Engineering Education* (with G. W. Ellis, M. A. Moriarty, and B. Mikic). He may be reached at arudnits@smith.edu.

○

*Jennifer L. Russell* is senior lead faculty developer at the Academy of Art University in San Francisco, California. She has taught in language and literacy programs at the University of California, Berkeley, Johannes Gutenberg-Universität Mainz, Mills College, and Concordia Language Villages. She holds an MA in TESOL from the Monterey Institute of International Studies. Current research interests include visual thinking skills, rubrics, the teaching of creativity, and contemplative pedagogy. She may be reached at jrussell@academyart.edu.

------------o------------

*Brian J. Rybarczyk* is the director of academic and professional development in the Graduate School at the University of North Carolina at Chapel Hill. He serves as the director of the Preparing International Teaching Assistants Program. He works with graduate students and postdoctoral scholars to develop professional skills necessary for a wide range of career outcomes; provides workshops on teaching, learning, and professional development; and is involved in assessing academic and professional support programs. He may be reached at brybar@unc.edu.

------------o------------

*David Sacks* has been a faculty/instructional consultant with the Center for the Enhancement of Teaching and Learning at the University of Kentucky since 2008. He received his PhD in educational studies from the University of Cincinnati emphasizing educational psychology. His current research interests include faculty development with instructional technology and best practices for assessing faculty instructional practices. He may be reached at David.Sacks@uky.edu.

------------o------------

*Peter A. Shaw* has taught English, French, and Spanish and trained language teachers around the world. He is professor of pedagogical magic in the Graduate School of Translation, Interpretation, and Language Education at the Monterey Institute of International Studies in Monterey California. His interest in learner-centered pedagogy and faculty development complements his academic and professional work in learning, instruction, and curriculum in language education. He may be reached at pshaw@miis.edu.

------------o------------

*Kevin M. Shea* is an associate professor of chemistry and director of the Sherrerd Center for Teaching and Learning at Smith College. He teaches courses in introductory and advanced organic chemistry. His research focuses on using the tools of synthetic organic chemistry to make new molecules, developing new advanced laboratory experiments, and investigating the history of organic chemistry. His recent results have been published in the *Journal of Organic Chemistry*, *Journal of Chemical Education*, and *Accounts of Chemical Research*. He may be reached at kshea@smith.edu.

○

*Marcia M. Tennill*, PhD, is an adjunct instructor for the Department of Educational Psychology, Research and Evaluation where she teaches a course on the psychology of learning. She is also a team member of the Partnership for Evaluation, Assessment, and Research at the University of Missouri–St. Louis, where she is facilitating the qualitative component of a program evaluation. Her professional interests are educational program evaluation and research. She may be reached at tennillm@umsl.edu.

○

*Judit Török* is the codirector of LaGuardia Community College's Making Connections National Resource Center, working with its Connect to Learning and the Making Transfer Connections projects; and she leads multidisciplinary faculty development for LaGuardia's Center for Teaching and Learning. She teaches courses in ethics and critical thinking; edited and published the Project Quantum Leap Sampler, a basic skills math curriculum resource; and has presented on professional development at international conferences. She may be reached at jtorok@lagcc.cuny.edu.

○

*Michael H. Truong* is executive director of the Office of Innovative Teaching and Technology in the Center for Teaching, Learning, and Assessment (CTLA) at Azusa Pacific University (APU) in Southern California. He provides leadership and direction for APU in the areas of online learning, instructional technology, and faculty engagement. The aim of his office is to engage, enable, and encourage faculty, departments, and schools to explore and employ innovative pedagogy and appropriate technology to transform teaching and learning at the university. He can be reached at mtruong@apu.edu.

○

*Kevin Yee* is director of the Academy of Teaching and Learning Excellence at the University of South Florida. His interests are widespread and include collecting interactive techniques and testing the tidal wave of online apps and programs that might be useful in the classroom. He publishes primarily on new technology tools for teaching, and his interest in gamification is a natural continuation of his one-time career in the video game industry. He may be reached at kyee@usf.edu.

○

*Michael J. Zeig* is a graduate research assistant at Michigan State University in the higher, adult, and lifelong education doctoral program. He was previously employed in the Michigan Governor's Office, where he worked with university trustee appointments and represented the governor on the State Board of Education. He has publications on how to support late-career and retired faculty and has also conducted research on the roles and responsibilities of university trustees. He may be reached at zeigmich@msu.edu.

# PREFACE

*To Improve the Academy: Resources for Faculty, Instructional, and Organizational Development (TIA) Volume 32* contains twenty-one contributions on a variety of topics from authors across an array of institutions. We have organized the chapters in this volume into seven parts based on our subjective reading of the topics and issues described after the chapters were accepted. As in the past, this organization provides some structure to assist understanding and application of the content presented. We have tried to fit part titles to chapter content so as not to constrain author creativity by forcing them to fit our predetermined structure. We hope that in this way, *TIA* reflects the richness of this work and captures the variety of levels at which we as developers have impact: developing new paradigms for faculty and organizational development, tailoring faculty development for different audiences and partners, refining faculty development programs for maximal impact, reflecting on and advancing what we do, responding to diverse graduate teaching assistant needs, assisting student learning, and advancing new pedagogical concepts.

## Part 1: New Paradigms for Faculty and Organizational Development

Chapter 1, by Terre H. Allen, Holly Harbinger, and Donald Para, posits that socialization and satisfaction are critical to retaining quality teacher/scholars and key to a well-functioning teaching-intensive, research-driven university. They report on a year-long research project aimed at investigating faculty work life and satisfaction at a large, urban, comprehensive state university to understand and support faculty work under "new normal" conditions characterized by reduced state funding and increased faculty workload. They propose a revitalized direction for faculty and explore directions for organizational development within the context of the new normal.

Gail A. Rathbun, Sally Kuhlenschmidt, and David Sacks in chapter 2 discuss an emerging role that faculty developers play in mediating differences between the seemingly exclusive cultures that university technologists and university teachers inhabit. Situated within a conflict theory perspective, activity theory embraces workplace conflict as normal and as contributing to organization health and adaptation, in contrast to a functionalist approach, which focuses on how to maintain system equilibrium.

In chapter 3, Beth Fisher, Carolyn Dufault, Michelle Repice, and Regina Frey discuss the crucial role that teaching and learning centers play in helping faculty learn about and apply research on learning. The approach they develop integrates discussion of recent research with specific recommendations for teaching modifications that can be adapted for different disciplines and courses. Preliminary evaluation suggests that this approach is fostering a growth mind-set about teaching—transforming faculty into scholars of teaching and learning and developing a collaborative, innovative culture that integrates research on teaching and learning with the practice of teaching.

## Part 2: Faculty Development Audience and Partners

In chapter 4, Gwendolyn Mettetal and Gail McGuire discuss a case study analyzing interviews with faculty and administrators to understand the formal and informal types of support that pretenure faculty use to gain tenure. By understanding the different types of support that pretenure faculty need, institutions can better address the diverse issues that junior faculty confront when preparing for tenure and can ensure that all candidates receive some type of support. They conclude that institutions need to be intentional about offering both formal and informal support to pretenure faculty at various points in their careers.

Michael J. Zeig and Roger Baldwin in chapter 5 discuss efforts to respond to the sharp increase in senior faculty. Historically faculty development programs have focused on early-career faculty, with less attention paid to more seasoned professors. Based on a national web-based investigation, this chapter reviews strategies some institutions have implemented to support senior faculty. It also provides recommendations for how senior faculty and their administrator colleagues can provide new meaning and purpose to this phase of academic life.

In chapter 6, Megan Palmer, Krista Hoffmann-Longtin, Amy Ribera, Tony Ribera, Tom Nelson Laird, and Mary Dankoski explore the level of faculty vitality in academic medicine and report on the results of a multi-institutional study where faculty were surveyed about climate and leadership, career and life management, satisfaction, engagement, productivity, and involvement in faculty development. Analysis reveals that, controlling for other factors, academic medicine faculty who participate regularly in faculty development activities are significantly more satisfied, engaged, and productive.

## Part 3: Faculty Development Programs

In chapter 7, Bret Eynon, Laura Gambino, and Judit Török discuss how the Connect to Learning project, an innovative hybrid professional development model using e-portfolios, online conversations, and face-to-face meetings, has strengthened e-portfolio initiatives on twenty-five diverse campuses nationwide. The model adapts a conceptual framework of inquiry, reflection, and integration to a hybrid context and addresses the challenge of developing local professional development leadership for classroom and institutional change.

In chapter 8, Al Rudnitsky, Glenn Ellis, Patricia Marten DiBartolo, and Kevin Shea describe a multiyear professional development effort undertaken by a learning and teaching center at a liberal arts college. Now in its fourth year, the seminar has had a significant impact on faculty participants and their thinking about teaching and learning. Moreover, the seminar has seeded a number of teaching and assessment initiatives at the college.

Marcia Tennill and Margaret Cohen in chapter 9 explore the long-term impact of a year-long faculty development program. Three guiding questions focused the study: In what ways did the program influence the professional lives of participants five years after completion? How did the participants integrate those experiences into their professional lives? and What recommendations for best practices in the field of faculty development can be drawn? Donald Kirkpatrick's four-level evaluation model was the template for this qualitative research. Results indicated that participants retained program learning over time.

## Part 4: Reflections on What We Do

In chapter 10, Kathryn Linder and Suzanna Klaf offer a retrospective view of our field through a timely analysis of the content published in *TIA* and editorial and authorship trends for the previous three decades. Frequency distributions identify the most published authors, their institutional affiliations, the most written-about topics, and patterns of collaborative authorship in volumes 1 (1982) through 30 (2011), while findings from a citation analysis of ten years of *TIA* (volumes 21–30) highlight trends in resources cited and types of resources.

Peter Felten, Deandra Little, Leslie Ortquist-Ahrens, and Michael Reder in chapter 11 discuss a heuristic to prompt quick yet generative examination of faculty development goals or programs in relationship to three key characteristics of effective educational development on three different institutional levels. They also describe uses and applications of the tool and reflective process, which allow developers to efficiently gain insight into their work and effectively frame priorities for planning and improvement.

While workshops and seminars are effective venues for introducing new pedagogical approaches or emerging technologies, faculty often have unique questions within specialized contexts that cannot be fully addressed in a large group setting. In such instances, a more personalized and customized level of support is needed. In chapter 12, Jason Rhode and Murali Krishnamurthi describe a database system for tracking and improving the effectiveness of such individual consultation services.

## Part 5: Graduate Teaching Assistants: Innovative Approaches

In chapter 13, Kathleen M. Brennan, Laura Cruz, and Freya Kinner assess graduate assistant competency in key skills that employers in and outside of academia value and examine whether these skills are developed in the context of the graduate assistantship at a specific state comprehensive university (SCU). Based on their findings, suggestions for addressing identified gaps in graduate teaching assistant training to facilitate graduate assistant development at SCUs are presented.

Warren Christian and Brian Rybarczyk in chapter 14 describe how undergraduates may be used in the training of international teaching assistants (ITAs) as conversation partners, classroom consultants, and guest instructors. Increasing contact between undergraduates and international graduate students before they meet in the classroom as, respectively, students and instructors can benefit each group. The authors also describe the roles that undergraduates may perform in training ITAs, explicate the benefits to both ITAs and undergraduates, and provide a list of best practices for including undergraduates in ITA training.

In chapter 15, Michael Palmer and Deandra Little describe the key elements of the University of Virginia's Tomorrow's Professor Today program and ongoing assessment efforts. Pre- and postprogram participant surveys from the first eight years show that this program is improving perceptions of preparedness in twenty-one competencies tracked; follow-up studies support long-term impact.

## Part 6: Enhancing Student Learning

Alison Cook-Sather and Praise Agu in chapter 16 describe a program, Students as Learners and Teachers, that developed academic and social spaces where deficit notions of people of color can be challenged and where a positive collegiate racial climate can be established and maintained for students and the faculty members with whom they work. The authors found that the students and their faculty partners used program counterspaces to explore links between their lived identities and pedagogical commitments and to share authority and responsibility in developing culturally sustaining pedagogy. In addition, the authors report on participants' experiences in these collaborations and how they legitimate the knowledge of students of color in faculty learning.

In chapter 17, Linda Nilson follows up on her previous *TIA* work that called into question the validity of student ratings as proxy measures for student learning and teaching effectiveness. She argues that because the overriding assessment criterion in accreditation and accountability is student learning, it makes sense to evaluate faculty by the same standard. This chapter explains and evaluates course-level measures of student learning based on data that are easy for faculty to collect and for administrators to use.

Michael Truong in chapter 18 provides guidance on how teaching and learning centers can help faculty and students acquire greater familiarity and fluency with just-in-time learning through mobile apps by creating informal, inviting, and informative learning spaces on their campuses. This chapter discusses the Mobile App Learning Lounge (MALL), a low-cost, high-impact initiative of a Center for Teaching and Learning at a California research university. Beyond sharing how MALL works, he offers practical suggestions and strategies for replicating a similar initiative at other institutions.

## Part 7: New Pedagogical Concepts

In chapter 19, Peter Shaw, Jennifer Russell, and Bob Cole propose a framework for "Slow learning and teaching" to address change in higher education, porous work/life boundaries, rapid developments in technology, and concerns about sustainability and to question assumptions and move beyond tips and tricks to more fundamental issues in curriculum and pedagogy.

Kevin Yee in chapter 20 describes how the principles of "gamification" can be applied to teaching and learning in online as well as face-to-face classes, resulting in educational experiences that have the best of both worlds: a game-based overlay without becoming too technical. Yee explains the concepts involved in successful games and provides ideas for translating those principles into practice in the classroom (or online) environment.

In chapter 21, Paula Kay Lazrus and Gretchen Kreahling McKay investigate the value of the Reacting to the Past pedagogy with regard to engaging first-year students. In recent years, calls to improve student engagement and active learning techniques have grown, and few others have been as successful in producing the desired results as Reacting to the Past. This chapter investigates why it is so successful in meeting the goals of high-impact practices that increase student engagement and learning. The authors also examine how the Reacting pedagogy and first-year seminars encourage problem solving, critical thinking, and writing among students.

———————— ○ ————————

*TIA* continues to be a primary source for faculty development professionals to disseminate their expertise, best practice, and research in the continuing effort to enhance teaching, learning, and the effectiveness of higher education. The true "spirit of POD" is reflected in the peer review process used to select the chapters in this book, as well as the willingness of our colleagues to share their wisdom with others. We hope this book serves as a handy and helpful resource in your efforts to give our practice more impact and make teaching and learning more effective.

POD, through its Core and Publication Committees and the *TIA* editorial team, strives to recognize and disseminate the scholarship of our interconnected field of faculty, academic, and organizational development. For the first thirty-two years of our organization's history, *TIA* and the *POD Quarterly*, its brief predecessor, have been the media through which this has been communicated. Publication of one's thoughts, words, and work in this peer-reviewed book is recognition both of one's past accomplishments and, more important, of one's future impact in shaping our field. However, heeding the words of the sage and seer of human behavior, Bob Dylan, "he who is not busy being born, is busy dying," POD continues to investigate new opportunities to share our work to maximize accessibility and impact. While the future of *TIA* is bright, its format may undergo revisions reflecting new communication channels and developing media conventions. Stay tuned!

# ACKNOWLEDGMENTS

*To Improve the Academy* would not be possible without the dedication and enthusiasm of myriad members of the higher education community whose work it reflects and advances. We received forty-eight manuscripts, all of them with significant merit, and our reviewers were indispensable in helping us make some very hard choices. As a result of a double-blind peer review process, the editorial team selected twenty-one manuscripts for publication. Each manuscript received, on average, four reviews from a total of 102 reviewers. Many experienced reviewers from *To Improve the Academy, Vol. 31* signed on again for this volume, as did many people who had also submitted manuscripts, and many new colleagues volunteered to join us. In the "spirit of POD," the reviews we received were timely, thorough, thoughtful, and constructive and reflected the diversity of perspectives that is one of the many strengths of our organization.

Those reviewers who worked so diligently to bring you the best possible *To Improve the Academy, Vol. 32* are Karen Adsit, Pamela Arrington, Isis Artze-Vega, Kola Babarinde, Dorothe Bach, Donna Bailey, Julianna Banks, Pamela Barnett, Gabriele Bauer, Danilo Baylen, Helen Bergland, Victoria Bhavsar, Phyllis Blumberg, Kate Brinko, Neal Bryan, Susanna Calkins, Rosemary Capps, Shiladitya Chaudhury, Chris Clark, Jeanette Clausen, Eli Collins-Brown, Kathryn Cunningham, Bonnie Daniel, Michele DiPietro, Rebecca Dueben, Angeles L. Eames, Sally Ebest, Phillip Edwards, Alev Elci, Elizabeth Evans, Joshua Eyler, Raichle Farrelly, Nancy Fire, Beth Fisher, Danielle (Danny) Fontaine, Brenda Frieden, Christopher Garrett, Judy Grace, Brian Greenwood, Kevin R. Guidry, Nira Hativa, Aeron Haynie, Jason Hendryx, Jennifer Herman, Sue Hines, Katherine Hoffman, Matthew Holley, Lily Hsu, Carol Hurney, Lisa Ijiri, Wayne Jacobson, David Jewell, Kathleen Kane, Wendi M. Kappers, Bruce Kelley, Susan Kleine, Bruce Larson, Jean Layne, Virginia Lee, Donna Gardner Liljegren, Kathryn Linder, Deandra Little, Debra Rudder Lohe, Jean Mandernach, Jean Martin-Williams, Christopher Mayer, Leslie McBride, Jeanette McDonald, Lillian McEnery, Sal Meyers, Joan Middendorf, Cheryl Miller, Linda B. Nilson, Leslie Ortquist-Ahrens, Patrick O'Sullivan,

Michael Palmer, Donna Petherbridge, Stacie Pittell, Susan Polich, Patricia Pulver, Marilyn Roberts, Michael Rogers, Brian Rybarczyk, Kenneth Sagendorf, Derina Samuel, David W. Schumann, Peter Shaw, Julie Sievers, Annie Soisson, D. Lynn Sorenson, Claudia J. Stanny, Susan Sullivan, Brigitte Valesey, William Vanderburgh, Kam Vat, Karen Ward, Beth Warrick, Stacie Williams, Laurel Willingham-McLain, Mary-Ann Winkelmes, Eva Wong, and Mary Wright.

Thanks are due to Hoag Holmgren, executive director of the POD Network, for supporting our efforts; the POD Publication Committee; and the entire editorial team at Jossey-Bass for their prompt responses and gentle reminders. My sincere appreciation goes to the Auburn University for professional support for this endeavor. Special thanks are due to Amy Vaughan for her efficiency, diligence, and editorial support for this project.

My collaboration with associate editor Laura Cruz has been exceptional. She has contributed editorial excellence to TIA and personal support to me, and I have enjoyed working with her for the past two years. TIA's future is bright under her leadership. This volume is truly a team effort, and its quality and comprehensiveness are attributable in no small measure to her work. With the completion of this volume, I pass *To Improve the Academy* into her capable hands.

Auburn, Alabama                                              James E. Groccia
August 1, 2013                                              Auburn University

# ETHICAL GUIDELINES FOR EDUCATIONAL DEVELOPERS

## Preamble

As professionals, educational developers (faculty, teaching assistant, organizational, instructional, and staff developers) have a unique opportunity and a special responsibility to contribute to the improvement of the quality of teaching and learning in higher education. As members of the academic community, they are subject to all the codes of conduct and ethical guidelines that already exist for those who work or study on campuses and those who belong to disciplinary associations. Educational developers have special ethical responsibilities because of the unique and privileged access they have to people and often to sensitive information. This document provides general guidelines to inform the practice of professionals working in educational development roles in higher education.

Educational developers in higher education come from various disciplinary areas and follow different career tracks. Some work as educational developers on a part-time basis or for simply a short time, but for others, educational development is a full-time career. The nature of their responsibilities and prerogatives as developers varies with their position in the organization, their experience, interests, and talents, and the special characteristics of their institutions. This document attempts to provide general ethical guidelines that should apply to most developers across a variety of settings.

Ethical guidelines indicate a consensus among practitioners about the ideals that should inform their practice as professionals, as well as those behaviors that would constitute misconduct. Between the ideal of exemplary practice and misconduct lies a gray area where dilemmas arise: choices may seem equally right or wrong; different roles and responsibilities may place competing, if not incompatible, demands on developers; or certain behaviors may seem questionable but no consensus can determine that those behaviors are examples of misconduct.

It is our hope that these guidelines complement typical programmatic statements of philosophy and mission and that educational developers can use the guidelines effectively to promote ethical practice. This document describes the ideals of practice, identifies specific behaviors that typify professional misconduct, and provides a model to think through situations that present conflicting choices or questionable behavior.

## Guidelines for Practice

### Ideals of Practice

Ideals that should inform the practice of educational developers include the following areas of professional behavior: providing responsible service to clients, demonstrating competence and integrity, ensuring that the rights of others are respected, maintaining the confidentiality of any information regarding contact with clients, and fulfilling responsibilities to the profession of educational development as a whole. It is expected that educational developers will understand and integrate these ideals into their daily practice. Even though the following categories are viewed as ideals of practice, many of the individual statements are quite concrete and practical, while others encourage educational developers to attain a high standard of excellence.

Educational developers evince a high level of responsibility to their clients and are expected to:

1. Provide services to everyone within their mandate, provided that they are able to serve all clients responsibly

2. Treat clients fairly, respecting their uniqueness, their fundamental rights, dignity and worth, and their right to set objectives and make decisions

3. Maintain appropriate boundaries in the relationship, avoid exploiting the relationship in any way, and be clear with themselves and their clients about their specific role

4. Protect all privileged information, obtaining informed consent from clients before using or referring publicly to client cases in such a way that the client could be identified

5. Continue service only as long as the client is benefiting, discontinue service by mutual consent, and suggest other resources to meet needs they cannot or should not address

## Competence and Integrity

Aspects of competence and integrity discussed in these guidelines include the behavior of educational developers, the skills and the boundaries they should respect and enforce, and the need for them to ensure the rights of their clients. Educational developers should also interact competently and with integrity in relationships with their coworkers, supervisees, and the community.

BEHAVIOR  In order to ensure evidence of competence and integrity, educational developers should:

a. Clarify professional roles and obligations

b. Accept appropriate responsibility for their behavior

c. Make no false or intentionally misleading statements

d. Avoid the distortion and misuse of their work

e. Clarify their roles and responsibilities with each party from the outset when providing services at the behest of a third party

f. Accept appropriate responsibility for the behavior of those they supervise

g. Model ethical behavior with coworkers and those they supervise and in the larger academic community

SKILLS AND BOUNDARIES  To practice effectively, educational developers need an awareness of their belief systems, personal skills, and personal knowledge base and cognizance of their own and their clients' boundaries. Ethical practice requires that educational developers:

a. Be reflective and self-critical in their practice

b. Seek out knowledge, skills, and resources continually to undergird and expand their practice

c. Consult with other professionals when they lack the experience or training for a particular case or endeavor or if they seek to prevent or avoid unethical conduct

d. Know and work within the boundaries of their competence and time limitations

e. Know and act in consonance with their purpose, mandate, and philosophy, integrating the latter insofar as possible

f. Strive to be aware of their own belief systems, values, biases, needs, and the effect of these on their work

g. Incorporate diverse points of view

h. Allow no personal or private interests to conflict or appear to conflict with professional duties or clients' needs

i. Take care of their personal welfare so they can facilitate clients' development

j. Ensure that they have the institutional freedom to do their job ethically

CLIENTS' RIGHTS   Because educational developers work in a variety of settings with a variety of clients and interact within different teaching and learning contexts, they must be sensitive to and respectful of intellectual, individual, and power differences. Educational developers should thus:

a. Be receptive to different styles and approaches to teaching and learning and to others' professional roles and functions

b. Respect the rights of others to hold values, attitudes, and opinions different from their own

c. Respect the right of clients to refuse services or to request the services of another professional

d. Work against harassment and discrimination of any kind, including race, ethnicity, gender, class, religion, sexual orientation, disability, age, nationality, etc.

e. Be aware of various power relationships with clients (e.g., power based on position or on information) and not abuse their power.

## Confidentiality

Educational developers maintain confidentiality regarding client identity, information, and records within appropriate limits and according to legal regulations. Educational developers should:

a. Keep confidential the identity of clients, as well as their professional observations, interactions, or conclusions related to specific clients or cases

b. Know the legal requirements regarding appropriate and inappropriate professional confidentiality (e.g., for cases of murder, suicide, or gross misconduct)

c. Store and dispose of records in a safe way; and comply with institutional, state, and federal regulations about storing and ownership of records

    d. Conduct discreet conversations among professional colleagues in supervisory relationships and never discuss clients in public places

## Responsibilities to the Profession

Educational developers work with colleagues in the local, national, and international arena. In order to ensure the integrity of the profession, they:

    a. Attribute materials and ideas to their creators or authors

    b. Contribute ideas, experience, and knowledge to colleagues

    c. Respond promptly to requests from colleagues

    d. Respect colleagues and acknowledge collegial differences

    e. Work positively for the development of individuals and the profession

    f. Cooperate with other units and professionals involved in development efforts

    g. Are advocates for their institutional and professional missions

## Professional Misconduct

The professional misconduct of educational developers would reflect gross negligence and disdain for the Guidelines for Practice stated above. Unethical, unprofessional, and incompetent behaviors carried out by educational developers should be brought to the attention of the association. Individual educational developers should take responsibility if or when they become aware of gross unethical conduct by any colleague in the profession.

## Ethical Conflicts in Educational Development

CONFLICTS ARISING FROM MULTIPLE RESPONSIBILITIES, CONSTITUENTS, RELATIONSHIPS, AND LOYALTIES　Educational developers may encounter conflicts that arise from multiple responsibilities, constituents, relationships, and loyalties. Because educational developers are responsible to their institutions, faculty, graduate students, undergraduate students, and themselves, it is inevitable that conflict will arise. For example, multiple responsibilities and relationships to various constituencies, together with competing loyalties, may lead to conflicting ethical responsibilities. The following examples point out situations in which conflicts may arise and identify the specific conflict:

    *Example 1:* An instructor is teaching extremely poorly, and students in the class are suffering seriously as a result. *Conflict:* In this situation, the educational developer is faced with a conflict between the responsibility of confidentiality to the client-teacher and responsibility to the students and the institution.

*Example 2:* A faculty member wants to know how a teaching assistant with whom the educational developer is working is progressing in his or her consultation or in the classroom. *Conflict:* In this situation, the educational developer is faced with a conflict between responding to the faculty member's legitimate concern and with maintaining confidentiality vis-à-vis the teaching assistant.

*Example 3:* The educational developer knows firsthand that a professor-client is making racist or sexist remarks or is sexually harassing a student. *Conflict:* In this situation, the educational developer is faced with a conflict between confidentiality vis-à-vis the professor-client and not only institutional and personal ethical responsibilities but responsibility to the students as well.

*Example 4:* A fine teacher who has worked with the educational developer for two years is coming up for tenure and asks that a letter be written to the tenure committee. *Conflict:* In this situation, the educational developer is faced with a conflict between rules regarding client confidentiality and the educational developer's commitment to advocate for good teaching on campus and in tenure decisions.

In such instances of conflict, educational developers need to practice sensitive and sensible confidentiality. It is best that they:

1. Consult in confidence with other professionals when they are faced with conflicting or confusing ethical choices.

2. Inform the other person or persons when they have to break confidentiality, unless doing so would jeopardize their personal safety or the safety of someone else.

3. Break confidentiality according to legal precedent in cases of potential suicide, murder, or gross misconduct. In such cases, to do nothing is to do something.

4. Decide cases of questionable practice individually, after first informing themselves to the best of their ability of all the ramifications of their actions.

5. Work to determine when they will act or not act, while being mindful of the rules and regulations of the institution and the relevant legal requirements.

CONFLICTS ARISING FROM MULTIPLE ROLES Educational developers often assume or are assigned roles that might be characterized as teaching police, doctor, coach, teacher, or advocate, among others. They are expected to be institutional models or even the conscience for good teaching on their campuses. Yet in their work with professors and graduate students, they endeavor to provide a safe place for their clients to work on their teaching. Another potential area for conflict arises from the fact that educational developers may serve as both faculty developers and as faculty members. As developers, they support clients in their efforts to improve their teaching; in their role as faculty, they often serve on review committees that evaluate other faculty. Either role may give them access to information that cannot appropriately be shared or communicated beyond the committee or the consultation relationship (even if it would be useful for the other role).

An important area of potential conflict exists in the case of the summative evaluation of teaching. Departmental faculty and campus administrators (chairs, deans, etc.) are responsible for the assessment of teaching for personnel decisions. Educational developers should not generally be placed in this situation because of the confidentiality requirements noted in the section on Guidelines for Practice. In general, educational developers do not make summative judgments about an individual's teaching. In particular, they should never perform the role of developer and summative evaluator concurrently for the same individual unless they have that person's explicit consent and with proper declaration to any panel or committee involved. However, educational developers may:

1. Provide assessment tools
2. Collect student evaluations
3. Help individuals prepare dossiers
4. Educate those who make summative decisions
5. Critique evaluation systems

## Conclusion

This document is an attempt to define ethical behaviors for the current practice of educational development in higher education. In creating this document the POD Network has referred to and borrowed from the Ethical Guidelines of the American Psychological Association, the American Association for Marriage and Family Therapy, Guidance Counselors, the Society for Teaching and Learning in Higher Education in

Canada, and the Staff and Educational Development Association in the United Kingdom. The association will continue to refine these guidelines in light of the changes and issues that confront the profession. The guidelines will be updated on a periodic basis by the Core Committee of the Professional and Organizational Development Network in Higher Education.

# TO IMPROVE THE ACADEMY

# PART ONE

# NEW PARADIGMS FOR FACULTY AND ORGANIZATIONAL DEVELOPMENT

# 1

# NAVIGATING THE NEW NORMAL

## EVIDENCE-BASED CHANGES IN FACULTY AND ORGANIZATIONAL DEVELOPMENT

---

*Terre H. Allen, Holly Harbinger, Donald J. Para*
*California State University, Long Beach*

*Faculty socialization and satisfaction are critical to retaining quality teacher/scholars and key to a well-functioning teaching-intensive, research-driven university (Ponjuan, Conley, & Trower, 2011). This chapter reports on a year-long research project aimed at investigating faculty work life and satisfaction at a large, urban, comprehensive state university. Our goal was to use empirical evidence to understand and support faculty work under the "new normal" conditions characterized by reduced state funding and increased faculty workload. We discuss the results in terms of a revitalized direction for faculty and explore directions for organizational development within the context of the new normal.*

---
o
---

Comprehensive, state-supported universities have a long history of providing higher education to support the professional employment needs of state and local communities (Finnegan, 1991). As such, faculty perceive the institutional cultures at comprehensive universities as weaker and less

---

We express our sincere gratitude to the members of the Ad Hoc Faculty Work Life Survey Committee. Please address all correspondence to terre.allen@csulb.edu.

satisfying, largely because of teaching loads that compete with faculty research. The current financial crisis and dwindling public support for higher education have created even more stress on faculty at public, comprehensive universities. Lustig (2002) asserted that reduced state budgets during the 1990s created heavier workloads for faculty at comprehensive universities, and the trend has not changed. The largest public, comprehensive university system in the United States is the California State University (CSU) with twenty-three campuses with approximately 40,000 faculty and 450,000 students. Lustig reported that within the CSU, there has been a steady increase in faculty workload since the 1990s. Student-faculty ratios have increased, student advising demands have increased, committee and governance work has increased, and expectations for publications and grant generation have increased. He found that economic downturns triggered faculty workload increases, but faculty workload did not drop with economic recovery.

The current economic downturn in California resulted in a CSU faculty furlough in 2009–2010 with faculty reducing their work and pay by approximately 10 percent. Furloughs were only one of several statewide and systemwide budget reductions. Today CSU campuses are searching for "the new normal," recognizing the reality of significantly reduced state support, fewer tenure-track hires, and increasing demands for an educated workforce. Nevertheless, the need for faculty development for new teaching and learning pedagogies and technologies is growing at an alarmingly fast pace. The stresses on the state comprehensive system and its faculty are tremendous. Resources that once provided token support for faculty research and creative and scholarly activities are gone. Course and student loads are at an all-time high, and fewer tenure-track positions place demands on the remaining tenured and tenure-track faculty to engage in increased faculty governance activities. What impact do these shifts in work have on faculty satisfaction, faculty work life, and faculty retention? What are the best ways to support faculty work under these new normal conditions?

Empirical evidence from a faculty work life survey at our institution, California State University, Long Beach (CSULB), administered to all faculty members, and the results from follow-up focus groups provided the data for navigating changes specific to faculty and organizational development. The data from that faculty work life survey and follow-up focus groups provided a road map for rethinking faculty development needs at our institution specific to challenges associated with navigating the new normal. The following sections provide a summary of the methods and results of the survey and focus groups. The final section describes how the survey led to refinement and revision of faculty organizational development activities.

# Method

## *The Survey*

The researchers reviewed several faculty satisfaction surveys and selected the Cornell Work Life Survey (Cornell University, 2006). Cornell granted permission for CSULB to adapt its survey to meet the needs of our campus. The provost and the associate vice president of faculty affairs appointed a ten-member ad hoc faculty work life committee to recommend changes to the Cornell survey to meet the needs and nomenclature of CSULB faculty work. The director of faculty development coordinated the project. The committee included representatives from each college, the library, and counseling and psychological services (all are included in the faculty collective bargaining unit). In addition, committee members represented part-time, tenure-track, and tenured faculty, as well as representative gendered, ethnic/cultural groups on campus. The committee met for two two-hour working lunches to adapt the Cornell survey. The resulting CSULB Work Life Survey consisted of fifty closed-ended items and two open-ended items adapted from the Cornell survey. The closed-ended items asked faculty to characterize workload, satisfaction with work, climate/work environment, stressors, and personal/family responsibilities. The two open-ended questions asked faculty to characterize the most and least satisfying aspects of their work at CSULB. The CSULB Faculty Work Life Survey received institutional review board (IRB) approval in spring 2011.

The survey provided descriptive data specific to the five categories and was not predictive of faculty work life. Rather, its intended use was for assessing faculty perceptions of their work life with the intention of using the data to inform decision making about efficient and effective faculty development and organizational development activities within difficult budgetary times. Scarce resources necessitate careful planning. Past planning surrounding faculty and organizational development was anecdotal rather than empirical in nature. The university had not previously undertaken any means of indexing faculty perceptions of workload, satisfaction, climate/work environment, stressors, and personal/family responsibilities.

The CSULB Faculty Work Life Survey was administered by campus site-licensed, electronic survey software. An e-mail was sent from the provost to all two thousand faculty inviting participation and providing the survey link, IRB information, ensuring anonymity, and indicating that all faculty who completed the survey would receive a coupon for a free coffee at an on-campus vendor (the coupon was donated by the vendor).

Two weeks following the initial e-mail, a reminder was sent, and a survey closing date was announced. The ad hoc faculty work life committee reviewed the results and recommended follow-up focus groups of new tenure-track faculty and newly tenured and promoted faculty. Chi-square analyses were used to determine if demographic, college-based, or appointment-type differences were reported. The campus community received results of the survey through presentations to the academic senate, deans, associate deans, and department chairs. Results were also posted on a university website.

## Focus Groups

The ad hoc committee concluded that follow-up focus groups (tenure-track faculty and newly tenured or promoted) would add more detailed and insightful qualitative data to the survey results. A question protocol was developed for addressing issues specific to results that required further exploration from the survey. All tenure-track and recently tenured or promoted faculty members were invited to a luncheon with the provost and to participate in one of three focus groups (based on appointment or tenure date). Extensive notes were taken, but no audio or video recording was done. Participants were encouraged to provide candid feedback to questions and were assured that no reporting of responses would identify them. A report of the summarized focus group results was submitted to the Office of Academic Affairs and delivered to college deans. In summer 2012 a focused discussion with all seventeen campus deans was conducted in order to explore college-based activities associated with survey results.

# Results

## The Survey

Five hundred twenty-nine faculty completed the survey, exceeding the number required for a confidence interval of 9 percent. Respondents represented, proportionately, faculty appointment levels, ranks, and colleges. Faculty academic ranks were represented within the sample as follows: part-time faculty ($n = 142$, 27 percent), full-time, nontenure/tenure track ($n = 48$, 9 percent), assistant professor ($n = 100$, 19 percent), associate professor ($n = 82$, 16 percent), and full professor ($n = 143$, 28 percent). The remainder opted not to respond to this item.

Faculty responding by college was proportionate to the number of faculty in each college: College of the Arts ($n = 63$, 13 percent), College of Business ($n = 25$, 5 percent), College of Education ($n = 49$, 10 percent), College of Engineering ($n = 20$, 4 percent), College of Health and Human Services ($n = 105$, 22 percent), College of Liberal Arts ($n = 167$, 35 percent), College of Natural Science and Math ($n = 35$, 7 percent), Counseling and Psychological Services ($n = 4$, 1 percent), and Librarians ($n = 14$, 3 percent).

The survey also included open-ended questions regarding gender identity and ethnic/cultural identity in an effort to capture the robust diversity of our campus. Two hundred ninety respondents characterized themselves as female, 192 respondents characterized themselves as male, and 47 respondents did not respond to this item. Two hundred seventy-four respondents characterized themselves as Caucasian or white, 192 respondents characterized themselves as nonwhite, and 51 different ethnic/cultural identities were reported. Seventy-four respondents did not report an ethnic/cultural identity. Respondents ranged in age from thirty to seventy-five, and the average age was forty-eight. More than 80 percent of the sample ($n = 431$) reported that their initial appointment at CSULB was either as a non-tenure-track faculty ($n = 228$) or assistant professor ($n = 203$). Other demographic items indicated the following: 75 percent of faculty respondents reported having a partner or spouse, 26 percent reported that they are in a "commuting" relationship with their spouse or partner some or all of the time, 54 percent reported that they are parents or legal guardians, and 18 percent reported that they are responsible for managing care for someone who is ill or disabled.

Respondents were asked several items about how they apportion their work time. Overall, across four general areas of faculty work, respondents reported that they spent the following percentages of their time engaged in instruction and instructionally related activities (56.8 percent, SD = 26.7); research, scholarly, and creative activities (17 percent, SD = 14.4); service activities, (13 percent, SD = 10.1); and assigned administrative duties (10.5 percent, SD = 20.2). The large standard deviations likely represent the diversity of the types of work done by various groups defined by the collective bargaining unit as faculty (e.g., department chairs, counselors, librarians, coaches).

Faculty responses to survey items regarding research productivity were highly consistent and similar regardless of college, academic rank, and appointment types. All items asked respondents to report on research work accomplished within the previous academic year. Respondents reported that their average number of articles published in peer-reviewed journals was 2 (SD = 1); average number of reviews, articles in edited volumes, encyclopedia entries, and reference articles was 2 (SD = 1.3); average number of textbooks, research reports, and manuals was 1.3 (SD = .64); average number of conference and other invited presentations was 2.6 (SD = 1.4); average number of performances or art exhibitions was 1.4 (SD = 1.2); and average number of grant proposals was 1.7 (SD = 1).

Overall, 71 percent (M = 5.29, SD = 1.7) of faculty expressed that they were satisfied with their work life at CSULB. Lecturers reported higher levels of work satisfaction than tenured and tenure-track faculty (M = 5.80) on seven-point Likert-type items. Full-time lecturers reported the highest level of satisfaction with work (M = 5.97). Other ranks were as follows: assistant professor (M = 5.0), associate professor (M = 4.9), and full professor (M = 5.02). College of Liberal Arts faculty reported less overall satisfaction than members of other colleges or units (M = 4.93). All other college means were slightly above 5. Overall, faculty reported a high level of satisfaction with life outside work (M = 5.1).

The survey also provided faculty with the opportunity to respond to several items that indexed their satisfaction or dissatisfaction with specific types of work activities. They reported most satisfaction with the opportunities to make a difference in students' lives (M = 6.06) and the intellectual stimulation of their work (M = 5.61). Faculty reported the least satisfaction with their opportunities to collaborate with colleagues outside their department (M = 4.29). Faculty reported that they place their highest value on teaching and their availability to their students (M = 4.71). They also reported that they place less value on service outside the university (M = 3.34), and mentoring junior faculty (M = 3.43). They reported that they were dissatisfied with university understanding of and support for their department (M = 2.88).

Several items asked faculty about their satisfaction with campus support for teaching, research, and service. They reported greater satisfaction with support for teaching and service-related activities than for support for research-related activities. The results were as follows: 56 percent of faculty reported satisfaction with support for teaching activities (M = 4.6, SD 1.6); 17 percent reported satisfaction with support for research, creative, and scholarly activities (M = 3.5, SD = 1.8); and 71 percent reported satisfaction with support for service activities (M = 5.2, SD = 1.7). The responses on all items indexing satisfaction with campus support were highly consistent across demographic groups, colleges, and appointment types.

Another category of items asked faculty to respond to items and questions concerning perceptions of their department or unit-level work climate and work environment. Overall, faculty reported feeling respected by their students (M = 4.28, SD = .8), immediate peers (M = 3.95, SD = 1.3), senior faculty (M = 3.81, SD = 1.65), and staff (M = 4.26, SD = .8). The results of the survey and follow-up focus groups indicated that faculty members are connected mainly at the department or unit level, and this is where the primary conditions of their work life are formed. Faculty perceived their department climate as supportive of opportunities for women faculty (M = 4.2, SD = 1.1) and that their department provided a supportive climate and opportunities for underrepresented minority faculty (M = 4.2, SD = 1.2).

Faculty reported feeling much less connected to the college and university units than to their department. They reported that their department was not adequately supported and valued by the university (M = 2.8, SD = 1.7). They also reported satisfaction with reappointment, tenure, and promotion requirements and processes (M = 4.5, SD = 1.5). But they also reported feeling stressed or overwhelmed that all aspects of their work representing "high priorities" by their department, unit, college, and university.

Two open-ended items asked faculty about the most and least satisfying aspects of their work life. Overwhelmingly they reported that "making a difference in the lives of students" and "teaching our students" was their most fulfilling work. Similarly, they responded in a highly consistent fashion to the question about work challenges, reporting that "department politics" and "difficult colleagues" were the most challenging and frustrating aspects of their work life.

## Faculty Focus Groups

Results from the faculty work life survey yielded numerous expected findings and several unexpected findings. We were interested in enriching the survey findings with qualitative data to help illuminate why so few faculty members reported being mentored, why faculty perceived "everything" to be a priority, and the impact these issues have on faculty who are advancing toward tenure and promotion.

Findings specific to dissatisfaction with support for research, scholarly, and creative activities were not surprising given budget cuts, but the provost was interested in how faculty were managing or not managing meeting reappointment and tenure demands in the face of diminished internal funding and support.

The associate vice president for faculty affairs arranged four focus group lunches for the following cohorts: faculty in their first year of tenure-track appointment, faculty in their second and third year on the tenure track, faculty who had received tenure and promotion to associate professor in 2012, and faculty who had just received promotion to full professor (effective fall 2012). A question protocol was developed to engage faculty in reflective discussion about their perceived experiences at the university, mentoring, successes, and challenges. The protocol was facilitated by the provost, associate vice president for faculty affairs, faculty development director, and academic senate chair. The focus groups took place during spring and early fall 2012. Sixty faculty members participated in the four focus groups. Informal transcripts provided qualitative data to add information and explanation related to survey findings.

The focus groups confirmed that dissatisfaction with support for research, scholarly, and creative activities largely came from diminished internal funding opportunities that once provided faculty with reassigned time from teaching duties to work on research, scholarly, and creative projects. Overwhelmingly, tenure-track and newly tenured faculty indicated that they were frustrated with diminished resources for research support. Most believed that when they were recruited for their tenure-track position, they were led to believe that there was ample support for faculty research and for scholarly and creative activities. However, they found that once they arrived on campus, obtaining research support was difficult, the processes for obtaining research support were complicated, and budget reductions had resulted in substantially fewer research support opportunities. These responses added important qualitative data to the survey results.

Tenure-track and newly tenured faculty indicated that one of the university's most useful support events for research, scholarly, and creative activities is the twice-yearly Scholarly Writing Institute (Ambos, Wiley, & Allen, 2009). They attributed manuscript completion, grant development activities, and conference paper completion to these university-sponsored events. They appealed to the provost to continue to fund the event despite difficult budget times. Several faculty members across all groups indicated that the teaching load was so demanding that they depended on the twice-yearly writing institutes to meet department and college publication requirements for tenure and promotion.

In addition, all focus group participants indicated frustration with the absence of a sense of community within their department, college, and the university in general. Isolation is not an uncommon experience for new faculty (Rice, Sorcinelli, & Austin, 2000). They expressed frustration with the lack of opportunities to develop relationships with department colleagues or colleagues within their hiring cohort (tenure-track faculty hired in the same year). Department and college colleagues were often described as "too busy" with their own overwhelming work life to have time to engage in social interaction with newcomers. As a result, tenure-track faculty believed that mentoring was not a department, college, or university priority. They also expressed difficulty in understanding how to prioritize work activities (teaching, research, service).

Tenure-track faculty noted that the degree to which they experienced isolation and the absence of a sense of community was largely a function of their relationship with their department chair. New faculty who felt the least isolated reported that their department chair was largely responsible for assisting them with developing interpersonal relationships with department, college, and university colleagues. They attributed a good deal of their socialization into the department as coming directly from the chair. New faculty who were more socialized into their departments and colleges reported that their chairs either served directly as a mentor or assigned a department faculty member to do so. Conversely, new faculty who reported feeling the most isolated reported that they had little or no communication or personal relationship with their department chair, did not feel socialized into their department or college, and had not established interpersonal relationships with department colleagues. Nevertheless, all new tenure-track faculty and newly tenured faculty reported experiencing some sense of isolation and lack of sense of community.

Tenure-track faculty also found few campus opportunities for social interaction and networking. Many were frustrated with the lack of sense of community in their department and college. In fact, several indicated that they rarely even saw many of their department colleagues, characterizing their colleagues as either Monday/Wednesday or Tuesday/Thursday faculty whose on-campus time is exclusively during their assigned teaching hours. The sense of isolation and lack of community was particularly frustrating for faculty who had only recently completed doctoral programs—almost the entire cohort. They said they were not prepared for a campus community that lacked the type of collaborative work environment they had experienced in their doctoral program of study.

All focus groups indicated that confusion about service requirements and information about opportunities was a major source of frustration. Messages regarding service requirements from senior colleagues, department chairs, deans, and university administrators were perceived as inconsistent. Most faculty felt that they were required to engage in service in every category listed among the university-defined areas for service (department, college, university, local community, and disciplinary/professional). Faculty of color felt additional obligations to serve their local communities and cultural/ethnic student groups. Some new faculty said that their department chair encouraged them to focus on teaching and research during the first few years of appointment, but that department and college reappointment and tenure committees had been critical of their lack of service during these years. Balancing service expectations with teaching and research expectations is an area for continued campus dialogue.

### Deans' Focused Discussion

All campus deans participated in a focused discussion facilitated by the director of faculty development and the provost. Deans were asked to report on how they engage, support, or foster faculty mentoring in their respective colleges. Only two of the seven deans reported any formalized activities intended to foster faculty mentoring in their colleges; several remarked that mentoring was "just not on my radar." Overall the deans were surprised that faculty reported a lack of value and commitment to mentoring activities.

## Discussion

Navigating the new normal requires assessing faculty work life and using those assessment data to inform faculty and organizational development. Baron (2006) explained that the effectiveness of faculty development is dependent on its ability to participate in organizational development. Our data indicate that faculty development has much value to add to organizational development while navigating the new normal. As a follow-up on Baron's recommendation, faculty development must provide faculty support for organizational development. Socialization of new faculty is critical to faculty satisfaction and success (Ponjuan et al., 2011). Faculty development events should be viewed as an opportunity for community building, socialization, and organizational learning, as well as individual improvement and learning opportunities.

In fact, our own reflections, debriefings, and discussion lead to the conclusion that managing issues related to our survey and focus group findings requires moving from a faculty development model that historically had focused on instructional and personal types of faculty development to one that also embraced organizational development activities. Bergquist and Phillips (1975) identified the organizational development approach as seeking to improve the institutional environment for learning and decision making for faculty and administration. This discussion is situated around how four themes have been used to establish organizational development activities.

Data from our faculty work life survey, faculty focus groups, and deans' focused discussion culminated in our identifying four faculty work life themes that would be used to shape faculty and organizational development activities in the coming three to five years. The survey data were reviewed by the ad hoc faculty work life survey committee, who discussed the survey results and concluded that the following themes were important interpretations of the results and should be the focus of planning for faculty and organizational development activities:

1. Faculty work life occurs dominantly at the department level.
2. New faculty too often experience isolation and lack socialization into the workplace.
3. Mentoring is not a priority at any level of the institution.
4. As a comprehensive state university with diminished resources, we struggle to be comprehensive, and faculty are overwhelmed with feeling "everything is a priority."

The ad hoc faculty work life survey committee recommended that a communication plan regarding the survey results should be developed by the associate vice president of faculty affairs and director of faculty development (in consultation with the provost) to engage the campus in dialogue about the results, themes, and plans to use the survey to make improvements in faculty work life and faculty development. Several members of the committee indicated that since the university had never before undertaken a faculty satisfaction or work life survey, a series of face-to-face presentations and discussions would be a good way to build community and create a narrative about faculty work life that is not derived from anecdotes alone. The provost, associate vice president for faculty affairs, and director of faculty development thus developed three goal-directed activities (1) using the survey results to build community, (2) redefining old and adding new faculty development activities, and (3) building a culture for mentoring relationships.

## Using the Survey Results to Build Community

A presentation reporting the survey selection and revision process and summarizing results of the survey was developed for faculty and academic administrators. Presentations were made from a wide variety of campus stakeholder groups, including academic affairs senior staff, the college deans' council, the associate deans' council, the academic senate executive committee, the academic senate, college faculty meetings, and retreats. Presentations offered the opportunity for questions, discussion, interpretation, and recommendations for future goals and actions. An informational website was also developed to provide survey methods, summarize results, and aggregate data for all items on the survey.

Discussions during the survey results presentations were thought provoking, spirited, and revealing. Most faculty and academic community members were surprised at the similarities among responses from faculty. In contrast to our data, conventional and anecdotal wisdom on campus maintained that faculty in the seven colleges vary greatly in terms of how they work and experience the university. Several discussions centered on how often we reflect on our differences and fail to recognize our similarities. Discussions also identified the challenges and difficulties of building and maintaining community within the context of reduced funding, reduced tenure-track hiring, increased retirements of tenured faculty, increased teaching loads, and obligations to students.

Notably, most members of the academic community were surprised at the high level of service activities reported. Each focus group spent a good deal of time discussing the confusion over expectations regarding faculty service activities, mixed messages from colleagues concerning the importance of service activities, and the difficulty that new(er) faculty have saying no and the degree to which they feel overwhelmed with service obligations. The data reporting and conversations have promoted much campuswide discussion.

## Redefining Old and Adding New Faculty Development Activities

Discussions among campus stakeholders revealed the need to address faculty development programming associated with the four themes. As a result, the traditional new faculty orientation was revised and content was moved to an online new faculty course, replaced with time spent directly with new faculty, deans, and department chairs interacting with one another. A series of new faculty happy hours was added to provide new faculty community building with informal wine and snacks with department chairs, the provost, and faculty development director. In addition, the faculty center and provost's office now offer faculty milestone luncheons to congratulate and seek feedback from faculty at the conclusion of their first year, on obtaining tenure and promotion to associate professor, and on obtaining promotion to full professor. During these luncheons, faculty are congratulated on their accomplishment and asked to reflect on their experiences past and future. These events are provided as a means of fostering socialization and networking opportunities. The faculty development director is also planning activities targeted to midcareer and late-career faculty to encourage leadership, mentoring, and socialization. These activities are not costly and provide needed opportunities for community building, dialogue, feedback, and collegial networking.

## Building a Culture for Developing Mentoring Relationships

Few efforts to create a culture conducive to mentoring relationships existed on our campus in the past. Faculty focus groups revealed a reluctance to seek mentoring because senior faculty appeared "too busy with their own work" to have time to mentor tenure-track faculty. In addition, mentoring by deans, chairs, and senior faculty was most likely viewed as something that was "done to" or "programmed for" faculty rather than a cultural element that gives rise to the development of interpersonal and work relationships that support organizational socialization and learning. We are working on developing a culture that is focused on the latter.

The Office of Faculty Affairs and the Faculty Center for Professional Development sponsored a panel discussion/workshop for department chairs on promoting a culture for mentoring of new probationary faculty. This was the first of its kind and was well attended. Attendees indicated that it was the best campus chairs' workshop they had ever attended. The event began with reflections on a mentoring culture from an associate dean, department chair, and director of faculty development. A substantial discussion and question-and-answer session provided department chairs the opportunity to reflect and raise questions, concerns, problems, and potential solutions. These events are ongoing, with the explicit goal of creating a culture of responsibility and value for mentoring relationships.

## Implications for Faculty Development Practice

Comprehensive state universities face numerous challenges: reduced budgets, diminished resources, increased student population demands, reductions in full-time faculty appointments, and more. Increased work demands limit time for collaboration, community building, and other opportunities for collegial interaction. Surviving this new normal for comprehensive universities requires reflection and purposeful, goal-directed change to a new environment for higher education. Proactive approaches must include empirical evidence to inform deliberate, strategic change. Understanding faculty support under the conditions that can give rise to change and potential areas of dissatisfaction are critical to a healthy organization.

The process of studying faculty work life and sharing the results with stakeholders in our academic community illuminated our need to be more proactive in creating and nurturing a sense of community. The consequences of a lack of interaction and community have resulted in little value being placed on mentoring. The lack of community results in new faculty members feeling isolated and lacking in opportunities for organizational socialization. This lack leads to new faculty members lacking in organizational knowledge and finding and using campus resources that can contribute to their success (e.g., teaching and research resources). Over time, all of these issues can contribute to faculty retention and job satisfaction problems.

The vast majority of new faculty members we hire are entry-level faculty and recent PhD or postdoc completers. The transition to an urban, commuter-style comprehensive university presents a number of challenges. Many new faculty members are the only department faculty member with teaching and research duties in their area of specialization. Departmental "one-and-only-ness" can further exacerbate feelings of isolation. The experience is often in sharp contrast to their PhD or postdoc experiences of working in groups or teams with a good deal of social and resource support. We must maintain mindfulness and direct action to foster community at our institution. We are still attempting to create cultural change to support more community-mindedness, particularly with respect to fostering opportunities for mentoring.

The department "one-and-only" phenomenon is particularly challenging for faculty of color. Faculty of color feel more pressed on for service activities associated with student cultural and ethnic groups and are also often called on by campus groups to "represent" a particular cultural or ethnic identity. New faculty members were candid about this during the focus groups. They also felt discomfort in serving as the representative voice for a particular culture or ethnicity and were concerned that service activities would take valuable time away from their research activities. Faculty ethnic diversity and service activities are all part of the landscape of the new normal for our university.

Faculty development activities play a critical role in providing opportunities that engage faculty in community building, socialization, organizational learning, and individual development. In particular, we found that blended (part face-to-face, part online) faculty learning communities (FLC) have provided our campus with community building and individual development without overwhelming faculty with meeting-intensive obligations. Faculty feel less burdened (and more participative) because participation in the blended FLC is more flexible than a traditional FLC. Our blended FLCs include three face-to-face luncheons (orientation, midpoint, and concluding), weekly common readings, online learning activities, and discussions. Typically we begin FLCs around the third week of instruction and conclude three weeks prior to the end of the semester. Therefore, the FLC spans ten weeks of a sixteen-week semester.

Faculty feedback indicated that faculty wanted FLCs that were made up of "near peers" or others who were teaching in similar content areas. Since all performance reviews of teaching are based at the department and college level, we believed that college-based FLCs were appropriate. We asked interested college faculty to determine a theme for their college-based blended FLC. The faculty development director designed the FLC framework and works with a few experienced faculty members in the college to identify discipline-specific readings and other material associated with the theme. All FLC content is housed and accessed through the campus learning management system. The FLC is made up of a series of modules, and each module includes readings, discussion boards, online learning activities, videos, and links to websites. All FLCs have a common set of modules, including campus student demographics, culturally responsive pedagogy, and assessment. The remaining modules in the FLC are theme specific (e.g., active and engaged learning, integrative learning, blended learning, and flipping) based on what the college has chosen. We anticipate that themes will change or evolve. Faculty participants are required to submit a course modification or redesign and assessment plan the semester following the FLC. Colleges are developing websites to house course redesigns and assessment data.

Thus far, faculty satisfaction with the college-based (blended) FLC model is extremely high. We have been overwhelmed by the level of communication activity in the FLC online discussions. Faculty report that they enjoy time spent in the online discussions because it is more flexible than a face-to-face workshop and affords them greater opportunities to reflect and respond. The faculty development director facilitates the FLC along with one or two faculty members from the college. We strive to select a diverse group of FLC participants each semester (rank, appointment level, and department). Mentoring relationships outside of departments are evolving as a result of the FLCs. In fact, faculty members in the College of Natural Science and Math have developed their own teaching and learning group of FLC graduates. They maintain contact with one another, often meet for teaching and learning brown bag sessions, take turns cofacilitating their college FLC, and provide peer classroom observations. This is particularly exciting because it marks the first time that any faculty member in the college can remember any effort by faculty to engage in community building or engage in regular dialogue about teaching and learning.

We view our research and faculty development activities as first steps in building a healthy, productive, and community-minded work environment for a twenty-first-century, teaching-intensive, research-driven university. We will continue to monitor the impact on our current programs and services. We recognize that there is a link among issues associated with a lack of mentoring and satisfaction with support for research, scholarly, and creative activities. We are hopeful that our new normal will be one that allows us to define ourselves as a productive and interconnected twenty-first-century comprehensive university.

REFERENCES

Ambos, B., Wiley, M., & Allen, T. H. (2009). Romancing the muse: Faculty writing institutes as professional development. In L. Nelson & J. Miller (Eds.), *To improve the academy: Resources for faculty, instructional, and organizational developers, Vol. 27* (pp. 135–149). San Francisco, CA: Jossey-Bass.

Baron, L. (2006). The advantages of a reciprocal relationship between faculty development and organizational development in higher education. In S. Chadwick-Blossey & D. R. Robertson (Eds.), *To improve the academy: Resources for faculty, instructional, and organizational developers, Vol. 24* (pp. 29–43). Bolton, MA: Anker.

Bergquist, W. H., & Phillips, S. R. (1975). *A handbook for faculty development.* Washington, DC: Council for the Advancement of Small Colleges.

California State University, Long Beach. (2011, April). *Faculty work life survey.* Retrieved from http://www.csulb.edu/divisions/aa/provost/faculty_survey/

Cornell University. (2006, November). *Faculty work life survey: Understanding faculty satisfaction.* Retrieved from http://www.advance.cornell.edu/documents/faculty_satisfaction_report.pdf

Finnegan, D. E. (1991). *Opportunity knocked: The origins of comprehensive colleges and universities.* Boston, MA: New England Resource Center for Higher Education Publications.

Lustig, J. (2002, Fall). Treadmill to oblivion? The coming conflict over academic workload. *Thought and Action*, 115–128.

Ponjuan, L., Conley, V. M., & Trower, C. (2011). Career stage differences in tenure track faculty perceptions of professional and personal relationships with colleagues. *Journal of Higher Education*, 82(3), 319–346.

Rice, R. E., Sorcinelli, M. D., & Austin, A. E. (Eds.). (2000). *Heeding new voices: Academic careers for a new generation* (Inquiry 7). Washington, DC: American Association for Higher Education.

# 2

# ENVISIONING CREATIVE COLLABORATION BETWEEN FACULTY AND TECHNOLOGISTS

Gail A. Rathbun
*Indiana University Purdue University Fort Wayne*

Sally Kuhlenschmidt
*Western Kentucky University*

David Sacks
*University of Kentucky*

*Faculty developers must often mediate conflicts resulting from differences between seemingly mutually exclusive cultures that university technologists and university teachers inhabit. Activity theory embraces workplace conflict as normal and as contributing to organizing health and adaptation, in contrast to a functionalist approach that focuses on how to maintain system equilibrium. Engeström's (1987) interpretation of activity theory provides a theoretically informed framework for understanding different forms of human activity, mediated by culturally molded rules, values, and division of labor, without suffering from the polarizing effects of an us-versus-them approach.*

---

When it comes to collaborative work between faculty members and technologists, fiercely defended professional and disciplinary boundaries often prevent the constructive collaboration that is required to make effective use of technologies in teaching and learning. Three groups are involved in resolving these work relationships: faculty, technologists, and faculty developers. Faculty come with a variety of backgrounds but always are grounded within a specific discipline, as well as in the general tasks of working with students. Technologists, such as help desk personnel, hardware and software installers, evaluators of university systems, and instructional designers, arrive as specialists in the application of technological tools to support the academic mission. Faculty developers, in their role of organization developers and managers of curriculum development teams, find themselves helping these two groups to communicate. University technologists and university teachers inhabit seemingly mutually exclusive cultures, each with its own vocabulary, style of communication, values, organization of work, and orientations toward control and authority.

Acquiring knowledge about and understanding of diverse professional cultures is the first step to resolving conflict and building collaboration. The ways in which we come to understand cultures different from our own, however, often depend heavily on characterization and stereotype. Activity theory, as interpreted by Yrjo Engeström (1987), a Finnish social psychologist, provides a theoretically informed analytical framework for developing an understanding of different forms of human activity, without suffering from the polarizing effects of an us–versus-them approach. Activity theory embraces workplace conflict as normal and as contributing to organization health and adaptation.

The Professional and Organizational Development (POD) Network identifies three areas in which faculty developers are active: providing assistance to individual faculty in their teaching, research, and professional well-being; supporting curriculum development teams; and organizational development ("Faculty Development Definitions," n.d.). In each of these areas, the faculty developer is often situated as a facilitator, team leader, or project manager. Faculty developers thus often occupy interstitial spaces within the academic organization, frequently acting as buffers and interpreters, playing multiple roles as advocates, defenders, and neutral parties to interactions between and among technologists, faculty, administrators, and students. These roles demand of the faculty developer skills in leadership, organization, mediation, and communication. Joint analysis of the disturbances and conflicts inherent in collaborations among individuals who are situated in different communities of practice gives rise to resolutions of conflicts and the possibility of innovations in the structure and processes of the shared activity.

## Conceptualizing Workplace Conflicts as Clashes between Cultures

Technological change inevitably produces conflict or, at the very least, discomfort. To those involved, what pundits refer to as "disruptive innovation" is painful. Testifying to this fact are numerous articles examining the barriers to technology adoption in higher education, among them organizational and individual resistance to technology, exacerbated by tensions between academic and nonacademic subcultures. For example, Nicole Matthews's (2008) account of an attempt to promote web-supported learning among arts and sciences faculty at an Australian university is a typical tale of high hopes and minimal results produced by cultural clashes between administration, academic disciplines, and technologists. In particular, faculty viewed institutional goals for the integration of virtual learning environments into 100 percent of academic programs by a certain date with deep suspicion because of a general fear and dislike of centralized control. Technologists, or anyone else perceived as carrying out the institutional goal of cultural change, became the enemy. In another example, uneasiness around the necessary alliance of academics and technologists surfaced spontaneously in a session that Eleta Exline (2009), a university archivist, led at a regional conference dedicated to forging digital partnerships among librarians and technologists. The failure of members of these two groups to work together became the dominant theme of the session and prompted Exline to devote a decade to developing partnerships with technologists, including writing a literature review on the topic (2009). Several case studies in her review identify differences in professional culture as an obstacle to creative collaboration. Further testimony to the persistent presence of these cultural undercurrents is the 2011 POD listserv discussion of how faculty developers might deal with the cultural gulf between faculty and technologists (S. Kuhlenschmidt, personal communication, February 6, 2011).

Shahron Williams van Rooij (2011) elaborates on the nature of higher education subcultures and their roles in hindering adoption of open source software at universities in the United States. She identifies faculty, nontechnical teaching and research support staff, and other nontechnical staff working under the chief academic officer as members of the "academic subculture" Fundamental values underpinning this subculture are academic freedom and the concept of tenure, shared governance, the knowledge creation imperative, academic honesty (Williams van Rooij, 2011; American Association of University Professors, 2007), creativity, and autonomy (Lin & Ha, 2009). The technologist subculture consists of information technology staff; other technical staff such as help desk workers who support campus computing; instructional technologists; and instructional designers. Concepts fundamental to this subculture include efficiency, rationality (Robey & Markus, cited in Leidner & Kayworth, 2006), equality, competency, community, and progressivism (Scholz, cited in Leidner & Kayworth, 2006). An earlier study by Williams van Rooij (2007) indicated that cultural conflict had been a significant hindrance to technology adoption at 772 institutions (Williams van Rooij, 2011). By 2011 a scarcity of resources had pushed the two cultures closer together, but the author concludes that maximizing the scarcer resources will depend on "striking a balance in which the drivers of one sub-culture are not realized at the expense of the other" (Williams van Rooij, 2011, p. 1182).

A mutually advantageous relationship between subcultures rests heavily on that cultural phenomenon called language and the ability to communicate clearly. In her essay, "The Techno-Humanist Interaction" (2010), Virginia Kuhn laments the communicative impasse between technologists and humanities scholars that impedes obvious synergies to be realized from collaboration. She describes a workshop bringing together supercomputing scientists and humanists in which the scientists "wondered how to manage data, whereas the [humanists] asked: 'Exactly what constitutes a datum?'" Kuhn continues, "While technologists imagine what *could* be, humanists imagine what *should* be" (p. 58). Miscommunication results in much wasted effort. Kuhn urges that we find a way to sustain "productive interaction . . . beginning in word and ending in action" (p. 58).

## Analyzing Cultural Conflict between Technologists and Academics

Within the higher education institution reside occupational cultures such as technologists and academics. An occupational culture is the set of values, norms, and beliefs that guide its members in the workplace. In academia, the overarching cultures are those of teaching and research, and within those we find the subcultures of disciplines. Technologists have a few subcultures, and faculty developers may fall in either or both groups, as well as having a distinct culture of their own. What follows is a discussion and a critique of some of the models and theories that have been used to analyze and diagnose this and other cultural conflicts in higher education organizations.

To study organizational culture at a university in the Midwest, Tierney (1988) applied a framework of six elements based on an ethnographic approach inspired by the methods of anthropologists: environment, mission, socialization, information, strategy, and leadership. Tierney believed that by surfacing the elements of culture along with its assumptions, administrators might better detect and resolve conflict. A further assumption is that the reduction of conflict produces a benefit to the organization. Tierney's study falls squarely within the functionalist perspective (LeCompte & Priessle, 1993), which holds as its major assumption that a system is composed of parts, each with a specific function that contributes to the overall health of the system. The goal of the functionalist analysis is to eliminate conflict and return the system to order. The case studies of conflict we will describe generally take a functionalist approach to examining the clash of information technology professional culture with faculty and academic cultures.

The study by Matthews (2008) is an example of a functionalist approach. The university that Matthews studied set as its goal to have 50 percent of all programs using virtual learning environments in two years and 100 percent of the university's programs within five years. Her critique is based on her identification of subcultures with widely varying values, goals, norms, and rules, and her recommendations are aimed at mitigating conflict between the fractious disciplinary "tribes" dwelling in the typical institution of higher education.

In another example of a functionalist approach. Davidson, Schofield, and Stocks (2001) studied the impact of professional cultures on collaboration between technologists and educators during a three-year project. They analyzed eighteen months of interviews, observations, and e-mails. From this analysis, they developed three meaningful cultural dimensions with which to interpret the behaviors and attitudes of the project members: routines, values, and orientations. Based on their findings, the researchers then offered insights into building successful collaborations and reducing conflict between technologists and educators.

Functionalist perspectives tend to focus on finding and describing different aspects of workplace culture, fragmenting the picture. The language and categories can be highly specialized. The functionalist approach does not integrate conflict, contradiction, and mutually influencing factors into its analysis. Finally, the approach tends to favor preservation of the status quo and perceives conflict as an aberration (LeCompte & Priessle, 1993). Studies completed from this perspective fail to provide a basis for change and innovation in a variety of work contexts.

Activity theory, an analytical framework that falls within the theoretical perspective of conflict theory, offers a major advantage in teaching people how to use conflict to collectively reconstruct organization practices (Engeström, 1987). Conflict theory overlaps with the functionalist perspective but adds concepts such as dialectic, change, and contradiction.

A conflict theory perspective argues that functionalism cannot fully explain change in social systems. Conflict theory embraces conflict and change as normal and as contributors to the overall health of a system. Given the disruptive innovations to higher education wrought by fast-moving technological change, the conflict theory perspective seems a better tool for addressing cultural conflict between faculty members and technologists. We did not find any exemplars in the literature of using this approach in facilitating the relationship between technologists and faculty members.

## A Brief Description of Activity Theory

Cultural historical activity theory (CHAT) sits squarely within the conflict theory perspective. In CHAT, human activity is understood as an ongoing set of negotiations and evolving relationships, set in motion by disturbances or contradictions within or from outside the activity system. From these disturbances arises the potential to innovate and therefore alter the activity system. In this chapter, we refer to CHAT simply as "activity theory." The activity system is the basic unit of analysis in activity theory (Engeström, 1987). The activity system, represented by a triangular diagram, is based on Soviet psychologist Leont'ev's (1981) conception, later enhanced by Vygotsky (cited in Engeström, 1987), of mediated human actions. Subjects—individuals or groups—perform an action on an object with a specific motive to obtain an outcome using mediating tools such as machines, gestures, writing, drawings, or music. Leont'ev's conception of the activity system is shown in figure 2.1 as

**Figure 2.1   Diagram of an Activity System**

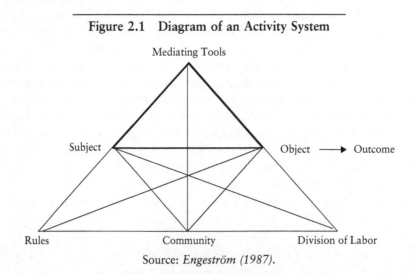

Source: *Engeström (1987).*

forming the tip of the triangle. Engeström widened the base of Leont'ev's simple triangle to include three primary elements of culture that influence the use of mediating tools:

- Rules, the explicit and implicit norms and conventions that enable and constrain action
- Community, which includes the individuals and groups that share the same object
- Division of labor, the horizontal division of tasks and vertical division of power and status

Activity theory emphasizes the key role of perspectives in understanding human activity, with these perspectives shaped by both the cultural and historical contexts of the activity. Understanding an activity requires analyzing the structure of the activity itself, how the cultural context shapes the activity, and the developmental history of that activity.

The elements of Engeström's conception (1987) of the activity system and examples of each element drawn from the context of higher education are shown in table 2.1.

## Applying Activity Theory in Workplace Contexts

In this section we present examples of ways in which practitioner-researchers have used activity theory to uncover the causes of workplace disturbances and at the same time use the process and its results to evolve innovative practices and altered activity systems. Our goal is to illustrate the benefits and advantages of the activity theory framework for effecting positive change in the academic workplace, with an eye to how that could be applied to the relationships of technologists, faculty, and faculty developers.

In an example from the context of higher education, Benson, Lawler, and Whitworth (2008) observed that using activity theory caused them to shift their perspective of a course management system as an object to that of a mediational element: a tool, a set of rules, and a reflection of a division of labor. This was the way that the users perceived the systems that the researchers were examining; thus, activity theory helped the researchers to reframe the study in a manner more appropriate to their goal of understanding the different ways in which the two systems mediated the activities of users—in this case, college teachers and their online students.

The usefulness of activity theory in reframing the problem space was again evident in Scanlon and Issroff's (2005) experimentation with it as a new approach to evaluating learning technologies. They suggest that

### Table 2.1   The Seven Elements of the Activity System

| Element | Description of Element | Example of the Element |
| --- | --- | --- |
| Subject | Individual or subgroup whose actions are being analyzed | Faculty member, technologist, media developer |
| Object | Problem or material receiving the action and which is molded into an outcome | The design of a course, a software application, instructional media |
| Outcome | Result of the subject's action on an object | Learning, a software selection, engagement |
| Rules | Norms and conventions, both implicit and explicit, that constrain action | Best practices, evaluation checklist, instructional theory |
| Tools | Mediating instruments and signs used by subject on object to achieve outcome | Syllabus, flowcharts, narratives |
| Community | Multiple individuals and subgroups sharing the same object and their shared values | Faculty in a discipline, instructional technologists, instructional media developers |
| Division of labor | Horizontal division of tasks and vertical division of power and status (complexity of the work, control of the work, task specialization) | Faculty controls all tasks (highly complex work); high specialization of tasks, coordinate work with others |

activity theory allowed them to address problems in the evaluation of learning technologies having to do with poor definitions of criteria for success and the effects of context in choosing appropriate technology. The evaluators were able to expand the types of evaluation criteria and explain evidence of these criteria in terms of contradictions among rules, tools, division of labor, and outcomes. The notion of a contextualized activity system provided a language and framework for their evaluation of technologies and a way of incorporating inherent contradictions.

Paul Warmington's 2011 report on the Learning in and for Interagency Working (LIW) research project took place in the context of improving children's social services in the United Kingdom. The purpose of the application of activity theory in this project was to analyze current work practices and develop new ones that would reach across multiple professional roles. Warmington enumerates the LIW project's concerns, which are similar to ours:

○ The identification of new professional practices emerging within multiagency/multiprofessional settings

○ The location of emergent multiagency/multiprofessional practice within an understanding of the changing character of service provision and user engagement

○ The creation, through joint developmental work research (dwr) interventions, of new professional knowledge that might be levered into more effective multiagency/multiprofessional working

○ The development and evaluation of activity theory/dwr derived methods as a tool both to analyze and to enhance professional learning. (p. 146)

Our last example has particular applicability for faculty development professionals. James Marken (2006) used Mwanza's (2001) eight-step model to guide the design and implementation of sales training for a Japanese sales force employed by a US Fortune 500 multinational company. In this case, cultural differences would be certain to emerge. Marken favored the use of Mwanza's model over Engeström's graphical representation for eliciting participation from teammates and clients. Marken's use (2006) of the eight-step model is summarized in table 2.2.

Mwanza (2001) then breaks down the activity triangle into what she calls the activity notation. Each activity notation includes an actor (subject or community), a mediator (tools, rules, or division of labor), and an object. Activity notations form small subactivities that are represented by lines drawn in the triangle between all of the elements of the activity system triangle.

When Marken plotted observations gained from using the eight-step model on the activity system triangle, he was able to explain relationships between contradictions and the mediating elements of the activity. The most important contradiction Marken's team had to resolve stemmed from a conflict between rules and division of labor. Social rules in Japan dictate that younger, less experienced people must not teach their elders, but all of the trainers were young and had not worked in Japan previously. The trainers received approval from senior Japanese leadership and made sure their trainees were aware of it. Marken claims that "by being able to name the contradiction we were able to bring the contradiction out and open it up for discussion" (p. 46). Other benefits from application of activity theory were a shared vocabulary and the ease with which members of the design team were able to use the idea of looking for contradictions to help them to solve problems.

Table 2.2    Marken's Use of Mwanza's Eight-Step Model

| Element of Activity | Identifying Question | Marken's Response |
|---|---|---|
| Activity of interest | What sort of activity am I interested in? | Training program/preparing for the program |
| Object or objective of activity | Why is this activity taking place? What will change as a result of this activity? | Coaching skills and support for business objectives |
| Subjects in this activity | Who is involved in carrying out this activity? | Japanese and US trainers, sales team leaders, sales managers, business unit managers |
| Tools mediating the activity | By what means are the subjects carrying out this activity? | Selling process workshop, district focus week review, role plays, case studies, equipment, room |
| Rules and regulations mediating the activity | Are there any cultural norms, rules, or regulations governing the performance of this activity? | Hierarchy in age and rank, don't speak first, share your experience, training must be relevant and realistic |
| Division of labor mediating the activity | Who is responsible for what, when carrying out this activity, and how are the roles organized? | Presenters and their tasks, debriefers and their tasks, technical support and their tasks |
| Community in which activity is conducted | What is the environment in which this activity is carried out? | Company, country of Japan, company units, peer companies |
| Outcome | What is the desired outcome from carrying out this activity? | Enhanced district sales manager performance, increased sales, increase in sales rank as compared with other companies |

## Activity Theory and Creative Collaboration

If college students are to receive the fullest benefit from their academic experience, faculty must be able to use the latest technologies well enough to craft meaningful learning experiences and pursue the scholarly work that informs and is informed by their teaching. Faculty development professionals play vital roles in providing interpretation of the role of technology in pedagogy and as scholars of teaching and learning. Activity theory is a useful addition to the developer's tool kit for improving communication and pedagogical effectiveness.

Some common activity systems in the faculty developer's work environment are teaching, consulting, learning, evaluation, relationship building, course design, and evaluation of teaching, to name a few. To determine whether activity theory as an analytical framework could lead to a less polarized perspective of faculty and IT professional cultures and help achieve the goal of creative collaboration, we developed several scenarios (we include one in this chapter) based on our own professional experiences as technologists, faculty members, faculty developers, and instructional designers, with additional input from faculty development colleagues participating in a 2011 POD listserv conversation (Sacks, Rathbun, & Kuhlenschmidt, 2011).

Our own analysis of the discussion revealed several broad areas in which faculty's and technologists' perspectives differed sharply. Each scenario featured a conflict between a faculty member and a technologist arising from one of the following orientations: toward time, toward process, and toward security of the information system. We then analyzed these conversations, identifying activity system elements and disturbances, using Engeström's (1987) graphical representation of an activity system. Because interactions between technologists and faculty frequently occur in the context of seeking and obtaining advice or recommendations concerning the use of computer hardware, software, and networks, we constructed an activity system of consulting viewed from two perspectives: that of the technologist and that of the faculty member. We applied the basic concepts of activity theory to this scenario:

Faculty: (on phone to IT help) I'm reviewing the drafts of some of my graduate research papers, and I'm having a very difficult time with the plagiarism detection software. I'm hoping you can help me.

Technologist: I'll sure try. Hang on a second, and I'll set up a remote session that will connect to your computer from my computer, if that's okay with you. That way we'll both have control over your desktop.

Faculty: (slowly, a little doubtful) Oh . . . okay, if you think that will help.

Technologist: (a few minutes pass) Just about there. Thanks for your patience. (another moment passes)

Technologist: Okay, you should be able to see my mouse on your screen. Now what's the problem?

Faculty: The software isn't checking the papers against professional journals, even though we have subscriptions in the library database. Is this feature turned off for some reason?

Technologist: Let me check into that. I'll go up here into the database list and see. Well, as you can see, the list of databases includes only things posted on the web and in paper mills on the Internet. There's not much I can do about not having professional journals in the list. These are what come with the program we bought. Can I do anything else to help you with this software?

Faculty: (starting to become visibly irritated) No. That isn't going to solve my problem. Who can help me with adding to the number of searchable databases?

Technologist: Uh, think the software specifications were drawn up by Tom in the academic software support unit. They do a thorough review of available options. Reviewing tech is their specialty.

Faculty: Did faculty have any input on the choice so that these issues about source being plagiarized were discussed? How was the final decision made?

Technologist: I don't know, but I am sure that Tom could answer your questions. Hold on, and I'll transfer you. I don't think he's gone for the day. If he is, you can leave a message.

Using Mwanza's activity notation, which includes an actor (subject or community), a mediator (tools, rules, or division of labor), and an object, we identified two subactivities within the activity system as the primary sources of disturbance. The first sign of disturbance (the gray triangle marked "1" in figure 2.2) is the faculty member's doubtful reaction to the eagerness of the help desk technician to fulfill his request for help with the plagiarism detection software. Following the rules of the help desk, the technician reacts speedily and asks permission to take control of the desktop, an established protocol for handling a question originating from the user's work station. Respectful of the technician's knowledge, the faculty member does not protest. The faculty member asks what seems like another technical question, at the same time indicating that he has already done some research into the problem, which seems to confirm that this is a technical question the help desk can answer. The rules of the help desk, reinforced by the values of the technologist community, do not satisfactorily mediate obtaining the faculty member's outcome. The technologist, however, may be able to record this interaction as "question answered," that is, outcome achieved.

Another rule of the help desk, asking if there is anything else the technician can do, actually serves to annoy the faculty member, providing a segue into the second disturbance (the gray triangle marked "2" in figure 2.2). Here the disturbance stems from the specialization of tasks

**Figure 2.2   Analysis of the Scenario from Two Perspectives**

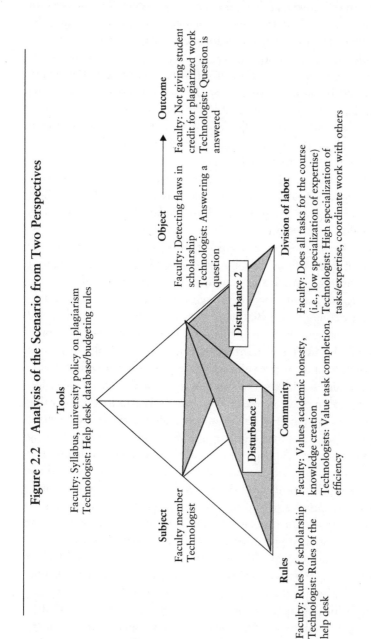

Tools

Faculty: Syllabus, university policy on plagiarism
Technologist: Help desk database/budgeting rules

Subject

Faculty member
Technologist

Rules

Faculty: Rules of scholarship
Technologist: Rules of the
help desk

Object ———→ Outcome

Faculty: Detecting flaws in
scholarship
Technologist: Answering a
question

Faculty: Not giving student
credit for plagiarized work
Technologist: Question is
answered

Disturbance 2

Disturbance 1

Community

Faculty: Values academic honesty,
knowledge creation
Technologists: Value task completion,
efficiency

Division of labor

Faculty: Does all tasks for the course
(i.e., low specialization of expertise)
Technologist: High specialization of
tasks/expertise, coordinate work with others

and expertise—the division of labor. The faculty member expects a greater breadth of knowledge from the technician, much like the breadth of knowledge expected of the faculty member. At the same time, the faculty member presumes that the academic software support unit does not have the appropriate knowledge to select plagiarism software. Responsibility for selecting this type of software, according to the faculty member, should be assigned to faculty. In this subactivity, neither the faculty member nor the technologist achieves his or her respective objectives or outcomes. The help desk rule that when the technician cannot answer a question he or she should find someone who can results in an unsatisfactory end to the interaction.

Our sample analysis of a typical technologist-faculty conversation isolated two nodes of conflict that technologists and faculty members could focus on together using a shared vocabulary. Using the methods described in this chapter, our scenario of a conflict of cultures may be reframed as a shared design problem—the design of processes and the organization of work—to achieve the outcomes of the activity system of technology consulting. In this situation, it is not necessary for all parties to have knowledge of activity theory, though it would be helpful. The faculty developer acting as a mediator or a team leader can meet with the help desk manager and the faculty member. The faculty developer could call attention to the difference in the technician's and the faculty member's intended outcomes and in the values guiding their respective behaviors. New shared values could emerge, such as the importance of precision and clarity in communication and suggestions for reprioritizing the value clarity over speed in help desk operations. A dialogue about the negative effects of task specialization could begin, and proposals for redrawing lines of communication between organization units could develop. The faculty developer is uniquely positioned to initiate and implement these changes in the organization of work and in work culture across boundaries of discipline, organizational functions, and professional cultures.

Faculty developers can take advantage of their roles as professional developers and scholarly practitioners to teach the basic activity theory concepts to their technologist and faculty colleagues, much as Marken (2006) did. He taught activity theory to the global sales and marketing team of a US multinational company as part of the development of a sales training retreat for the Japanese affiliate. Marken used Mwanza's (2001) eight-step model to introduce the fundamental concepts. Team members found this approach easier to use than the Engeström (1987) model, though they did employ the framework somewhat. As part of the process of development, team members interviewed Japanese managers and analyzed these interviews and their own considerable knowledge of Japanese culture using activity theory. Potential cultural conflicts were uncovered that changed the design of the training and shaped the expectations of the trainers (Marken, 2006). In a similar fashion, the faculty developer might bring together representatives of the technologist and faculty cultures to learn activity theory together and jointly analyze their shared workplace. From such joint systematic study, the potential for organization change is created.

## Conclusion

Painstaking analyses of occupational subcultures from a functionalist theoretical perspective have shed much light on the structure of institutions of higher education, their goals for instructional technologies, and the nature and impact of occupational subcultures. Understanding the role of professional culture, however, does not necessarily lead to constructive adaptation to technological change or to the development of innovative work processes. The theoretical perspective of activity theory, building on functional analysis of the workplace, integrates conflict, disturbances, and contradictions into a coherent description of shared work activity. At the same time, activity theory provides a way for coworkers residing in diverse communities of practice to collaboratively envision new ways to transform the academic workplace in support of achieving institutional goals.

The case studies, including our own scenario presented here, illustrate the negative effects of conflicts between the technologists and faculty members on the design and implementation of technologies in higher education. Divergent ways of defining and solving a particular problem can lead to confusion, mistrust, disappointment, and failure to resolve anything. Faculty give up trying to use technologies that could be helpful or quit consulting with technologists for help, and technologists lose respect for faculty work or fail to consult with them when it is needed for the better functioning of the university. How much better education would be if these two divergent viewpoints, this diversity, could be meshed to create stronger, more effective pedagogy and more efficient uses of technology.

REFERENCES

American Association of University Professors. (2007). *Informal glossary of AAUP terms and abbreviations.* Retrieved from http://www.aaup.org /AAUP/about/mission/glossary.htm

Benson, A., Lawler, C., & Whitworth, A. (2008). Rules, roles and tools: Activity theory and the comparative study of e-learning. *British Journal of Educational Technology, 39*(3), 456–467.

Davidson, A. L., Schofield, J., & Stocks, J. (2001). Professional cultures and collaborative efforts: A case study of technologists and educators working for change. *Information Society, 17,* 21–32.

Engeström, Y. (1987). *Learning by expanding: An activity-theoretical approach to developmental research.* Helsinki, FI: Orienta-Konsultit.

Exline, E. (2009). Working together: A literature review of campus information technology partnerships. *Journal of Archival Organizations, 7,* 16–23.

Faculty Development Definitions. (n.d.). Retrieved from http://www.podnetwork .org/faculty_development/definitions.htm

Kuhn, V. (2010). The techno-humanist interaction. *Educause Review, 45*(6), 58–59.

LeCompte, M. D., & Priessle, J. (1993). *Ethnography and qualitative design in educational research.* San Diego, CA: Academic Press.

Leidner, D. E., & Kayworth, T. (2006). A review of culture in information systems research: Toward a theory of technology culture conflict. *MIS Quarterly, 30*(2), 357–399.

Leont'ev, A. N. (1981). The problem of activity in Soviet psychology. In J. V. Wertsch (Ed.), *The concept of activity in Soviet psychology* (pp. 37–71). Armonk, NY: Sharpe.

Lin, C., & Ha, L. (2009). Subcultures and use of communication information technology in higher education institutions. *Journal of Higher Education, 80*(5), 564–590.

Marken, J. A. (2006). An application of activity theory: A case of global training. *Performance Improvement Quarterly, 19,* 27–49.

Matthews, N. (2008). Conflicting perceptions and complex change: Promoting web-supported learning in an arts and social sciences faculty. *Learning, Media and Technology, 33*(1), 35–44.

Mwanza, D. (2001). *Where theory meets practice: A case for an activity theory based methodology to guide computer system design.* Retrieved from http:// kmi.open.ac.uk/publications/techreports.html

Sacks, D., Rathbun, G., & Kuhlenschmidt, S. (2011). *Bridging faculty and IT cultures.* Retrieved from https://sites.google.com/a/podnetwork.org /wikipodia/Home/topics-for-discussion/bridging-faculty-and-it-cultures

Scanlon, E., & Issroff, K. (2005). Activity theory and higher education: Evaluating learning technologies. *Journal of Computer Assisted Learning, 21,* 430–439.

Tierney, W. G. (1988). Organizational culture in higher education: Defining the essentials. *Journal of Higher Education, 59*(1), 2–21.

Warmington, P. (2011). Divisions of labour: Activity theory, multi-professional working and intervention research. *Journal of Vocational Education and Training, 63*(2), 143–157.

Williams van Rooij, S. (2007). Open source software in higher education: Reality or illusion? *Education and Information Technologies, 12*(4), 191–209.

Williams van Rooij, S. (2011). Higher education sub-cultures and open source adoption. *Computers and Education, 57*, 1171–1183.

3

# FOSTERING A GROWTH MIND-SET

## INTEGRATING RESEARCH ON TEACHING
## AND LEARNING AND THE PRACTICE OF TEACHING

*Beth A. Fisher, Carolyn L. Dufault, Michelle D. Repice,*
*Regina F. Frey*
*Washington University in St. Louis*

*Centers for teaching and learning have a crucial role to play in helping faculty learn about and apply research on learning. The approach we have developed integrates discussion of recent research with specific recommendations of teaching modifications that can be adapted for different disciplines and courses. Preliminary evaluation suggests the effectiveness of this approach in fostering a growth mind-set about teaching—a mind-set that helps faculty develop, implement, and assess effective teaching modifications, thereby transforming faculty into scholars of teaching and learning and further developing a collaborative, innovative culture that integrates research on teaching and learning with the practice of teaching.*

○

Current interest in research on learning has opened up new avenues for improving teaching and learning in higher education. However, many faculty members have limited opportunities to learn about this research unless they are in fields such as cognitive science, neuroscience, education, or the learning sciences. Given their limited opportunities to learn about this research and consider how it might apply to their teaching, faculty often do not understand teaching and research on learning as mutually informing enterprises. Centers for teaching and learning have an essential and unique role to play in shifting the faculty mind-set about research on learning and its relation to their own developing pedagogical methods.

At the Teaching Center at Washington University, we have developed an integrative approach to working with faculty to develop, implement, and assess instructional modifications based on recent research on learning. Our approach integrates our expertise as experienced educators with research that is conducted in the learning sciences, discipline-specific educational research, and cognitive science. Our approach has these objectives:

- To help faculty develop and refine effective pedagogy
- To advance faculty knowledge of research on teaching and learning
- To advance faculty knowledge of how to incrementally incorporate instructional modifications that are informed by this research and adaptable for different disciplines
- To help faculty learn how to assess such modifications, either informally or in formal scholarship of teaching and learning (SoTL) projects

Preliminary evaluation using a faculty survey reveals enthusiasm about the potential of our approach to foster innovation in teaching and help faculty become scholars of teaching and learning.

Our approach builds on the work of scholars who have identified research-based principles that educators can use to improve instruction in higher education (Ambrose, Bridges, DiPietro, Lovett, & Norman, 2010; Angelo, 1993) and in K–12 classrooms (Bransford, Brown, & Cocking, 2000; Pashler et al., 2007). However, rather than presenting principles based on research, we select recent studies that are relevant to higher education teaching and then present details from the studies—including the methods and results—directly to faculty in our workshops, symposia, and consultations. This approach helps faculty develop a conceptual understanding of how researchers in various fields understand and measure learning. When faculty gain this conceptual understanding, they are better equipped to determine whether specific research findings can inform the design of pedagogical approaches in their own courses. This new understanding can also lead them to transform their knowledge of research on teaching and learning into what Bransford et al. (2000) describe as "useable knowledge"—knowledge that instructors can transfer, adapt, and modify as they work to improve and refine their teaching over time. In addition, learning about research on teaching and learning helps faculty make what can otherwise be a challenging leap—to become scholars of teaching and learning who understand research on learning and how it is conducted and are equipped to develop and assess instructional methods informed by this research, whether on their own or in consultation with teaching center staff.

Our approach has increased the number of faculty participating in our programs, including workshops, consultations, and iteach, a biennial teaching symposium. It has also helped faculty develop what William Buhro, professor and chairperson of chemistry, refers to as a "growth mind-set about teaching." Buhro has consulted extensively with the Teaching Center on the use of active learning and technology in his courses (Fisher, Miller, Buhro, Frank, & Frey, 2012), and he has regularly attended our teaching symposium. The term *growth mind-set* is borrowed from Carol Dweck's (2006) concept of the distinction between "a growth versus a fixed mind-set." When asked to comment on the 2012 teaching symposium, Buhro noted:

> I initially believed that one either had a knack for teaching, or sadly, did not. I believed that everything that could possibly be known about teaching had been discovered a long time ago, and endlessly discussed since. I have more recently developed a "growth mindset" about effective teaching, which I now see as the product of knowledge and skills developed over time. Participating in *iteach* and in the [Washington University] teaching community has fed that growth, giving me new insights into recent advances in research on cognition and learning—and new teaching methods that can be used to increase student motivation and learning in tough curricula. (personal communication, November 21, 2011; see also "2012 *iteach*," 2011)

Our approach to developing workshops, consultations, and teaching symposia is informed by our participation in collaborations bringing together four groups of experts at Washington University: the Teaching Center staff, researchers in the learning sciences, researchers in cognitive science, and faculty teaching in the disciplines. Each group brings a distinct area of expertise that is essential to a shared goal of improving teaching and learning. Staff at the Teaching Center—with PhDs in the sciences, the social sciences, and the humanities—bring expertise in SoTL and in designing, implementing, and assessing pedagogy across the disciplines. Learning scientists bring knowledge of

**Figure 3.1   Collaboration among Experts Leads to Continual Integration of Effective Pedagogical Practices and Research on Teaching and Learnings**

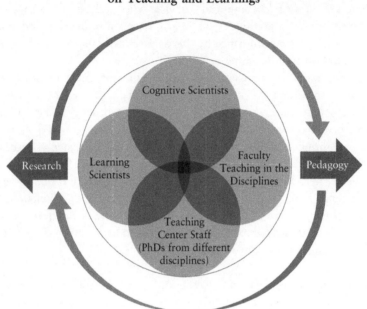

research on how to design and assess curricula and classrooms that promote learning. Cognitive scientists bring conceptual models of learning derived from experimental research in the laboratory. Faculty teaching in the disciplines bring knowledge of specific teaching and learning challenges, drawn from their experiences designing and teaching courses and from their knowledge of discipline-specific educational research and SoTL. Collaboration among these four groups takes shape in multiple configurations. The results include new research, as well as the refinement of effective pedagogical practices, as research on teaching and learning and the practice of teaching inspire and feed into one another, in a collaborative process that fosters a growth mind-set in all of us (figure 3.1).

The resulting collaborations, some of them research collaborations, typically involve two or more groups but can involve all four. For example, Regina Frey, the executive director of the Teaching Center, and Florence E. Moog, professor of STEM (science, technology, engineering, and mathematics) education, conduct educational research with collaborators from the learning sciences and cognitive science, as well as with faculty from different disciplines. These collaborations signal the emergence of a campus culture focused on integrating teaching and research. This culture can be seen in the 2008 founding of the Washington University STEM Education Research Group (ERG), in which faculty from STEM departments, including psychology, and the Department of Education meet weekly to discuss their educational research (Fisher & Frey, 2011). This culture can also be seen in the 2011 creation of the Center for Integrative Research on Cognition, Learning, and Education (CIRCLE), which provides an additional structure for collaborative research involving cognitive scientists, discipline-education researchers, and faculty from across the disciplines. This center is codirected by Frey and professor of psychology Mark McDaniel.

The collaborative research of these four types of experts has also informed the Teaching Center's approach to working with faculty to design and assess instructional modifications that apply recent research on learning. Whether we are developing faculty workshops or working with faculty in individual consultations on teaching or on SoTL projects, we first identify specific challenges that faculty face when designing courses and curricula. These challenges may pertain to specific learning objectives for students, such as learning dense areas of new knowledge or building the critical-thinking skills needed to solve complex problems, build analytical arguments, and synthesize disparate facts and ideas into an original proposal.

The next step is multifaceted: we draw on our own knowledge of effective pedagogical practices as we investigate what recent research can tell us about how to improve student learning. This research includes classroom-based studies, drawn from relevant discipline-specific educational studies and from the learning sciences. Keith Sawyer, associate professor of education, who has conducted collaborative research with Frey, has been instrumental in defining the relatively new field of the learning sciences. Sawyer (2005) describes the learning sciences as an interdisciplinary field that brings together "researchers in psychology, education, computer science, and anthropology, among others" (p. 3). The "goal of the learning sciences is to better understand the cognitive and socio-cultural processes that result in the most effective learning, and to use this knowledge to redesign classrooms and other learning environments so that people learn more deeply and effectively" (Sawyer & Nathan, in press). Working primarily with educators in K–12 schools, learning scientists use an iterative design process that draws on current research on teaching and learning to redesign learning environments and assess how students learn in the redesigned environment (R. K. Sawyer, personal communication, November 12, 2012).

We also incorporate recent cognitive science research. In this field, researchers develop models of how learning occurs based on carefully designed laboratory experiments. These experiments are not designed to replicate how learning occurs in the messy world of the classroom; they are designed to isolate and control for specific variables and study whether manipulating those variables has any effect on learning. However, over the past decade, cognitive scientists have become interested in bridging the gap between laboratory research and the real-world environment of the classroom (Mayer, 2008; Mestre & Ross, 2011). Some have published reviews of current cognitive science research that suggests specific teaching and learning strategies that may improve learning outcomes (Dunlosky, Rawson, Marsh, Nathan, & Willingham, 2013; Mayer, 2008; Pashler et al., 2007; Willingham, 2009). These researchers include faculty from our Department of Psychology, such as McDaniel, Kathleen McDermott, and Henry Roediger (McDaniel, Roediger, & McDermott, 2007; Roediger, Agarwal, McDaniel, & McDermott, 2011; Roediger, McDermott, & McDaniel, 2011). Although much of the work integrating cognitive science with classroom practice is addressed to K–12 educators, many cognitive scientists are conducting laboratory research that engages directly with learning in higher education (McDaniel, Anderson, Derbish, & Morrisette, 2007). Cognitive scientists are also beginning to collaborate with higher education faculty to measure the effectiveness of instructional modifications that apply learning theory (M. McDaniel, personal communication, November 13, 2012; Mestre & Ross, 2011).

There is clearly a need for faculty to work with faculty developers to learn about research on learning and use this knowledge to modify and improve their instructional methods; in addition, there is a need for researchers in cognitive science and the learning sciences to collaborate with faculty developers and faculty in order to better understand authentic teaching and learning challenges. Such collaboration is central to improving teaching and learning in higher education.

## "Show Me the Data": Disseminating Recent Research on Learning in Faculty Workshops

Our faculty interact with the Teaching Center using multiple pathways, including workshops, consultations, teaching symposia, and research collaborations. Our most extensive teaching collaborations with faculty occur in workshops and consultations. In the workshops, typically sixty to ninety minutes long, we present research on learning and facilitate group discussion of the research and its implications for the participants' teaching. Because our staff have PhDs with teaching expertise in multiple disciplines, we can work as a team to identify research on learning, as well as specific instructional modifications that are flexible enough to be applied in courses of various sizes and in different disciplines. To promote a growth mind-set about teaching and learning, we begin workshops by presenting study details, such as participant demographics and study conditions (e.g. classroom or laboratory based, level of experimental control). In addition, we describe the study methods and present the relevant data or results. We have found that faculty are curious not only about the ideas that can be drawn out of research on learning; they are also curious about how this research is conducted. Discussing the study details helps faculty assess the significance of the data and its relevance for their teaching, as well as develop a better sense of how to read and understand research on learning when they embark on their own investigations of this research after the conclusion of the workshop.

When presenting study details, we strive to help faculty transform knowledge of recent research on learning into knowledge that they can adapt and modify as they refine their teaching over time. To accomplish this transformation, translating terminology is often crucial. For example, the terminology used in cognitive science literature may not be recognized as specialized language. In fact, there is a potential for misunderstanding precisely because cognitive scientists use terms that are widely used in education (e.g., *study* and *test*). However, in the cognitive science literature, these terms have more specific meanings than they do when educators use them more broadly. For instance, "to study" often means "to read," while "to test" often means to measure retention or transfer. (Retention tests measure how much knowledge a learner retains and can retrieve from memory; transfer tests measure how well a learner can apply newly learned knowledge to a novel situation.) Translating these terms by explaining their specific meanings within the primary literature is one of the most important aspects of our approach, and it represents one of the primary areas in which the cross-disciplinary knowledge of faculty developers can have a significant impact on efforts to disseminate research on learning to faculty across disciplines.

## Translating Research into Practice: Recommendations

When developing and delivering workshops and working with faculty individually in consultations, we follow discussions of the selected studies with specific recommendations of instructional modifications informed by the studies. Our recommendations are designed to help faculty develop ideas for modifying their own teaching to improve learning. For example, several of our workshops have included discussion of laboratory-based experiments that have compared how college students performed on retention tests when they engaged in retrieval practice, that is, to recall information they had just read or heard, compared to students who reread the text one or more additional times but did not engage in retrieval practice before being tested (Karpicke & Blunt, 2011; Lyle & Crawford, 2011; Roediger & Karpicke, 2006). The positive effects of retrieval practice have been shown not only in student performance on questions that require recall of factual information from a previously read text, but also on questions that ask students to make inferences based on facts presented in the text they have already read (Karpicke & Blunt, 2011).

When we present these findings to faculty, we facilitate discussion of multiple strategies that suggest how retrieval practice and other concepts can be incorporated into teaching. For example, we describe strategies such as starting class with a low-stakes quiz or series of questions that prompt students to generate information they have just learned, or combining short lectures with group work designed to help students remember and apply what they have just learned in the lecture. We describe such strategies not as prescriptions but as flexible approaches that can be incorporated incrementally. In addition, we include specific logistical recommendations, stressing the importance, for example, of structuring group work by limiting groups to three to four students, giving clear instructions and time limits, and asking the groups to report and discuss the results of their work. This approach incorporates strategies drawn from education literature on classroom-assessment techniques and active learning (e.g., Angelo & Cross, 1993; Eberlein et al., 2008). However, it takes these strategies in a new direction by helping faculty understand concepts from learning and memory research that they can use to ensure that these strategies help students build and retain new knowledge and skills. Understanding these concepts also helps faculty adapt these strategies for their own courses and students and devise plans for assessing and modifying these implementations over time.

## Preliminary Evaluation: Survey of Faculty Workshop Participants

In 2012, we presented four faculty workshops entitled Applying Cognitive Science to Improve Teaching. Two of the workshops were for multidisciplinary faculty from arts and sciences, business, medicine, and engineering, and two were for medical faculty. We have also integrated information from research on learning into workshops on such topics as incorporating active learning, teaching with PowerPoint, and teaching with lectures.

In November 2012, we administered a survey to faculty who had participated in one of the faculty workshops on applying cognitive science research to improve teaching (the only participants not invited had attended a medical faculty workshop, for which attendance records were not available). We invited seventy-seven workshop participants to complete the survey, which asked respondents to indicate their perceptions of the usefulness of the workshop content and the extent to which the workshop increased their likelihood to incorporate specific instructional modifications based on the presented studies. The response rate was approximately 36 percent, with twenty-eight faculty members responding. The demographic representation of the survey respondents was similar to that of the seventy-seven survey invitees. Respondents came from sixteen departments, representing the humanities, social sciences, natural sciences, and medicine. A majority of the respondents (fifteen) had tenure-line faculty appointments at or above the level of assistant professor. Nearly two-thirds of the respondents were women.

The survey respondents found each of the major workshop components to be useful (figure 3.2). More specifically, when asked to rate the usefulness of the group discussions on how to apply the research findings to teaching, 69 percent responded "useful" or "very useful." When asked to rate the usefulness of "specific, detailed recommendations for applying cognitive-science findings to classroom teaching," 74 percent responded "useful" or "very useful." Nearly all (89 percent) reported that the "review and explanation of data from recent cognitive-science studies on learning and memory" was "useful" or "very useful." Respondents also reported increases in their likelihood to incorporate the recommended modifications: 82 percent reported being more likely to use active learning activities, and 59 percent reported being more likely to use weekly quizzes (figure 3.3).

The survey included open-ended questions about whether the participants had already incorporated the recommended modifications. Responses to these questions suggest several themes, as illustrated by the comments that follow:

> I wanted to incorporate in-class group work, but received a fair amount of redirection from colleagues. But after this workshop, I was determined to figure it out. I had 3 in-class group assignments with 98 students, and they loved it! It worked out just as I had hoped. They retained the information through [the] active-learning activity rather

Figure 3.2   Percentage of Survey Respondents Who Rated the Relative Usefulness of Each of the Major Workshop Components

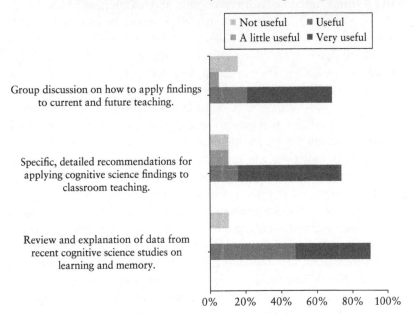

than [through my] lecturing with PowerPoint on how to develop and implement a study.

This semester, I will incorporate more of [the recommended strategies] in both lecture content and their homework assignments. Actually, taking this survey at this time is REALLY helpful as I am now redoing the syllabus for the spring semester and can make sure I incorporate some of the insights from this workshop.

I build in more active elements, including ungraded midsession quizzes to practice retrieval just minutes after material is presented. This seems to work well in that students do recall correct answers, and it generates conversation when there is confusion. I will continue to use this method.

I am now giving short quizzes to improve memory recall. I have active learning activities either in each class or at least every week. I would use the modifications again in my teaching.

When I first told the students that there would be in-class group work, they were not happy. I told them it would work out and it did.

Figure 3.3    Percentage of Survey Respondents Indicating Whether Participating in the Workshops Made Them More Likely to Implement Pedagogical Modifications Recommended in the Workshops

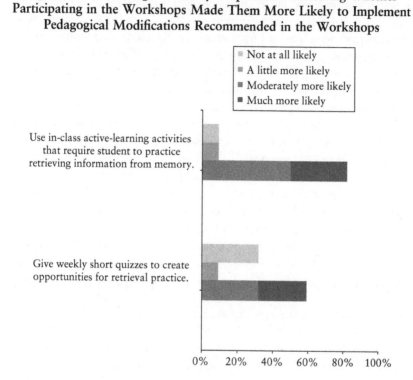

But I made sure to get the housekeeping and logistics all settled before I actually had them do an in-class group assignment. That meant getting them into small groups through sign-up sheets and e-mails, then setting up the lecture hall to facilitate their group seating arrangement.

First, the comments conveyed clear enthusiasm about incorporating the modifications, as well as appreciation for the provided guidance on the logistical aspects of how to incorporate these modifications.

Second, when asked about barriers they had encountered when incorporating—or attempting to incorporate—the recommended modifications, the respondents cited time constraints and resistance by students and colleagues. Notably, a few of the respondents said that taking an incremental approach to incorporating modifications, as well as sharing with students and colleagues the rationale behind the modifications, helped faculty to overcome these barriers. In addition, a quarter of the respondents reported that after participating in the workshops, they were "more likely to have informal discussions with colleagues about applying cognitive science to improve teaching." Several respondents also reported mentoring other faculty in this area, as well as working with co-instructors to adapt and implement the recommended modifications. In other words, the survey responses suggested that workshop participants had started to develop a growth mind-set about teaching and were becoming scholars of teaching and learning.

While the survey represents a preliminary evaluation of our workshops on applying research on learning, the results are encouraging. Most notably, they point to the increased likelihood of implementing instructional modifications integrating concepts from cognitive science and learning sciences research. In addition, they speak to the faculty's need for guidance on the logistical aspects of adapting these modifications incrementally and effectively. The results also suggest that faculty workshop participants are excited about continuing to incorporate, adapt, refine, and assess the concepts and strategies they learned in the workshops.

## "Practical, Hard-Nosed Advice": Consultations with Faculty

Without specific, detailed recommendations for modifying their teaching, faculty might be intrigued by research on learning but remain unsure of how to apply this research in their own teaching. Therefore, they often need advice from centers for teaching and learning staff on how to devise a feasible plan for implementing and assessing modifications based on the research. At the Teaching Center, we provide such advice not only in workshops and symposia but also in individual faculty consultations. During consultations, we use a taxonomy of learning drawn from education theory (Anderson et al., 2001; Bloom, 1956) to help faculty members identify course goals and then determine how well the their current instructional approach aligns with these goals. Looking carefully at the faculty member's lecture notes and other materials, we discuss whether and how specific instructional modifications, informed by research on learning, could improve student learning in the course. In addition, we help the faculty member identify specific points at which retrieval practice or other modes of active learning could be incorporated into each class session.

Susan Fitzpatrick, who teaches neuroscience in the departments of anatomy and neurobiology and in the program in occupational therapy, has reflected on her experience with this process. As a result of her research expertise, as well as her work as vice president of the James S. McDonnell Foundation, which supports research and scholarship in brain science and human cognition, Fitzpatrick has a high level of knowledge about cognitive science and its potential for improving teaching and learning. However, she notes that implementing pedagogical modifications based on cognitive science or other research on learning can be a daunting prospect for faculty. Furthermore, faculty are unlikely to implement their new knowledge of the research if they do not get practical advice on "what [they] can *actually do*." Describing her experience of redesigning her course to incorporate questions prompting students to use retrieval practice and incorporate more active learning exercises, Fitzpatrick notes that consultations with the Teaching Center's executive director provided her with "practical, hard-nosed advice" from someone who has been "on the ground"—an experienced instructor who brings expertise in teaching as well as knowledge about research on learning. Fitzpatrick appreciates that the recommendations are flexible, so implementing them does not mean faculty are "locked into a complex curriculum or system." Instead, they can implement modifications in a way that fits the individual instructor's discipline, course, teaching style, and students; in addition, an instructor can readily understand how to make additional modifications to fit each new course or group of students. The result is "a more dynamic, adaptable system . . . and therefore a more resilient classroom" (personal communication, November 19, 2012).

Consultation with the Teaching Center also enables the faculty member to create a plan for assessing the effectiveness of the planned modifications. Discussing and learning about how research on teaching and learning is conducted—whether in cognitive science, the learning sciences, or discipline-specific education research—helps faculty members think about how they can assess learning in their own courses. The assessment may begin informally with the faculty member's reflections on student work and student evaluations (or other feedback), or with observation and feedback by staff from the Teaching Center. Continued consultation can guide this process, which in some cases develops into a formal evaluation study or a SoTL project, designed in collaboration with either the Teaching Center or CIRCLE.

After laying the groundwork in workshops, consultations, or teaching symposia for faculty to think about how research on teaching and learning is conducted, we find that faculty are primed to think about how to design a study to assess learning in their own courses. Our discussions with them about research on learning not only give us a deeper sense of specific teaching and learning challenges and the extent to which current research on learning may suggest new ways to meet those challenges; these discussions also reveal areas of teaching and learning that the research has not yet examined—prompting ideas for new research. In other words, at the same time that research on learning can suggest new ways to invigorate teaching, our collaborative efforts to refine and improve teaching points to gaps in the research that can be addressed by new classroom- or laboratory-based studies.

## Recommendations

The recommendations that follow for faculty developers who are engaged in efforts to help faculty learn about and apply research on teaching and learning highlight strategies that can foster a growth mind-set about teaching and lead faculty to become scholars of teaching and learning:

1. In workshops, consultations, and symposia or other programs that incorporate research on learning, help faculty understand the research study details, think conceptually about the results of this research, and consider how the results can be applied when developing and refining effective teaching practices.
   - Present the study details, such as number of participants, study conditions (e.g. classroom or laboratory based; degree of experimental controls employed), methods, and results.
   - Facilitate discussion of the study results and their potential for improving teaching and learning in specific disciplines.
   - Be attuned to linguistic barriers that may make it difficult for faculty from different disciplines to understand the terminology employed by researchers from cognitive science or the learning sciences (e.g. *study* and *test*). Define terms when needed to promote mutual understanding of what the research does—and does not—suggest about how learning occurs and to clarify specific practices that instructors and students can use to maximize learning.
   - Present specific, elaborated recommendations of instructional modifications that are applicable and feasible in different disciplines and courses. These recommendations should include suggestions on the logistical aspects of the implementations, how these modifications may be implemented incrementally, and ideas about how faculty can assess these modifications.
2. Expand your knowledge of research on teaching and learning from the learning sciences, cognitive science, and educational research in the disciplines.
   - Read recent literature from all of these research areas and seek out opportunities to discuss this literature with colleagues from

these fields. Your colleagues can help you determine the research areas that are most relevant to teaching and learning in higher education. We expect that they will be enthusiastic to talk with you, as will faculty in all other disciplines who are interested in discussing how this research might help them improve student learning in their courses.

○ Seek out opportunities to develop collaborative research on teaching and learning with colleagues from your institution or elsewhere.

○ Form research groups that bring together colleagues from all of the above areas to discuss their research on teaching and learning. Develop a structure that enables these groups to meet on a regular basis to present their research and to collaborate with one another, both formally and informally (Fisher & Frey, 2011; Huber & Hutchings, 2005).

3. Continue to refine your teaching expertise by modifying and assessing your own pedagogical methods—whether in courses or in the development of workshops, seminars, or other learning opportunities for faculty and graduate students. Learning about the research is only the first step. Developing pedagogical modifications that can work and be assessed in the classroom is often a more challenging step. Your expertise as an experienced educator will help you develop specific recommendations for modifying teaching that are not only informed by research but also designed in a way that can be readily adapted, implemented, and assessed by faculty teaching across disciplines. Continuing to teach will also allow you to develop logistical suggestions on how to implement these recommendations.

## Conclusion

We intend this description of our approach to provide a broad philosophy, as well as concrete ideas and strategies, that others may adapt and modify as they expand and diversify their own efforts to improve teaching and learning by integrating research and pedagogy. The ultimate goal of our approach is to solidify what is beginning to emerge at our university— a collaborative culture in which scholars across disciplines understand research on teaching and learning and the practice of teaching as vibrant, evolving, mutually informing enterprises. The development of this culture is akin to the emergence of a space for multidisciplinary discussions about the scholarship of teaching and learning that Huber and Hutchings

(2005) call the "teaching commons." We understand this culture of collaboration as just one manifestation of a broader movement toward integrating research and teaching—a movement that is advancing in multiple directions across many different institutions.

REFERENCES

2012 *iteach* offers faculty opportunity to exchange ideas on teaching. (2011, December 6). *Record*. Retrieved from http://news.wustl.edu/news/Pages/23074.aspx

Ambrose, S. A., Bridges, M. W., DiPietro, M., Lovett, M. C., & Norman, M. K. (2010). *How learning works: Seven research-based principles for smart teaching.* San Francisco, CA: Jossey-Bass.

Anderson, L. W., Krathwohl, D. R., Airasian, P. W., Cruikshank, K. A., Mayer, R. E., Pintrich, P. R., Rath, J., & Wittrock, M. C. (2001). *A taxonomy for learning, teaching, and assessing: A revision of Bloom's taxonomy of educational objectives.* New York, NY: Longman.

Angelo, T. A. (1993). A "teacher's dozen": Fourteen general, research-based principles for improving higher learning in our classrooms. *AAHE Bulletin, 45*(8), 3–13.

Angelo, T. A., & Cross, K. P. (1993). *Classroom assessment techniques: A handbook for college teachers.* San Francisco, CA: Jossey-Bass.

Bloom, B. (1956). *Taxonomy of educational objectives: Vol. 1. Cognitive domain.* New York, NY: McKay.

Bransford, J., Brown, A. L., & Cocking, R. R. (Eds.). (2000). *How people learn: Brain, mind, experience, and school.* Washington, DC: National Academy Press.

Dunlosky, J., Rawson, K. A., Marsh, E. J., Nathan, M. J., & Willingham, D. T. (2013). Improving students' learning with effective learning techniques: Promising directions from cognitive and educational psychology. *Psychological Science in the Public Interest, 14*(1), 4–58. doi:10.1177/1529100612453266

Dweck, C. S. (2006). *Mind-set: The new psychology of success.* New York, NY: Ballantine Books.

Eberlein, T., Kampmeier, J., Minderhout, V., Moog, R. S., Platt, T., Varma-Nelson, P., & White, H. B. (2008). Pedagogies of engagement in science. *Biochemistry and Molecular Biology Education, 36*(4), 262–273. doi:10.1002/bmb.20204

Fisher, B. A., Miller, K. G., Buhro, W. E., Frank, D. J., & Frey, R. F. (2012). Collaborating with faculty to design active learning with flexible technology. In J. E. Groccia & L. Cruz (Eds.), *To improve the academy: Resources* for faculty, instructional, and organizational development, Vol. 31 (pp. 329–346). San Francisco, CA: Jossey-Bass/Anker.

Fisher, B. A., & Frey, R. F. (2011). Adapting a laboratory research group model to foster the scholarship of teaching and learning. In J. E. Miller & J. E. Groccia (Eds.), To improve the academy: Resources for faculty, instructional, and organizational development, Vol. 30 (pp. 99–111). San Francisco, CA: Jossey-Bass/Anker.

Huber, M. T., & Hutchings, P. (2005). The advancement of learning: Building the teaching commons. San Francisco, CA: Carnegie Foundation for the Advancement of Teaching and Jossey-Bass.

Karpicke, J. D., & Blunt, J. R. (2011). Retrieval practice produces more learning than elaborative studying with concept mapping. Science, 331(6018), 772–775.

Lyle, K. B., & Crawford, N. A. (2011). Retrieving essential material at the end of lectures improves performance on statistics exams. Teaching of Psychology, 38(2), 94–97. doi:10.1177/0098628311401587

Mayer, R. E. (2008). Applying the science of learning: Evidence-based principles for the design of multimedia instruction. American Psychologist, 63(8), 760–769.

McDaniel, M. A., Anderson, J. L., Derbish, M. H., & Morrisette, N. (2007). Testing the testing effect in the classroom. European Journal of Cognitive Psychology, 19(4–5), 494–513.

McDaniel, M., Roediger, H., & McDermott, K. (2007). Generalizing test-enhanced learning from the laboratory to the classroom. Psychonomic Bulletin and Review, 14(2), 200–206.

Mestre, J., & Ross, B. H. (Eds.). (2011). Cognition in education. San Diego, CA: Academic Press.

Pashler, H., Bain, P. M., Bottge, B. A., Graesser, A., Koedinger, K., McDaniel, M., & Metcalfe, J. (2007). Organizing instruction and study to improve student learning. IES practice guide. Washington, DC: National Center for Educational Research, Institute of Education Sciences, US Department of Education.

Roediger, H. L., Agarwal, P. K., McDaniel, M. A., & McDermott, K. B. (2011). Test-enhanced learning in the classroom: Long-term improvements from quizzing. Journal of Experimental Psychology: Applied, 17(4), 382–395. doi:10.1037/a0026252

Roediger, H. L., & Karpicke, J. D. (2006). Test-enhanced learning. Psychological Science, 17(3), 249–255.

Roediger, H. L., McDermott, K., & McDaniel, M. A. (2011). Using testing to improve learning and memory. In M. A. Gernsbacher, R. Pew, L. Hough, & J. R. Pomerantz (Eds.), Psychology and the real world: Essays illustrating *fundamental contributions to society* (pp. 65–74). New York, NY: Worth Publishers.

Sawyer, R. K. (2005). Introduction: The new science of learning. In R. K. Sawyer (Ed.), *Cambridge handbook of the learning sciences* (pp. 1–16). Cambridge: Cambridge University Press.

Sawyer, R. K., & Nathan, M. J. (in press). Teaching and the learning sciences. In D. Gitomer & C. Bell (Eds.), *Handbook of research on teaching* (5th ed.). Washington, DC: American Educational Research Association.

Willingham, D. T. (2009). *Why don't students like school? A cognitive scientist answers questions about how the mind works and what it means for your classroom.* San Francisco, CA: Jossey-Bass.

PART TWO

# FACULTY DEVELOPMENT
# AUDIENCE AND PARTNERS

4

# FORMAL AND INFORMAL SUPPORT FOR PRETENURE FACULTY

## RECOMMENDATIONS FOR ADMINISTRATORS AND INSTITUTIONS

*Gwendolyn Mettetal, Gail M. McGuire*
*Indiana University South Bend*

*We analyze interviews from sixty-five faculty and administrators to understand the formal and informal types of support that pretenure faculty use to navigate their way to tenure. By understanding the different types of support that pretenure faculty need, institutions can better address the diverse issues that junior faculty confront when preparing for tenure and can ensure that all candidates receive some type of support. We conclude that institutions need to be intentional about offering both formal and informal support to pretenure faculty at various points in their careers.*

o

For most academics, the tenure decision is the most critical and anxiety-producing time in their career. Fortunately, there are many books with advice for pretenure faculty members, including suggestions on how to maintain scholarly productivity, be collegial, and balance competing demands (Diamond, 2004; Lang, 2005; Toth, 2009; Whicker,

We thank Indiana University South Bend for its financial support of this project.

59

Kronenfeld, & Strickland, 1993). Certainly tenure advice books for candidates are helpful, but they focus on the aspects of the tenure process that are largely under the control of the pretenure faculty member. Little scholarship offers guidance to the administrators who are supervising the tenure process and the institutions within which faculty are seeking tenure. We contend that many of the choices pretenure faculty members make depend on the options their institutions provide. Successfully navigating the tenure process therefore depends on both the individual choices that faculty members and the opportunities their institutions provide.

This chapter offers guidance to administrators and institutions on how best to support pretenure candidates as they progress toward tenure. Our case study identifies a range of formal and informal sources of support for pretenure faculty that an institution should consider offering. The multiple types of support we identify can assist institutions in addressing the diverse issues (balancing teaching, research, and service; documenting performance) that candidates face when preparing for tenure. We share both the strengths and weakness of the tenure support provided by our institution so that others can craft an effective portfolio of tenure support for their pretenure faculty. While pretenure candidates are responsible for meeting the standards for tenure in their institution, institutions also have a responsibility to inform candidates of these standards and offer them support in reaching them. This study is unique in focusing on recommendations to administrators and institutions and recognizing the importance of both formal and informal support for pretenure faculty members.

## Methods

One of us (Mettetal) conducted an action research study on the support that faculty received as they worked toward tenure on our campus. Action research aims to address people's practical concerns (in this case, getting tenure) and contribute to broader knowledge in a collaborative research context (Griffiths & Davies, 1993; Rapoport, 1970). Mettetal interviewed thirty-two of the forty-three faculty members who had received tenure in the past five years. Although the original focus of these semistructured interviews was a tenure dossier preparation group, the scope soon expanded to ask about all forms of support for achieving tenure. In addition, Mettetal interviewed five coleaders of the dossier preparation group and six administrators (deans, directors, and chairs), and held two focus groups with twenty-two pretenure faculty members. Interviewees represented a variety of disciplines, including arts, natural sciences, social sciences, education, business, and humanities. Interviews lasted an average of one hour and were audiotaped. The university's institutional review board approved both the original protocol and the revisions. Using qualitative methods that Glesne and Peshkin (1992) recommended, we both independently reviewed transcripts and looked for emergent themes. After discussion, we identified several major themes and then returned to the data to look for specific evidence of those themes. Although our suggestions are based primarily on these data, we also draw on Mettetal's eleven years of experience as a coleader of the tenure dossier prep group on our campus and the experience both of us have had as campus administrators.

Indiana University (IU) South Bend is a comprehensive public university in north central Indiana and the third largest campus in the IU system. The university has approximately eighty-three hundred students and offers over one hundred majors. The campus employs about 300 full-time faculty members and about 260 part-time faculty members. Tenure-track faculty members are generally required to spend 75 percent of their time teaching (three courses per semester).

## Results and Discussion

Our research identified both formal and informal support for tenure on our campus. Sources of formal support included written documents, chairs and deans, formal mentors, a tenure dossier preparation group through the teaching center, third-year feedback from the academic senate tenure committee, new faculty orientation, and participation on a tenure committee. Sources of informal support included senior faculty members and peers.

### Formal Support for Tenure

Our campus provides a number of formal sources of support to pretenure faculty ranging from a faculty handbook to a tenure preparation group. Faculty in our study were generally aware of these formal sources, but the helpfulness of each source varied with individual circumstances.

WRITTEN DOCUMENTS    When new faculty arrive on campus, they are given documents that discuss tenure procedures and expectations. Sections of the IU and the IU South Bend academic handbooks describe policies and procedures and also provide an outline of materials that must be included in the tenure dossier. In addition, new faculty receive copies of their unit tenure expectations, which are more specific. According to our interviewees, these documents were useful in preparing a tenure dossier. For example, one faculty member said, "I got the faculty handbook, and somebody pointed out a list to follow—that list as you start to put together your dossier, and I did that from my very first submission." Another interviewee noted, "One of the nice things about our department is that we have a document that outlines what is considered excellence in teaching, what is considered excellence in research . . . We have a very clear departmental document." In sum, formal tenure documents were useful for identifying the general contents of dossier and in some cases for articulating standards for excellence.

About half of the faculty members we interviewed were in units that ask for a complete dossier for each reappointment, which occurs almost every year. Several of those faculty mentioned that they used the same outline for their tenure dossiers that they did for their reappointment dossiers, which helped them keep materials organized. A unit's process for reappointment therefore can also influence the difficulty or ease of preparing a tenure dossier.

CHAIRS AND DEANS   Department chairs (or deans in smaller units) were another source of formal support for pretenure faculty in our study. Faculty members are formally reviewed by their chair every spring based on their annual report of accomplishments in teaching, scholarship, and service. Faculty are also reappointed approximately once a year, and although reappointments go through all of the levels of a tenure decision, the most detailed feedback usually comes from the department chair. (In one unit, the unit's promotion, tenure, and reappointment committee provides that detailed feedback to the candidate.) If the chair takes this role seriously, these multiple opportunities for feedback and discussion can play a key role in helping junior faculty members build a strong case for tenure. Chairs can also use this occasion to offer guidance, provide resources, and point out opportunities that will benefit the pretenure faculty member. One professor remarked, for instance, "I got a lot of good information from my annual reviews from the school's tenure committee." The committee gave detailed feedback on his strengths and weaknesses and suggested actions he could take to strengthen his case for tenure.

Not all interviewees had supportive chairs or deans. In some cases, the problem was a lack of mentoring and social skills or benign neglect. In other instances, candidates reported having adversarial relationships with their supervisors. According to one interviewee, "I've had these pretty vocal arguments with the chair, so he might have reappointed me with reservations . . . and then I understand that he instructed my dean not to reappoint me the year before my tenure." Another interviewee was in a unit with an unsupportive dean. When that dean left the year before the tenure decision, a professor from a different unit stepped in as interim dean. The interviewee said, "I believe God sent him to me! He had the experience; he knew exactly what needed to be done, when; what we needed. You don't have to know the discipline to mentor someone to tenure. You have to know academia. You have to know the system." This interim dean explained exactly what was going to be needed for tenure, including teaching documentation, scholarship, and external letters.

FORMAL MENTOR   Chairs and deans can be important formal sources of support if they are competent and have a good relationship with the candidate. Because an institution cannot always assume either of these, it is important to have other formal mentors available to candidates. Mentors are "individuals with advanced experience and knowledge who are committed to providing support and upward mobility to their protégés' careers" (Ragins, 1999, p. 349). In a formal mentor program, individuals are assigned to each other, some official expectations of the relationship are communicated, and the relationship has a limited duration (Baugh & Fagenson-Eland, 2007).

The history of formal mentoring on our campus offers a cautionary tale about how to make formal mentor programs effective. For many years, each unit on our campus assigned senior faculty as mentors for incoming faculty. When the University Center for Excellence in Teaching (UCET) was founded, it took over that responsibility, but three years later, the deans took back this task. In the following years, assignment of mentors was erratic, depending on the unit. UCET continues to arrange mentors for any faculty who request one, which helps fill the gaps. These formally assigned mentors could be very useful in explaining campus culture to new faculty, but according to our interviewees, they were not very helpful when it came to tenure issues.

Although some of the interviewees reported that formal mentors were helpful, most interviewees did not get much assistance from their mentors or were never assigned a mentor. On the positive side, a faculty member said, "I met with my mentor and got some honest feedback. Umm, some really good suggestions." This faculty member was encouraged by her mentor to collaborate with her new colleagues and to have a colleague observe her teaching, for instance. However, another interviewee said, "That faculty mentor position was very helpful to me my first semester in making that transition. But in terms of tenure, particularly because he had gone up for tenure a long time ago . . . Umm, I wasn't really looking for people who had gone ten or twenty years ago."

Inconsistent and unclear expectations for formal mentors likely explain the variation in their helpfulness with tenure. When UCET assigned mentors, a mentor training workshop discussed the needs of new faculty members and best practices in mentoring. Campus units, in contrast, did not provide that structure. The result was often benign neglect by the formal mentor, as one interviewee noted: "The mentor was always available to me and was always interested in answering my questions, but the mentor didn't necessarily seek me out to just kind of check in with me or to, you know, share some ideas that he might have had. So I had to make the effort to go by and say what about this, or explain this to me and so, I mean, he was very willing to do that, but I had to instigate it."

Another problem with our formal mentor structure was in how mentors were assigned to junior faculty members. The usual unit practice was to assign one of the most senior faculty in a unit as a mentor, but that person might not be the best choice. Senior faculty may be too busy, too removed from the tenure process, or not interested in fulfilling this role. Finally, because most senior faculty on our campus are white, they might not understand the challenges of the increasingly diverse junior faculty (Bowman, Kite, Branscombe, & Williams, 1999).

UCET TENURE DOSSIER PREPARATION GROUP   Our campus teaching center, UCET, sponsors a group to assist faculty in tenure dossier preparation every year. Faculty are invited to join the group in the November before they submit their dossier. Co-mentors who are experienced in many aspects of the tenure process lead these meetings, which take place every two to four weeks until dossiers are submitted in mid-August. The agenda includes drafting and commenting on vita and teaching and research statements, providing information on the tenure process (e.g., time line, soliciting letters), and tips on the mechanics of dossier preparation (e.g., assembling dossier binders) not easily found elsewhere. Because group mentors and participants come from a variety of disciplines, they must explain their teaching and research to colleagues from other areas. These discussions are particularly helpful in clarifying teaching and research statements. The usefulness of joint reflection was highlighted in McBride and Voegele's (2012) description of a faculty learning community focused on tenure and promotion.

According to those who participated in the UCET group, the most important benefit of participation was not the actual information provided, but the interactive aspects of the group process. One participant commented, "The direct instruction was probably the least important part and the 'active learning' part was the part that I found invaluable." One of the major activities of the group is to give feedback on each other's materials, and the group format seems to be conducive to this process. According to one participant, "I think that the group format is beneficial not just for the social comparison but also to see that it puts the criticism of your dossier in the context of, well, everybody's getting criticism and it's all supportive and made it easier I think, as opposed to let's say if I'd had you and X helping me and say 'there's this problem with your dossier.'" Other benefits of participation interviewees mentioned were relieving stress, making new friends, and providing a time line and deadlines.

Not all participants found the UCET group helpful. Sometimes one or two highly anxious group members would monopolize the sessions, and their anxiety could be contagious. Several participants did not like the interdisciplinary nature of the group because they thought the discussions about teaching and research in other disciplines were not relevant to them. Finally, comments suggest that in some years, the group was too unstructured and consequently not very helpful. However, these comments tended to come from the people who had attended only a few of the sessions. Of those who did not attend the group, half said that they either felt that they knew what they were doing or that they already had quite a bit of help from other sources. Others mentioned time conflicts or other factors as reasons for not attending.

THIRD-YEAR FEEDBACK FROM ACADEMIC SENATE TENURE COMMITTEE    Our faculty handbook states that faculty in their third year can submit a dossier to the senate promotion, tenure, and reappointment committee (our campus PTR committee) and receive feedback about progress toward tenure. The dossier is usually assigned to one or two members of the committee for confidential feedback. Of those who took advantage of this option, most thought it was useful, especially if the candidate had no other source of feedback before tenure. One person said, "That was very helpful, and I've encouraged everybody to take advantage of that . . . It seems like you got a letter which gives you a limited amount of information, and then you can contact the person for a meeting. And it's the meeting that's always more helpful." During the meeting, some PTR members gave detailed feedback on the candidate's progress toward tenure, as well as dossier organization. One interviewee mentioned that the third-year review was an impetus to begin working on the tenure dossier early.

Like formal mentoring, however, the quality and quantity of feedback from the PTR committee varied widely, depending on who was on the committee. "I think a third-year review might or might not be useful depending on the kind of feedback that you get," said one interviewee. Based on our own experience, we know that the PTR committee did not always know they were supposed to offer this service. In fact, one year the committee sent the notice of this service out so late that candidates did not have time to compile a dossier. A handful of faculty members also said that compiling a dossier for the third-year review took too much time and effort. One said, "I took a look at that, and the thought [was] that it looked onerous or worrisome or too much for me to think about." Faculty members in our sample who decided not to participate in a third-year review were from units that did not turn in a complete dossier for reappointments, so they would be assembling a dossier from scratch. In units requiring a reappointment dossier, it was very easy to submit a midcareer dossier to the senate PTR committee.

NEW FACULTY ORIENTATION   The University Center for Excellence in Teaching provides an orientation for new faculty, and most new faculty attend all or most of the sessions. The format has varied widely, from an intensive week to several days spread out over several weeks, but it always includes a brief discussion of the tenure process. One popular feature of the orientation is a panel discussion by pretenure faculty in their second or third year. They speak on many issues, from teaching concerns to setting up a laboratory to work/life balance, but they always mention thinking ahead to tenure. The main point they make about tenure is that faculty must begin documenting their teaching, research, and service early in their careers. A few interviewees recalled that the orientation urged them to save datebooks, syllabi, thank you letters, and other documents that they could eventually use to document their contributions.

PARTICIPATION ON A TENURE COMMITTEE   Several interviewees mentioned serving on or observing a promotion and tenure committee as useful in preparing a dossier. At our institution, we recognize that PTR service can be helpful to junior faculty members, and chairs often suggest to junior faculty members that they serve a term on a PTR committee before going up for tenure. One faculty member said that serving on his unit's PTR committee helped him better understand the personalities in his unit: "You understand people a little better when you hear [them] vocalize their thoughts and you see a particular spin they might be interested in and how they look at things." Other faculty members explained that serving on a PTR committee helped them see what committee members pay attention to and how they evaluate materials. For instance, one junior faculty member said that she did not realize the importance of annual reports until she served on a PTR committee. Finally, one interviewee said that serving on a PTR committee taught her how to write for a general audience: "I think probably amongst the most useful things I got out of being on the PT&R Committee . . . was to realize just how little people outside my field understand not just the gory details of what it is I do but the whole culture of how my kind of science operates." Finally, serving on a PTR committee gave pretenure faculty the opportunity to review many dossiers—good and bad. Candidates reported that it was helpful to know that there was not just one right way to put a dossier together, but that there were also certain practices that made a dossier ineffective or unimpressive.

## Informal Support for Tenure

While IU-South Bend has a fairly extensive system of formal support for tenure, the participants in this study took advantage of informal sources of support as well. Senior colleagues within the university were the most common source of informal support, followed by peers within the university.

SENIOR FACULTY MEMBER Although the university handbook and departmental documents describe the general contents of the tenure dossier, they cannot possibly list all items that might be included in a dossier. Senior colleagues helped to fill this gap by informing candidates what materials to keep and how to document teaching, research, and service. For instance, one junior faculty member described how a senior colleague told her to document everything she did. Based on the authors' experience, this was good advice because when a junior faculty member starts on the tenure track, she or he might not be completely certain about her or his area of excellence. For instance, when one of our colleagues started on the tenure track on our campus, she had assumed that her area of excellence would be research. However, when her research articles took longer than expected to get published, she was grateful for the senior faculty member who encouraged her to document her teaching excellence because she declared teaching as her area of excellence for tenure.

Formal PTR documents typically do not describe different strategies to employ in creating a dossier, in particular, how to categorize one's research, teaching, and service activities (e.g., does a teaching publication go in the research or teaching section of the dossier?). Senior faculty made their own tenure dossiers available to candidates so that they could envision how to organize a dossier, demonstrate excellence, and write for a general audience. These colleagues also helped junior faculty understand and navigate the informal PTR guidelines. One interviewee obtained feedback from senior colleagues on what she called "the hidden rules about what counts as service at IUSB and what counts as scholarship." These rules are not in the handbook or formal PTR guidelines, but rather are determined by the culture of each academic unit. Finally, senior faculty helped pretenure faculty view their dossier from the perspective of their evaluators. One junior faculty member said that a senior colleague told him what people on PTR committees looked for and how they evaluated dossiers.

Senior colleagues also gave pretenure faculty copies of their annual reports for review and offered advice on what to put in their annual reports. These evaluations are foundational documents in the dossier because they are the record of one's yearly progress toward tenure. It is in these reports that faculty begin to build their case for excellence in research, teaching, or service. It would be extremely difficult to claim excellence in teaching for tenure, for instance, without documenting one's teaching activities and development every year.

Some pretenure faculty reported being anxious about how to put the actual dossier together—how to organize it, format it, what tabs to use, and so on. Senior colleagues demystified this aspect of the tenure process by helping candidates with these nuts-and-bolts issues of the dossier. For instance, one interviewee reported that two senior colleagues "talked about what they did and how long it took them and what they spent the most time on." Another senior colleague described "what was in his dossier and how he did it and how he thought about it." This information made the junior faculty member feel more confident that she would not "set off any red flags."

Senior faculty also helped junior colleagues by reviewing their dossiers. Their attention helped untenured faculty members identify what was missing from their dossier and what was unnecessary for it. One faculty member explained that a senior colleague helped her include "invisible labor," such as teaching outside the classroom and noncommittee service. In some cases, senior colleagues also edited dossier statements. One interviewee said this was particularly important for her because English was her second language.

The encouragement of senior colleagues was an important aspect of informal support in the tenure process as well. For instance, a senior colleague told one interviewee, "You've done these good things . . . don't feel nervous about this. You know this [going through tenure] is an opportunity for you to reflect." Another junior faculty member said, "One of the reasons why I got plenty of good nights' sleep over the process is just that I really simply had helpful and supportive senior colleagues who made it clear for me . . . that they had confidence in me." Similarly, one untenured faculty member said, "I feel like they [senior colleagues] want you to succeed and they're very supportive. The expectation is that you will succeed." Encouragement from senior faculty who had survived the tenure process helped to decrease pretenure faculty members' anxiety and instill confidence in them at this vulnerable time.

Among the interviewees who relied on senior colleagues for help was a small subgroup who considered their senior colleague mentors. An interviewee with a vulnerable tenure case (she had little support from her chair and dean) said that her mentor had stood up to the administration on her behalf and told them that the junior faculty member was being treated unfairly. According to the interviewee, "Had she not done that, I probably wouldn't have gotten promoted." Another interviewee described the help she received from her mentor on the politics of the PTR process: "Another thing that was important about her mentoring is she has such a good sense of the ins and outs of this university, the politics. She's been on the PTR committee." One faculty member described how his mentor took him and a few other junior faculty "under her wing" and told them what to do and what not to do in regard to the different people in their unit. He said that his mentor warned him, "Be careful, don't step on this land mine, don't say too much about that because X doesn't like it." In other words, his mentor helped him navigate the political landscape in his academic unit.

PEERS    The most common type of support that peers gave to each other was emotional and social. Some faculty members said they took comfort knowing that their peers were experiencing similar hardships and anxiety. For example, one interviewee said that it felt good knowing "that you're not the only person going through this pain and suffering . . . Misery likes company, and it felt good that you're not the only one walking the halls on the weekends."

According to our data, peers often served as sounding boards for pretenure faculty, which helped the latter interpret tenure expectations. One candidate and a few other pretenured faculty members in his unit formed an informal support group to exchange ideas about what to include in the dossier. Another pretenured person said that she and a peer, who came from work backgrounds different from those of many of her other colleagues at the university, talked a lot about "the different cultural expectations" in their old and current work environments.

In some cases, peers assisted each other with the statements in their dossiers as well. One faculty member described a lot of informal interaction (e.g., meeting for coffee) among the untenured folks in his unit and that he "picked up on things just from those kind of discussions." His peers sat on different committees, including PTR, and shared information from those experiences that helped him write his statements for a general audience. Another interviewee asked a junior faculty member in her department to read her research statement. She said, "I was concerned about my research statement being intelligible to people completely outside the field." She felt that if this person could understand her research statement, then others outside of her area probably would as well.

## Conclusion

Pretenure faculty members differ in their strengths, needs, and willingness to use available resources. Units also differ in regard to the types of support they offer pretenure faculty members. Given all of these variables, institutions should create a wide web of support for pretenure faculty, including formal and informal sources. While formal documents provide the general framework for tenure and dossier preparation, informal mentors and peers help candidates navigate the politics of tenure, clarify expectations for their units, and provide emotional support. Building this kind of web will decrease the likelihood that a candidate will fall through the cracks. This case study also highlights the need to offer support to pretenure faculty at various points in their careers. Faculty orientations and tenure documents can be important in introducing ideas to junior faculty early on that chairs, mentors, and dossier support groups can later reinforce. While many of the faculty in our study reported more benefits from informal than formal sources, it is critical to offer formal sources of help for faculty who have unsupportive supervisors or work in hostile environments.

Whatever sources of support that institutions offer to pretenure faculty, they need to be intentional about how they do it. For instance, if institutions want chairs to be primarily responsible for guiding pretenure faculty through the tenure process, they need to communicate this expectation to chairs and prepare chairs to provide this support. They should also ensure that mentoring junior faculty is one of the criteria on which chairs are evaluated. If an institution decides to institute a formal mentor program, it needs to carefully consider program design, including training, structures of accountability, and communication of expectations (Lottero-Perdue & Fifield, 2010).

Our interviewees reported that informal sources of tenure support were more beneficial than formal sources, which suggests that institutions need to pay particular attention to the social climate on their campus. Administrators cannot make people like each other, of course, but they can create opportunities that will increase the likelihood that informal bonds will develop between faculty members. For instance, an all-day or overnight retreat could allow faculty to have more in-depth conversations than they would in the hallway. We recommend holding a retreat in a location with leisure activities available, such as walking, golfing, swimming, and having a glass a wine. Offering opportunities for faculty to share a meal or cup of coffee is another way to foster informal connections. When one of us (McGuire) was a junior faculty member, she was invited to attend a monthly gathering of faculty from her college at a local coffee house as well as a monthly ethnic potluck that drew faculty from across the campus. The relaxed nature of these occasions often led to off-the-record conversations about other faculty members and administrators, as well as explanations of how the university "really" operated. Finally, administrators should not underestimate the importance of physical space for fostering informal relations. We have faculty lounges scattered across our campus, which are often equipped with microwaves, refrigerators, coffee makers, and tables for eating. These amenities encourage faculty members to interact outside meetings regularly and create opportunities for personal conversations.

In sum, we recommend that institutions review the different sources of tenure support they offer junior faculty. While our results suggest that informal sources of support are more effective than formal sources of support, we recommend that institutions offer a variety of both types of support in order to meet the diverse needs of pretenure faculty. Being intentional about offering formal and informal support for pretenure faculty will help institutions create an effective web of support for junior faculty members as they work through the tenure process.

## REFERENCES

Baugh, A. G., & Fagenson-Eland, E. A. (2007). Formal mentoring programs: A "poor cousin" to informal relationships? In B. R. Ragins & K. E. Kram (Eds.), *The handbook of mentoring at work: Theory, research, and practice* (pp. 249–271). Thousand Oaks, CA: Sage.

Bowman, S. R., Kite, M E., Branscombe, N. R., & Williams, S. (1999). Developmental relationships of black Americans in the academy. In A. J. Murrell, F. J. Crosby, & R. J. Ely (Eds.), *Mentoring dilemmas: Developmental relationships within multicultural organizations* (pp. 21–46). Mahwah, NJ: Erlbaum.

Diamond, R. M. (2004). *Preparing for promotion, tenure, and annual review: A faculty guide* (2nd ed.). San Francisco, CA: Jossey-Bass.

Glesne, C., & Peshkin, A. (1992). *Becoming qualitative researchers: An introduction.* White Plains, NY: Longman.

Griffiths, M., & Davies, C. (1993). Learning to learn: Action research from an equal opportunities perspective in a junior school. *British Educational Research Journal, 19*(1), 43–76.

Lang, J. M. (2005). *Life on the tenure track: Lessons from the first year.* Baltimore, MD: John Hopkins University Press.

Lottero-Perdue, P., & Fifield, S. (2010). A conceptual framework for higher education faculty mentoring. In L. B. Nilson & J. E. Miller (Eds.), *To improve the academy: Resources for faculty, instructional, and organizational development, Vol. 28* (pp. 37–62). San Francisco, CA: Jossey-Bass.

McBride, L. G., & Voegele, J. D. (2012). Reflecting together about tenure and promotion: A faculty learning community approach. In J. E. Miller & J. E. Groccia (Eds.), *To improve the academy: Resources for faculty, instructional, and organizational development, Vol. 30* (pp. 43–53). San Francisco, CA: Jossey-Bass.

Ragins, B. R. (1999). Gender and mentoring relationships: A review and research agenda for the next decade. In G. N. Powell (Ed.), *Handbook of gender and work* (pp. 347–370). Thousand Oaks, CA: Sage

Rapoport, R. (1970). Three dilemmas of action research. *Human Relations, 23*(6), 499–513.

Toth, E. (2009). *Ms. Mentor's new and evermore impeccable advice for women and men in academia.* Philadelphia: University of Pennsylvania Press.

Whicker, M. L., Kronenfeld, J. J., & Strickland, R. A. (1993). *Getting tenure.* Newbury Park, CA: Sage.

# 5

# KEEPING THE FIRE BURNING

## STRATEGIES TO SUPPORT SENIOR FACULTY

*Michael J. Zeig, Roger G. Baldwin*
*Michigan State University*

*Recent reports indicate that at some colleges and universities, as many as one in three professors are age sixty or older. This increase in senior faculty raises the question of what institutions do to support this large and important cohort. Historically, faculty development programs have focused on early-career faculty, with less attention paid to more seasoned professors. Based on a national web-based investigation, this chapter reviews the strategies some institutions have implemented to support senior faculty. It also provides recommendations for how senior faculty and their administrator colleagues can provide new meaning and purpose to this phase of academic life.*

---

As baby boomers approach retirement age, many organizations, including higher education institutions, face an increasingly older workforce. While this means that some organizations will face high turnover rates in the coming years, higher education institutions face a unique challenge in dealing with an aging professoriate. The growing number of older professors, combined with the end of mandatory retirement, an increasing life span, economic uncertainty, and a love for their profession, is resulting in a large number of older professors putting off retirement.

In fact, the *Chronicle of Higher Education* recently reported, "At some universities . . . more than one in three tenured or tenure-track professors are now 60 or older" (June 2012, para. 4). Colleges and universities may face an increasing number of retirements as professors continue to age, but they also face the question of how to support older professors who remain employed at their institutions.

In *The Vitality of Senior Faculty Members: Snow on the Roof—Fire in the Furnace*, Bland and Berquist (1997) argued that senior professors are a vital force with much to contribute to their institutions and profession. This chapter explores the varied ways in which institutions currently support the distinctive needs of senior faculty. There are many ways to identify a senior faculty member through indicators such as rank, age, and years of service. For this reason, definitions vary across institutions. For the purposes of this chapter, we define a senior faculty member as an individual who is fifty-five years or older with many years (fifteen or more) of service in the academic profession.

## Brief History of Faculty Development

Historically faculty development programs have focused primarily on early-career, tenure-track faculty. The needs and concerns of early-career faculty have been chronicled in great depth (Austin, 2003; Boice, 1992; Brown, 2006). Although early-career faculty encounter many challenges during the beginning years of their employment, they also often receive significant start-up funds for research projects, protection from time-consuming committee work, mentoring, and other forms of development support for their teaching. Colleges and universities often view early-career faculty as one of their highest priorities and offer many programs and services designed to address early-career challenges.

In recent years, interest in faculty development has expanded to include a focus on midcareer faculty. Baldwin and Chang (2006) identified strategies colleges and universities have implemented to support mid-career faculty, including support to move research in new directions or develop new teaching skills. Baldwin, DeZure, Shaw, and Moretto (2008) studied midcareer faculty at a research university and outlined distinctive challenges these professors face, including the lack of a clear direction following the attainment of tenure. The researchers also identified support strategies that institutions, especially department chairs, can use to support faculty in the middle of their careers.

Support for faculty development now extends beyond the formal boundaries of an academic career. For example, many doctoral institutions have created their own future faculty preparation programs (Preparing Future Faculty, 2012) as a means to prepare graduate students more thoroughly for a faculty career by enhancing the culture of doctoral education and the professional socialization process (Austin, 2002; Pruitt-Logan & Gaff, 2004). On the back end of the career is a new focus on how to support faculty in their transition to retirement along with initiatives to make the retirement years engaging and fulfilling. In a nationwide study, Baldwin and Zeig (2012) identified 180 retired faculty organizations providing a range of services and activities for emeritus professors. There is also a national organization, the Association of Retirement Organizations in Higher Education (2012), dedicated to supporting campus efforts to serve retired faculty.

The many ways faculty are supported from their time in graduate school through their early- and middle-career phases and in retirement are all important to faculty careers. Unfortunately, much less attention has been paid to faculty during the latter stages of their employment despite the fact that faculty in their fifties and sixties may still work for another ten to fifteen years. Although the needs of senior professors may be different from those of younger faculty, these needs should not be discounted or ignored. If institutions are serious about supporting strong faculty performance at all career stages, it is important to consider the needs of senior late-career faculty and examine strategies designed to support this important group of professors. Gappa, Austin, and Trice (2007) argued that "in order to work creatively and effectively in a rapidly changing context, faculty must engage in continuous learning so as to constantly expand their repertoires of talents and skills" (p. 84). Colleges and universities have an important role to play in facilitating this continual learning and development.

## Needs of Senior Faculty

The professional needs of senior faculty often differ from those of early- or midcareer faculty. Although some senior faculty may still be interested in pursuing goals comparable to those of their junior colleagues, others may be focused on new aspects of their career. Bland and Berquist (1997) indicated that senior faculty often wish to contribute to their institutions in different capacities such as renegotiated teaching duties, service roles, or mentoring new faculty members, which may differ from earlier priorities in their careers when they were more focused on their own research productivity. Berberet, Bland, Brown, and Risbey (2004) found that many senior faculty are interested in more flexible workload arrangements, as well as contributing to their institutions through service

activities in areas where they may have well-developed skills and expertise. In addition, some senior faculty are interested in having opportunities to learn entirely new roles through on-campus "internships" or
other opportunities that allow them to explore new ways to contribute to
their institutions in administrative or other professional roles (Berberet
et al., 2004).

Besides looking for new ways to contribute to their institutions, senior
faculty may also desire support services more closely aligned with their
distinctive needs. Bataille and Brown (2006) argued that senior faculty are
particularly sensitive to resource allocation issues and may have a strong
desire for access to research funds to jump-start or move their research
in new directions. In terms of teaching support, Schuster and Finkelstein
(2006) noted that many senior faculty are interested in learning new
instructional technologies but do not receive proper training on how to
integrate those technologies in the classroom. Trower (2011) found that
many senior faculty desire more support and encouragement from
administrators and peers to help them "remain vital, productive, and
engaged" (p. 11). This can include better communication about expectations and priorities and continuity in those expectations even during
leadership changes within the university (Trower, 2011). Despite the
growing documentation of the needs of senior faculty, little is known
about how institutions actually support faculty in the latter stages of
their careers.

## Support for Senior Faculty

In order to gain a better understanding of the current forms of support for
senior faculty, we conducted a national web-based search for senior
faculty development programs, policies, and services. The search was
conducted during spring 2012 using search terms such as "senior faculty
programs," "senior faculty development," and "support for late-career
faculty." We focused on identifying institutions with forms of support
targeted specifically at senior faculty, although institutions often defined
senior faculty differently. We did not review monetary retirement incen-
tives or buy-outs since those options are focused on encouraging retirements rather than developing faculty.

We discovered that many faculty development offices indicate they
offer programs for faculty from early-through late-career stages, although
they often do not make clear specifically how senior faculty are supported
differently from faculty at other career stages. It is less common for
institutions to maintain programs and services specifically aimed at senior

---

**Table 5.1   Examples of Institutional Support for Senior Faculty**

---

*Development programs*

Carleton College (https://apps.carleton.edu/handbook/facultyapp/?policy_id= 864379#864439)

Marquette University (http://www.marquette.edu/phil/documents/SeFacRevPro tocols.pdf)

University of Georgia (http://www.ctl.uga.edu/faculty/ctl_senior_teaching_fellows)

Western Michigan University (http://www.wmich.edu/facdev/Programs /Communities.html)

*Mentoring*

University of Michigan (http://www.provost.umich.edu/faculty/faculty_mentor ing_study/ideas.html)

University of North Carolina-Greensboro (http://www.uncg.edu/tlc/mentoring/)

*Research support*

Dartmouth College (http://www.dartmouth.edu/~dof/jjf_sfg_2011memo_rev .pdf)

Elon University (http://www.elon.edu/e-web/faculty/faculty_funding/replacement .xhtml#senior)

Georgetown University (http://admin.maincampusresearch.georgetown.edu /index.php/Grant-Senior_Faculty_Research_Fellowships)

Illinois State College of Fine Arts (http://www.cfa.ilstu.edu/faculty_staff/grants .shtml)

*Workload adjustment*

Appalachian State University (http://www.hubbard.appstate.edu/senior-faculty)

Drake University (http://www.drake.edu/academics/policies/pdf/srfacultystatus .pdf)

*Recognition*

Ohio State University (http://www.osu.edu/universityawards/2012/scholar.html)

University of Michigan (http://www.rackham.umich.edu/faculty_staff/awards /faculty_awards/henry_russel_lectureship/)

---

faculty. Our search did, however, identify five main categories of support provided for senior faculty: development programs, mentoring, research support, workload adjustments, and recognition. We highlight examples of each form of support within each category. We chose the examples to highlight a variety of types of well-developed programs and services from multiple institutional types. Table 5.1 provides web URLs of selected examples within each category.

## Development Programs

One method institutions use to support senior faculty is through development programs designed to address the unique interests and needs of senior faculty. Many of these programs provide forums for reflecting on professional roles, duties, and future directions. For example, Carleton College's (2012) Senior Faculty Development Forum "provides a regular opportunity for faculty who are Full Professors to reflect on teaching, scholarship, creative and service activities and to plan a course of professional development for the future" (para. 3). These reflective activities often focus on honing new skills related to teaching and learning. At Western Michigan University, the faculty development office established senior faculty learning communities to discuss teaching innovations. The University of Georgia's senior teaching fellows program focuses on sharing ideas across disciplines related to undergraduate instruction. This program also involves creating an instructional project "to strengthen courses and teaching methods in each participant's academic department" (University of Georgia Center for Teaching and Learning, 2012, para. 2).

Some institutions include department chairs in a reflective developmental review process with senior faculty, with the emphasis clearly on professional development, not evaluation. At King's College, the senior faculty development program provides senior faculty members an opportunity to create a professional development plan outlining long-term goals and how those goals align with the needs of the department and college. Similarly, Marquette University's (2012) philosophy department maintains a policy for reviewing senior faculty that encourages a "frank and candid discussion regarding the enhancement of a faculty member's career, working conditions, and satisfaction at Marquette" (para. 1).

Some development programs include monetary support. The programs at Carleton and Georgia provide faculty members with five hundred dollars and two thousand dollars, respectively, for supporting faculty members' professional development or for completing projects related to their development goals. Although King's College does not indicate a specific monetary amount, its program does make a general commitment to provide faculty members with resources to achieve mutually beneficial goals within their development plans. These funds, although often in small amounts, send an important message to senior faculty that their continued developmental needs are not only recognized but also supported financially.

## Mentoring

Another way institutions use senior faculty is to involve them in mentoring their junior colleagues. These programs typically pair an experienced, tenured faculty member with a newly hired assistant professor. The senior faculty member may provide guidance to the newer professor on teaching, research, or other professional roles. Although mentoring programs usually emphasize benefits to the junior partner, these programs can also offer developmental opportunities for the senior faculty mentor. For example, at the University of North Carolina-Greensboro, the New Faculty Mentoring Program is described as a mutually beneficial opportunity. The senior faculty mentors receive summer training in mentoring, meet monthly with the other senior faculty mentors, and receive five hundred dollars in an academic expense account. In this program, the senior faculty have an opportunity to grow and develop as mentors. This opportunity may help them beyond their immediate mentoring of a junior colleague and can also help them in future student mentoring activities as well.

At the University of Michigan, the provost's office provides a list of ideas related to mentoring intended for deans, associate deans, and department chairs to consider in establishing their own mentoring programs. Among the suggestions, the office recommends that senior faculty who provide mentoring services receive course release time or appropriate recognition during annual reviews for their mentoring activities as a university service, or both. Ensuring that mentoring activities are beneficial to both the mentor and mentee can help mentoring become more than an additional task for senior faculty. It also can provide an opportunity for senior faculty to reflect on their years of practice and, through mentoring, learn from their junior colleagues as well. This can be particularly important in fields with quickly changing technological advances, such as journalism, computer science, and marketing. When senior faculty take part in co-mentoring they can learn from their younger colleagues about the latest advances in their fields and innovative research methods while they help their junior colleagues learn about teaching, institutional service, and professional norms.

## Research Support

Support for research activities is another way institutions can aid senior professors. At some institutions these awards are fairly straightforward. At Elon University, senior faculty research fellowships are available for post-probationary faculty with seven or more years of experience. At the Illinois State College of Fine Arts, a senior faculty research award program provides research funds of up to four thousand dollars for senior faculty. Other institutions provide awards that grant release time for senior faculty. Dartmouth College (2012), for example, "provides one term of released time for senior members of the faculty who have established reputations in a given field or are venturing into a new field outside their accustomed area of study" (para. 4). At Georgetown University, senior faculty research fellowships are provided to allow seasoned professors to pursue a project in the creative arts.

## Workload Adjustment

During the latter stages of their career, some professors may wish to reallocate the amount of time they spend on certain activities or decrease their work commitment partially. Appalachian State University's (2012) faculty development office website states, "It is not uncommon for senior faculty who have firmly established a national reputation in their field to become less interested in scholarship and more interested in service to the University or profession, and/or mentoring students and younger colleagues" (para. 5). Appalachian State provides opportunities for senior faculty to develop new teaching skills or take on new responsibilities to mentor and advise students. These opportunities can provide a new sense of purpose and help energize senior faculty.

Drake University offers another way to adjust one's workload in the latter stages of the career. At Drake, senior faculty can participate in a program that allows them to teach a two-thirds load at two-thirds pay for up to two years. This program differs from Drake's retirement benefits program, which is a more traditional retirement incentive program. Instead, its senior faculty status program allows faculty wishing to remain productively engaged in the latter stages of their career to begin to taper off responsibilities while still remaining an active part of the academic workforce.

## Recognition

Several institutions honor senior faculty through awards and other forms of recognition. Although awards are not developmental in and of themselves, many of the awards are signs of appreciation of senior faculty for their years of hard work and service to the institution. At some institutions, awards are combined with a monetary prize. At the University of

Michigan, the Henry Russel Lectureship is considered among the highest honors a senior faculty member can receive. Recipients are selected by a campus committee and formally approved by the board of regents, an indication of the importance the university places on this award. Honorees receive a monetary prize of two thousand dollars and deliver a lecture to the campus community. At Ohio State University (2012), the distinguished scholar award "recognizes exceptional scholarly accomplishments by senior professors who have compiled a substantial body of research" (para. 1). Along with their formal recognition and award, recipients receive a three-thousand-dollar and a twenty-thousand-dollar research grant.

## Sizing Up Support for Senior Faculty

Senior faculty can provide many benefits to their institutions. Yet our research shows that institutions provide limited forms of support specifically designed to help senior faculty continue to grow, develop, and prosper. The examples we have presented highlight some of the ways institutions try to support senior faculty members. From the senior faculty initiatives we identified, several themes emerge about the purpose and structure of senior faculty support programs and policies:

- The lack of a consistent definition of *senior faculty* means that some "senior" faculty programs are not designed specifically for the late-career senior faculty member whom we define as fifty-five years or older with fifteen or more years of experience in the academic profession.

- Programs often focus more on recognition or how to use senior faculty rather than how to help senior faculty grow and develop.

- There are multiple ways to support senior faculty development at different levels within an institution.

- Very few institutions take a comprehensive developmental approach to addressing the distinctive needs of senior faculty.

Many of the "senior" faculty programs we reviewed may not actually serve the most seasoned faculty. The programs reviewed offer many different definitions of senior faculty ranging from any associate or full professor to individuals who are within a few years of retirement. It is possible that an individual could be an associate professor by his or her midthirties and would need much different support from a long-serving professor who is fifty-five or older. It is noteworthy that some institutions develop "senior" faculty programs, but the lack of a consistent definition about who senior faculty members are makes it difficult to truly determine how many support services exist for late-career faculty. Furthermore, this lack of a precise definition may lead institutions and departments to overlook the distinctive professional needs of this important group of faculty.

Our research revealed that many programs for senior faculty are not intentionally developmental in nature. Mentoring, for example, can be a mutually beneficial experience. However, mentoring programs usually emphasize support of junior faculty. Honors and recognition, while nice to receive, are ways to acknowledge senior faculty contributions, but not necessarily to support faculty in a new phase of their career. Awards programs may also neglect long-serving professors who do not stand out from their colleagues for their professional achievements. These types of support services are important to continue, but they are not necessarily sufficient to meet the diverse developmental needs of senior faculty. In contrast, some of the programs we reviewed that encourage senior faculty to reflect on their careers and identify new strategies for remaining productive in teaching, research, and service provide opportunities for learning and growth more consistent with the needs and desires of faculty in the latter stages of their careers.

We also found a variety of ways to support senior faculty across different levels of an institution. We identified senior faculty support services offered out of the provost's office, at the department level, and through faculty development offices. For example, the provost's office at the University of Michigan serves as a repository of information on mentoring programs that deans and chairs across campus can tailor to support the senior faculty in their academic units. Marquette University's philosophy department conducts a developmental review of senior faculty work conditions and satisfaction. At other institutions, such as Appalachian State and Western Michigan, faculty development offices take the lead in coordinating support for senior faculty. This variety of service options at different levels across an institution demonstrates the multiple avenues through which senior faculty can be supported. Every institution has its own unique culture. However, with a variety of options available to support senior faculty, each institution can develop ways to support long-serving professors that are consistent with its mission and culture.

Finally, it is clear from our study that notable strategies are being employed at some institutions to support senior faculty, but this support is not widespread. For example, Berberet et al. (2004) argued that some senior faculty may desire opportunities to learn and develop new skills through internships that allow them to explore new career opportunities, but we did not find any explicit examples of this practice. Some of the development programs we found provide opportunities for personal reflection and discussion with peers and chairs, but not necessarily opportunities to explore new professional roles as part of a formalized program. In addition, while the research support provided for senior faculty at some institutions is beneficial, it is not always targeted specifically to meet the research needs of faculty late in their careers. Bataille and Brown (2006) argued that many senior faculty desire research funding specifically enabling them to jump-start research in new areas. This may require different types of institutional funding programs from what is typical of traditional in-house grants that often favor faculty with well-developed research ideas and a record of achievement in a particular specialty area. Overall, the forms of support provided for senior faculty that we identified are a good starting point for addressing the needs of this cohort of faculty, but they do not address all the needs of senior faculty and are not prevalent across many institutions.

## Recommendations

Although the growing number of senior faculty at many colleges and universities often raises the question of how institutions can best maintain a steady flow of academic talent, it should also provide an opportunity for institutions to consider how they can best support their current faculty even at the latter stages of faculty careers. Blaisdell and Cox (2004) argued that it is important not to automatically assume that the cohort of senior faculty is "somehow lacking, deficient, or not fully vital" (p. 138). There may be some senior faculty members who are beyond their greatest years of productivity and may need to be gently nudged toward retirement, but other senior faculty members have much to contribute to their institutions, students, and academic fields. Developing support programs, policies, and services for this group of faculty, even in a limited fashion, can help ensure that senior faculty have the tools necessary to be productive and fulfilled in their final years of employment. In order for programs to be successful, there are important issues for both faculty and administrators to consider. We offer the following recommendations:

### Recommendations for Faculty

- *Be reflective about your career.* Faculty entering the latter stages of their careers should take time to consider what their goals are for their remaining years of service. Many senior faculty find new priorities during the latter stages of their careers. Senior faculty should be explicit about outlining what their priorities are and what support they need to achieve those priorities. Priorities could include engaging in more undergraduate teaching and mentoring or concluding a long-term research or writing project prior to retirement. Regardless, senior faculty must reflect on their priorities before they are able to identify what support services they need.

o *Reconsider what success means in late career.* For many highly productive senior faculty, the latter stages of their career may result in the need to redefine success. For example, faculty winding down their academic careers may find it difficult to pursue or receive as many major grant awards. While this may become a source of dissatisfaction for some faculty members, it is important for those faculty to find other ways to contribute professionally. Senior faculty may be able to use their experience and knowledge to serve in other ways. They may find a renewed sense of vitality in teaching, mentoring, working with alumni, or supporting institutional advancement. It is important for senior faculty to understand that they can continue to be contributing members of the academy in the latter stages of their careers even if in new and different ways than they were previously.

o *Seek out co-mentoring opportunities.* Much of the discussion on mentoring focuses on how senior faculty can mentor younger professors and students. These opportunities are important, but it is also important for senior faculty to find their own mentors, often from a younger cohort of colleagues. Younger professors can help senior faculty learn new technologies, new teaching techniques, and the latest trends in their fields. Mentoring should be a two-way street: senior faculty often have as much to learn as they have to offer others.

o *Recognize that it may take faculty initiative to secure proper departmental or institutional support for senior faculty.* Since most faculty development support is aimed at early-career faculty, senior faculty can often be overlooked. Senior faculty desiring more development and support for teaching, research, or other professional endeavors should be explicit with their department chairs and deans about what support they need. Many of the support services senior faculty may desire, such as co-mentoring opportunities, senior faculty learning communities, or teaching technology workshops, can be accomplished at little or no cost and could be spearheaded by senior faculty themselves as a starting point. While costs are always a concern, there are many ways to support the growth and development of senior faculty peers on a smaller scale, with the hopes of growth in these programs in the future if successful and cost-effective.

### Recommendations for Chairs, Deans, and Faculty Development Offices

○ *Recognize that senior faculty are not a homogeneous group.* Some senior faculty may remain highly productive in their research, while others may wish to focus more on teaching or other roles in the latter stages of their careers. It is important to recognize these differences and identify ways for all senior faculty to contribute productively to the institution.

○ *Help senior professors rejuvenate and revitalize their interests.* It would be a mistake to view senior faculty as professionals past their prime who merely need to show up to teach their required courses and do little else. Viewing senior faculty in this light may lead to a self-fulfilling prophecy. In reality, with appropriate support and development opportunities, senior faculty can remain an engaged and vital part of the academy. This may require negotiation with individual senior professors to develop new professional goals and determine what resources, such as money, time, and learning opportunities, will be necessary to reach these goals.

○ *Recognize the difference between offering generic support services for faculty across the career and support targeted specifically for faculty in the latter stages of their careers.* Many colleges and universities offer teaching and research support programs regardless of faculty age or rank. It is important, however, just as it is with early-career faculty, to offer forms of support specifically responsive to the circumstances and needs of late-career faculty. A workshop on integrating technology into instruction for early-career faculty may need to cover different issues from one for late-career faculty. While some support services can include professors across age and rank, it is important to recognize that senior faculty also have their own distinctive needs that should be addressed in ways appropriate to their career stage and professional status.

○ *Be cognizant of costs, but also of cost-effectiveness.* In a time of constrained resources, it is easy to write off the development of senior faculty programs as too costly or not a good investment compared to developing early-career faculty. Many senior faculty development programs, however, may simply require the formation of workshops or learning communities that require minimal expenditure. Although there may be costs in developing some senior faculty support programs, it may be more costly to ignore this cohort of faculty and not receive maximum productivity in return. At every institution there are probably some senior faculty members whom administrators wish would simply retire. However, there are probably many more senior professors whom institutions want to retain as productive and engaged faculty members. Those are the senior faculty members whom administrators should work to keep energized, satisfied, and productive.

o *Keep open lines of communication with senior faculty and develop mutually agreeable, clear, and consistent expectations.* The latter stages of one's career can often bring uncertainty for both the individual faculty member and the institution. In order to maximize the talents of these faculty, clear expectations and goals can help alleviate some of the stresses of uncertainty. It can also help senior faculty members feel like valued members of the academic community if there are mutually agreeable opportunities identified for continued engagement, contribution, and productivity in the latter stages of one's career.

o *Recognize the valuable contributions of senior professors and show your institution's appreciation.* Late-career faculty sometimes feel neglected and unappreciated as their younger colleagues take over important teaching assignments, move into leadership roles, and gain stature through their research achievements and national service roles. While this developmental process is inevitable, it is important to acknowledge the valuable work senior professors continue to perform and recognize the significant contributions they have made over a long career. Academic leaders can support the morale of senior colleagues and their institutional community as a whole by recognizing the achievements of late-career professors with awards, citations, small grants, and personal notes that demonstrate the work of late-career faculty is visible and valued.

## Conclusion

Senior faculty have a great deal to contribute to their institutions due to their years of experience, vast store of knowledge, and accumulated professional wisdom. This group of faculty also has its own distinctive challenges and needs. Many late-career senior professors can benefit from flexible forms of support to help them address those needs. This chapter outlines the varied ways institutions can assist senior faculty. However, support targeted specifically at senior faculty remains relatively rare across higher-education institutions. We hope this chapter provides a case for focusing more precisely on senior faculty. Colleges and universities cannot afford to waste any of their valuable human resources. Policies, programs, and services designed to support the work and careers of late-career faculty can enrich the academic community by maintaining professors' vitality all the way to retirement.

REFERENCES

Appalachian State University Faculty and Academic Development. (2012). *Senior faculty*. Retrieved from http://hubbard.appstate.edu/senior-faculty

Association of Retirement Organizations in Higher Education. (2012). *About AROHE*. Retrieved from http://arohe.org/wp/about-us/

Austin, A. E. (2002). Preparing the next generation of faculty: Graduate school as socialization to the academic career. *Journal of Higher Education, 73*(1), 94–122.

Austin, A. E. (2003). Creating a bridge to the future: Preparing new faculty to face changing expectations in a shifting context. *Review of Higher Education, 26*(2), 119–144.

Baldwin, R. G., & Chang, D. A. (2006). Reinforcing our "keystone" faculty: Strategies to support faculty in the middle years. *Liberal Education, 92*(4), 28–35.

Baldwin, R. G., DeZure, D., Shaw, A., & Moretto, K. (2008). Mapping the terrain of mid-career faculty at a research university: Implications for faculty and academic leaders. *Change, 50*(5), 46–55.

Baldwin, R. G., & Zeig, M. J. (2012). Making emeritus matter. *Change, 44*(5), 28–34.

Bataille, G., & Brown, B. (2006). *Faculty career paths: Multiple routes to academic success and satisfaction.* Westport, CT: Praeger.

Berberet, J., Bland, C. J., Brown, B. E., & Risbey, K. (2004, April). *Preliminary report: Senior faculty perceptions and practices during the late career and planning for retirement.* Paper presented at the TIAA-CREF Institute Conference, New York, NY.

Blaisdell, M. L., & Cox, M. D. (2004). Midcareer and senior faculty learning communities. Learning throughout faculty careers. In M. D. Cox & L. Richlin (Eds.), *New directions for teaching and learning: No. 97. Building faculty learning communities* (pp. 137–148). San Francisco, CA: Jossey-Bass.

Bland, C. J., & Berquist, W. H. (1997). *The vitality of senior faculty members: Snow on the roof–fire in the furnace.* ASHE-ERIC Higher Education Report 25(7). Washington, DC: George Washington University, Graduate School of Education and Human Development.

Boice, R. (1992). *The new faculty member.* San Francisco, CA: Jossey-Bass.

Brown, B. E. (2006). Supporting and retaining early-career faculty. *Effective Practices for Academic Leaders, 1*(9), 1–16.

Carleton College. (2012). *Senior faculty development forum.* Retrieved from https://apps.carleton.edu/handbook/facultyapp/?policy_id=864379#864439

Dartmouth College. (2012). *Applications for faculty fellowships and senior faculty grants.* Retrieved from http://www.dartmouth.edu/~dof/jjf_sfg _2011memo_rev.pdf

Gappa, J. M., Austin, A. E., & Trice, A. G. (2007). *Rethinking faculty work: Higher education's strategic imperative.* San Francisco, CA: Jossey-Bass.

June, A. W. (2012, March 23). Aging professors create a faculty bottleneck. *Chronicle of Higher Education.* Retrieved from http://chronicle.com/article /Professors-Are-Graying-and/131226/

Marquette University Department of Philosophy. (2012). *Policy for review of regular senior faculty.* Retrieved from http://www.marquette.edu/phil /documents/SeFacRevProtocols.pdf

Ohio State University. (2012). *University awards and recognition.* Retrieved from http://www.osu.edu/universityawards/2012/scholar.html

Preparing Future Faculty. (2012). *The Preparing Future Faculty Program.* Retrieved from http://www.preparing-faculty.org

Pruitt-Logan, A. S., & Gaff, J. G. (2004). Preparing future faculty: Changing the culture of doctoral education. In D. H. Wulff & A. E. Austin (Eds.), *Paths to the professoriate: Strategies for enriching the preparation of future faculty* (pp. 177–193). San Francisco, CA: Jossey-Bass.

Schuster, J., & Finkelstein, M. (2006). *The American faculty: The restructuring of academic work and careers.* Baltimore, MD: Johns Hopkins University Press.

Trower, C. A. (2011). *Senior faculty vitality.* New York, NY: TIAA-CREF Institute.

University of Georgia Center for Teaching and Learning. (2012). *CTL senior teaching fellows program.* Retrieved from http://www.ctl.uga.edu/faculty /ctl_senior_teaching_fellows

6

# ENHANCING VITALITY IN ACADEMIC MEDICINE

## FACULTY DEVELOPMENT AND PRODUCTIVITY

Megan M. Palmer, Krista Hoffmann-Longtin, Tony Ribera, Mary E. Dankoski
Indiana University School of Medicine

Amy K. Ribera, Tom F. Nelson Laird
Indiana University School of Education

*The prevalence of low satisfaction and increased stress among faculty in academic medicine makes understanding faculty vitality in this field more important than ever before. To explore the contributors to and outcomes of faculty vitality, we conducted a multi-institutional study of faculty in academic medicine (N = 1,980, 42 percent response rate). Faculty were surveyed about climate and leadership, career and life management, satisfaction, engagement, productivity, and involvement in faculty development. Analysis reveals that controlling for other factors, academic medicine faculty who participate regularly in faculty development activities are significantly more satisfied, engaged, and productive.*

о

Compared with other faculty members across higher education, those in academic medicine face both common and unique challenges. Common challenges include increased calls for institutional accountability from the public and an increasingly diverse and technologically savvy student body. Academic physicians are expected to meet the same bar for promotion and tenure as other faculty across academe yet must also simultaneously meet expectations to generate clinical revenue.

Because faculty are the greatest resource of any academic institution, medical schools must recruit, retain, and advance the most talented faculty possible in order to meet the urgent and complex demands of health care education today. This includes developing new educational models to train the next generation of scientists and physicians in a rapidly shifting, political health care environment, generating research that improves health amid intense competition for funding, and developing increasingly efficient models of care delivery. The environment can be described as high stakes, competitive, fast paced, complex, and constantly changing. As such, recent research shows that faculty in academic medicine report increased stress, depression, and decreased satisfaction (Kelly, Cronin, & Dunnick, 2007; Schindler et al., 2006). Furthermore, challenges in faculty life are often magnified for underrepresented minorities (URM) and women. URM faculty comprise less than 10 percent and women less than 36 percent of all current medical school faculty (Castillo-Page, 2012; Joliff, Leadley, Coakley, & Sloane, 2012), and these groups are promoted and tenured at lower rates than majority or male faculty. Given the importance of faculty in creating a better future for health professions education and the strain faculty are currently under, the need to improve our understanding of faculty vitality has never before been greater.

## Defining Faculty Vitality

The concept of faculty vitality has been discussed in the higher education literature since the mid-1980s. Despite multiple studies in the past twenty-five years using a variety of proxy indicators such as satisfaction or productivity (Baldwin, 1990; Bland, Seaquist, Pacala, Center, & Finstad, 2002; Chan & Burton, 1995; Pololi, Conrad, Knight, & Carr, 2009; Woods, Reid, Arndt, Curtis, & Stritter, 1997), the construct is still imprecise and lacks a predictive model (Clark, Boyer, & Corcoran, 1985). Clark and Lewis (1985) offered this early description: "those essential, yet intangible positive qualities of individuals and institutions that enable purposeful production" (p. 176). Elsewhere faculty vitality has been defined as "faculty members' commitment to and ability to achieve both their own goals and their institution's goals" (Bland et al., 2002, p. 369).

Over the past five years, we have developed the Faculty Vitality Survey and a resulting model of faculty vitality (Dankoski, Palmer, Nelson-Laird, Garver, & Bogdewic, 2012). (The survey is in the chapter appendix.) In this model, *faculty vitality* is defined as the synergy between high levels of satisfaction, productivity, and engagement that enables faculty members to maximize their professional success and achieve goals in concert with institutional goals. Not only is it critical for faculty developers to understand what makes faculty members highly engaged, productive, and satisfied, it is also important to expand our knowledge about how faculty development programs may aid in sustaining vitality.

## Assessing Outcomes of Faculty Development

Despite the importance of faculty development, assessing its outcomes can be difficult. Unfortunately, many faculty development programs track relatively simplistic metrics such as attendee satisfaction and faculty contacts, without conducting more rigorous analyses such as linking programs to student learning outcomes, assessing for learning or behavioral change, or mapping efforts to institutional measures (Birch & Gray, 2009; Chism & Szabo, 1997–1998). Without more sophisticated studies, faculty developers are hard-pressed to know how to best invest precious programming dollars or address questions about the value of faculty development to individual faculty members and the institution.

There is, however, a small but growing body of literature in academic medicine about faculty development assessments and outcomes. For instance, studies comparing participants and nonparticipants in part-time, off-site, cohort-based programs have shown that participants have higher academic promotion rates (Smith, Barry, Dunn, Keefe, & Weismantel, 2006), increased collegial relationships (Morzinski & Fisher, 2002), and increased attainment of leadership roles (Simpson, Bragg, Biernat, & Treat, 2004). A recent literature review on faculty development initiatives designed to promote leadership had a similar conclusion: leadership development program completers often obtain new leadership positions and also self-report attitude changes and knowledge gains (Steinert, Naismith, & Mann, 2012).

Studies of local programs (those conducted at participants' home institutions) have also shown important outcomes. One such program that combined career planning, scholarly writing, and peer mentoring yielded increased publication rates among participants (Pololi, Knight, Dennis, & Frankel, 2002). Similarly, a program targeted toward faculty retention and academic productivity showed positive results in both of these areas (Morzinski & Simpson, 2003); another program focused on scientific writing among medical school faculty was found to be effective in improving confidence, writing ability, and productivity (Dankoski et al., 2012). Many medical schools offer structured programs for junior faculty members and formal mentoring programs, both of which aid in the retention of faculty (Ries et al., 2012; Wingard, Garman, & Reznik, 2004) and greater research productivity (Bland, Weber-Main, Lund, & Finstad, 2005). A qualitative analysis investigated the role of a longitudinal faculty development program in the growth of an "academic identity" among health professions faculty (Lief et al., 2012). Furthermore, several programs intended to improve teaching abilities have yielded significant gains in faculty teaching skill, commitment, and confidence (Barratt & Moyer, 2004; Berbano, Browning, Pangaro, & Jackson, 2006; Knight et al., 2005; Pololi & Frankel, 2005). As one way to explore faculty development outcomes, Palmer, Dankoski, Smith, Brutkiewicz, and Bogdewic (2011) compared indicators related to faculty satisfaction, mentoring, feeling valued, and career planning between two points in time during which multiple new faculty development initiatives had been launched.

Although not meeting the full definition of return on investment analyses, using more rigorous assessment methods such as those described moves faculty developers away from simply reporting reactions or satisfaction to measuring important institutional results (Bothell & Henderson, 2004). The purpose of our study was to investigate the relationship between engagement in faculty development and the construct of faculty vitality as another approach to exploring the result of institutional investment in faculty development.

## Purpose

This study examines responses from 1,980 faculty members in academic medicine to better understand faculty engagement in faculty development and the relationship between that engagement and faculty productivity. Three research questions guided this work:

1. How often do faculty in academic medicine participate in faculty development activities?

2. What topical areas are faculty members most or least likely to attend?

3. Does participating in professional development activities have an effect on faculty productivity?

# Methods

In spring 2011, faculty members at four academic medical centers participated in an administration of the Faculty Vitality Survey. The survey instrument asks faculty about their perceptions and experiences with various aspects of their work. The self-report survey contained demographic variables (gender, race/ethnicity, academic rank, track) and subscales measuring perceptions of institutional climate and leadership, career and life management, satisfaction, engagement, and productivity. The survey also included questions about the frequency of attendance at various types of faculty development programs for an analysis regarding how participation in such programs may be related to faculty vitality. Specifically, participants were asked to indicate approximately how many times over the previous academic year they had participated in professional development activities (e.g., workshops, conferences, online tutorials) related to each of the following areas: promotion and tenure, teaching and learning, research, advancement of women, and other diversity issues. The focus of this chapter is on the extent to which faculty in academic medicine engage in faculty and professional development activities.

# Sample

This study was limited to academic medicine at four public medical schools in the United States. After removing cases with a large number of missing responses, the final sample consisted 1,980 faculty members in academic medicine (institutional response rates ranged from 31 percent to 78 percent). Table 6.1 shows sample characteristics.

The majority of our participants were employed full time by their institutions (93 percent, $n = 1,743$). The majority were male (62 percent, $n = 1,147$) and white (71 percent, $n = 1,313$). Approximately one-sixth of the sample (15 percent, $n = 276$) were Asian, and a much smaller percentage identified as black or African American (2 percent, $n = 39$) or Latino or Hispanic (3 percent, $n = 60$). The largest number of faculty in the sample were assistant professors (42 percent, $n = 769$). Associate rank faculty (26 percent, $n = 489$) and full professors (28 percent, $n = 519$) were less represented in our sample. The majority of faculty in the sample spent 30 percent or more of their time on clinical duties (53 percent, $n = 1,055$) while 38 percent ($n = 757$) spent 30 percent or more of their time on research. Faculty in the sample spent less time on teaching (17 percent, $n = 330$) and administrative duties (17 percent, $n = 339$).

Table 6.1   Descriptive Statistics of Faculty Respondents in Academic Medicine

|  | Count | Percentage |
|---|---|---|
| Gender |  |  |
| Male | 1,147 | 62 |
| Female | 691 | 38 |
| Employment status |  |  |
| Full time | 1,743 | 93 |
| Part time | 122 | 7 |
| Race or ethnicity |  |  |
| Asian | 276 | 15 |
| Black or African American | 39 | 2 |
| Latino or Hispanic | 60 | 3 |
| White | 1,313 | 71 |
| Other | 161 | 9 |
| Academic rank |  |  |
| Assistant | 769 | 42 |
| Associate | 489 | 26 |
| Full | 519 | 28 |
| Other | 72 | 4 |
| Percentage of faculty time spent[a] |  |  |
| Research focused | 757 | 38 |
| Teaching focused | 330 | 17 |
| Clinical focused | 1,055 | 53 |
| Administrative focused | 339 | 17 |

[a]Percentage who spent 30 percent or more of their time on research, teaching, clinical, or administrative duties. Since there is potential that faculty could spend more than 30 percent of their time in different areas, the total percentage exceeds 100 percent.

## Selected Measures and Analyses

To answer our first research question, we examined faculty responses to the item, "To what extent are you currently engaged in faculty development activities?" We report the percentage of faculty who indicated engaging in these activities very little, some, quite a bit, or very much. For our second research question, "How often do faculty in academic medicine participate in faculty development activities?" we looked at the number of activities in which faculty participated. Faculty members were asked to indicate how many times they participated in seven specific types of professional development activities (see table 6.4 for a complete list).

Table 6.2   Item-level Descriptive Statistics of Productivity Scales

|  | N | Mean | SD |
|---|---|---|---|
| **Research productivity (alpha = .81)** | | | |
| Participation in professional organizations in my field | 1,784 | 3.28 | 1.13 |
| Translating research into practice | 1,709 | 3.04 | 1.17 |
| Securing external funding | 1,739 | 2.72 | 1.31 |
| Number of peer-reviewed publications | 1,772 | 2.93 | 1.35 |
| Number of peer-reviewed conference presentations | 1,754 | 3.02 | 1.28 |
| **Teaching and service productivity (alpha = .67)** | | | |
| Teaching evaluations | 1,723 | 3.74 | 1.00 |
| Number of learners with whom I interact | 1,762 | 3.65 | 1.02 |
| Participation in university/department/school service | 1,771 | 3.45 | 1.15 |

Faculty could select 0, 1 to 3, 4 to 6, 7 to 9, or more than 10. To answer our third research question, "Does participating in professional development activities have an effect on faculty productivity?" we conducted a linear regression to better understand the effect engagement in faculty and professional development activities had on faculty productivity.

Two productivity scales were used in this analysis: research productivity (alpha = .81) and teaching and service productivity (alpha = .67). The research productivity scale combines five items indicating the extent to which faculty engage in research-related activities (e.g., securing external funding) and the amount of scholarship (e.g., number of peer-reviewed publications). The teaching and service productivity scale combines three items capturing faculty members' self-rated performance on teaching evaluations and the extent to which they interact with learners and participate in university, department, and/or school service related to the education mission. Productivity items are described in table 6.2.

## Results

Frequencies in table 6.3 suggest that most faculty members in academic medicine engage in faculty development activities at least "some." When asked about the extent to which they engage in faculty development activities, close to seven out of ten (66 percent, $n = 1,143$) indicated they do this "some," "quite a bit," or "very much." Among this group, 28 percent ($n = 480$) reported that they engage in these activities frequently ("quite a bit" or "very much"). Approximately one-third of the sample (34 percent, $n = 579$) indicated that they participated in faculty development activities very little.

## Table 6.3    Level of Engagement in Faculty Development Activities

|  | Number | Percentage |
|---|---|---|
| Very Little | 579 | 34 |
| Some | 663 | 38 |
| Frequently[a] | 480 | 28 |

[a]Combined response options "quite a bit" and "very much."

## Table 6.4    Average Yearly Participation in Professional Development by Topical Area

| Topical Area | Average Yearly Participation |
|---|---|
| Research | 3.4 |
| Teaching and learning | 3.4 |
| Leadership | 1.9 |
| Promotion and tenure | 1.3 |
| Other diversity issues | 0.8 |
| Advancement of women | 0.7 |
| Advancement of underrepresented minority | 0.7 |

Although these findings suggest that most faculty members in academic medicine engage in at least some faculty development activities, we are also interested in the focus of these activities. Table 6.4 illustrates the average participation in faculty development activities by topical area. Among a list of seven topical areas, research ($M = 3.4$) and teaching and learning ($M = 3.4$) had the highest average yearly participation. Activities focused on the advancement of women ($M = 0.7$), the advancement of underrepresented minorities ($M = 0.7$), and other diversity issues ($M = 0.8$) had the lowest average yearly participation.

These findings provide valuable information on the type of professional development activities in which medical school faculty engage. It is not surprising, given the demands of academic medicine, that events focused on supporting faculty in their research and teaching are among the most widely attended. However, due to the quantitative nature of this study, it is unclear what might contribute to average yearly participation.

Table 6.5 shows the results of the regression analyses. Model 1 explained a significant portion of the variance in research productivity

Table 6.5 Effects of Participation in Faculty Development on Productivity in Research and Teaching and Service

| | Research Productivity (Model 1) | | | Teaching and Service Productivity (Model 2) | | |
|---|---|---|---|---|---|---|
| | Beta | SE (Beta) | Significance (Beta) | Beta | SE (Beta) | Significance (Beta) |
| Constant | 0.00 | 0.02 | | 0.00 | 0.03 | |
| Female | -0.02 | 0.05 | | -0.05 | 0.05 | |
| Race or ethnicity | | | | | | |
| Asian/Asian American | 0.03 | 0.07 | | -0.18 | 0.07 | * |
| African American | 0.02 | 0.17 | | 0.02 | 0.18 | |
| Latino or Hispanic | 0.15 | 0.13 | | -0.22 | 0.14 | |
| White (reference group) | | | | | | |
| Full-time employment | 0.10 | 0.10 | | 0.31 | 0.11 | ** |
| Academic rank | | | | | | |
| Assistant | -0.54 | 0.06 | *** | -0.25 | 0.07 | *** |
| Associate | -0.35 | 0.07 | *** | -0.01 | 0.07 | |
| Full (reference group) | | | | | | |
| Other rank | -0.67 | 0.14 | *** | -0.64 | 0.15 | *** |
| Focus of work | | | | | | |
| 30 percent or more of time spent on teaching | -0.27 | 0.06 | *** | 0.44 | 0.07 | *** |
| 30 percent or more of time spent on researching | 0.61 | 0.05 | *** | -0.09 | 0.05 | |
| 30 percent or more of time spent on admin. duties | -0.18 | 0.06 | ** | 0.09 | 0.07 | |
| Engagement in faculty development | | | | | | |
| Participate very little (reference group) | | | | | | |
| Participate some | 0.15 | 0.06 | ** | 0.37 | 0.06 | *** |
| Participate frequently | 0.53 | 0.06 | *** | 0.57 | 0.07 | *** |
| Adjusted $R^2$ | 0.24 | | | 0.13 | | |
| F-change | 33.7*** | | | 17.3*** | | |

*Note:* Medical faculty (valid $N = 1,385$). The dependent variables were standardized prior to the analyses. All dichotomous independent measures were grand mean centered. $*p < .05$, $**p < .01$, $***p < .001$.

among faculty ($F = 33.7$, $p < .001$; adjusted $R^2 = 0.24$). Results suggested gender, race or ethnicity, and employment status were not significant predictors of research productivity. However, academic rank, focus of work, and, most important, engagement in faculty development were all found to be significantly related to research productivity.

Similar to previous studies on faculty vitality, full professors were more productive in research than assistant and associate faculty. Model 1 indicates that on average, assistant professor faculty scored half of a standard deviation lower and associate rank faculty scored over one-third of a standard deviation lower than full professors. Model 1 also shows a small negative effect on research productivity if faculty spent more than 30 percent of their time on teaching (beta = $-27$; $p < .001$) or administrative duties (beta = $-.18$; $p < .01$). Yet a medium positive effect on research productivity was found among faculty who spent 30 percent or more of their time on research (beta = $.61$; $p < .001$).

We also found a positive relationship with engagement in faculty development and research productivity. That is, faculty who "frequently" engaged in professional development produced half a standard deviation more research than those who engaged in professional development "very little." A significantly positive but smaller effect on research productivity was found among those who only participated in "some" professional development (beta = $15$; $p < .01$).

For faculty productivity in teaching and service, model 2 explained a significant but smaller portion of the variance ($F = 17.3$, $p < .001$; adjusted $R^2 = 0.13$). After controlling for gender, race or ethnicity, employment status, rank, and focus of work, we found that participation in faculty development had a significant and positive effect on faculty productivity in teaching and service. Specifically, faculty who are frequent participants in faculty development engaged in teaching and service three-fifths of a standard deviation more than faculty who participated in faculty development "very little." The model also shows a positive significant effect on teaching and service productivity when faculty participate in only "some" faculty development activities (beta = $37$; $p < .001$). Other notable findings were significant differences by race/ethnicity, rank, and work focus. Compared to white faculty, Asians (beta = $-.18$; $p < .05$) engaged in teaching and service slightly less when controls were introduced. The model also indicated that assistant professors engaged in teaching and service slightly less than full professors. Furthermore, spending 30 percent or more time on research was not significantly related to productivity in teaching service. However, the model showed a significant positive effect (beta = $.44$;

$p < .001$) on productivity in teaching and service if faculty spent more than 30 percent of their time on teaching.

## Conclusion

The findings from this study reveal that faculty developers, at least in academic medicine, have more work to do to reach the majority of the faculty. The fact that slightly over one-third of the respondents indicated that they participate in faculty development "very little" raises three key questions:

- What should faculty developers expect in terms of the amount and level of participation in faculty development programming?
- Are the current faculty development offerings not meeting the needs of nearly one-third of the faculty, which may explain their low levels of participation?
- In what ways does or could the reward structure encourage faculty to participate in development activities?

With regard to anticipated levels of participation in faculty development, there likely is not a single answer because this is dependent on institutional resources and culture. Yet it is worth having local and national conversations about what the benchmarks should be in terms of the number of faculty reached and the ideal extent of faculty involvement in faculty development activities. This is a particularly important discussion given the positive relationship between engagement in faculty development and productivity.

Faculty developers in academic medicine, and likely developers in other areas, should determine why participation levels vary. That is, are the offerings not relevant to a subgroup of faculty? Or perhaps the timing of the workshops or events doesn't work well for faculty who are responsible for taking care of a large number of patients. It could be useful for faculty developers to conduct surveys or focus groups with non-participants to better understand this issue.

Finally, faculty developers should examine how the reward structures encourage or discourage participation. For example, to what degree are department chairs actively inviting or discouraging faculty to participate in development activities? Similarly, are faculty recognized when they take, or are expected to take, their professional development seriously? Is language present in promotion and tenure documents that require that faculty document their engagement in professional development activities?

Faculty members were most likely to attend workshops and events focused on teaching and research. Activities related to diversity and the advancement of women were not as widely attended. Given the nature of this research, we cannot be certain what contributes to the level of participation in each of the areas measured. It is possible that this may have less to do with the interests of individual faculty members and more to do with the number of programs offered in these areas at each institution. With this perspective, it could be that faculty participation in programs focused on the advancement of URM faculty is low because of a lack of offerings at the institutions in this sample when compared to research or teaching and learning programs. Conversely, faculty may be less interested in or less comfortable attending workshops or events related to diversity and women's issues. More research is needed to better understand faculty interests and the amount and types of professional development activities at academic medical centers. Deeper understanding regarding this matter could assist faculty developers in better meeting the needs of the faculty and potentially provide insight into the values of the medical school faculty with regard to diversity and the advancement of women.

Faculty developers are, of course, interested in the impact of faculty development activities on outcomes that matter (in this case, productivity), and the results of this study provide good news. Based on the findings, we can conclude that not only faculty in academic medicine benefit from engagement in professional development; the institution also benefits. That is, faculty who engage in faculty development activities report greater levels of productivity. It is not difficult to argue that productivity is the coin of the realm in academic medicine. Therefore, the results of this study can assist faculty developers in demonstrating the benefit of engagement in faculty development. Furthermore, these results can be used when speaking with junior faculty, department chairs, and institutional leaders regarding why engagement in faculty development activities is important. The results of the study also provide evidence that investment in faculty development within medical schools is paying off.

More work can and should be done regarding the return on investment for faculty development. This study, focused on academic medicine, provides faculty developers with some additional insight regarding the outcomes of the work and why faculty development remains a critical piece of the equation in ensuring that each faculty member can be a success story.

## Appendix: Faculty Vitality Survey, 2011, Indiana University School of Medicine

Many of the following items inquire about your experiences, perceptions, and satisfaction with the academic environment in what you consider to be your primary unit; that is, the unit you feel most closely affiliated.

———— o ————

Please consider the following options and identify one as your primary unit. Response options: School, Department, Division, Regional Center, Other.

Consider your work over the *last academic year*. Approximately what percentage of your time was devoted to activities related to the following areas (must add to 100%)?

Teaching

Research

Patient care/clinical work

Administrative duties (including committee service)

Consider your experiences over the *last academic year*, and rate to what extent you agree with the following statements. Response options: Strongly agree, Somewhat agree, Neither agree nor disagree, Somewhat disagree, Strongly disagree, Not applicable/I don't know.

Colleagues are fully engaged in their work in my primary unit.

Opportunities for faculty development are offered by my primary unit.

Fair mechanisms for acknowledging achievements are in place in my primary unit.

Women have an equal opportunity for advancement as men in my primary unit.

Minority faculty are provided equal opportunities for advancement as white faculty in my primary unit.

Effective recruitment strategies are in place for attracting the best talent to my primary unit.

There is a shared vision in my primary unit.

My primary unit is comprised of a well-developed network of colleagues.

My contributions are valued by the leaders in my primary unit.

Consider your experiences over the *last academic year*, and rate to what extent you agree with the following statements. Response options: Strongly agree, Somewhat agree, Neither agree nor disagree, Somewhat disagree, Strongly disagree, Not applicable/I don't know.

Effective strategies to retain productive faculty are employed by leaders of my primary unit.

Faculty achievements are often recognized by the leaders of my primary unit.

An inclusive environment is created by the leaders of my primary unit.

Conflict is effectively handled by the leaders of my primary unit.

Faculty feel empowered to act by the leaders of my primary unit.

My opinions are routinely solicited by the leaders of my primary unit.

The leaders of my primary unit are highly regarded by others *within* the unit.

The leaders of my primary unit are highly regarded by others *outside* the unit.

The leaders of my primary unit are willing to challenge the status quo.

The leaders of my primary unit provide me guidance to improve.

Consider your experiences over the *last academic year*, and rate to what extent you agree with the following statements. Response options: Strongly agree, Somewhat agree, Neither agree nor disagree, Somewhat disagree, Strongly disagree, Not applicable/I don't know.

I ask for assistance when I need it.

I balance personal and professional demands.

I am able to negotiate in complex situations.

I am internally driven.

I have a plan for achieving my academic career goals.

I have a tolerance for change.

I have input into how I spent my time.

I sought out a mentor.

I personally see more opportunities than challenges.

I set appropriate boundaries to maintain productivity.

I routinely solicit feedback on my professional growth.

I considered leaving academic medicine.

Over the *last academic year,* about how many times have you participated in professional development activities (e.g., workshops, conferences, online tutorials) related to the following areas? Response options: 0, 1–3, 4–6, 7–9, More than 10, Not applicable/I don't know.

Promotion and tenure

Teaching and learning

Research

Leadership

Advancement of women

Advancement of underrepresented minorities

Other diversity issues

To what extent are you currently engaged in the following activities? Response options: Very much, Quite a bit, Some, Very little, Not applicable/I don't know.

Professional organization(s) in your field

Mentoring colleagues

Committee work at the school or campus level

Collaborations with colleagues in my primary unit

Serving as a mentor to learners

Faculty development activities

Given the expectations in your primary unit, how do you currently rate yourself? Response options: Well below, Slightly below, At expectations, Slightly above, Well above.

Relative value units (RVUs) benchmarks

Securing external funding

Teaching evaluations

Number of peer-reviewed publications

Number of peer-reviewed conference presentations

Number of learners with whom I interact

Participation in university/department/school service

Participation in professional organizations in my field

Translating research into practice

Consider your experiences over the *last academic year,* and please rate your level of satisfaction with the following items: Very satisfied, Somewhat satisfied, Neither satisfied nor dissatisfied, Somewhat dissatisfied, Very dissatisfied, Not applicable/I don't know.

Efforts to promote diversity in my primary unit

Sense of community in my primary unit

Promotion and tenure process

My overall level of productivity

Overall, how satisfied are you with your career? Response options: Very satisfied, Somewhat satisfied, Neither satisfied nor dissatisfied, Somewhat dissatisfied, Very dissatisfied, Not applicable/I don't know. Responses to the following demographic items will be reported only in the aggregate, and no individual respondent will be identifiable.

School

Division

Department

Enter the number of years as faculty at your current institution. Write in.

Enter the number of years as faculty at any other institution. Write in.

Degree(s). Response options: DDS, MD, PhD, MBA, MPH, MA/ MS, MLS, RN, BSN, MSN, Other (write in).

Track: Tenure track, Clinical (non–tenure track), Lecturer, Academic Specialist, Research/scientist track, Librarian, Other.

Faculty Rank: Assistant, Associate, Full Professor, Other.

Gender: Response options: Male, Female.

Race/ethnicity. Response options: American Indian or other Native American; Asian, Asian American, or Pacific Islander; black or African American; white (non-Hispanic); Mexican or Mexican American; Puerto Rican; other Hispanic or Latino; multiracial; Other; I prefer not to respond.

Employment status. Response options: Full time, Part time.

If you have any additional comments you would like to make, please type them below.

REFERENCES

Baldwin, R. G. (1990). Faculty vitality beyond the research university. *Journal of Higher Education, 61*(2), 160–180.

Barratt, M. S., & Moyer, V. A. (2004). Effect of a teaching skills program on faculty skills and confidence. *Ambulatory Pediatrics, 4* (1 Suppl.), 117–120.

Berbano, E. P., Browning, R., Pangaro, L., & Jackson, J. L. (2006). The impact of the Stanford Faculty Development Program on ambulatory teaching behavior. *Journal of General Internal Medicine, 21*(5), 430–434.

Birch, A. J., & Gray, T. (2009). Ten ways to use a relational database at a faculty development center. In L. B. Nilson & J. E. Miller (Eds.), *To improve the academy: Resources for faculty, instructional, and organizational development, Vol. 27* (pp. 72–87). San Francisco, CA: Jossey Bass.

Bland, C. J., Seaquist, E., Pacala, J. T., Center, B. A., & Finstad, D. (2002). One school's strategy to assess and improve the vitality of its faculty. *Academic Medicine, 77*(5), 368–376.

Bland, C. J., Weber-Main, A. M., Lund, S. M., & Finstad, D. A. (2005). *The research-productive department: Strategies from departments that excel.* San Francisco, CA: Jossey-Bass/Anker.

Bothell, T. W., & Henderson, T. (2004). Evaluating the return on investment of faculty development. In C. M. Wehlburg & S. Chadwick-Blossey (Eds.), *To improve the academy: Resources for faculty, instructional, and organizational development, Vol. 22* (pp. 52–70). Bolton, MA: Anker.

Castillo-Page, L. (2012). *Diversity in medical education: Facts and figures 2012.* Association of American Medical Colleges. Retrieved from https://www.aamc.org/initiatives/diversity/

Chan, S. S., & Burton, J. (1995). Faculty vitality in the comprehensive university: Changing contexts and concerns. *Research in Higher Education, 36*(2), 219–34.

Chism, N.V.N., & Szabo, B. (1997–98). How faculty development programs evaluate their services. *Journal of Staff, Program, and Organizational Development, 15*(2), 55–62.

Clark, S. M., Boyer, C. M., & Corcoran, M. (1985). Faculty and institutional vitality in higher education. In S. M. Clark & D. Lewis (Eds.), *Faculty vitality and institutional productivity: Critical perspectives for higher education* (pp. 3–24). New York, NY: Teachers College Press.

Clark, S. M., & Lewis, D. R. (Eds.). (1985). *Faculty vitality and institutional productivity: Critical Perspectives for higher education.* New York, NY: Teachers College Press.

Dankoski, M. E., Palmer, M. M., Banks, J., Brutkiewicz, R. R., Walvoord, E., Hoffmann-Longtin, K., Bogdewic, S. P., & Gopen, G. D. (2012). Academic writing: Supporting faculty in a critical competency for success. *Journal of Faculty Development, 26*(2), 47–54.

Dankoski, M. E., Palmer, M. M., Nelson-Laird, T., Garver, A., & Bogdewic, S. P. (2012). An expanded model of faculty vitality in academic medicine. *Advances in Health Science Education, 17*(5), 633–649.

Joliff, L., Leadley, J., Coakley, E., & Sloane R. A. (2012). *Women in U.S. academic medicine and science: Statistics and benchmarking report 2011–2012.* Association of American Medical Colleges. Retrieved from https://www.aamc.org/members/gwims/statistics/

Kelly, A. M., Cronin, P., & Dunnick, N. R. (2007). Junior faculty satisfaction in a large academic radiology department. *Academic Radiology, 14*(4), 445–454.

Knight, A. M., Cole, K. A., Kern, D. E., Barker, L. R., Kolodner, K., & Wright, S. M. (2005). Long-term follow-up of a longitudinal faculty development program in teaching skills. *Journal of General Internal Medicine, 20*(8), 721–725.

Lief, S., Baker, L., Mori, B., Egan-Lee, E., Chin, K., & Reeves, S. (2012). Who am I? Key influences on the formation of academic identity within a faculty development program. *Medical Teacher, 34*(3), e208–215.

Morzinski, J. A., & Fisher, J. C. (2002). A nationwide study of the influence of faculty development programs on colleague relationships. *Academic Medicine, 77*(5), 402–406.

Morzinski, J. A., & Simpson, D. E. (2003). Outcomes of a comprehensive faculty development program for local, full-time faculty. *Family Medicine, 35,* 434–439.

Palmer, M. M., Dankoski, M. E., Smith, J. S., Brutkiewicz, R. R., & Bogdewic, S. P. (2011). Exploring changes in culture and vitality: The outcomes of faculty development. *Journal of Faculty Development, 25*(1), 21–27.

Pololi, L., Conrad, P., Knight, S., & Carr, P. (2009). A study of the relational aspects of the culture of academic medicine. *Academic Medicine, 84*(1), 106–114.

Pololi, L. H., & Frankel, R. M. (2005). Humanizing medical education through faculty development: Linking self-awareness and teaching skills. *Medical Education, 39*(2), 154–162.

Pololi, L. H., Knight, S., Dennis, K., & Frankel, R. (2002). Helping medical school faculty realize their dreams: An innovative, collaborative mentoring program. *Academic Medicine, 77*(5), 377–384.

Ries, A., Wingard, D., Gamst, A., Larssen, C., Farrell, E., & Reznik, V. (2012). Measuring faculty retention and success in academic medicine. *Academic Medicine, 87*(8), 1046–1051.

Schindler, B. A., Novack, D. H., Cohen, D. G., Yager, J., Wang, D., Shaheen, N. J., & Drossman, D. A. (2006). The impact of the changing health care environment on the health and well-being of faculty at four medical schools. *Academic Medicine, 81*(1), 27–34.

Simpson, D. E., Bragg, D., Biernat, K., & Treat, R. (2004). Outcomes results from the evaluation of the APA/HRSA Faculty Scholars Program. *Ambulatory Pediatrics, 4* (1 Suppl.), 103–112.

Smith, M. A., Barry, H. C., Dunn, R. A., Keefe, C., & Weismantel, D. (2006). Breaking through the glass ceiling: A survey of promotion rates of graduates of a primary care faculty development fellowship program. *Family Medicine, 38*(7), 505–510.

Steinert, Y., Naismith, L., & Mann, K. (2012). Faculty development initiatives designed to promote leadership in medical education. A BEME systemic review. BEME Guide 19. *Medical Teacher, 34*(6), 483–502.

Wingard, D. L., Garman, K. A., & Reznik, V. (2004). Facilitating faculty success: Outcomes and cost benefit of the UCSD National Center of Leadership in Academic Medicine. *Academic Medicine, 79* (10 Suppl.), S9–S11.

Woods, S. E., Reid, A., Arndt, J. E., Curtis, P., & Stritter, F. T. (1997). Collegial networking and faculty vitality. *Family Medicine, 29,* 45–49.

PART THREE

# FACULTY DEVELOPMENT PROGRAMS

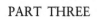

7

# CONNECT TO LEARNING

## USING E-PORTFOLIOS IN HYBRID PROFESSIONAL DEVELOPMENT

*Bret Eynon, Judit Török*
*LaGuardia Community College*

*Laura M. Gambino*
*New Community College*

*Based at LaGuardia Community College, the Connect to Learning (C2L)*
*project has developed an innovative hybrid professional development*
*model using e-portfolios, online conversations, and face-to-face meetings*
*to support campus leadership teams as they strengthen e-portfolio*
*initiatives on twenty-five diverse campuses nationwide. The C2L model*
*adapts a conceptual framework of inquiry, reflection, and integration to a*

We thank the U.S. Department of Education Fund for Improvement of Post-
Secondary Education for its support of the C2L project and are grateful to the
participating faculty, staff, and institutions of the C2L community for their
dedication to innovation and collaboration. Our thanks also to those whose
insightful comments on drafts helped us clarify our thinking, including Randy
Bass, Trent Batson, Alison Carson, Helen Chen, Peter Felten, Pat Hutchings,
Mary Huber, Terry Rhodes, and Howard Wach.

109

*hybrid context and addresses the challenge of local professional development leadership for classroom and institutional change.*

———— o ————

E-portfolios have emerged as an innovative feature of today's higher education landscape. The promise of enhanced student learning and authentic assessment has made e-portfolios broadly attractive. Data show that the number of colleges offering e-portfolio services tripled from 2003 to 2010 (Green, 2011). Using e-portfolios effectively can be challenging, however. Many colleges approach e-portfolios only as a technology and fail to grasp that the value depends on sophisticated pedagogy and institutional practice.

The Connect to Learning project (C2L), funded by the Fund for the Improvement of Secondary Education (FIPSE), assembles a diverse national network to address these challenges, linking e-portfolio leadership teams from twenty-five campuses to build a community of practice and develop a national resource site for e-portfolio initiatives. Launched in 2011, C2L is spearheaded by LaGuardia Community College, City University of New York (CUNY), working with the Association for Authentic, Experiential and Evidence Based Learning, an international e-portfolio organization, and twenty-four partner campuses from across the United States.

To do national professional development with limited resources, C2L employs a hybrid structure, linking online seminars and face-to-face meetings with campus experimentation. Campus e-portfolios created by each team unify the hybrid process. Three design principles—inquiry, reflection, and integration—inform our professional development process. Preliminary evidence suggests that this approach is helping C2L campus teams strengthen their work with hundreds of faculty, deepening e-portfolio practice that serves tens of thousands of students, and builds engagement in key integrative learning processes.

## The C2L Professional Development Model

C2L builds on LaGuardia's successful e-portfolio project (Eynon, 2009) and three years of the Making Connections project (2007–2010), a professional development effort to help New York City–area campuses launch e-portfolio initiatives. Holding monthly face-to-face meetings at LaGuardia, Making Connections worked with sixty campuses over three years, helping teams explore issues related to e-portfolio use, including integrative learning pedagogy, reflection, professional development techniques, technology, and authentic outcomes assessment.

In 2011, LaGuardia's Making Connections National Resource Center launched a new FIPSE-funded project: Connect to Learning: e-Portfolio, Engagement, and Student Success. This new effort expands to campuses nationwide and focuses on campuses that have e-portfolio initiatives already well under way. The primary goal is to create a community of practice where, guided by a leadership team based at LaGuardia's Making Connections Center, campus teams explore relevant scholarly literature and share their own practices, learning from each other to deepen their e-portfolio work (Sherer, Shea, & Kristensen, 2003). A secondary goal is to harvest the learning and practices to create a national resource website available to the larger e-portfolio field.

Selected in a competitive application process, the C2L campuses range from two-year colleges such as CUNY's Queensborough Community College to private liberal arts colleges such as Manhattanville College and Research I campuses such as the University of Delaware and San Francisco State University. Each campus has an active e-portfolio initiative, addressing campus-specific goals. The leaders of those initiatives—two to four members per campus—take part in C2L activities.

To help teams deepen their knowledge of e-portfolio practice, the C2L leadership used online tools to design a hybrid professional development model with four components:

- ○ *Campus practice.* Each team works with students, faculty, and staff on their campus, using e-portfolios to enhance pedagogy and strengthen outcomes assessment. The C2L process seeks to surface campus practices and make them more visible, conscious, and intentional. At the same time, C2L asks campus teams to experiment with new practices, developing plans and trying out strategies to advance campus initiatives.

- ○ *Face-to-face meetings.* After an initial face-to-face launch meeting, C2L has held annual summer institutes, gathering teams for discussion, exchange, and collaborative work.

- ○ *Online forum.* The Making Connections website hosts a Moodle-based threaded discussion forum; each year, C2L organizes five to six conversations, called "Jams," focusing on specific topics related to e-portfolio practice, such as designing reflective pedagogy for e-portfolio-enhanced courses or e-portfolios for outcomes assessment.

- ○ *Campus e-portfolios.* While helping campus teams use e-portfolios with their students, C2L also employs e-portfolios in its professional development process. Every campus has created a C2L project portfolio that is used to post campus information, practices, plans, and reflections. Examined during the online Jams and the face-to-face institutes, the recursive use of the campus e-portfolios serves as a unifying element for the entire process.

The forum and the campus e-portfolios are related but distinct. While Jams are temporal events, the campus portfolios endure, helping campuses make connections across issues and topics. The e-portfolios link the online and face-to-face exchange back to the tasks of scaling up campus e-portfolio initiatives, grounding project-wide conversation in evolving campus practice.

C2L's conceptual framework is grounded in three complementary design principles: inquiry, reflection, and integration. These three principles are applicable to e-portfolio pedagogy and practice on the campuses; at the same time, they inform the C2L professional development process. In this sense, we follow Thomas Angelo's (2001) precept: to model in the professional development process the pedagogies we seek to nurture in the classroom.

The concepts of inquiry, reflection, and integration are well developed in the literature. By inquiry, we mean the investigative, problem-based learning described by David Kolb and others—a cyclical process of asking questions about authentic problems, analyzing relevant evidence, creating and presenting evidence-based solutions, reflecting on the learning process, and developing new questions and plans for further inquiry (Dewey, 1938b; Kolb, 1984). At its best, e-portfolio pedagogy engages students in a recursive inquiry into their own learning and their evolving identities as learners and simultaneously supports institutional inquiry into learning through holistic outcomes assessment. Meanwhile, inquiry has a rich history in professional development (Butler & Schnellert, 2012). Programs with an emphasis on collective inquiry ask faculty and staff to raise questions, explore issues, and use their classrooms as laboratories for scholarly experiments with new pedagogies (Palmisano, 2012). Through sustained collective inquiry, faculty and staff construct new knowledge and understandings.

Reflection can be linked with inquiry but can also stand alone. From a Deweyan perspective, reflection complements experience; the purpose of reflection is to make connections among experiences, deepening continuities and empowering the meaning-making process (Dewey, 1938a; Rodgers 2002a). Reflection is pivotal to meaningful student e-portfolios, which function as sites for prompting, documenting, and sharing students' reflection on their learning. In a professional development process, reflective activities help participants learn from their experiences and develop as reflective practitioners (Rodgers, 2002b; Schön, 1983).

Integration, or integrative learning, has gained new visibility in higher education. For students, integrative learning involves making connections and transferring knowledge across courses, disciplines, and semesters, linking academic learning with lived experience into a more intentional whole (Huber & Hutchings, 2005). Guided by integrative pedagogy, students use e-portfolios to bring together work from multiple contexts, consider the relation between their classrooms and their lives outside class, and construct new identities as learners. In professional development, integration not only engages faculty and staff in the effort to employ integrative strategies with students; it also asks these professionals to transfer their own knowledge and insight from specific instances to broader contexts and applications. C2L sees integration in the process of moving from seminar to classroom, deepening and sustaining innovations, turning creative, one-shot experiments into broadly adopted changes in practice (Hutchings, 2006). For e-portfolio projects, integration demands going beyond individual classrooms to address institutional curricula, structure, and culture—issues that involve campus leaders, budgets, and governance. As Randy Bass (2012) writes, "We must fully grasp that students will learn to integrate deeply and meaningfully only insofar as we design a curriculum that cultivates that; and designing such a curriculum requires that we similarly plan, strategize and execute integratively across the boundaries within our institutions" (p. 32).

Because these three design principles speak to rich and adaptive processes of both student and professional learning, we believe they are broadly applicable in professional development. Moreover, we have found that these design principles amplify the value of e-portfolio use in professional development. The e-portfolio is inherently well suited to support professional inquiry into learning, the deepening of reflective practice, and the connective process central to integration. Used with social pedagogy, e-portfolios enrich collaboration as participants move through recursive cycles of inquiry, reflection, and integration.

## The C2L Model in Action

### Campus Activity

The C2L process is grounded in the experience of campus teams working in diverse settings. Each team works to advance the use of e-portfolios on its campus, addressing campus-specific goals and conditions. Some campus teams have been active for a decade; others are two to three years old. Most teams lead campus professional development, using a range of approaches to address self-selected topics that may include reflection, integrative pedagogy, and holistic outcomes assessment. A set of snapshots suggests the work of campus teams:

○ Three Rivers Community College (TRCC) in southeast Connecticut launched its e-portfolio project in 2004, focused on career portfolios for nursing students. The nursing faculty who lead the project explain that in 2006, their focus "shifted from technology to pedagogy." Adding courses each semester, they integrated e-portfolios program-wide. Students were introduced to program outcomes when they began their portfolios. Particular attention was given to reflection; the goal is for "students to reflect on action and develop reflective in action abilities." E-portfolios have served TRCC well in nursing professional accreditation, and its team has opened a conversation with the TRCC general education committee about using e-portfolios for broader outcomes assessment.

○ Manhattanville College, a liberal arts college in New York's Hudson Valley, began exploring e-portfolios in 2009 to reinvigorate the long-standing use of paper portfolios. The team seeks to "develop skills of reflection, self-assessment and integrative thought, utilizing e-portfolio." Aiming to build a systemic initiative, the team has used teaching and learning circles to nurture pockets of sophisticated e-portfolio use, such as the first-year seminar, the Center for Career Development, and a doctoral program in educational leadership. Recognizing the value of "the voice of students who have worked with e-portfolio in their classes," Manhattanville uses student "e-terns" to help faculty and peers. A growing number of majors have expressed interest in using e-portfolio to do "authentic and holistic outcomes assessment, designed to improve student learning."

○ Salt Lake Community College (SLCC), a multicampus Utah college, serves sixty thousand credit and noncredit students per year. In 2009, faculty approved a requirement that students use an e-portfolio in all general education courses. Since then, over thirty-five thousand student e-portfolios have been created. The SLCC team focuses on three main goals: "promoting engagement and intentionality among our students, adding coherence to our General Education program, and assessment of General Education." Encouraging sophisticated e-portfolio pedagogy needs ongoing attention, but the SLCC initiative has grown in unexpected ways. E-portfolios have been woven into developmental math and technical education programs and have become an integral part of how students document service-learning experiences. A handful of faculty now use e-portfolios to create tenure portfolios.

○ Boston University (BU) began using e-portfolios in 2008 in its College of General Studies, a two-year core curriculum program enrolling eleven hundred students each year; it is now a requirement, supporting assessment and helping students "make connections among their classes, reflect on their learning, enhance their academic projects with videos and other images, and archive their writings and extra-curricular activities." In 2011, BU assessed a large set of student e-portfolios, gathering quantitative and qualitative data on patterns of student progress. Pleased with their assessment work and the use of e-portfolios "to facilitate student-centered learning," the team acknowledges the challenge of sustaining faculty and student support. Looking ahead, they'll focus on engaging students through a peer mentor program and a student e-portfolio showcase.

Campus work is the site for professional learning; implementation is part of the inquiry process, a chance to test theory in the diverse campus contexts. Those campus contexts present challenges as well as opportunities. Campus teams confront not only tight budgets and resistance to change, but also the complexity of e-portfolio as an educational innovation. The most dynamic e-portfolio initiatives balance sophisticated pedagogy, digital technology, and holistic outcomes assessment. E-portfolio learning spans disciplines and semesters, linking academic and cocurricular learning, cognition, and affective development. Integrative e-portfolio practice asks faculty to step outside the comfort zone of individual courses and disciplinary training. Developing a meaningful e-portfolio initiative requires sustained cross-campus collaboration and systemic thinking by campus stakeholders. To deepen and scale e-portfolio initiatives, C2L's campus teams must recursively engage students, faculty, staff, and campus leaders, helping them focus on holistic student learning and its implications for campus structure and culture—what John Tagg (2000) called "double-loop" learning. Recognizing the importance of this task, C2L seeks to help campus teams build not only understanding of e-portfolio pedagogy and practice but also skills as educational change agents, working to promote a campuswide culture of learning (Butler & Schnellert, 2012).

## Face-to-Face Meetings

To help campus teams develop and test effective strategies for this campus work, C2L asks them to engage in a sustained process of collective inquiry and exchange, examining the literature, their own practices, and others' practices. Reflecting on this inquiry, the process asks them to take what they learn and integrate it back into their own campus activities.

Shared inquiry and exchange takes place face-to-face and online. Four face-to-face meetings were included in the project's three-year time line. In January 2011 we held a face-to-face kick-off meeting that brought together our new community, building trust among a diverse group of campuses, and introducing our hybrid structure. We have now held two summer institutes, bringing teams together for practice sharing, discussions of shared challenges, and development of strategies for evaluating the impact of e-portfolio activity.

Prior to the meetings, teams use their campus e-portfolios to post campus plans and goals for the upcoming year and review each other's plans. During the institute, teams build on this exchange, meeting with other teams to provide feedback; they then return to their own plans, using insights from the exchange to advance their campus initiatives more effectively. Team planning time and cross-campus community building are built into each institute. After each institute, teams use their campus e-portfolios to post reflections on their learning as well as revised campus plans.

## Online Forum

Recognizing that annual meetings are not sufficient to support its community of practice, C2L uses a Moodle-based forum for online conversation, collaboration, and collective inquiry. In the forum, C2L hosts threaded asynchronous discussions—the Jams. It holds five to six time-limited Jams per year, each running seven to ten days, focusing on a specific theme such as reflective pedagogy (see table 7.1).

Most Jams involve a review of relevant literature, multimedia presentations, small group discussion, sharing campus practices, and team reflection. They often begin with readings of key texts from the relevant literature. For example, in a fall 2011 Jam that explored linkages between e-portfolios and high-impact practices (particularly capstone and first-year experience programs), teams read articles from *Peer Review* (Carey, 2006) focused on the first college year; selections from Gardner and Van der Veer's (1998) *The Senior Year Experience: Facilitating Integration, Reflection, Closure, and Transition;* and a piece by George Kuh (2008).

### Table 7.1 Jam Topics and Dates, 2011 and 2012

| Dates | Topic |
| --- | --- |
| 2/25–3/7/2011 | Reflective Pedagogy for e-Portfolio Classrooms |
| 4/7–4/18/2011 | Best Practices in Integrative Faculty Development |
| 6/1–6/9/2011 | Goals and Plans: Building Your 2011–12 e-Portfolio Initiative |
| 9/19–9/29/2011 | From Beginning to End: Integrative e-Portfolios in First Year Experience and Capstone Courses |
| 11/1–11/11/2011 | Strengthening our Evaluation Practices: Sharing Revised Plans, Getting Assistance |
| 1/17–1/25/2012 | E-Portfolio and Social Pedagogy: A Conversation with Randy Bass |
| 2/27–3/7/2012 | C2L's National Development Model of e-Portfolio Practice: A Structured Resource for the Field |
| 4/16–4/30/2012 | Polishing Our Reflective e-Portfolio Practices: Deepening Our Work, Preparing to Go Public |
| 6/4–6/12/2012 | Becoming a Learning College: E-Portfolios for Outcomes Assessment |
| 9/27–10/5/2012 | Scaling Up: Strategies for Institution-Wide e-Portfolio Integration |
| 11/12–11/20/2012 | Professional Development Polished Practices |

Virginia Tech and LaGuardia shared multimedia presentations on their first-year and capstone e-portfolio programs. After watching these presentations on their own time, teams used the forum to discuss the presentations and readings and consider implications for their own work. Engagement in the Jams has been high; in this Jam, for example, participants posted more than two hundred comments.

## Campus e-Portfolios

Using the Digication platform, each campus team has created its own C2L e-portfolio, customizing it with images and information about its campus, its project, and its leadership team. Teams construct their portfolios recursively, regularly adding plans, reports, evaluation evidence, practice descriptions, and reflections. Rich with detail, evidence, and reflection, the campus e-portfolios support the inquiry processes taking place face-to-face and online, building integrative connections with ongoing campus practice.

Teams use their e-portfolios to document campus practice, preparing detailed descriptions of integrative and reflective activities and attaching samples of faculty and student work, including assignments, grading rubrics, and student portfolios. The inclusion of student work (shared by permission) grounds the descriptions in real artifacts of student learning. Descriptions include reflections on strengths and challenges. C2L teams have a wealth of knowledge and experience; developing their e-portfolios prompts them to articulate their insights, making tacit knowledge more explicit and accessible.

In C2L, e-portfolios are more than static repositories. We ask teams to share their e-portfolios, making them sites for interactive social learning. The e-portfolios are often used in Jams, alongside the forum. Building on questions raised in the forum, teams deepen their inquiry by sharing examples of relevant e-portfolio practice. They work in small groups, using the e-portfolios to read each other's practices. They use Digication's commenting feature to ask questions and provide detailed, grounded observations. This process not only provides access to concrete examples of practice; it also supports peer critiquing. Initial practice descriptions are seen as drafts; after engaging in discussion, teams rethink, refine, and polish their write-ups.

As the last step in each Jam, teams post written reflections to their e-portfolio. We ask participants to think about what they learned from each part of the Jam: the readings, forum, shared practices, and comments. This reflective process prompts participants to articulate their own learning and growth, become more reflective practitioners, and translate this learning to their own campus activity.

Campus e-portfolios document not only classroom practices but also the team's broader work: the intentional process of strategically building an e-portfolio project. C2L asks teams to engage in a yearly cycle of developing campus plans and evaluation reports and posting them in their e-portfolios. Developing a campus plan requires careful reflection; teams examine their campus work from many angles, thinking about ways they might integrate knowledge acquired from the C2L process into their project. In annual reports, teams summarize accomplishments and provide evaluation data. The evaluations ground inquiry with evidence, encouraging a more structured action research process; this process gains depth by combining inquiry at multiple levels of granularity, from individual practice to institutional structure and culture. Shared in e-portfolios, plans are reviewed by other teams and discussed at institutes. This advances the cycle of inquiry, reflection, and integration across multiple levels of collaboration; campus e-portfolios help unify a multi-layered community of practice focused on learning.

Campus e-portfolios thus serve an integrative function, linking other elements of the C2L model. Useful in and of themselves, they are most valuable in the ways they connect campus practices to institutes and the forum. When teams share practices during the Jams, they contribute to the project's multilayered collective inquiry. At the same time, the e-portfolios facilitate the process of reflection and integration, helping teams bring their learning back from the community exchange and apply it to the advancement of local initiatives.

## Preliminary Findings

As C2L begins its third year, preliminary evidence suggests that it is advancing toward its goals. Participant surveys, student outcomes data, and campus activity reports suggest that the process supports professional learning about e-portfolio pedagogy and practice and helps teams to build their campus initiatives.

One way to assess the program's value to participants is to ask for feedback. In January 2012, after twelve months of project activity, C2L leaders administered an online evaluation with open-ended and multiple-choice items. Three-quarters of the forty-eight respondents (76.1 percent) reported that overall, their participation in C2L had been either "very helpful" or "quite helpful." On another item, 97.8 percent "agreed" or "strongly agreed" that the C2L experience had "deepen[ed] my insights into e-portfolio Pedagogy." Nearly four-fifths (78.2 either) either "agreed" or "strongly agreed" that taking part in C2L had "spurr[ed] our team to focus on planning and evaluation."

Qualitative feedback adds nuances to our understanding of the value of the C2L experience. While some comments offered constructive suggestions for making the Jams more efficient and others noted the challenge of taking part in a demanding process while also leading a campus project, most highlighted the value of the process. Following is a selection of responses to the question, "How would you summarize the most interesting thing you learned through C2L?"

> "The readings and discussion on social pedagogy deepened and renewed my commitment to the concept and stimulated me to consider more ways to increase collaboration and reflection through e-portfolios as well as other classroom activities."

> "Being part of this project has ensured that the e-portfolio 'agenda' has been moving forward on our campus in a focused and timely manner."

"The wealth of practices around the country. I think we innovate well, but I'm always surprised by the ways to use e-portfolios that I hadn't thought of."

"The best part of C2L is having the opportunity to share practices and exchange ideas with other campus teams. This opportunity provides new ideas to bring back and work with on our own campus."

Feedback suggests that the combination of face-to-face, online, and campus-based activity in C2L is highly meaningful for participants. C2L teams are not only developing new insights into e-portfolio pedagogy and practice but also see the process as directly relevant to their campus work.

Campus reports represent another major data source. These annual reports provide data on the scope of the campus implementations, student learning outcomes, and narrative accounts of C2L-related activities. They indicate that teams drew on C2L processes as they engaged large numbers of faculty in e-portfolio-related professional development and teaching, serving large numbers of students in e-portfolio-intensive courses. In the 2011–12 academic year, over 860 faculty members participated in campus-based C2L-related professional development; over 760 instructors used e-portfolios in 895 course sections linked to C2L, which served over twenty thousand students in 2011–12.

The 2012 reports began to examine the impact of e-portfolio practice on student learning, but the evidence was limited in some respects. Proving a causal connection between professional development and change in student learning is always challenging (Fink, 2013). C2L campus teams have limited staff and budgets; they are not trained as evaluators and can be overwhelmed by the tasks of leading complex projects while also meeting other campus responsibilities. Getting campus institutional research offices to evaluate the impact of e-portfolios can be difficult. Aware of these challenges, C2L has used Jams and institute workshops to help teams plan ways to gather evidence of the impact of e-portfolios on student learning. Most C2L teams have begun to collect and analyze evidence, such as student and faculty surveys, retention rates, and GPA data—for example:

○ At Tunxis Community College, a year-long comparison between e-portfolio and non-e-portfolio sections of developmental English courses showed a 3 to 5 percent increase in student pass rates and an almost 6 percent increase in retention rates.

○ At Manhattanville College, the average GPA of students participating in an e-portfolio pilot was 3.097, while in a comparable, non-
e-portfolio cohort, the average GPA was 2.771.

○ At Indiana University-Purdue University Indianapolis, the one-year
fall-to-fall retention rate for students who complete an e-portfolio
(80 percent) was significantly higher than for students who did not
(72 percent).

To complement the examination of student outcomes, C2L developed
a network-wide C2L Core Student Survey, piloted in 2011–2012.
Responses to e-portfolio-specific questions suggest that nearly two-thirds
(64.8 percent) of the 4,137 student respondents felt the e-portfolio
experience had been valuable in helping them to deepen their learning
and "agreed" or "strongly agreed" with the statement, "Building my
e-portfolio helped me to think more deeply about the content of this
course." In addition, 63.8 percent "agreed" or "strongly agreed" with,
"Building my e-portfolio helped me to make connections between ideas."

E-portfolio-specific questions were flanked by a set of questions about
integrative learning used with permission from the National Survey of
Student Engagement (NSSE). Since the NSSE and the Community College
Survey of Student Engagement (CCSSE) are nationally normed, we could
use weighted national means from the NSSE First Year and the CCSSE
to do a preliminary comparison. The results suggest that students in C2L-
related courses were more likely than students nationwide to report
engagement in integrative learning. For example, in response to the
question, "To what extent has your experience in this course emphasized
synthesizing and organizing ideas, information and experiences in new
ways," 79.4 percent of C2L-related students responded "quite a bit" or
"very much." Nationally the comparable figure (on a weighted average of
national NSSE/CCSSE scores) was 64.1 percent. Similarly, on a question
about whether their experiences had "emphasized applying theories or
concepts to practical problems or in new situations," an indication of
knowledge transfer and integration, 74.3 percent of C2L students
responded "quite a bit" or "very much," compared to a national figure of
63.5 percent. On a question asking whether their experiences had "contributed to your knowledge, skills, and personal development in understanding yourself," indicating a connection between academic learning
and identity, the difference was even larger: 78.2 percent of C2L students
responded "quite a bit" or "very much," compared to a national figure of
58.5 percent. While rough and preliminary, these figures may be evidence

that C2L's campus teams are using e-portfolios to foster integrative learning. For now, these figures are best understood as an indication of the value of further research.

In campus reports, teams describe what they did in the past year to advance their local e-portfolio implementations. They report on the strategy and focus of their professional development processes and their work with e-portfolios around outcomes assessment. They discuss efforts to work with student groups, departments, administrators, and teaching centers to scale their e-portfolio initiatives and nurture a campuswide learning culture. On each of these issues, campus reports discussed what they did to deepen their work and address issues raised in the Jams.

Does the C2L experience shape these practices? The reports provide evidence that the processes of inquiry and reflection advance integration of C2L approaches into campus practice. In their reports, campuses explicitly identified ways that C2L participation had shaped plans and activities. The following excerpts suggest the breadth of the integration process:

> Participation in C2L has been essential to the success we have had with our e-portfolio launch at Manhattanville College. Indeed, we could not have rolled out e-portfolio to the entire freshman class this year without the support that C2L provides. The Manhattanville team has used C2L activities as a model when working in our Teaching/ Learning Circles (TLCs). In our TLCs, we use many of the readings we've used in C2L, including Lewis and Fournier's "A Catalyst without a Mandate," Carol Rogers' essay on "John Dewey and Reflective Thinking," and "Designing Learning Activities" from AAC&U's Electronic Portfolios and Student Success. (Manhattanville College)

> Though the changes are slow, I believe the one thing that C2L is encouraging us to do that we would not do otherwise is to base our activities in real data—to determine what has been effective and what has not and to develop our program based on that data. (Virginia Tech)

> The most substantive part of the C2L participation for us has been the opportunity to view other colleagues' practices . . . These concrete examples are extremely valuable to us as teachers as is the feedback we receive on our own practices. (Northwest Connecticut Community College)

> The SLCC team has taken quite a few meaningful ideas away from our C2L participation regarding assignments & reflection,

project planning, faculty development, assessment, and using social pedagogy in the classroom . . . Sharing how other campuses use e-portfolios for assessment also helped us . . . modify and strengthen our assessment this year. (Salt Lake Community College)

Our participation in C2L has enhanced our understanding of the importance of reflection in the learning process and the key role e-portfolios can play in facilitating students' self-reflections. We have implemented self-reflection assignments at the end of both the freshman and sophomore years now, and we probably would not havedone so, or done so this quickly, without the work of C2L. (Boston University)

These excerpts indicate some of the ways the C2L process appears to affect campus e-portfolio initiatives. The deepest impact so far has been on reflective e-portfolio pedagogy. But the effects ripple out from there, shaping faculty development, outcomes assessment, programmatic evaluation, work with stakeholders, linkages with high-impact practices, and other aspects of institutional e-portfolio integration. While not conclusive, this evidence, along with the feedback survey and other data provided by campuses, suggests that C2L's professional development model has already begun to demonstrate its effectiveness.

## Implications

Guided by the design principles of inquiry, reflection, and integration, C2L's hybrid, e-portfolio-based model shows signs of being a meaningful professional development process. Working effectively within this multicampus partnership, the C2L model may offer opportunities in other professional development contexts as well. First, the C2L hybrid model takes proven face-to-face practices and, using e-portfolio, translates them into an online environment. Second, C2L provides a design framework for structuring conversations around teaching practices that can be used with individual faculty, small groups, and larger organizations.

The use of the e-portfolio as a tool and a pedagogy for guiding professional development could be adapted to a wide range of settings and topics. In a hybrid professional development context, it complements threaded discussion, grounding it more firmly in practice. The detailed practice write-ups and campus reports included in the campus e-portfolios give depth and specificity to the professional development conversation. The connection to student work facilitates a focus not only on teaching but also on learning. Used with social pedagogy, e-portfolio-based interaction creates a wealth of commentary that is directly attached to practice. This grounded commentary stays with the e-portfolio, easily accessed as participants reflect and revise. In an online or a face-to-face setting, the use of the e-portfolio as a professional learning tool can strengthen continuity and connections between collective discourse and foster a sustained and recursive process of change.

Similarly, the design principles of inquiry, reflection, and integration have application in other professional development settings. The value of inquiry and reflection in professional learning is widely recognized. Adding integration recognizes the importance of integrative learning not only for students but also for professionals and institutions. It transforms the processes of inquiry and reflection, highlighting the importance of connecting individual and episodic innovation to sustained institutional change. In a period when colleges are under great pressure to make large-scale changes and improve student learning, professional development models that help educators examine and address the connections between classroom change and institutional transformation may prove to be critical to the future of higher education.

REFERENCES

Angelo, T. (2001). Doing faculty development as if we value learning most: Transformative guidelines from research and practice. In D. Lieberman & C. Wehlburg (Eds.), *To improve the academy: Resources for faculty, instructional and organizational development, Vol. 19* (pp. 97–112). San Francisco: CA: Jossey-Bass.

Bass, R. (2012). Disrupting ourselves: The problem of learning in higher education. *Educause Review Online.* Retrieved from http://net.educause.edu/ir/library/pdf/ERM1221.pdf

Butler, D., & Schnellert, L. (2012). Collaborative inquiry in teacher professional development. *Teaching and Teacher Education, 28*(8), 1206–1220.

Carey, S. (Ed.). (2006). *Peer Review, 8*(3).

Dewey, J. (1938a). *Experience and education.* New York, NY: Macmillan.

Dewey, J. (1938b). *Logic: The theory of inquiry.* New York, NY: Holt.

Eynon, B. (2009). "It helped me see a new me": e-portfolio, learning and change at LaGuardia Community College. *Academic Commons.* Retrieved from http://www.academiccommons.org/commons/essay/e-portfolio-learning-and-change

Fink, L. (2013). Innovative ways of assessing faculty development. In C. McKee, M. Johnson, W. Ritchie, & W. Tew (Eds.), *New Directions for Teaching and Learning: No. 133. The breadth of current faculty development practitioners' perspectives* (pp. 47–59). San Francisco, CA: Jossey-Bass.

Gardner, J., & Van der Veer, G. (1998). *The senior year experience: Facilitating integration, reflection, closure, and transition.* San Francisco, CA: Jossey-Bass.

Green, K. (2010). *2010 Campus computing report.* Encino, CA: Campus Computing Project.

Huber, M. T., & Hutchings, P. (2005). *Integrative learning: Mapping the terrain.* Washington, DC: Association of American Colleges and Universities.

Hutchings, P. (2006). *Fostering integrative learning through faculty development.* Carnegie Foundation for the Advancement of Teaching. Retrieved from http://gallery.carnegiefoundation.org/ilp/uploads/facultydevelopment_copy.pdf

Kolb, D. (1984). *Experiential learning: Experience as the source of learning and development.* Englewood Cliffs, NJ: Prentice Hall.

Kuh, G. (2008). High impact practices: What they are, who has access to them, and why they matter. *Leap.* Retrieved from http://www.aacu.org/leap/hip.cfm

Palmisano, M. (2012). *Collaborative inquiry differs from traditional professional development.* Retrieved from http://www.literacyinlearningexchange.org/collaborative-inquiry-differs

Rodgers, C. (2002a). Defining reflection: Another look at John Dewey and reflective thinking. *Teachers College Record, 104*(4), 842–866.

Rodgers, C. (2002b). Seeing student learning: Teacher change and the role of reflection. Voices inside schools. *Harvard Educational Review, 72*(2), 230–253.

Schön, D. (1983). *The reflective practitioner: How professionals think in action.* New York: Basic Books.

Sherer, P. D., Shea, T. P., & Kristensen, E. (2003). Online communities of practice: A catalyst for faculty development. *Innovative Higher Education, 27,* 183–194.

Tagg, J. (2007). Double-loop learning in higher education. *Change, 39*(4), 36–41.

8

# DEVELOPING A FACULTY LEARNING COMMUNITY GROUNDED IN THE SCIENCE OF HOW PEOPLE LEARN

## A YEAR-LONG, FACULTY-LED TEACHING AND LEARNING SEMINAR

*Al Rudnitsky, Glenn W. Ellis,*
*Patricia Marten DiBartolo, Kevin M. Shea*
*Smith College*

*This chapter describes a multiyear professional development effort undertaken by a learning and teaching center at a liberal arts college. As part of its founding mandate, the center helps faculty improve teaching by paying attention to the current literature about how people learn. This core commitment of our center is pursued through support of a year-long faculty seminar. Now in its fourth year, the seminar has had a significant impact on its faculty participants and their thinking about teaching and*

We thank the teaching and learning seminar faculty participants for the insights and thoughtful reflections they shared with us over the past few years. Thanks also to Mary Dean Sorcinelli for feedback on earlier versions of this chapter. Finally, we thank the Sherrerd family and the Davis Educational Foundation for their generous support of this work.

*learning. Moreover, the seminar has seeded a number of teaching and assessment initiatives at the college.*

---
○
---

Smith College has initiated an effort to improve teaching and learning by sustaining faculty engagement with the learning sciences through a teaching and learning seminar. By "the learning sciences," we mean the multidisciplinary efforts to understand better the learning process, in particular the learning process that leads to deep learning on the part of students. Also included in the learning sciences are developing ideas about how to design environments that support this kind of learning (Sawyer, 2006; Schwartz, Bransford, & Sears, 2005). Faculty members are introduced to these ideas as part of a community that meets regularly over the course of a year to discuss teaching in the context of each other's practice.

The seminar is best understood in relation to professional development efforts sponsored and organized by Smith College's Sherrerd Center for Learning and Teaching. The center, established in 2009, has a mission that explicitly recognizes three distinct areas of development:

○ Craft knowledge (Bereiter, 2002a), which includes the skills, techniques, methods, and tools that can be used to structure and support pedagogy

○ The human element of teaching, which includes support for the affective and social relationship realms of teaching and learning

○ Theoretical knowledge, aimed at supporting the kind of teaching Sawyer (2004) refers to as "disciplined improvisation" and is explicitly grounded in the latest advances in the science of learning and teaching

The prominence of theoretical knowledge in the center's mission reflects an underlying premise shared by the faculty who created the center that good teaching is inherently problematic, teaching can always be improved, and teaching takes place in a dynamic environment. It also recognizes that few college faculty have any formal education in pedagogy or learning theory and thus have neither shared knowledge nor the accompanying language for thinking and talking productively about teaching and learning. Without empirically and theoretically grounded ideas, instructional "innovations" tend to be implemented in surface and sometimes counterproductive ways. Innovations, even good ones, can become what Ann Brown (Brown & Campione, 1996, p. 292) referred to as "lethal mutations." Current calls for improving teaching in higher education also emphasize the role of the learning sciences (e.g., American Association for the Advancement of Science, 2011; Association of American Medical Colleges, 2009; Association of American Colleges and Universities, 2011).

In a recent review of the literature on faculty development, Amundsen and Wilson (2012) summarize the findings of other literature reviews on the same topic conducted over a thirty-year period. They concluded that earlier reviews produced little in the way of clear conclusions about what efforts result in effective faculty development. Amundsen and Wilson think the problem is that these reviews clustered heterogeneous professional development efforts by factors like duration or format (e.g., workshop, one-to-one consultations) and relied heavily on self-report outcome measures. In response, they conducted a review of 137 reports about faculty development published since 1995. Although they found little new from their own review, Amundsen and Wilson suggested that any potential findings were obscured because of the way the research was clustered. They offer a different scheme for categorizing professional development that is based on the nature of the goals pursued. In their reconceptualization, they identify six clusters of professional development: a skills focus, a method focus, a reflection focus, an institutional focus, a disciplinary focus, and an action research focus. Studies that fall into the skill, method, and institutional clusters emphasize outcomes. Studies that fall in the reflection, disciplinary, and action research clusters emphasize process.

An emphasis on outcomes, typical of a skill focus, often entails helping faculty develop a repertoire of tips, tools, routines, and instructional techniques that are often embedded in the latest technology. Examples of such tools range from the use of lecture clickers to the use of peer review as an effective tool in teaching writing. Teachers need craft knowledge, and supplying faculty a wide array of possible pedagogical tools and techniques is reflected in many professional development programs in higher education.

In contrast to outcomes, more process-oriented faculty development aims at developing a deeper understanding of teaching and learning. A process orientation conceptualizes the work of teaching as having to solve complex problems of design and making ongoing adjustments as teaching unfolds. This kind of teaching calls for a theoretical kind of knowledge—the kind of knowledge that Hatano and colleagues (Hatano & Inagaki, 1986; Hatano & Osuro, 2003) see as the basis for adaptive expertise.

Ken Bain (2004), author of *What the Best College Teachers Do*, makes a strong case for theoretical knowledge as he discusses the obstacles to good teaching:

> Perhaps the second biggest obstacle (the biggest obstacle is harboring the belief that one either is or is not born with the ability to teach) is the simplistic notion that good teaching is just a matter of technique . . . Such ideas make enormous sense if you have a transmission model, but it makes no sense if you conceive of teaching as creating good learning environments . . . In short, we must struggle with the meaning of learning within our disciplines and how best to cultivate and recognize it. For that task, we don't need routine experts who know all the right procedures but adaptive ones who can apply fundamental principles to all the situations and students they are likely to encounter, recognizing when invention is both possible and necessary and that there is no single "best way" to teach. (p. 175)

Despite the recognition that theoretical knowledge is important, evidence indicates that higher education devotes more resources to the development of skills by way of workshops or minicourses highlighting the newest advances in instruction, technology, or assessment than they do to introducing faculty to current scholarship about learning and teaching (Levinson-Rose & Menges, 1981; Steinert et al., 2006; Stes, Min-Leliveld, Gijbels, & Van Petegem, 2010).

There have been notable professional development efforts that are process oriented. Faculty learning communities (FLC) are a well-established organizational approach to professional development that is both collaborative and reflective (Cox, 2001). These communities have been shown to be effective in initiating and supporting pedagogical innovation (Furco & Moely, 2012; Richlin & Cox, 2004). Smith College's teaching and learning seminar is an instance of an FLC, and its organization includes many of the developmental steps that Richlin and Cox (2004) recommended. These include applying for membership, having an opening and closing retreat, preparing for the start of the school year, and scheduled presentations by participants. Cox (2004) cites two kinds of FLC organization. One form of organization is by cohort (e.g., midcareer faculty). The other form of organization, and the one Cox advocates, is topic based and focuses for a year on a problem or theme (e.g., teaching research skills across the curriculum, teaching foreign languages). Many of the features and steps found to support the establishment of an effective FLC have been incorporated into the design of our teaching and learning seminar. There are aspects, however, that distinguish it from many other FLCs. Among them is its explicit focus on ideas from the learning sciences and a commitment to the development of principle-based teaching. Seminar leaders are guided by the learning sciences in creating a set of readings and beginning discussion topics that initiate the work of the seminar. Also, rather than being topical, the seminar addresses a variety of problems or issues depending on the community's faculty participants. The liberal arts context of the seminar means that participants represent a wide range of liberal arts disciplines. The exploration of underlying principles of learning and teaching is enriched by the diversity of perspectives. The seminar represents the Sherrerd Center's first step in pursuing the principle-based part of its mission.

# Method

## Faculty Participants

While the popularity of the seminar has not flagged since its inception in 2009, the seminar is kept intentionally small (usually ranging from nine to thirteen participants plus two group leaders) in order to foster cohesion and discussion. Since 2009, forty-two faculty and three staff members are participating or have participated in the seminar. The faculty members represent almost half (twenty of forty-five) of the departments and programs at the college (see table 8.1 for more detail) and every level of faculty rank—twelve participants at full, sixteen at associate, eight at assistant professor—and six lecturers or staff members. Compensation for year-long participation in the seminar is modest for participants (five hundred dollars) and leaders (one thousand dollars).

## Seminar Organization and Core Readings

Consistent with our emphasis on idea improvement and adaptive expertise in the classroom, the structure and the readings of the seminar have changed each year to best meet faculty needs; nonetheless, an overall organization has taken shape with a number of core readings identified. The seminar begins with a half-day August workshop in which readings are used to introduce some of the big ideas in the seminar and to begin developing a shared language from the learning sciences. Recent readings include an overview of the learning sciences (Sawyer, 2006), an introduction to transfer-in and transfer-out—including assessment and implications for the classroom (Schwartz et al., 2005), and the changing role of education in a knowledge society (Bereiter, 2002a, 2002b).

Table 8.1   Department and Program Representation in the Sherrerd's Teaching and Learning Seminar, 2009-Present

| Division | Number of Faculty Participating (% of total faculty participants) | Number of Departments and Programs with at Least One Faculty Participant | Departments and Programs Represented |
|---|---|---|---|
| Humanities | 11 (24.44%) | 7 | Afro-American studies, Art, Classics, East Asian studies, East Asian Languages and Literatures, English, French, History |
| Social sciences | 9 (20.00%) | 5 | Anthropology, Economics, Education and Child Study, Government, Sociology |
| Natural sciences | 22 (52.38%) | 8 | Biology, Chemistry, Computer Science, Geosciences, Engineering, Mathematics and Statistics, Physics, Psychology |

After the initial workshop, the seminar meets twice a month throughout the school year. Discussions in the fall semester meetings focus on shared readings about topics such as conceptions of teaching and learning (Bruner, 1996; Richardson, 2005), teaching as storytelling (Egan, 2004), idea-centered education (Bereiter, 2002a, 2002b), and knowledge building (Bereiter & Scardamalia, 2006; Scardamalia, 2002; Scardamalia & Bereiter, 2003, 2006).

Discussion emerges from topics with current relevance to the participants (e.g., designing effective midsemester student feedback) or arises from student discourse that unfolds over the course of the semester. At other times, discussion is seeded through the use of videos that address varied teaching and learning issues, such as the challenges of addressing misconceptions that students bring to the classroom (Schneps & Sadler, 2003) or the importance of students learning to formulate problems (Meyer, 2010).

The spring semester begins with a half-day workshop in January with more extensive preparatory readings such as Bain's *What the Best College Teachers Do* (2004) and other readings that explore fall semester topics in greater depth. At this point, the participants begin to take on more of a leadership role in the seminar discussions and largely run the subsequent bimonthly meetings, take turns leading discussions, and share their own classroom experiences and ideas they plan to try out in their upcoming classes.

The seminar recognizes the importance of developing the learning community, supporting its members, and sustaining extended discourse. Indeed, faculty members cycling out of the seminar in spring 2010 voiced an interest in continuing to maintain connections and opportunities for reflection provided by the seminar's regular meeting times. For this reason, all past and present participants are now invited to attend several meetings throughout the year. Although the topics vary, often past participants share in these meetings how they have applied ideas from the seminar. Examples include a faculty member who led her department in developing an assessment instrument to measure deep learning in psychology and several faculty members who shared online knowledge building student discourse from their classes.

## Central Principles of the Teaching and Learning Seminar

Based on the premise that teaching can always be improved, the teaching and learning seminar was designed to encourage discussions about learning, sustained over extended periods of time, among faculty from diverse disciplines. Fundamental principles about teaching and learning that shape seminar discussions came from readings within the learning sciences. These central principles include the following:

- Learners must learn what and how they think because different kinds of thinking lead to different learning outcomes. Ultimately learning depends on what learners do, not what teachers do.
- Learners' existing knowledge has a profound effect on their current thinking and learning.
- Effective learners are metacognitive in that they set goals for themselves and engage in self-monitoring and self-regulation.
- Learning is socially situated and mediated. It begins in participation with others through substantive discourse, and the edge of individual competence is marked by what a learner can do with support from others.

○ Instruction is most productively conceived as designing complex learning environments that support good learner thinking, with recognition that evaluation and assessment exerts a powerful influence on the learning environment.

○ Understanding and deep learning that allow for better knowledge transfer and preparation for future learning are privileged educational outcomes.

Many faculty participants come to the seminar already beginning to raise questions about their teaching and student learning. Over the course of the seminar, most begin to see how heavily didactic approaches to teaching often result in shallow, superficial kinds of student learning. In fact, the problem of knowledge transfer, both within and across courses, is often the impetus for faculty involvement in the seminar, as they become increasingly concerned about student learning across time and contexts.

This evolving understanding of teaching and learning is in keeping with the general direction of pedagogical reform in higher education. That is, the direction of reform is away from teacher-centered didacticism to a more student-centered constructivism. In most cases, moves away from teacher-centered pedagogy have typically emphasized putting students in more active learning roles, often working together in collaborative groups. Among the approaches reform recommendations employ are reenactment, problem-based learning, project-based learning, inquiry-based pedagogy, the use of case studies, and writing across the curriculum. All of these approaches represent movement in a progressive direction. Nonetheless, seminar readings and discussions have helped faculty identify ways this activity-centered teaching can be improved.

Much of the improvement centers on what faculty, through reading, discussion, and experience, have come to recognize as a weakness common to these approaches: students in an activity-centered learning environment tend to adopt a product rather than a learning orientation. Research (Bereiter, 2002a, 2002b; Bransford, 2000; Bruner, 1996; Doyle, 1983) indicates that students typically see their task as one of doing well in a course. When that means producing a good product or performance, then that is where students direct their efforts. Producing a good product can require learning, but the learning is often incidental to the more central production goal. In the interest of efficiency and effectiveness, students often rely on their own well-learned routines, skills, and knowledge. When working in groups, they tend to divide the labor rather than engage in extended collaborative discourse, thereby short-circuiting the kind of intentionality, reflectiveness, and engagement that deep learning requires.

Through the teaching and learning seminar, many faculty have found the principles and ideas associated with knowledge building (Scardamalia, 2002; Scardamalia & Bereiter, 2006) an appealing conceptual framework for crafting powerful learning environments—environments that might help students develop a deeper understanding of core disciplinary concepts and principles. Knowledge building is a pedagogical approach that emphasizes the importance of ideas and collaborative discourse in helping students learn more deeply by asking them to work on idea improvement while grappling with interesting and important knowledge problems.

Ordinarily most school learning finds students working in belief mode (Bereiter & Scardamalia, 2006) wherein ideas are seen as fixed entities and student engagement is a matter of memorizing, resolving doubt, or making arguments for or against. In contrast, idea improvement is the essence of what Bereiter and Scardamalia (2006) call operating in design mode, where ideas are treated as conceptual artifacts, invented to serve a purpose, and as inventions, subject to improvement. As Scardamalia and Bereiter (2003) state, "Knowledge building may be defined as the production and continual improvement of ideas to a community, through means that increase the likelihood that what the community accomplishes will be greater than the sum of individual contributions and part of broader cultural efforts . . . If learners are engaged in process only suitable for a school, then they are not engaged in knowledge building" (p. 1370).

Given that faculty often engage in knowledge building as scholars within their respective disciplines, it is not surprising that the notion of idea improvement resonates with seminar participants. Most faculty see themselves as participants in a discourse community whose goal is to advance knowledge. Having students engage in the kind of thinking that occurs at a discipline's cutting edge is often a stated goal for students, especially advanced students. A knowledge-building approach, with its emphasis on good discourse, idea improvement, and collective cognitive responsibility, advances this goal.

## Outcomes

### Evaluation Data from Three Cohorts of Participants

We surveyed the first three cohorts who participated in the Teaching and Learning Seminar between 2009 and 2012 and received responses from nineteen of the thirty participants. We asked about ideas from the seminar that had an impact on their thoughts about teaching and learning, changes they made in their classes, and differences in student learning and engagement after making changes.

The seminar affected individual faculty participants in a variety of ways. Faculty reported that they are lecturing less, having students complete self-directed projects and get more prepared for class, focusing less on content and more on big, central questions, and empowering students to take ownership of their own learning. One participant stated that she "takes risks . . . and jettisons a lot of busy work to leave more time for deeper learning related to the central themes," while another focuses on trying "to get students to do a better job coming up with ideas and exploring questions that don't have obvious answers."

One of our goals was to help faculty develop a more sophisticated conception of teaching focused on results from the learning sciences. Indeed, sixteen of the nineteen respondents mentioned learning science concepts that had an impact on their thoughts about teaching and learning, including knowledge building, idea-centered teaching, collective idea improvement, knowledge transfer, understanding prior knowledge, bringing research into the classroom, encouraging half-formed thoughts, being transparent, and efficiency versus innovation.

Sixteen faculty implemented significant teaching changes based on their participation in the seminar. For example, they designed more challenging assignments, were mindful of preparation for future learning, and highlighted subtlety and complexity of problems. Many also reported highlighting the importance of student-formulated questions and working in groups on real problems. Overall, faculty focused on getting students to participate in learning through knowledge-building assignments or the use of online discourse communities to enable sustained conversations outside of class.

Overall, faculty believed that students were learning more, despite the fact that some students struggled to change existing ideas and accompanying habits about teaching and learning. Faculty believed that students who did embrace the changes gained a better understanding of what it means to do research (even at the introductory level of the curriculum) and had better ideas about how knowledge is created and advanced in different disciplines. One participant reported that students were more willing to discuss concepts and problems and that there was a richer exchange of ideas in class. This was a key point, with many faculty reporting improved in-class discussions. Outside class, course changes "fostered a greater engagement and independence in my students."

Others commented that students and recent alums were "articulating the connections between their learning and their careers after Smith," "I have been getting increasing feedback from students that their level of conceptual understanding feels deeper," and "last spring's transformed colloquium was certainly one of the most successful I have ever taught. Students from the course have continued to be in touch all summer whenever they encountered ideas which related to it."

## Reflections on the Seminar

Faculty reflections on the teaching and learning seminar were positive, some enthusiastically so, with only two respondents unhappy with their experiences in the seminar. Participants have also been forthcoming with critical feedback, in keeping with our philosophy that all teaching can be improved. Four participants were unhappy with what they saw as too great a focus on knowledge building. With the formation of a (now) grant-funded group pursuing knowledge building, the seminar has made an effort to represent a range of thinking and pedagogical ideas. The seminar needs to be a place that can give birth to collaborative faculty efforts like those of the knowledge-building group. At the same time, the seminar needs to be careful not to focus too narrowly. Other faculty "struggled with how to apply the big ideas from the seminar to the practicalities of teaching." This is a concern and a constant reminder of how difficult principle-based teaching is.

Participants who were most positive reported, "The ongoing nature of the seminar [beyond the initial year] is also extremely valuable as these ideas and their implementation take time," "I have and continue to grow a lot in my approach to teaching and in how I understand the process of learning. I know there's a long way to go, so having an ongoing group at Smith is very important," and "I appreciated meetings and the opportunity to talk to colleagues across disciplines about their challenges and successes." We do not know whether there is a critical mass at which point the nature and pace of this work changes. The evidence points to a growing conversation among faculty. We think this is a good thing.

## Additional Assessments of Seminar Impact on Participants

DEVELOPMENT OF A KNOWLEDGE-BUILDING COMMUNITY FOR FACULTY PARTICIPANTS The teaching and learning seminar has created an opportunity to participate in a collaborative learning environment for its faculty participants. They grapple with new ideas and philosophies while attempting to implement similar models in their own classes. The learning sciences highlight the importance of sustained discourse for idea improvement, and our faculty cohorts report the value of discourse with their peers as they strive to improve their conception of teaching and implement strategies to enhance student learning. One participant commented that "a significant component of these seminars is . . . the fact that a group of interested and thoughtful colleagues gets together to talk about these ideas in a sustained way. I've learned and been inspired by my fellow teachers." Another stated, "The seminar was worthwhile in deepening the quality of my own thoughts about teaching and better grounding them in evidence from research." These outcomes highlight the value of the learning environment created as part of the teaching and learning seminar and demonstrate outcomes we hope we will see among students in our classes.

DEVELOPMENT OF KNOWLEDGE BUILDING ACROSS THE CURRICULUM  As a result of collaborative discussions within the context of the teaching and learning seminar, four faculty members realized their shared desire to provide greater support for student- and idea-centered teaching initiatives across campus. Together with the Sherrerd Center, they launched an effort to pursue and ultimately received grant funding from the Davis Educational Foundation to support the development of these pedagogies across the curriculum. Our first cohort of eleven Davis fellows and four faculty teaching mentors has begun its work. Beginning with a series of day-long workshops in summer 2012 and continuing throughout the academic year with biweekly meetings, these fellows have committed to a significant course revision that privileges idea-centered learning and outcomes. All mentors and fellows are previous teaching and learning seminar participants or leaders who were inspired to put into action the ideas cultivated by the seminar.

Most of the faculty pursuing knowledge building use Knowledge Forum (KF), software that helps to foster and capture student discourse. Faculty use of KF databases is an additional measure of how many courses are involving students in idea-centered pedagogy. KF is now being used by twenty faculty members (all former or current teaching and learning seminar participants) in over thirty courses (see figure 8.1).

SCHOLARSHIP OF TEACHING AND LEARNING  To date, former seminar participants have published a peer-reviewed journal article and given eight presentations at conferences or universities (see DiBartolo, 2011; DiBartolo & Rudnitsky, 2012; DiBartolo, Rudnitsky, & Shea, 2012;

Figure 8.1   Growth in Knowledge Forum Databases in Sustaining Student-Centered Learning

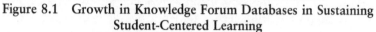

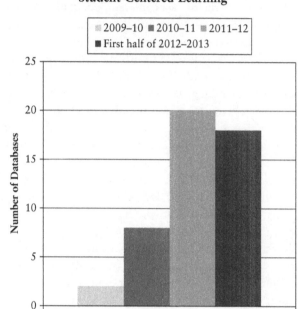

Ellis, DiBartolo, & Yu, 2012; O'Sullivan, 2012; Shea, 2011, 2012a, 2012b, 2012c). This work has involved five faculty members and one undergraduate student. Moreover, ideas from the teaching and learning seminar created some interest in building discipline-specific assessments that would examine deep learning, including transfer of knowledge and preparation for future learning. Thus far, two departments on campus (Chemistry and Psychology) are working to develop direct assessments of learning that look across courses at students' understanding of the core principles and practices of the discipline (i.e., to think like a psychologist or chemist). So far, these faculty groups have shared their data only within the college, but we anticipate they will seek a broader audience in the near future.

## Discussion

Our experiment with a sustained faculty development seminar based on the science of teaching and learning has fostered positive change at the individual, departmental, and college levels. Outcomes include changes in pedagogical practices and the way faculty think about teaching. Some faculty have pursued the scholarship of teaching and undertaken initiatives that support putting theory into practice, in particular, a grant-supported effort to investigate idea-centered pedagogies. Several departments have implemented creative summative assessments of their student majors based on discussions initiated in the seminar and focused on higher-order capacities and learning outcomes. In addition, the college revised its student course evaluation form to align more with learning science principles by including short-answer questions focused on student learning and moving away from traditional quantitative questions.

' Our model for this seminar, similar to a faculty learning community, should be amenable to implementation at a variety of institutions. We anticipate that many colleges have groups of faculty eager to explore the learning sciences with supportive, motivated, and inspiring colleagues. Like us, the ultimate destination for these group discussions will be unclear. In fact, each institution will likely give rise to participants whose deliberations will lead them in unique directions. Nonetheless, we are convinced that long-term faculty engagement with the ideas from the learning sciences will ultimately transform our academic institutions into more vibrant teaching and learning communities for our faculty and, most important, our students.

## REFERENCES

American Association for the Advancement of Science. (2011). *Vision and change in undergraduate biology education: A call to action.* Washington, DC: Author.

Amundsen, C., & Wilson, M. (2012). Are we asking the right questions? A conceptual review of the educational development literature in higher education. *Review of Educational Research, 82,* 90–126.

Association of American Colleges and Universities. (2011). *The LEAP vision for learning: Outcomes, practices, impact, and employers' views.* Washington, DC: Author.

Association of American Medical Colleges. (2009). *Scientific foundations for future physicians.* Washington, DC: Author.

Bain, K. (2004). *What the best college teachers do.* Cambridge, MA: Harvard University Press.

Bereiter, C. (2002a). *Education and mind in the knowledge age.* Hillsdale, NJ: Erlbaum.

Bereiter, C. (2002b). Liberal education in a knowledge society. In B. Smith (Ed.), *Liberal education in a knowledge society* (pp. 11–34). Peru, IL: Carus Publishing Company.

Bereiter, C., & Scardamalia, M. (2006). Education for the knowledge age: Design-centered models of teaching and instruction. In P. A. Alexander & P. H. Winne (Eds.), *Handbook of educational psychology* (2nd ed., pp. 695–713). Mahwah, NJ: Erlbaum.

Bransford, J. D. (Ed.). (2000). *How people learn: Brain, mind, experience, and school.* Washington, DC: National Academy Press.

Brown, A. L., & Campione, J. C. (1996). Psychological theory and the design of innovative learning environments: On procedures, principles, and systems. In L. Shaublean & R. Glaser (Eds.), *Innovations in learning: New environments for education* (pp. 289–325). Mahwah, NJ: Erlbaum.

Bruner, J. (1996). *The culture of education.* Cambridge, MA: Harvard University Press.

Cox, M. D. (2001). Faculty learning communities: Change agents for transforming institutions into learning organizations. In D. Lieberman & C. Wehlburg (Eds.), *To improve the academy: Resources for faculty, instructional and organizational development, Vol. 19* (pp. 69–93). San Francisco, CA: Jossey-Bass.

Cox, M. D. (2004). Introduction to faculty learning communities. In M. D. Cox & L. Richlin (Eds.), *New directions for teaching and learning: No. 97. Building faculty learning communities* (pp. 5–25). San Francisco, CA: Jossey-Bass

DiBartolo, P. M. (2011). *In pursuit of deep learning: Using knowledge building to teach research methods.* Paper presented at the meeting of the Consortium on High Achievement and Success Faculty Forum, Smith College, Northampton, MA.

DiBartolo, P. M., & Rudnitsky, A. N. (2012). What happens when a college instructor meets the learning sciences. *International Journal of University Teaching and Faculty Development, 2,* 155–180.

DiBartolo, P. M., Rudnitsky, A., & Shea, K. (2012). *Knowledge Forum: Facilitating development of idea-centered learning environments.* Workshop presented at the New England Faculty Development Conference Consortium, East Greenwich, RI.

Doyle, W. (1983). Academic work. *Review of Educational Research, 53,* 159–199.

Egan, K. (2004). *An imaginative approach to teaching.* San Francisco, CA: Jossey Bass.

Ellis, G. W., DiBartolo, P. M., & Yu, Y. (2012). *Designing learning environments that prepare students for the knowledge age.* Workshop presented at the Association of American Colleges and Universities conference, Seattle, WA.

Furco, A., & Moely, B. E. (2012). Using learning communities to build faculty support for pedagogical innovation: A multi-campus study. *Journal of Higher Education, 83,* 128–153.

Hatano, G., & Inagaki, K. (1986). Two courses of expertise. In H. Stevenson, H. Azuma, & K. Hakuta (Eds.), *Child development and education in Japan* (pp. 262–272). New York, NY: Freeman.

Hatano, G., & Osuro, Y. (2003). Reconceptualizing school learning using insight from expertise research. *Educational Researcher, 32,* 26–29.

Levinson-Rose, J., & Menges, R. J. (1981). Improving college teaching: A critical review of research. *Review of Educational Research, 51,* 403–434.

Meyer, D. (2010). *Math class needs a makeover.* Retrieved from http://www.ted .com/talks/dan_meyer_math_curriculum_makeover.html

O'Sullivan, R. (2012). *Using "Knowledge Forum" to promote discussion and group work.* Paper presented at the Second Annual National Conference on Teaching Economics, Boston, MA.

Richardson, J.T.E. (2005). Students' approaches to learning and teachers' approaches to teaching in higher education. *Educational Psychology, 25,* 673–680.

Richlin, L., & Cox, M. D. (2004). Developing scholarly teaching and the scholarship of teaching and learning through faculty learning communities. In M. D. Cox & L. Richlin (Eds.), *New directions for teaching and learning: No. 97. Building faculty learning communities* (pp. 127–135). San Francisco, CA: Jossey-Bass.

Sawyer, R. K. (2004). Creative teaching: Collaborative discussion as disciplined improvisation. *Educational Researcher, 33,* 12–20.

Sawyer, R. K. (2006). The new science of learning. In R. K. Sawyer (Ed.), *The Cambridge handbook of the learning sciences* (pp. 1–16). Cambridge: Cambridge University Press.

Scardamalia, M. (2002). Collective cognitive responsibility for the advancement of knowledge. In B. Smith (Ed.), *Liberal education in a knowledge society* (pp. 67–98). Peru, IL: Carus Publishing Company.

Scardamalia, M., & Bereiter, C. (2003). Knowledge building. In J. W. Guthrie (Ed.), *Encyclopedia of education* (pp. 1370–1373). New York, NY: Macmillan Reference.

Scardamalia, M., & Bereiter, C. (2006). Knowledge building: Theory, pedagogy and technology. In R. K. Sawyer (Ed.), *The Cambridge handbook of the learning sciences* (pp. 97–115). Cambridge: Cambridge University Press.

Schneps, M. H., & Sadler, P. M. (2003). *A private universe: Minds of our own.* Cambridge, MA: Harvard-Smithsonian Center for Astrophysics.

Schwartz, D. L., Bransford, J. D., & Sears, D. (2005). Efficiency and innovation in transfer. In J. Mestre (Ed.), *Transfer of learning: Research and perspectives* (pp. 1–51). Charlotte, NC: Information Age Publishing.

Shea, K. M. (2011). *Knowledge building: Application of the science of teaching and learning.* Paper presented at the New England Faculty Development Consortium, College of the Holy Cross, Worcester, MA.

Shea, K. M. (2012a). *Empowering students to learn chemistry: My journey to improvisational student- and idea-centered teaching.* Paper presented at University of Central Florida, Orlando.

Shea, K. M. (2012b). *Empowering students to learn chemistry: My journey to student and idea-centered teaching.* Ed Mellon Lecture presented at Florida State University, Tallahassee, FL.

Shea, K. M. (2012c). *Getting new faculty and their mentors to talk about teaching and learning.* Workshop presented at the AALAC meeting, Northfield, MN.

Steinert, Y., Mann, K., Centeno, A., Dolmans, D., Spencer, J., Gelula, M., & Prideaux, D. (2006). A systematic review of faculty development initiatives designed to improve teaching effectiveness in medical education. *Medical Teacher, 28,* 497–526.

Stes, A., Min-Leliveld, M., Gijbels, D., & Van Petegem, P. (2010). The impact of instructional development in higher education: The state-of-the-art of the research. *Educational Research Review, 5,* 25–49.

# 9

# ASSESSING THE LONG-TERM IMPACT OF A PROFESSIONAL DEVELOPMENT PROGRAM

---

*Marcia M. Tennill, Margaret W. Cohen*
*University of Missouri–St. Louis*

*This study was designed to explore the long-term impact of a year-long faculty development program on participants. Three guiding questions focused the study: In what ways did the program influence the professional lives of participants five years after completion? How did the participants integrate those experiences into their professional lives? and What recommendations for best practices in the field of faculty development can be drawn? Donald Kirkpatrick's four-level evaluation model was the template for this qualitative research. Results indicated that participants retained program learning over time.*

---

○

---

This program evaluation explored the long-term impact of faculty development in higher education and is situated in the context of a specific program: the University of Missouri's New Faculty Teaching Scholars Program (NFTS). Although this research was based on the experiences of faculty who participated in that specific program, it also broadly addressed the concept of faculty development and its general relevance to higher education. Faculty development programs in higher education broadly refer to activities that focus on enhancing the professional success of faculty members as teachers, scholars, professionals, and individuals. While each of these areas is valuable and worthy of study, exploring all of them presented a task that exceeded the goals of the research. Instead, data collection addressed four of the five NFTS programmatic goals that were directed at supporting the faculty member's teaching role.

## New Faculty Teaching Scholars Program

The 2001 strategic plan of the University of Missouri (UM) called for the development of campus environments focused intentionally on student learning. One response was the systemwide NFTS. Initiated in the 2001–2002 academic year, NFTS continued annually until it was suspended for budgetary reasons during the 2008–2009 academic year. The program was administered through the UM system office of academic affairs and coordinated by a director on each of the four campuses (Columbia, St. Louis, Kansas City, and Rolla). New and early-career faculty members in their second, third, or fourth years of appointment were eligible to participate. At the time of application, both the faculty member and the department chair acknowledged in writing the time commitment necessary to participate fully in the program. Approximately fifty faculty members participated annually.

The program acclimated new faculty members to their roles and responsibilities on their own campuses and across the university system. As noted in the program brochure (New Faculty Teaching Scholars, 2004), the NFTS had these goals:

1. To support individual campus activities that help new faculty members become effective teachers and scholars.
2. To promote engaged instructional strategies that support student-centered learning environments.
3. To assist in the development of campus and systemwide networks that are essential for success in today's academic world.
4. To support increased faculty research, teaching productivity and faculty retention.
5. To support efforts to develop a "culture of teaching" on each campus and throughout the University of Missouri.

The NFTS program spanned the nine-month academic year. Three two- to three-day systemwide retreats were scheduled—one each fall, winter, and spring. Two of the retreats convened in locations removed from each of the campuses. Expenses associated with travel, accommodations, meals, and materials were funded by the UM System. The fall retreat focused on course design and offered participants opportunities to learn about, develop, and apply active and learner-centered teaching strategies to their courses. The winter retreat was held concurrently with a teaching renewal conference on the Columbia campus, where NFTS participants participated in conference workshops and instructional presentations facilitated by experts in the fields of teaching and learning. The spring retreat focused participants on creating an academic portfolio describing and documenting their academic accomplishments and professional development. The portfolio serves as a foundation for promotion and tenure dossiers. In addition, each director sponsored monthly presentations and discussions for his or her campus's participants. Although these events were scheduled to reflect the NFTS goals, directors had the flexibility to tailor events to meet the needs of their campus group. For example, events on the Rolla campus, now Missouri University of Science and Technology, might focus programs on its research mission, devoting attention to National Science Foundation funding.

Thus, NFTS convened the faculty participants multiple times during the year as a single cohort and as campus cohort groups. University administrators and the program directors hoped to nurture a culture of teaching across the university system. They sought to foster environments where early-career faculty engaged with students and one another in learner-centered environments. The program was designed to expand faculty members' collegial networks by creating relationships that might lead to joint research or teaching collaborations. Ultimately administrators wanted NFTS to engage, encourage, and entice early-career faculty to stay at the university until they attained tenure and beyond.

Based on the strategic plan set forth by the University of Missouri System (Pacheco, 2001) and the goals of the NFTS program (New Faculty Teaching Scholars, 2004), the yearly evaluations of the NFTS program generally reflected outcomes found in the literature. At the end of each program year, participants completed a comprehensive evaluation of the activities, the content, and the perceived effect of the program on their professional development. During the seven years of the program, 395 faculty members attended and completed the program. Of those faculty participants, 74 percent responded to the end-of-program evaluative surveys. Those participants agreed that NFTS had a positive impact on their teaching (average agreement, 89 percent), their collegial relationships (average agreement, 89 percent), and their professional development as related to promotion and tenure (average agreement, 57 percent for the three years that issue was surveyed). These data are compiled from the annual evaluation reports from each program year (University of Missouri System, 2001–2008).

Nevertheless, a larger question remained: "How does this program impact the professional lives of participants on a long-term basis?" One means of determining long-term program impact is to follow up with participants after a period of time has passed.

## Guiding Questions

Qualitative research methods explore the details of selected issues in depth. The purpose of this research study, then, was not to measure, compare, or quantify outcomes of the program but to explore with participants how and in what ways the program has affected them on a long-term basis. The following guiding questions served as the template for this qualitative research study:

1. In what ways has NFTS influenced the professional lives of participants five years after completing the program?
2. How have participants integrated NFTS experiences into their professional lives?
3. How do the results of this study offer recommendations for best practices in the field of faculty development?

## Review of the Literature

Faculty development is now regarded as integral to higher education. Broadly, the term is used to describe activities that focus on the multiple roles of faculty in the current educational environment. These roles encompass teaching, research, scholarship, and service within the educational system and in the community (Amundsen et al., 2005). The literature subsumes many documented evaluations of faculty development programs, and most reported outcomes are positive. Faculty who participated generally found them helpful in several areas. They appreciated the opportunities to learn and implement classroom strategies that contribute to improved teaching and relevant learning for their students. Participants reported that their teaching skills improved (Camblin & Steger, 2000; Davidson-Shivers, Salazar, & Hamilton, 2005; Pittas, 2000), and they were more confident and satisfied with their teaching

(Knight, Carrese, & Wright, 2007). They also valued the collegial relationships that often developed through these programs. Participants established social and professional relationships with peers and mentors (Morzinski & Fisher, 2002; Pittas, 2000), created cooperative partnerships across disciplines (Camblin & Steger, 2000), and had stronger personal communication with colleagues (Knight et al., 2007).

## Importance of Follow-Up Evaluation

The majority of faculty development program evaluations stop with a one-time assessment on the completion of a program, whether it was a one-day workshop or a year-long series. However, there is a persistent call in the literature for long-term evaluations of faculty development programs (Knight et al., 2007; Morzinski & Simpson, 2003; Steinert, 2000). For the purposes of this study, the terms *follow-up evaluation* and *long-term evaluation* are used interchangeably to indicate an evaluation that takes place after a given period of time has passed after program completion.

While it is essential and often valuable to get a snapshot assessment of the impact of a program at its conclusion, it is equally vital to explore the long-term effects of a program on participants to see if and how they are transferring recently acquired skills and knowledge to their current professional situations. For example, initial effects of training may fade over time if participants are no longer in an ideal and supportive environment. In other instances, there may be a delay in how participants implement newly acquired knowledge. Some participants may not report an immediate impact of a program but may realize important positive outcomes at a later date. Consequently, a follow-up evaluation of a program not only explores the continuing effects of a program but also has the potential to identify outcomes experienced only after the program has ended. This program evaluation was a formal, summative exploration of the impact of NFTS on participants five years after completing the program. We based our design of this evaluation on Kirkpatrick's (1975) four-level model of training evaluation.

## Methodology

Based on the study's purpose and the questions guiding our inquiry, qualitative methods were ideal for this study. While quantitative methods concentrate on testing specific hypotheses (Worthen, Sanders, & Fitzpatrick, 1997) and generally seek "explanations and predictions that will generalize to other persons and places" (Thomas, 2003, p. 2), qualitative methods, including qualitative evaluations, "permit the evaluator to study selected issues in depth and detail" (Patton, 1990, p. 13). Patton suggests that studying a small number of cases enables qualitative researchers to generate detailed information that can lead to a better understanding of the cases or of the topic being studied. Based on the guiding questions, this study's purpose was not to predict or generalize the impact of the NFTS program to other populations, but rather to explore in detail what types of impacts the program had on participants and how those program experiences affected participants' professional lives. Therefore, qualitative methodology was the appropriate choice for this study.

Document review, interviews, and observations are inherent sources of data for qualitative research and evaluation (Patton, 1990). These three methods provided information to meet all four levels of the evaluation model, and each was incorporated into the design. We used purposeful random sampling to select twelve participants from two program years and interviewed them to learn how the NFTS program had affected them over the long term. We also reviewed CVs and one course syllabus for each participant and identified professional activities that reflected and supported their interview responses. We observed in the classrooms of two participants from the study. These data points served as a triangulation of the data sources. Interviews with selected participants, review of their CVs and course syllabi, and classroom observations provided evidence of the impact the NFTS program had on their professional lives and how that initial impact continued to affect their professional behaviors.

## Kirkpatrick's Model

Kirkpatrick's (1975) model of training evaluation offers a standard for evaluating industry and business training programs. It is based on four levels of measurement: reaction, learning, behavior, and results. Kirkpatrick notes that measuring any one of these program stages is informative, but he argues that an evaluation of all four levels provides a more complete picture of a program's effectiveness.

Kirkpatrick's (1998) model has been used successfully to evaluate training programs in business and industry and is regarded as applicable to academic evaluations (Boyle & Crosby, 1997; Naugle, Naugle, & Naugle, 2000). Morzinski and Simpson (2003) applied the four-level model to evaluate longitudinal outcomes of a faculty development program for family medical practitioners. Their application of all four levels illustrates its applicability to our study.

We addressed the guiding questions of this research using Kirkpatrick's model in the following manner:

1. *Reaction: What did the selected participants think about the retreats and campus events?* We reviewed and summarized the annual evaluation reports from the two years selected to gather information reflective of participants' perceptions about the program. During the interviews, we gathered retrospective data when we asked participants to offer their thoughts about their year of participation in the NFTS program.

2. *Learning: What did the selected participants learn? Did the selected participants learn more about teaching? Did their attitudes about teaching change? Did they learn additional skills?* Participant responses to these questions were gathered as we reviewed and summarized annual evaluation reports from the two years selected for this study. During interviews, we asked study participants to reflect on and discuss what they had learned from the program.

3. *Behavior: How has the professional behavior of the selected participants changed? How is it different? Did it change in the classroom? Did it change in relation to peers? Did it change their professional activities?* This level of the evaluation model was addressed during in-depth interviews with study participants. We also reviewed their CVs and a syllabus and observed in several classrooms.

4. *Results: How has the NFTS program affected the selected participants, their departments, their campus, or the university?* This level of the evaluation model was probed during individual, in-depth interviews conducted with each participant.

## Participants and Sample Size

We relied on a purposeful random sample of study participants. Randomly selecting participants from even a small population indicates that the researcher is reporting data in advance of knowing outcomes (Patton, 1990). Patton argues that it is critical to understand that this is a purposeful random sample, not a representative random sample. This type of small random sample offers credibility to the data, not representativeness or generalization to other populations.

We invited faculty members who completed the NFTS program during the 2004 and 2005 academic years to participate. Approximately 50 faculty members participated in the NFTS program each academic year, and targeting these two program years yielded 106 faculty members as potential participants. Since face-to-face interviews and classroom observations were part of data collection, only the 89 faculty participants who were still working on a UM campus were included.

Three participants from each of the four UM campus NFTS groups were randomly selected as potential participants, resulting in a sample size of twelve. While there is minimal guidance in the literature regarding the number of interviews that are ideal for a qualitative research project, guidance came from an extensive review of the academic and medical literature conducted by Guest, Bunce, and Johnson (2006). Their study on data saturation in qualitative interviewing concluded that twelve interviews generally suffice when a researcher's intention is to explore common perceptions and experiences of a relatively homogeneous group of individuals. This reinforced our reasoning to include twelve participants in this study.

Males and females were evenly represented in the sample. Their teaching experience ranged from teaching assistant experience to more than nine years of full-time teaching. They represented twelve different departments and professional programs. Six had attained tenure, and three were tenure-track assistant professors. Two were in non-tenure-track positions, and one had already committed to moving to a position outside the UM system.

## Analysis

Content analyses were used to analyze the results of this study. We relied on inductive analysis techniques, which allowed patterns, themes, and categories to emerge from the data (Patton, 1990). We used document review to analyze existing evaluations from the two NFTS program years selected for study and analyze participant CVs and syllabi. The interviews were analyzed using cross-case analysis. The interview guide served as an analytical framework for the data. We also used cross-case analysis as a strategy to analyze the classroom observations.

## Results

On all four levels of Kirkpatrick's evaluation model, NFTS produced positive results for most participants.

REACTION  The general reaction to the NFTS program was positive. Participant responses on the end-of-year surveys and study participants' interview comments mostly reflected satisfaction and an appreciation for the program. The majority of both participant groups welcomed the opportunities provided by NFTS to improve their teaching and expand their peer networks. One person commented:

> So it was nice to have space and time dedicated to thinking about teaching. I felt that the program, especially the fall retreat, focusing on active engagement of students and student centered learning, I felt like that was really helpful. Actually, I still have a book they gave us and I pull it out once in a while: active learning. I think that was really great.

Others appreciated the guidance offered for their career advancement and the efforts of the university to welcome them as new faculty. Positive reactions from the study participants were similar to those from surveyed participants four or five years ago. This indicated that positive feelings about the program were basically held constant over time for many of the participants. As Kirkpatrick (1998) stated, those who liked and enjoyed a program have the potential to reap the greatest benefits.

Although there were no surveyed participants who expressed disappointment in the program, three of the study participants had suggestions that reflected a less positive reaction to the program. All three comments reflected a lack of connection with the program on some level. One participant mentioned that he was the only one in his field, another commented that the content presented didn't apply to his educational strategies, and the last stated that he had more teaching experience than the other participants.

LEARNING   Most participants from both groups, those who responded to the end-of-year surveys and those who participated in this study, responded in a similar manner when asked what they had learned from the NFTS program. They noted that their attitudes toward teaching shifted to be more active and engaging and identified specific teaching strategies that they incorporated into their classrooms. Some participants learned to modify an existing course strategy, and others learned to implement new ones. One person mentioned:

> Specifically, I teach large lecture classes, so I learned how to make them student centered, how to make them active, the think-pair-share thing. I think that was the first year I started using clickers in the classroom, and there was a presentation that gave me some kind of real tangible ways of using the clickers and ways that I hadn't thought about before: using them for opinion-like thought questions instead of

> just attendance or quiz-like questions. It pushed me to use them in ways that I hadn't done before. Now I use them in a completely different way than I used to. Now I use them to gather evidence from the students to demonstrate a theory that we're discussing in class.

According to Kirkpatrick's (1998) model, such positive responses are evidence that these participants did in fact have a learning experience during the program.

Not all comments about what was learned during NFTS were positive. Several survey participants indicated that their NFTS experience resulted in minimal learning. Again, the comments reflected a lack of connection with the program at some level. One participant said the program content dealt with class sizes that did not match his, a few thought the content of the program was too general to apply to their own courses, and another said the program was better suited to inexperienced teachers. One study participant reiterated again that his teaching strategies were very different from those presented at NFTS and that he would continue teaching in that way. It is worth noting that most of the negative comments regarding the program came from the same few participants.

BEHAVIOR Participants in this study mostly agreed that NFTS had changed their professional behaviors in some way. Expanding on the discussions of what they learned in the program, most agreed that their professional behaviors in the classroom have changed to include instructional strategies focused on active and engaged learning. They also mentioned that they benefited from conversations and discussions about teaching strategies with their NFTS peers. Some of those participants said that the strategies they learned and implemented from NFTS had a positive impact on student learning in their classes.

Three of the twelve study participants acknowledged that NFTS had not made any specific difference in their classroom and teaching behaviors. Of those three, the same participant reiterated that his teaching strategies differed from those presented at NFTS, one commented that he would continue teaching based on his previous experience, and the other noted that NFTS had more of an impact on relationships with his peers. The inference of no connection with program content is evident again.

All study participants acknowledged that their social or professional peer networks expanded during the NFTS program year. One participant explained:

> I can call my NFTS friend who's in another college and say: "You know, I've got this student here, and this is the situation, this is what

happened, and this is the argument they're making and this is what I'm thinking. What do you think? Is this appropriate or not?" . . . That's the greatest thing about that network, having that support and people you can trust to go to and be vulnerable. That's the big thing, too, is there's ego involved. Having a network with people you can go to and trust and be comfortable with, possibly exposing yourself as an idiot . . . Most of my networking is peer networking, the NFTS contacts.

Some enjoyed new relationships with colleagues on their home campuses, and others forged collaborations with NFTS colleagues across the UM system. However, several participants lamented that those peer relationships were not sustained after the end of the program year. Ten of the twelve participants agreed that networking was a vital part of their professional lives. They revealed that networking occurred in a variety of ways, but most of them acknowledged that the most productive opportunities to network took place at planned events. Supporting evidence from CV and syllabi reviews and from classroom observations corroborated the behavior changes discussed by participants. Based on Kirkpatrick's (1998) model, these behavior changes are indications of a positive program effect.

## Benefits of the Experience

The study participants thoughtfully discussed the benefits of their NFTS experiences. On a personal level, some agreed that their instructional knowledge and classroom confidence increased because of NFTS. Others acknowledged that the social and professional relationships developed during NFTS were both enjoyable and beneficial, and a few participants appreciated the guidance offered for their own career advancement. Interestingly, two participants who fully participated and embraced the NFTS program mentioned that their focus on improved teaching would probably delay their promotions, explaining that some aspects of the university culture continue to undervalue teaching.

Most participants recognized that their personal benefits from the program extended into their departments as well. They said that improved and engaged teaching positively affected their departments by attracting and retaining more students. One person commented:

> Students that are in dynamic classrooms and have mentoring relationships with faculty are by definition more engaged. More engaged students are going to participate more on campus and they're going to

have greater allegiances to the university. It's funny, if you ask the students who's the chancellor or who's the provost, they usually don't know, but they can tell you who teaches Psych 101. This is my perspective as a faculty member, but I think faculty are the face of the university for the students, and in many instances, the universe for the students. So if you make faculty more effective in teaching and make them more open to adult learning, then I think the students have a better experience, they're more engaged in the university, and that benefits everyone.

Participants also mentioned that expanded networking broadened and brought a more global perspective to their departments. Some participants noted that these same types of benefits carried over to their home campuses, adding that benefits from NFTS could also have a positive effect on faculty retention. Although most of the participants had difficulty envisioning a connection between NFTS and benefits to the university system, a few added that the positive program outcomes could also contribute to alumni support. These results reflected Kirkpatrick's (1998) model by identifying outcomes that are beneficial on multiple levels.

While it is invaluable to assess a program at its conclusion, it is increasingly important to explore the long-term impact of a program on participants. This allows the evaluator to see if and how program participants are applying recently acquired skills and knowledge to their current professional situation. This study met the call for long-term evaluations of faculty development programs (Knight et al., 2007; Morzinski & Simpson, 2003; Steinert, 2000), and the results provided evidence that the NFTS program continued to have positive impacts on its participants over time.

## Discussion and Recommendations

This qualitative study offers participants' personal narratives about their program participation. Exploring experiences over time offers insight into how such programs continue to have an impact on the professional lives of faculty. While participants identified behavioral changes in their professional lives following program participation, it is possible that such changes relate to multiple sources. We learn from theories of motivation how difficult it is to attribute change to a single event or experience.

Our results suggest that the success of this faculty development program, and perhaps other similar programs, might share several common themes. Successful programs offer content that is current, relevant, and

accessible to all participants. The program brought together heterogeneous groups of early-career faculty, offering opportunities to experience
and share active and engaged teaching and learning strategies. Program
participants came from four campuses and differed in discipline, teaching
experience, and preparation. The diversity of participants' experiences
enhanced social and professional conversations during the program, but
that diversity may also have isolated or hindered several participants from
fully experiencing the program. It is ideal to advise program planners to
help individual participants access and integrate program content into
their own professional lives. However, it is far more practical to remind
program planners of their responsibility to be transparent and explicit
about the program's objectives and content so that applicants can make
informed decisions about participation. For example, why would an
experienced teacher opt to participate fully in the program?

We propose that successful programs present opportunities for participants to build relationships on both social and professional levels. This
program provided multiple opportunities for discussion and conversations among participants. The structured retreats and topical campus
meetings offered opportunities for participants to share and engage in
professional and academic conversations. These gatherings also incorporated a social component, which allowed the faculty to broaden their
personal networks within the UM system. Participants often mentioned
networking as an important benefit of the program.

We also suggest that successful programs provide structured follow-up
activities for program participants. Many participants commented on the
value of networking and expressed an interest in continued connections
with their peers after the conclusion of the program. Program planners
could incorporate follow-up events to provide continuing opportunities
for program alumni to maintain social and professional relationships with
their peers.

The results of this study also pose considerations for future research
related to long-term evaluations of faculty development programs. Future
studies could use multiple perspectives by expanding data sources to
include discussions with students, peers, supervisors, and appropriate
campus administrators. Future studies could explore whether collecting
data using different methods, such as written or online surveys or phone
calls, would yield similar responses. Researchers could explore whether
five years after a program is long enough to measure the impact of
development programs.

Multiple factors emerged that might have affected the participants'
successes in the program. Participants listed a wide range of previous

teaching experience, training in education, working in a variety of disciplines, and instructional obligations encompassing teaching small graduate classes to large lecture ones. One could investigate how these differences contribute to positive experiences in programs like this one. In addition, researchers could ask whether veterans of such programs are more likely to participate in future faculty development or professional development programs. One could also assess the cultures of campuses that support programs like NFTS to see if those cultures are shifting to a system that appreciates and rewards teaching activities. One could also explore whether programs like this result over time in more effective teachers and subsequently increased student learning.

## Conclusion

This qualitative study explored the long-term impact of a faculty development program. The study focused on participants from the University of Missouri's New Faculty Teaching Scholars program five years after the program. Kirkpatrick's (1998) four-level evaluation model was used to gather data for the study. Although the Kirkpatrick model was created to evaluate training programs in business, this research reinforced previous studies that found the model to be an effective tool in evaluating educational programs as well. Through document review, interviews, and observations, the study results provided evidence that the NFTS faculty development program continued to have positive impacts on the participants over time.

REFERENCES

Amundsen, C., McAlpine, L., Weston, C., Krbavac, M., Mundy, A., & Wilson, M. (2005). *The what and why of faculty development in higher education: An in-depth review of the literature.* Retrieved from http://www.sfu.ca /rethinkingteaching/publications/CAmundsen.etal.pdf

Boyle, M. A., & Crosby, R. (1997). Academic program evaluation: Lessons from business and industry. *Journal of Industrial Teacher Education, 34*(3), 81–85.

Camblin Jr., L. D., & Steger, J. A. (2000). Rethinking faculty development [Electronic version]. *Higher Education, 39,* 1–18.

Davidson-Shivers, G. V., Salazar, J., & Hamilton, K. H. (2005). Design of faculty development workshops: Attempting to practice what we preach [Electronic version]. *College Student Journal, 39*(3), 528–539.

Guest, G., Bunce, A., & Johnson, L. (2006). How many interviews are enough? An experiment with data saturation and variability. *Field Methods, 18*(1), 59–82.

Kirkpatrick, D. L. (1975). *Evaluating training programs: A collection of articles from the Journal of the American Society for Training and Development* Alexandria, VA: American Society for Training and Development.

Kirkpatrick, D. L. (1998). *Evaluating training programs: The four levels* (2nd ed.). San Francisco, CA: Berrett-Koehler.

Knight, A. M., Carrese, J. A., & Wright, S. M. (2007). Qualitative assessment of the long-term impact of a faculty development programme in teaching skills [Electronic version]. *Medical Education, 41,* 592–600.

Morzinski, J. A., & Fisher, J. C. (2002). A nationwide study of the influence of faculty development programs on colleague relationships [Electronic version]. *Academic Medicine, 77*(5), 402–406.

Morzinski, J. A., & Simpson, D. E. (2003). Outcomes of a comprehensive faculty development program for local, full-time faculty [Electronic version]. *Family Medicine, 35*(6), 434–439.

Naugle, K. A., Naugle, L. B., & Naugle, R. J. (2000, Fall). Kirkpatrick's evaluation model as a means of evaluating teacher performance [Electronic version]. *Education, 121*(1), 135–144.

New Faculty Teaching Scholars. (2004). *General goals.* University of Missouri: Academic Affairs. Retrieved from http://www.umsystem.edu/ums/departments /aa/nfts/goals.shtml

Pacheco, M. T. (2001). *Design for the future: Creating the learner-centered research University—University of Missouri System Strategic Plan.* University of Missouri System: Office of the President.

Patton, M. Q. (1990). *Qualitative evaluation and research methods* (2nd ed.). Newbury Park, CA: Sage.

Pittas, P. A. (2000). A model program from the perspective of faculty development [Electronic version]. *Innovative Higher Education, 25*(2), 97–110.

Steinert, Y. (2000). Faculty development in the new millennium: Key challenges and future directions [Electronic version]. *Medical Teacher, 22*(1), 44–50.

Thomas, R. M. (2003). *Blending qualitative and quantitative research methods in theses and dissertations.* Thousand Oaks, CA: Corwin Press.

University of Missouri System. (2001–2008). *New faculty teaching scholars annual evaluation reports.* Unpublished reports. Academic Affairs.

Worthen, R. D., Sanders, J. R., Fitzpatrick, J. L. (1997). *Program evaluation: Alternative approaches and practical guidelines* (2nd ed.). White Plains, NY: Longman.

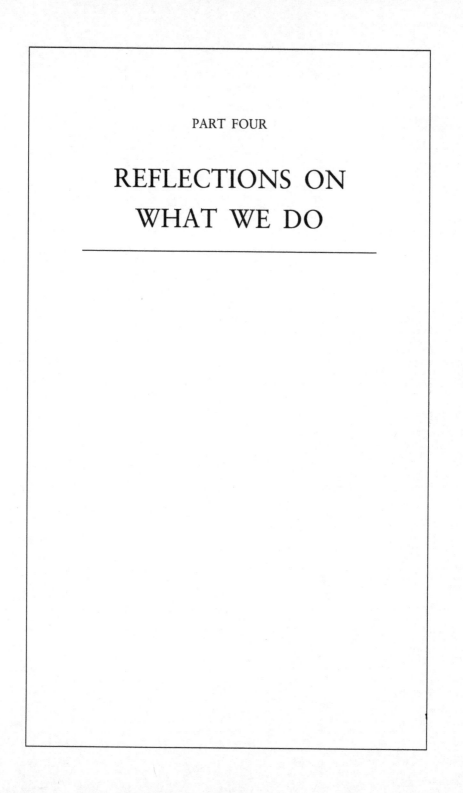

PART FOUR

# REFLECTIONS ON WHAT WE DO

10

# FACULTY DEVELOPMENT SCHOLARSHIP

## AN ANALYSIS OF *TO IMPROVE THE ACADEMY*, 1982–2011

*Kathryn E. Linder*
*Suffolk University*

*Suzanna Klaf*
*Fairfield University*

As To Improve the Academy *enters its thirty-second year, this chapter offers a retrospective to honor the history of the field through a timely analysis of the content published in TIA and editorial and authorship trends over the previous three decades. Frequency distributions identify the most published authors, their institutional affiliations, the most written about topics, and patterns of collaborative authorship in volumes 1 (1982) through 30 (2011), and findings from a citation analysis of ten years of TIA (volumes 21–30), highlight trends in resources cited and types of resources.*

o

The volumes of *To Improve the Academy* (*TIA*) have been an important set of resources to introduce us to the fields of professional, faculty, and organizational development. With fewer than ten years of faculty development experience between us, we find ourselves frequently looking to *TIA* to inform us about best practices with program development, assessment, classroom practice, and the scholarship of teaching and learning, among other topics, as we establish ourselves as professionals within the field (both of us work in teaching centers—one as a director and the other as an associate director). Robert Boice (2000) advises new faculty to "learn about academic culture early, patiently" (p. 211). As junior scholars in faculty development, we have found *TIA* to be a foundational tool generally, and especially for those early in their faculty development careers. On reflection, we realized that an analysis of *TIA* volumes, similar to those conducted in other fields (see Blancher, Buboltz, & Soper, 2010; Pelsma & Cesari, 1989; Tight, 2009; Williams & Buboltz, 1999), would help us to explore our profession even further.

This retrospective also honors the history of the field, for it is through looking back and reflecting on the past that we can look ahead, begin a dialogue, and explore together the future directions for scholarship in *TIA*. If *TIA* is to expand beyond what appears to be its current purpose as a repository for chapters by practitioners in the field of faculty development, and particularly POD members, then now is a time to begin to explore how it compares with other publications in the field, the contributors it attracts, and the most frequent topics published in it. This chapter is not an exhaustive analysis of the past thirty years of *TIA* (due to time and resource constraints, this was not a possibility), but we do offer a jumping-off point for further conversations and analysis of one of our field's primary publications, certainly a standard reference for both of us.

Our research questions and analysis were primarily designed to help us discover *TIA* trends. Some topics seem to appear more than others in *TIA*, and certain authors are frequent contributors, but what is the actual breakdown of themes, editor and author demographics, and citation sources for this publication that is now thirty years old? Other questions guided our analysis as well:

- What trends can we identify in editorship and authorship in *TIA*?
- What is the publication frequency of individual authors in *TIA*?
- How diverse is the author base?
- What resources are authors citing in *TIA* chapters?
- What seem to be the trusted sources of information in terms of both medium and particular titles?
- What are the most popular topics that are published in *TIA*? Does the popularity of certain topics change over time?

This analysis seeks to answer some of these questions. We present these data to two main audiences: members of POD who have previously published in *TIA* or plan to publish in it in the future and the leadership of the POD organization, who may find the results helpful in shaping of the role of *TIA* within POD in the future.

We first explore the editorship of the journal to learn more about editors and associate editor characteristics over time. Second, we use frequency distributions to identify the most published authors and their institutional affiliations, the most written-about topics, and patterns of collaboration across institutions in volumes 1 (1982) through 30 (2011). Third, we discuss the findings from a citation analysis of ten years of *TIA* (volumes 21–30), noting the most frequently cited resources, as well as trends concerning the types of resources being cited. At the conclusion of the chapter, we explore what some of these trends may mean for current and future scholars of faculty development.

## Three Decades of *TIA*, 1982–2011

For the editor, author, section, and topic coding analysis of this chapter, we include thirty volumes (see table 10.1), which amount to 587 chapters,

### Table 10.1    *TIA* by Volume and Year of Publication

| Volumes 1–10 (1982–1991) | | Volumes 11–20 (1992–2002) | | Volumes 21–30 (2003–2011b) | |
|---|---|---|---|---|---|
| Volume | Year | Volume | Year | Volume | Year |
| Volume 1 | 1982 | Volume 11 | 1992 | Volume 21 | 2003 |
| Volume 2 | 1983 | Volume 12 | 1993 | Volume 22 | 2004 |
| Volume 3 | 1984 | Volume 13 | 1994 | Volume 23 | 2005 |
| Volume 4 | 1985 | Volume 14 | 1995 | Volume 24 | 2006 |
| Volume 5 | 1986 | Volume 15 | 1996 | Volume 25 | 2007 |
| Volume 6 | 1987 | Volume 16 | 1997 | Volume 26 | 2008 |
| Volume 7 | 1988 | Volume 17 | 1998 | Volume 27 | 2009 |
| Volume 8 | 1989 | Volume 18 | 2000 | Volume 28 | 2010 |
| Volume 9 | 1990 | Volume 19 | 2001 | Volume 29 | 2011a |
| Volume 10 | 1991 | Volume 20 | 2002 | Volume 30 | 2011b |

*Note:* The publication years conflict in the print volumes versus online citations of *TIA*. Hoag Holmgren, executive director of the Professional and Organizational Development Network, clarified the correct dates for each volume through e-mail correspondence. There are two 2011 publications because Jossey-Bass, the publisher, changed the publication conventions with volume 30. Traditionally *TIA* was published in October for the POD Network Conference but carried the next year's date. Starting with volume 30, the listed publication date is the same as the actual publication date. Thus, both volumes 29 and 30 have a 2011 publication date.

Figure 10.1   Number of Chapters per TIA Volume, 1982–2011b

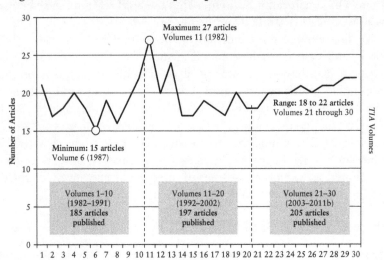

48 unique editors and associate editors, and 808 unique authors. For the citation analysis, we focus on ten volumes (21–30) and analyze 4,485 citations from 205 chapters.

Between 1982 and 2011b, 587 chapters have been published in *TIA*. The number of chapters published has increased over this three-decade period from 185 published between 1982 and 1991 to 205 published between 2003 and 2011b (see figure 10.1).

Also worth noting is the publication's audience. During its first decade (1982–1991), *TIA* provided "resources for student, faculty, & institutional development," and from 1992 onward, it shifted focus to providing "resources for faculty, instructional, and organizational development."

## Methods

To facilitate our analysis, an Access database was created, and all 587 chapters published in volumes 1 through 30 were entered into a table (fields included volume, year of publication, authors, author affiliation, author gender, chapter title, and TIA section title). Baseline data were generated from this initial table (including totals, averages, and frequencies).

For the topic analysis conducted on all chapter published in *TIA* (1982–2011b), all 587 chapter titles were entered into an Excel spreadsheet. In order to analyze the chapter topics, a coding scheme was developed based on the topic designations that were offered for the POD

2012 conference: adjunct professional development; administration; assessment; diversity; faculty professional development; graduate student professional development; organizational development; POD professional development; programs; research; retention; the scholarship of teaching and learning; start-up; sustainability; teaching and learning; and technology (see table 10.2 for descriptions of each topic). We added two

### Table 10.2 Topic Coding Categories for Chapters, 1982–2011b

| Topic | Description |
|---|---|
| Adjunct professional development | Practices, processes, theories, techniques, programs pertaining specifically to adjunct or part-time faculty development |
| Administration | Budgeting, funding, management, planning, performance appraisal, staff and faculty recruitment and retention, and other issues concerning the administration of a center or other unit |
| Assessment | Measuring the effectiveness of an aspect of practice or outcomes in order to improve (designate other topics to indicate the subject of assessment—e.g., teaching and learning, programs, faculty professional development) |
| Diversity | Addressing underrepresented or minority populations on campus, in the classroom, in administration |
| Ethics[a] | Discussions of the ethics of faculty development and teaching and learning practices, processes, theories, and techniques |
| Faculty professional development | Practices, processes, theories, techniques, programs pertaining to faculty development |
| Graduate student professional development | Practices, processes, theories, techniques, programs pertaining specifically to graduate and professional student development |
| Higher education[a] | Faculty development in the larger framework of higher education; teaching and learning issues in higher education |
| Organizational development | Practices, processes, theories, or techniques related to the systemic development of institutions and organizations |
| POD professional development | Practices, processes, theories, techniques, programs pertaining to the development of those in the professions represented by POD (e.g., center staff, technologists) |

*(Continued)*

## Table 10.2. *Continued*

| Topic | Description |
|---|---|
| Programs | Organization, implementation, practices, theories, techniques related to programs and services (in centers and other units) |
| Research | Systematic, generalizable investigations into clearly defined questions, employing accepted methods for data collection and analysis |
| Retention | Practices, processes, theories, techniques related to retaining students and improving graduation rates |
| Scholarship of teaching and learning | Practice of, results of, and programs supporting the scholarship of teaching and learning |
| Start-up | Practices, processes, organizational ideas related to establishment and growth of centers, programs, or other projects |
| Sustainability | Incorporating principles of environmental and programmatic sustainability into educational development work |
| Teaching and learning | Practices, processes, theories, techniques related to classroom and other teaching and learning |
| Technology | Explorations of current and new technologies that can support teaching, program, or organizational development |

[a]Topic coding categories added to the POD categories.

categories based on a brief review of the chapter: ethics, which we describe as discussions of the ethics of faculty development and teaching and learning practices, processes, theories, and techniques; and higher education, which we describe as faculty development in a larger framework of higher education or teaching and learning issues in higher education. We coded each chapter independently, with up to three categories chosen to represent the topics covered. When titles were insufficient to locate topics—for example, titles such as "Silk Purses" (1985) and "Do You See What I See?" (1994)—we looked to chapter abstracts to assist in categorizing each piece.

Given time and resource constraints, citation analysis was conducted on only one decade of *TIA* publications (2003–2011b); all 4,485 citations from the 205 chapters published in volumes 21 through 30 were entered into a separate table in Access. In order to analyze the citations, a coding scheme was developed to categorize the different citation sources and formats; the main categories are books, journals, monograph series, web materials, and other (e.g., conference papers, reports, magazines, news-letters, conference proceedings). We recognize that these categories are subjective; however, we cross-checked the citation source with publisher and library databases in order to verify categorizing conventions and the actual terms used when referring to published materials (e.g., *TIA* is categorized as a book, not a journal; *New Directions in Teaching and Learning* is categorized as a monograph series).

## Results

### Editorship, 1982–2011

In thirty years of publication, *TIA* has had thirty-three editors and forty-eight combined editors and associate editors. The current editorial structure of one editor and one associate editor was established in 1995 with volume 14. Before this structure, *TIA* would have as many as two editors and six associate editors for one volume.

Overall the number of total editors and associate editors has decreased over the years. Between 1995 and 1997, the associate editor served a one-year term as associate and subsequently one year as editor of *TIA*. Since 1998, individuals serve four-year terms: each associate editor serves a two-year associate editor term prior to a two-year term as editor. Early volumes of *TIA* also included "invited reviewers" who were listed in the editorial matter along with editors and associated editors (invited reviewers were not included in the data analysis of editors and associate editors).

LOCATION AND PROFESSIONAL ROLE   The forty-eight unique *TIA* editors and associate editors over the course of the past three decades have been affiliated with forty-seven institutions; forty-five of those institutions are located in twenty-three states in the United States (the largest regions represented were the Midwest, with fourteen institutions represented, and the South, with twelve institutions represented), and two institutions located in Canada. Since 2002, editors and associate editors of *TIA* have held administrative or faculty positions, and several have also served within the POD organization on the Core Committee or as POD president.

GENDER   An analysis of the gender of editors and associate editors in *TIA* over the past three decades illustrates that the leadership of women has remained steady at over two-thirds representation since *TIA*'s original publication in 1982 (table 10.3). Women have predominated as editors and associate editors of TIA over three decades. Of the thirty-three editors

Table 10.3   Gender of Editors and Associate Editors by Decade

| | Volumes 1–10 (1982–1991) ($n = 28$) | | Volumes 11–20 (1992–2002) ($n = 22$) | | Volumes 21–30 (2003–2011b) ($n = 6$) | |
|---|---|---|---|---|---|---|
| | Number | Percent | Number | Percent | Number | Percent |
| Women | 17 | 61% | 16 | 73% | 4 | 67% |
| Men | 11 | 39% | 6 | 27% | 2 | 33% |

of *TIA* over three decades, 70 percent were women and 30 percent were men. Similarly, of the sixteen associate editors of *TIA* over three decades, 62.5 percent were women and 37.5 percent were men.

## Contributors, 1982–2011

Of the 587 chapters published between 1982 and 2011b, there were 808 unique authors, 57.2 percent of whom were unique first-listed authors. The number of authors published in *TIA* has increased over time, from 175 in the first decade (1982–1991), to 277 in the second (1992–2002), and 356 in the most recent decade (2003–2011b).

GENDER   We analyzed the gender of authors in *TIA* both overall and by looking at only first authors and found a steady growth in the inclusion of women. Since its original publication, *TIA* has gone from an overall women authorship of 43.8 percent from 1982 to 1991 to 63.3 percent in the most recent decade (2003–2011b). The numbers of female first authors mirror this growth with 45.4 percent (1982–1991) and 68.3 percent (2003–2011b).

COLLABORATIVE AUTHORSHIP   While a slight majority of chapters in *TIA* have had one author (51.4 percent), dual authorship is also prominent, with 29.8 percent of chapters authored by two individuals (see table 10.4). Collaborative authorship has also increased over time. Of the 185 chapters published between 1982 and 1991, 36.2 percent were authored by two or more individuals. In the volumes spanning 1992 to 2002, 48.7 percent of the 197 published chapters were authored by two or more individuals. In the most recent decade, 59.5 percent of the 205 chapters published were authored by two or more individuals. Single authorship has also decreased from approximately 64 percent in the decade 1982 to 1991 to approximately 40 percent in the most recent decade. Authorship of five to eight authors emerged in the 1990s and continues through the present day.

Table 10.4  Singular and Collaborative Authorship by Chapters Published across Three Decades of TIA

| | Volumes 1–10 (1982–1991) ($n = 185$) | | Volumes 11–20 (1992–2002) ($n = 197$) | | Volumes 21–30 (2003–2011b) ($n = 205$) | | Total ($n = 587$) | |
|---|---|---|---|---|---|---|---|---|
| | Number of Chapters | Percent | Number of Chapters | Percent | Number of Chapters | Percent | Number of Chapters | Percent |
| One author | 118 | 63.8 | 101 | 51.3 | 83 | 40.5 | 302 | 51.4 |
| Two authors | 54 | 29.2 | 61 | 31 | 60 | 29.3 | 175 | 29.8 |
| Three authors | 11 | 5.8 | 23 | 11.7 | 38 | 18.5 | 72 | 12.3 |
| Four authors | 2 | 1.1 | 7 | 3.6 | 13 | 6.3 | 22 | 3.7 |
| Five authors | – | – | 3 | 1.5 | 7 | 3.4 | 10 | 1.7 |
| Six authors | – | – | 1 | 0.5 | 2 | 1 | 3 | 0.5 |
| Seven or more authors | – | – | 1 | 0.5 | 2 | 1 | 3 | 0.5 |

FREQUENCY OF PUBLICATION BY AUTHORS   In the early years of *TIA* in particular, it was common for authors to publish multiple pieces in the journal over a period of years. For example, in the first decade of *TIA*'s publication, about 31 percent (54 of 175) of the authors published in *TIA* had two or more chapters published in that decade. Between 1992 and 2002, 14.8 percent (41 of 277) authored multiple chapters, and between 2003 and 2011b, 12.4 percent (44 of 356) did so.

With the number of unique authors included in *TIA* at 175 in the first decade, to 277 in the second, and 356 in the most recent decade, the likelihood of authors publishing multiple chapters in *TIA* decreased by about 10 percent (see table 10.5). As the field of faculty development grew to include more practitioners, the proliferation of journals on teaching and learning in those decades may have offered more publication outlets on issues relevant to faculty development.

CROSS-INSTITUTIONAL AFFILIATIONS   Similar to the increase in collaborative authorship in *TIA*, the number of cross-institutional affiliations for coauthored chapters has also grown over time, doubling between the first and last decades of publication. Although chapters written by authors from one institution still remain the most prevalent, at 66.7 percent of all *TIA* chapters published in the thirty years reviewed, it has become more common to see collaboratively written chapters with between two and five institutional affiliations (see table 10.6). Of the chapters published between 1982 and 1991, 27.9 percent were the result of cross-institutional collaborations. This number rose to 35.4 percent in the volumes published between 1992 and 2002. Contributions that brought together three or more institutional affiliations rose from 4.9 percent between 1982 and 1991 to 11.5 percent between 2003 and 2011b.

INTERNATIONAL AFFILIATIONS   Over the three decades, thirty-five chapters published in *TIA* were written by one or more authors with international affiliations. These authors were affiliated with the following countries: Australia (three authors); Canada (twenty-five authors); Great Britain, including England and Scotland (four authors); Germany (three authors); Israel (three authors); and Thailand (three authors). From 1983 through 1991, ten internationally affiliated authors published in *TIA*, fifteen such authors did so between 1992 and 2002, and an additional ten internationally affiliated authors did so between 2003 and 2011b.

SELF-CITATION OF AUTHORS IN *TIA*   Of the 587 chapters published in *TIA*, 255 (43.4 percent) included author self-citations (see table 10.7).

Table 10.5 Authorship or Coauthorship of Two or More Publications in *TIA*, 1982–2011b

| | Volumes 1–10 (1982–1991) (*n* = 54) | | Volumes 11–20 (1992–2002) (*n* = 41) | | Volumes 21–30 (2003–2011b) (*n* = 44) | | Total (*n* = 139) | |
|---|---|---|---|---|---|---|---|---|
| | Number of Authors | Percent | Number of Authors | Percent | Number of Authors | Percent | Number | Percent |
| Two chapters | 34 | 63 | 23 | 56.1 | 25 | 56.8 | 82 | 59 |
| Three chapters | 9 | 16.7 | 10 | 24.4 | 9 | 20.5 | 28 | 20.1 |
| Four chapters | 7 | 13 | 6 | 14.6 | 8 | 18.2 | 21 | 15.1 |
| Five chapters | 3 | 5.6 | 1 | 2.4 | 2 | 4.5 | 6 | 4.3 |
| Six chapters | 0 | 0 | 1 | 2.4 | 0 | 0 | 1 | 0.7 |
| Seven or more chapters | 1 | 1.9 | 0 | 0 | 0 | 0 | 1 | 0.7 |

Table 10.6  Number of Institutional Affiliations for Coauthored Chapters, 1982–2011

| Number of Institutions | Volumes 1–10 (1982–1991) (n = 61)[a] | | Volumes 11–20 (1992–2002) (n = 96) | | Volumes 21–30 (2003–2011b) (n = 122) | | Total (n = 279) | |
|---|---|---|---|---|---|---|---|---|
| | Number of Chapters | Percent | Number of Chapters | Percent | Number of Chapters | Percent | Number of Chapters | Percent |
| 1 | 44 | 72.1 | 62 | 64.6 | 80 | 65.6 | 186 | 66.7 |
| 2 | 14 | 23 | 27 | 28.1 | 28 | 23 | 69 | 24.7 |
| 3 | 2 | 3.3 | 4 | 4.2 | 9 | 7.4 | 15 | 5.2 |
| 4 | 1 | 1.6 | 3 | 3.1 | 3 | 2.5 | 7 | 2.5 |
| 5 | 0 | 0 | 0 | 0 | 2 | 1.6 | 2 | 0.7 |

[a]Excludes data for 1982 (affiliations not available).

Table 10.7   *TIA* Chapters with Self-Citations, 1982–2011

| | Volumes 1–10 (1982–1991) (*n* = 185) | | Volumes 11–20 (1992–002) (*n* = 197) | | Volumes 21–30 (2002–2011b) (*n* = 205) | | Total (*n* = 587) | |
|---|---|---|---|---|---|---|---|---|
| | Number | Percent | Number | Percent | Number | Percent | Number | Percent |
| Chapters with self-citations | 58 | 31.4 | 96 | 48.7 | 101 | 49.3 | 255 | 43.4 |

Self-citations have increased over the decades, with an average of 3.2 self-citations per chapter, ranging from 1 to 21 citations in a given chapter, and a minimum of one self-citation. Authors who have published on specific topics in both *TIA* and other publications are the ones who self-cite, thus indicating expertise in an area.

## Chapter Topic Analysis: How TIA Topics Have Changed over Time

After independently coding 587 chapters using eighteen coding categories (specified in the methods section; see table 10.2), coding each chapter with up to three of the eight coding categories, we had an 89 percent agreement rate on one or more of the three categories. All chapters were coded into at least one category (see table 10.8 for a data summary). According to this categorizing method, the majority of the chapters published in *TIA* over the three decades have consistently focused on faculty professional development (274 chapters), teaching and learning (252 chapters), POD professional development (179 chapters), and programs (157 chapters). These results are not surprising given the aims of *TIA* and the intended audience of POD members. Perhaps more interesting are the chapter themes that were infrequent: sustainability (10 chapters), ethics (8 chapters), faculty development program start-up (8 chapters), adjunct professional development (6 chapters), and student retention (1 chapter). There has been an increase over the past three decades in the number of chapters published that focus on POD professional development, assessment, program start-up, and adjunct professional development (see table 10.8).

Noteworthy are the topics that we thought would be more prominent across the decades, including assessment, scholarship of teaching and learning, and technology, which seem to have risen in popularity and predominate in contemporary discussion in other publications. For instance, technology was the focus of less than 5 percent of the chapters published in *TIA*. These are gaps in the literature that perhaps future *TIA* authors will consider. Overall, these findings raise the questions of how *TIA* has responded to trends in higher education and will do so in the future.

CITATION ANALYSIS   Of the 587 chapters analyzed, 56 (nine percent) include no cited references to other literature in the field. The majority without cited references were published before 2000, with only two chapters (one in 2002 and one in 2010) citing no outside literature. The average number of citations in volumes 1 through 30 (1982–2011b) is 15.8 citations per *TIA* chapter (see figure 10.2). The number of citations has increased over the past three decades of TIA, from an average of 9.85 citations in the 1980s to an average of 21.81 citations in the 2000s.

Based on an analysis of 4,485 citations from 205 chapters in ten volumes (21–30), fifty-three authors and two organizations have been cited ten or more times between 2003 and 2011b. Of these, six authors have been cited thirty or more times in *TIA* chapters (Hutchings, Schulman, Boyer, Cox, Sorcinelli, and Boice). Seven authors have been cited twenty to twenty-nine times in *TIA* chapters (Millis, Palmer, Weimer, Rice, Nuhfer, Fink, and Huber). Forty authors and two organizations (Association of American Colleges Universities and POD) have been cited ten to nineteen times in *TIA* chapters.

The majority of sources cited by authors in volumes 21 through 30 (2003–2011b) were books (47 percent of all citations) and journals (29 percent). The most cited source was TIA, cited 258 times; followed by the monograph series *New Directions for Teaching and Learning*, cited 142 times; and the magazine *Change*, cited 89 times. The five most cited journals were the *Journal of Higher Education* (cited 65 times), *Innovations in Higher Education* (cited 39 times), *Research in Higher Education* (cited 31 times), *College Teaching* (cited 28 times), and the *International Journal for Academic Development* (cited 23 times). (See figure 10.3.)

VISIBILITY OF *TIA*   Further exploration reveals that *TIA* is infrequently cited in the teaching and learning journals that are most frequently cited in *TIA*. Through an analysis of the top five journals over a five-year period (2007–2011), we found that only three *TIA* chapters were cited in the *Journal of Higher Education*; twelve *TIA* chapters in *Innovations in Higher Education*; one *TIA* chapter in *Research in Higher Education*; six *TIA* chapters in *College Teaching*; and seven *TIA* chapters in the

Table 10.8  Number (and Percent) of Chapters by Coding Categories

| Coding Category | Volumes 1–10 (1982–1991) (n = 185) | | Volumes 11–20 (1992–2002) (n = 197) | | Volumes 21–30 (2003–2011b) (n = 205) | | Total (n = 587) | |
|---|---|---|---|---|---|---|---|---|
| | Number | Percent | Number | Percent | Number | Percent | Number | Percent |
| Faculty professional development | 91 | 49.2 | 105 | 53.3 | 78 | 38 | 274 | 46.7 |
| Teaching and learning | 81 | 43.8 | 88 | 44.7 | 83 | 40.5 | 252 | 42.9 |
| POD professional development | 40 | 21.6 | 65 | 33 | 74 | 36.1 | 179 | 30.5 |
| Programs | 51 | 27.6 | 49 | 24.9 | 57 | 27.8 | 157 | 26.7 |
| Organizational development | 31 | 16.8 | 50 | 25.4 | 33 | 16.1 | 114 | 19.4 |
| Research | 33 | 17.8 | 21 | 10.7 | 28 | 13.7 | 82 | 14 |
| Diversity | 26 | 14.1 | 24 | 12.2 | 27 | 13.2 | 77 | 13.1 |
| Assessment | 14 | 7.6 | 24 | 12.2 | 37 | 18 | 75 | 12.8 |
| Higher education | 27 | 14.6 | 17 | 8.6 | 18 | 8.8 | 62 | 10.6 |
| Scholarship of teaching and learning | 22 | 11.9 | 13 | 6.6 | 25 | 12.2 | 60 | 10.2 |
| Administration | 8 | 4.3 | 4 | 2 | 18 | 8.8 | 30 | 5.1 |
| Technology | 4 | 2.2 | 13 | 6.6 | 11 | 5.4 | 28 | 4.8 |
| Graduate professional development | 8 | 4.3 | 5 | 2.5 | 9 | 4.4 | 22 | 3.7 |
| Sustainability | 2 | 1.1 | 0 | 0 | 8 | 3.9 | 10 | 1.7 |
| Ethics | 2 | 1.1 | 2 | 1 | 4 | 2 | 8 | 1.4 |
| Start-up | 2 | 1.1 | 2 | 1 | 4 | 2 | 8 | 1.4 |
| Adjunct professional development | 0 | 0 | 3 | 1.5 | 3 | 1.5 | 6 | 1 |
| Retention | 0 | 0 | 1 | 0 | 0 | 0 | 1 | <1 |

Figure 10.2    Average Number of Citations per *TIA* Volume,
1982–2011b

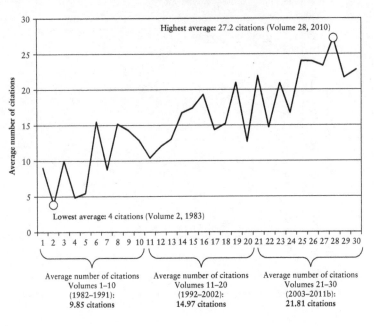

Average number of citations
Volumes 1–10
(1982–1991):
9.85 citations

Average number of citations
Volumes 11–20
(1992–2002):
14.97 citations

Average number of citations
Volumes 21–30
(2003–2011b):
21.81 citations

Figure 10.3    Types of Sources Cited in *TIA*, 2003–2011b

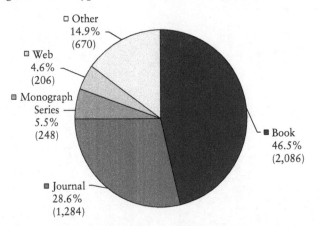

*Note:* N = 4,485. The category "Other" includes conference papers (3.1 percent); reports (3 percent); magazines (2.7 percent); newsletters (1.7 percent); newspapers (1.4 percent); and occasional papers, dissertations, unpublished manuscripts, center for teaching and learning materials, media, conference proceedings, POD Ethical Guidelines, keynote presentations, e-mail communication, survey, directory, and software manuals (all under 0.5 percent).

*International Journal for Academic Development.* Comparatively, the top five journal citations were 4 percent of overall citations in *TIA* chapters, whereas *TIA* citations comprised less than 1 percent of the citations in the top five journals. In a five-year period, *TIA* was cited 29 times in 19 chapters out of a total of 25,727 citations and 881 chapters analyzed. Not surprisingly, the authors citing *TIA* in other journals were frequently those who had been previously published in *TIA* (though they rarely cited their own work).

## Limitations

The data analysis in this study has some limitations. First, all efforts were made to ensure that the *TIA* data were properly entered into a database; however, data entry errors and resulting calculation errors may be a slight possibility. Second, although we used the POD conference themes to categorize *TIA* chapters, the qualitative analysis can be considered subjective. For instance, we interpreted the categories differently, and this led to differences in how chapters were coded; moreover, no interrater reliability was established for conference themes. Third, the citation analysis is limited to one decade of *TIA* (2003–2011b), as is the exploration of other sources that cite *TIA* chapters. This is due to time and resource constraints, though future researchers may want to tackle the citations of all chapters published in *TIA* between 1982 and 2002.

## Conclusion

This study examined trends over three decades of *TIA* publication: 1982 to 2011b. By reflecting backward, we have a better understanding of the history of *TIA* as a publication for professional developers to publish in and as a resource to inform their practice. Noteworthy trends have included the regularization of editorship roles, a shift in target audience, an increase in collaborative authorship, an increase in the number of citations referenced per chapter, consistent emphasis on particular chapter topics and themes, and an increase in self-citation practices.

### Opportunities for POD Members

Brew (2002) notes the "centrality of inquiry to everything developers do" (p. 116). For many faculty developers, *TIA* has played a significant role in promoting the inquiries of POD members and contributing to POD professional development. Research continues to be central to the practice of academic developers and a matter of credibility in the field. Reflecting forward, it is worth exploring the potential ways in which *TIA*, through its editors, authors, and readers, contributes to moving research on teaching and learning forward in higher education. There appear to be great opportunities for collaboration, increased visibility of *TIA* beyond POD members, and potential authors to write about underresearched topics and themes.

There are also several opportunities for further studies regarding *TIA*. First, a more in-depth citation analysis covering all decades of *TIA*'s publication may lead to additional findings regarding how *TIA* has followed various citation trends, such as the rise in online references. Second, additional coding is needed on the chapters that are being referenced by other higher education journals. Because these chapters are so few, looking back beyond five years to find which chapter themes have been the most prevalent in these citations could yield new information about how authors are using *TIA* citations in their work and how *TIA* is being represented in other scholarly publications. Based on these analyses, we offer the following additional recommendations.

## Recommendations

While researching three decades of *TIA,* we encountered difficulty accessing past issues; however, the discovery of digitized volumes (1982–1998) hosted on the University of Nebraska-Lincoln DigitalCommons open access site (http://digitalcommons.unl.edu/podimproveacad/) proved to be indispensable. Making *TIA* more accessible, ideally online, is worth exploring if the intent is for the knowledge generated to be shared with a wider audience. It is imperative that *TIA* chapters be more easily found and referenced.

*TIA* is said to be the most important peer-reviewed resource for professional developers. Yet the questions posed by this research study persist: Who is citing *TIA*? What are the latest developments? The majority of *TIA* citations found in other higher education publications are in chapters by POD members. Faculty development researchers should cite *TIA* whenever applicable and whenever possible in their own work, but also in work that they coauthor with others outside of the field who may not be familiar with *TIA*. Consideration should be given to citation indexing, as there is currently no way to determine the impact that *TIA* is having on the literature and the field. By making *TIA* both accessible and increasing its visibility, there may be increased potential for cross-fertilization, collaboration, creation of new knowledge, and advancement of the field.

We embarked on this research study eager to discover the history of *TIA*. Our exploration of the editor, author, chapter, and citation trends proved to be a time-consuming exercise but one that *TIA* may consider routinely engaging in, as such introspection is what may sustain the publication by attracting a new generation of readers and authors.

REFERENCES

Boice, R. (2000). *Advice for new faculty members: Nihil nimus.* Boston: Allyn and Bacon.

Blancher, A. T., Buboltz, W. C., & Soper, B. (2010). Content analysis of the *Journal of Counseling and Development,* volumes 74–84. *Journal of Counseling and Development 88,* 139–145.

Brew, A. (2002). Research and the academic developer: A new agenda. *International Journal for Academic Development, 7,* 112–122.

Pelsma, D., & Cesari, J. P. (1989). Content analysis of the *Journal of Counseling and Development,* volumes 48–66. *Journal of Counseling and Development, 67,* 275–278.

Tight, M. (2009). The structure of academic research: What can citations studies tell us? In A. Brew & L. Lucas (Eds.), *Academic research and researchers* (pp. 55–65). New York, NY: McGraw-Hill.

Williams, M. E., & Buboltz, W. C. (1999). Content analysis of the *Journal of Counseling and Development,* volumes 67–74. *Journal of Counseling and Development 77,* 344–349.

## 11

# PROGRAM PLANNING, PRIORITIZING, AND IMPROVEMENT

## A SIMPLE HEURISTIC

*Peter Felten*
*Elon University*

*Deandra Little*
*University of Virginia*

*Leslie Ortquist-Ahrens*
*Berea College*

*Michael Reder*
*Connecticut College*

*As educational developers working with multiple constituencies and demands on our time, how can we efficiently and creatively improve our programming and prioritize our efforts? In this chapter, we offer a simple heuristic to prompt quick yet generative examination of our goals or*

---

The authors are listed in alphabetical order, and all contributed equivalently to the ideas and writing of this chapter. We ask that any citation of this article list all four authors.

*programs in relationship to three key characteristics of effective educational development on three different institutional levels. We then describe uses and applications of the tool and reflective process, which allow developers to efficiently gain insight into their work and effectively frame priorities for planning and improvement.*

---

o

---

Higher education is in a state of unusual flux, confronting a rapidly changing environment with increasingly limited resources. Christensen and Eyring (2011) contend that this is a moment of "disruptive innovation" that will lead to sudden, fundamental change similar to that experienced recently by newspapers, bookstores, and record companies. This turbulence presents a distinct challenge to our profession. More than ever before, we need to determine frequently, quickly, and creatively what activities and programming we should prioritize (Sorcinelli, Austin, Eddy, & Beach, 2006). We must consider not only how to do things better but when and how to do better things, including identifying emerging opportunities and discovering our gaps and blind spots. While these pressures can feel threatening and ominous, they also present distinct opportunities for us as individuals and as a field.

As educational developers, we are familiar with managing change. We routinely advocate for the kind of scholarly, reflective approaches that are essential in the face of disruptions. And we champion evidence-informed innovation at our institutions as our field has become more scholarly by developing increasingly sophisticated approaches for evaluating programs and measuring impact (Chism, 1998; Chism, Holley, & Harris, 2012; Debowski, 2011a; Stefani, 2010). Such assessment efforts help us adapt to changing conditions while also documenting the impact of our work for ourselves and for broader audiences.

Yet rapidly evolving environments and institutions require us to be ever more nimble and to make adjustments even before undertaking full-scale program reviews or annual assessments. Short of traditional, time-intensive planning activities, how can we reflect on the work we do in our institutions in efficient and generative ways? Research suggests that developers "would welcome more opportunities for scholarly reflection on practice" (Sorcinelli et al., 2006, p. 166), but what tools do we have to help guide that work? Moreover, how do we make time for the kind of considered reflection characteristic of deep learning and necessary for understanding the complicated and often messy ideas and problems we encounter (Moon, 1999) or for the kind of structured analysis that will help us align the theories and values we espouse with those we actually employ (Schön, 1983, 1987)?

## A Tool for Creative and Critical Reflection

Our framework emerged out of conversations we had in preparation for a 2011 AAC&U conference presentation on the characteristics of effective educational development programs in the changing landscape of higher education (Felten, Little, Ortquist-Ahrens, & Reder, 2011). We brought to those conversations our own professional experiences in diverse institutional contexts, as well as perspectives from the literature. Because that conference draws more deans and other senior administrators than it does developers, we could not assume our audience had an intimate knowledge of educational development practices or frameworks. We needed to highlight the most salient aspects of our field in ways that would explain our work to a diverse group of professionals from a wide variety of institutions.

As we refined and applied that draft framework on the heels of the conference, we found it to be surprisingly useful as a heuristic—a tool that supports an exploratory approach to problem solving that may lead to discovery, one that involves trial and error and creative thinking as much as critical analysis. Since that initial AAC&U session, we have used this framework on our own campuses and tested it in the 2011 POD conference anchor session (Ortquist-Ahrens, Felten, Foster, Little, & Reder, 2011) and again in a session at the 2012 conference (Felten, Little, Ortquist-Ahrens, & Reder, 2012).

This heuristic is not a comprehensive framework for assessment but rather a tool to prompt guided reflection and discussion; it can serve as a point of departure for noticing patterns, locating gaps, and strategically envisioning future possibilities. The heuristic encourages divergent thinking that can facilitate a shift in perspective, helping us see the familiar in new ways or hinting at different possibilities for routine practices (Cropley, 2006). As Tosey (2006) argues, the intense and continuous change we face requires us to be more creative and agile than ever before, even if we operate in a system that can inhibit novelty and tend toward conservatism. This heuristic also provides an effective task constraint (Cropley, 2006; Tosey, 2006), an open-ended problem or challenge with rules to help sort through possibilities—creating an interplay of convergent thinking, which Cropley asserts "always generates orthodoxy," with divergent thinking, which "always generates variability" (2006, p. 392).

## The Structure of the Heuristic

Vertically our grid features three characteristics of effective educational development programs: people focused, context sensitive, and evidence informed. Horizontally the grid contains three perspectival levels on which our programming, influence, or leadership can operate and that need to be considered when designing programs or prioritizing our involvement for any campus: the individual, departmental, and institutional (table 11.1).

### Characteristics

Each of the three major characteristics highlighted along the left side of the heuristic plays a role in the emerging agenda that Sorcinelli et al. (2006) sketch for the future of educational development in "the Age of the Network" (p. 157). Even as we broaden the scope of traditional faculty development, we should remain fundamentally focused on the people involved—though perhaps in new ways and with an eye toward redefining diversity. Furthermore, to be most effective, we will need to be responsive to local context as well as grounded in scholarship (Sorcinelli et al., 2006).

PEOPLE FOCUSED  Our work first involves the individuals and groups of stakeholders that it affects directly and indirectly: from faculty and graduate students at the individual level, to departmental life, undergraduate students, senior administrators, and other stakeholders at the institutional level. For each, we must take into consideration people's needs and their potential for growth. Filling out this cell in the heuristic means answering such questions as: Which individuals or groups are involved in or served by the program? What are their characteristics, needs, or contributions? Asking questions like these keeps institutional perspectives on students and their learning at the forefront, even when designing programs for individual faculty. It also means thinking developmentally about faculty needs at different career stages and then providing appropriate programming and support (Debowski, 2011a). Focusing on people highlights how our work serves as a bridge between the sometimes conflicting interests of different stakeholders—for example, between faculty and administrators (Little & Green, 2012)—and means that we are often called on to help facilitate organizational change (Chism, 1998; Latta, 2009). Even as we work on a microlevel, we must take a larger view of the complex interests and needs that both

**Table 11.1   The Heuristic**

| | Individual Perspective (focusing primarily on individual needs of the people we work with one-on-one) | Departmental Perspective (concentrating on needs and issues of groups within an institution, such as departments or programs) | Institutional Perspective (considering systemic issues or trends from a broader perspective, including the perspectives of multiple stakeholders at or beyond the institution) |
|---|---|---|---|
| People focused: Planning with the needs of stakeholders in mind, including faculty, staff, and administrators, as well as students and others | | | |
| Context sensitive: Taking into consideration institutional type, mission, size, specific student body, history and traditions, challenges, and goals | | | |
| Evidence informed: Drawing on the scholarship of higher education, faculty and student success, and using evidence from data collected locally about teaching, learning, and programming | | | |

inform and drive our work. The heuristic also emphasizes that a developer's role often operates on different levels, from professional or instructional development (individual) to midlevel unit development (departmental, curricular) to broader organizational development (institutional) (Debowski, 2011a, 2011b; Schroeder and Associates, 2011).

CONTEXT SENSITIVE  Effective educational development programs fit to (and help shape) the culture, mission, opportunities, and constraints at each level of the institution. For this reason, programs or approaches cannot simply be transplanted from one college or university to another without careful modulation (what Carew, Lefoe, Bell, & Armour, 2008, describe as "Elastic Practice"; Sorcinelli et al., 2006). Programs and services need to be carefully tailored to an institution's distinctive priorities, culture, values, and resources (Latta, 2009; Milloy & Brooke, 2004) and for the individuals within that system. This row of cells on the heuristic opens up such questions as: What contexts do the individuals consulting with us come from, work within, need, or need to adjust to in order to thrive? What efforts would help the institution thrive as well?

Being context sensitive means that the work we do is shaped by the setting in which we are working and the circumstances of audience, politics, timing, or external pressures that inform it. Our work needs to take into consideration the environment, relationships, and power dynamics at each level in which we operate.

EVIDENCE INFORMED  Our work must be informed by evidence about effective faculty development, as well as research on teaching and learning, including institution-specific information about student learning and experiences. This part of the heuristic raises questions such as: What literature or models are we drawing on to design and deliver our programs? How do we know they are effective and for whom? To succeed "in claiming and deserving the right to respect and credibility," we must, as Bath and Smith (2004) argue, "make explicit the research underlying both the theories of [our] discipline and [our] pragmatic engagement with the day-to-day teaching problems" we help others resolve (p. 24). Specifically, being evidence informed means drawing and building on a base of research and scholarship about student learning (Ambrose, Bridges, DiPietro, Lovett, & Norman, 2010; Brownwell & Swaner, 2010; Hutchings, Taylor Huber, & Ciccone, 2011; Kuh, 2008) as well as research on effective educational development practices (Chism et al., 2012; Kreber & Brook, 2001). If we are to meaningfully advocate for evidence-informed teaching and curricular approaches, we too must approach our work in an intentionally scholarly manner, inquiring systematically into its effectiveness, collecting our own evidence to learn how well our efforts are working, and then using that evidence to improve (Chism & Szabo, 1997; Debowski, 2011b; Felten, Kalish, Pingree, & Plank, 2007; Hines, 2009, 2011; Stefani, 2010). Being informed by evidence means taking a scholarly approach to our work by using our knowledge of relevant research and contributing to it through ongoing assessment of our programs and services.

## Perspectives

Again following the lead of Sorcinelli et al. (2006), we frame educational development as having the potential to foster both individual and institutional change. Many campus programs focus on one-on-one or small group work with faculty, driven by the needs of participants and operating within a culture of confidentiality. This attention to the individual faculty member or on the needs of specific groups makes educational development "safe" and ground-up, two essential values for many developers; it also makes our work sustainable in places where educational development resources, both people and funding, are scarce. However, this ethos can create barriers to broad-scale organizational development work, particularly when developers are perceived to be on the margins of campus, far from (and perhaps deliberately avoiding) places of influence and power (Chism, 1998, 2011; Schroeder & Associates, 2011). We recognize that developers need to consider multiple perspectival levels simultaneously, and we represent these in three columns: individual, departmental, and institutional. Working through the columns of the heuristic raises questions about who else would benefit directly or indirectly from a program (and at what level), and it leads us to wonder who else we could involve or inform about it.

INDIVIDUAL    Faculty development work has traditionally targeted the growth of individual faculty members. To do this effectively, we acknowledge our colleagues' diversity related to individual identity and power (race/ethnicity, gender, sexuality, age, experience, ability, tenured/untenured) as well as personality type and disposition. In addition, we consider the different disciplinary backgrounds, expectations, and preferences that characterize the particular contexts in which they teach. Our work must recognize that effective teaching can take various shapes and honor these differences, rather than advocate for any one right way to teach (Reder, 2007, p. 11).

DEPARTMENTAL  While supporting individuals may remain central to our work, typically the academic department is a particularly relevant place for individual faculty members, whose identity often is deeply embedded in a disciplinary context and whose first loyalty is to a department. Wergin (2003) argues that engaged departments are one of the six key elements of a quality institutional climate and that the key to creating a successful department is engaging diverse constituencies in particular ways. As educational developers, we can play a role in improving the ways departments support individual faculty and design their curriculum, majors, and courses, helping them make evidence-informed decisions to improve student experiences.

While most colleges and universities have departments, we recognize that at many institutions, there are other significant organizational units that may warrant inclusion in this portion of the heuristic, such as major programs, divisions, or colleges. Although on many campuses the department is primary for individual faculty members and mediates their relationship to the institution as a whole, this is not always the case; thus, this category should be modified as appropriate.

INSTITUTIONAL  Effective educational development efforts also reach beyond individual needs to the overall health and effectiveness of the organization, remaining cognizant of priorities for student learning and the academic program. Sorcinelli et al. (2006) note that educational development work often is about making connections. In serving the needs of a changing professoriate and an increasingly diverse student body, teaching centers are more and more engaged in brokering collaborations among various constituencies across campus—departments, student and residential life, academic technologies, writing and quantitative programs, student affairs, institutional research, and libraries—in support of student learning. The potential for an educational development program to serve as a change agent within an institution should not be underestimated, especially at a time when the very nature of teaching and learning in higher education is being examined and discussed as never before (Arum & Roksa, 2011; Bass, 2012; Debowski, 2011a; Latta, 2009).

## Reflective Planning for Prioritizing and Improvement

We offer this heuristic to colleagues as a new tool. We have consciously aimed to keep it simple so that it can support short bursts of creative reflection, formative assessment, dialogue, and planning. In describing a sophisticated strategic planning model for educational development, Hunt (2006) asks a question that evokes a familiar dilemma: "What do you do when it seems that everything should be done at once?" (p. 75). Hunt (2006), Sorcinelli et al. (2006), Schroeder and Associates (2011), and others offer detailed planning frameworks to guide developers as we negotiate often competing requests that come from the top down and the bottom up at our institutions. Similarly, other authors offer a range of analytical tools for and approaches to summative program assessment (Hines, 2009; Plank & Kalish 2010; Stefani, 2010; Walvoord 2004) as they describe in-depth evaluation metrics for programming and services. Our heuristic is not intended to replace these comprehensive models but to complement them, providing an efficient perspective-taking exercise that can capture how educational development units are engaging stakeholders at different levels and how well our programming matches our goals, constituent needs, and institutional priorities.

Successful educational development programs must be agile in responding to change. As a holistic tool supporting creative reflection on experience and practice, our heuristic functions as an instrument that can be used with a relatively low investment of time and other scarce resources. Moreover, it is designed to be flexible, so that developers in a range of situations can use or modify it to reflect their own contexts. We intend the heuristic as a guide to reflection that allows us to quickly assess some aspect of our programming or services. Times like these, Claxton (2006) contends, "do not succumb to methodological problem-solving using familiar constructs," but rather require the "soft creativity" necessary to navigate multifaceted, "ill-defined and open-ended" situations (p. 357). As a heuristic rather than a script, this framework supports brainstorming and thinking beyond the familiar.

## Suggestions for Using the Heuristic

When we experimented with the heuristic ourselves, we each followed a simple process. We allotted ourselves ten to fifteen minutes to identify a single program as a focus and then consider that program through the perspective of each cell in the grid. We discovered that some cells were more easily and quickly populated than others, particularly those in the "Individual Perspective" column; determining what we might include in others sometimes felt puzzling. We then discussed our thoughts and findings with each other and clarified in that exchange any new insights that emerged. For example, asking what a particular program had to do with the departmental perspective led us to ask new questions that we might not have fully considered before: How does our work with individuals or cohorts relate to departments, or, conversely, what impacts do departmental cultures have on our work? Should we plan programming at the department level or in concert with departments rather than working more exclusively with individuals or cohorts? Such previously unarticulated questions often prompted us to come to surprising and generative insights, and the entire process took only about thirty minutes from start to finish.

When we offered the heuristic as an invitation for guided reflection and dialogue at the 2011 and 2012 POD conferences, we urged colleagues to take an attitude of curiosity toward their work. We varied the initial prompts for each conference session. In both, we asked participants to begin with a particular point of departure—one to two specific programs they wished to assess (POD 2011) or a central goal, value, or mission for their work (POD 2012). Then we asked them to spend fifteen minutes filling out the heuristic individually with this program or goal in mind, using these prompts:

- Which individuals or groups are involved in or served by the program? What are their characteristics? Their needs? Their contributions?

- What contexts do they come from? Work within? Need to thrive in?

- Who else would benefit directly or indirectly from the program? Individuals? Department or units? The larger institution?

- Who else might be informed or involved in programming?

- What literature or models are you drawing on in designing and delivering your program?

- How do you know about your program's effectiveness?

As it had for us, this stage of the process proved vexing but productive for participants. The heuristic does not provide a simple grid to fill out with numbers of events or program goals; instead, it invites the user to determine the salient features of each category, how the categories relate, and which theories, implicit or explicit, might be shaping one's practice. Using the heuristic is less about applying known data than articulating key questions and discovering possibilities.

Next, participants reflected, individually and in pairs, on what they discovered from using the heuristic, by considering the following questions: What do you notice? Where are the gaps or opportunities? What are the implications of what you notice for that program or your center more broadly? During this step, participants considered and discussed how the heuristic helped them understand aspects of their program, whether there were important things not represented in the grid, and what this all meant for their decisions about prioritizing and determining where to focus energies or resources. For the final step in the process, participants committed to concrete actions in response to this reflection cycle, naming what needed to be done, setting deadlines, and specifying the first action they would take toward that goal.

## Applying and Adapting the Heuristic

We intend our heuristic to be neither prescriptive (not all cells must be filled in) nor definitive. It is meant as a starting point for others to adapt for their own contexts as appropriate. For example, when we each used the heuristic to examine new faculty programming on our various campuses, we found that although we shared similar goals and some program design features and discovered similar areas to address, we found differences in how we planned to act on those insights within our individual institutional contexts. When applying the heuristic to new faculty programming, each of us discovered that completing the column in the heuristic from the individual and institutional perspectives was very easy, but the departmental perspective presented a challenge.

For all of us, the heuristic revealed that our new faculty workshop or seminar was doing little to address the stakeholders within the departments themselves. So we asked ourselves: Are there new ways to engage departments in new faculty programming to highlight complementary departmental efforts or initiatives? Are we taking advantage of opportunities to communicate with departments and other important constituencies about our work with new faculty? As individuals, we came up with different answers to these questions. One of us decided to improve communication with departments about the seminar on a broader scale through a quick announcement at a meeting of department chairs and a follow-up e-mail with more information. Another of us decided we needed to cultivate relationships with a few key department chairs on an individual basis to learn how our programming was anticipating and responding to the needs of their new faculty. In these cases, the heuristic helped make sense of granular data about our programs by looking at that program in a larger context. That "view from ten thousand feet" yielded insight and suggested improvements in communication that will improve the program's effectiveness and save our time in the long run, but it also took different forms more appropriate to our individual work at the local level.

Many participants in both the 2011 and 2012 conference sessions offered further adaptations and uses: to diagnose the relative contribution of multiple programs to the mission of the center; for assessing programs and also for analyzing the multiple relationships developed in the role as center director; to revisit the same program or goal at different moments and thus add a valuable temporal element to the insights gained. Still others found that layering different programs onto the grid allowed them to reflect on and assess center-wide programming in order to discover stakeholder needs that were not being met or places where the degree of focus on a particular group or need did not match the importance afforded it in broader institutional strategic priorities. Colleagues from Fairfield University left energized in 2011 by insights gained through the exercise, which they used as a gateway instrument that they built on with additional work in program evaluation and assessment, when they realized that the in-depth analysis they wanted necessitated a more comprehensive tool (Klaf, Miners, & Nantz, 2012). These examples do not constitute an exhaustive inventory of ways to adapt the heuristic, but rather hint at the possibilities of how it might be used.

Beyond the time-effective nature of the approaches to using the heuristic, it is a fruitful means for stimulating reflection and structuring conversations among colleagues about program planning and assessment from a wide-angle perspective. Based on insights generated through reflection, developers may choose not only which programs to redesign but also which initiatives and projects have the greatest likelihood of positive outcomes for multiple stakeholders and at multiple levels.

## Conclusion

Our experience, coupled with that of our colleagues at various institutions who have now used the heuristic, suggests that the small investment of time using this simple tool for guided reflection can lead to valuable new perspectives and reframing of our work. Even thirty minutes of concentrated periodic reflection with the heuristic can uncover insights that will inform our practices and priorities—helping us to see where we might make adjustments to improve communication with multiple stakeholders; to deepen, broaden, or improve offerings; to work to effect systemic change or participate in departmental or institutional initiatives; or simply to avoid offering a scattered and unsystematic menu of options.

No single tool is appropriate in all settings and for all tasks, of course, and even with this tool, the reasoning and ultimate decisions of individual developers may differ significantly based on which specific values or groups of people hold priority within a particular institutional context. We have found the heuristic can help us clarify our priorities as well as articulate how different programs fit within the broader framework of our educational development work. The heuristic's structure captures essential aspects of our field and might be used as a foundation for those seeking to undertake extensive assessment and strategic planning exercises, and also as a theoretical basis for research on educational development.

While the heuristic is no substitute for the systematic evaluation of an external review or a major assessment of our programs, it provides a productive tool for responding to the dynamic forces confronting our field today. Being an agile and effective educational developer requires both deeply immersive planning and sustainable brief bursts of generative thinking. Efficient tools like this heuristic will help all of us to imagine possibilities and take new perspectives on our work, allowing us to contribute to, and perhaps even to lead, positive change at our institutions and in higher education.

REFERENCES

Ambrose, S. A., Bridges, M. W., DiPietro, M., Lovett, M. C., & Norman, M. K. (2010). *How learning works: Seven research-based principles for smart teaching.* San Francisco, CA: Jossey-Bass.

Arum, R., & Roksa, J. (2011). *Academically adrift: Limited learning on college campuses.* Chicago, IL: University of Chicago Press.

Bass, R. (2012). Disrupting ourselves: The problem of learning in higher education. *Educause Review, 47*(2), 23–33.

Bath, D., & Smith, C. (2004). Academic developers: An academic tribe claiming their territory in higher education. *International Journal for Academic Development, 9*(1), 9–27.

Brownwell, J. E., & Swaner, L. E. (2010). *Five high-impact practices: Research on learning outcomes, completion, and quality.* Washington, DC: AAC&U.

Carew, A. L., Lefoe, G., Bell, M., & Armour, L. (2008). Elastic practice in academic developers. *International Journal for Academic Development 13*(1), 51–66. doi:10.1080/13601440701860250

Chism, N.V.N. (1998). The role of educational developers in institutional change: From basement office to front office. In M. Kaplan (Ed.), *To improve the academy: Resources for faculty, instructional, and organizational development, Vol. 17* (pp. 141–154). Stillwater, OK: New Forums Press and the Professional and Organizational Development Network in Higher Education.

Chism, N.V.N. (2011). Getting to the table: Planning and developing institutional initiatives. In C. M. Schroeder & Associates, *Coming in from the margins: Faculty development's emerging organizational development role in institutional change* (pp. 47–59). Sterling, VA: Stylus.

Chism, N.V.N., Holley, M., & Harris, C. J. (2012). Researching the impact of educational development: Basis for informed practice. In J. Groccia & L. Cruz (Eds.), *To improve the academy: Resources for faculty, instructional, and organizational development, Vol. 31* (pp. 385–400). San Francisco, CA: Jossey-Bass/Anker.

Chism, N.V.N., & Szabo, B. (1997). How faculty development programs evaluate their services. *Journal of Staff, Program, and Organizational Development, 15*(2), 55–62.

Christensen, C. M., & Eyring, H. J. (2011). *The innovative university: Changing the DNA of higher education from the inside out.* San Francisco, CA: Jossey-Bass.

Claxton, G. (2006). Thinking at the edge: Developing soft creativity. *Cambridge Journal of Education 36*(3), 351–362. doi:10.1080/03057640600865876

Cropley, A. (2006). In praise of convergent thinking. *Creativity Research Journal 18*(3), 391–404. doi:10.1207/s15326934crj1803_13

Debowski, L. (2011a). Emergent shifts in faculty development: A reflective review. In J. Miller & J. Groccia (Eds.), *To improve the academy: Resources for faculty, instructional, and organizational development, Vol. 30* (pp. 306–322). San Francisco, CA: Jossey-Bass/Anker.

Debowski, L. (2011b). Locating academic development: The first step in evaluation. In L. Stefani (Ed.), *Evaluating the effectiveness of academic development* (pp. 17–30). New York, NY: Routledge.

Felten, P., Kalish, A., Pingree, A., & Plank, K. (2007). Toward a scholarship of teaching and learning in educational development. In D. Robertson & L. Nilson (Eds.), *To improve the academy: Resources for faculty, instructional, and organizational development, Vol. 25* (pp. 93–108). Bolton, MA: Anker.

Felten, P., Little, D., Ortquist-Ahrens, L., & Reder, M. (2011). *Linking faculty development with global learning and student success.* Paper presented at the annual meeting of the Association of American Colleges and Universities, San Francisco, CA.

Felten, P., Little, D., Ortquist-Ahrens, L., & Reder, M. (2012). *Prioritizing your center's time and resources to meet 21st century demands.* Paper presented at the meeting of the Professional and Organizational Development Network in Higher Education, Seattle, WA.

Hines, S. R. (2009). Investigating faculty development assessment practices: What's being done and how can it be improved? *Journal of Faculty Development, 23*(3), 5–19.

Hines, S. R. (2011). How mature teaching and learning centers evaluate their services. In J. Miller and J. Groccia (Eds.), *To improve the academy: Resources for faculty, instructional, and organizational development, Vol. 30* (pp. 277–289). San Francisco, CA: Jossey-Bass/Anker.

Hunt, L. (2006). A community development model of change: The role of teaching and learning centres. In L. Hunt, A. Bromage, & B. Tomkinson (Eds.), *The realities of change in higher education: Interventions to promote learning and teaching* (pp. 64–77). New York, NY: Routledge.

Hutchings, P., Taylor Huber, M., & Ciccone, A. (2011). *The scholarship of teaching and learning reconsidered: Institutional integration and impact.* San Francisco, CA: Jossey-Bass.

Klaf, S., Miners, L., & Nantz, K. (2012). *Using POD's heuristic: Finding the big picture in the pixels.* Paper presented at the meeting of the Professional and Organizational Development Network in Higher Education, Seattle, WA.

Kreber, C., & Brook, P. (2001). Impact evaluation of educational development programmes. *International Journal of Academic Development, 6*(2), 96–108.

Kuh, G. D. (2008). *High-impact educational practices: What they are, who has access to them, and why they matter.* Washington, DC: Association of American Colleges and Universities.

Latta, G. F. (2009). Maturation of organizational development in higher education: Using cultural analysis to facilitate change. In L. B. Nilson & J. E. Miller (Eds.). *To improve the academy: Resources for faculty, instructional, and organizational development, Vol. 18* (pp. 32–71). San Francisco, CA: Jossey-Bass/Anker.

Little, D., & Green, D. A. (2012). Betwixt and between: Academic developers in the margins. *International Journal for Academic Development, 17,* 203–215.

Milloy, P. M., & Brooke, C. (2004). Beyond bean counting: Making faculty development needs assessment more meaningful. In C. Wehlburg & S. Chadwick-Blossey (Eds.). *To improve the academy: Resources for faculty, instructional, and organizational development, Vol. 22* (pp. 71–92). Bolton, MA: Anker.

Moon, J. (1999). *Reflection in learning and professional development.* London: Kogan Page.

Ortquist-Ahrens, L., Felten, P., Foster, L., Little, D., & Reder, M. (2011). *Conceptualizing our work: Characteristics of effective teaching and learning programs.* Paper presented at the meeting of the Professional and Organizational Development Network in Higher Education, Atlanta, GA.

Plank, K. M., & Kalish, A. (2010). Program assessment for faculty development. In K. Gillespie, D. L. Robertson, & Associates (Eds.), *A guide to faculty development* (2nd ed., pp. 135–149). San Francisco, CA: Jossey-Bass.

Reder, M. (2007). Does your college really support teaching and learning? *Peer Review, 9*(4), 9–13.

Schroeder, C. M., & Associates. (2011). *Coming in from the margins: Faculty development's emerging organizational development role in institutional change.* Sterling VA: Stylus.

Schön, D. A. (1983). *The reflective practitioner: How professionals think in action.* New York, NY: Basic Books.

Schön, D. A. (1987). *Educating the reflective practitioner.* San Francisco, CA: Jossey-Bass.

Sorcinelli, M. D., Austin, A. E., Eddy, P. L., & Beach, A. L. (2006). *Creating the future of faculty development: Learning from the past, understanding the present.* Bolton, MA: Anker.

Stefani, L. (Ed.). (2010). *Evaluating the effectiveness of academic development.* New York, NY: Routledge.

Tosey P. (2006). Interfering with the interference: An emergent perspective on creativity in higher education. In N. Jackson, M. Oliver, M. Shaw, & J. Wisdom (Eds.), *Developing creativity in higher education: An imaginative curriculum* (pp. 29–42). New York, NY: Routledge.

Walvoord, B. E. (2004). *Assessment clear and simple.* San Francisco, CA: Jossey-Bass.

Wergin, J. F. (2003). *Departments that work: Building and sustaining cultures of excellence in academic programs.* Bolton, MA: Anker.

# 12

# A CONSULTATIONS TRACKING DATABASE SYSTEM FOR IMPROVING FACULTY DEVELOPMENT CONSULTATION SERVICES

*Jason Rhode, Murali Krishnamurthi*
*Northern Illinois University*

*The role of the faculty development center in supporting the academic environment of the institution often includes creating or sustaining a culture of teaching excellence, responding to individual faculty members' needs, and advancing new initiatives in teaching and learning (Sorcinelli, Austin, Eddy, & Beach, 2006). The varied programs, resources, and services offered routinely result from efforts to meet the expressed needs of faculty. While workshops and seminars are effective for introducing new pedagogical approaches or emerging technologies, faculty often have unique questions within specialized contexts that cannot be fully addressed in a large group setting. In such instances, a more personalized and customized level of support is needed. This chapter describes a*

We express our sincere appreciation to the staff of the Faculty Development and Instructional Design Center at Northern Illinois University for their contributions to and support of this effort. We are especially grateful to program coordinator Brenda Hodges for her coordination of the center's assessment efforts and preparation of assessment and annual reports.

*database system for tracking and improving the effectiveness of individual consultation services.*

———— o ————

One rewarding and time-consuming form of faculty development is consulting with faculty members on a one-to-one basis. It is through such individualized encounters that support can be tailored to specific expressed needs (Lewis, 2002). Requests for assistance from faculty can consist of a wide variety of formats, ranging from formally scheduled one-on-one meetings to requests by phone, e-mail, or virtual means for technical assistance. During an individualized consultation, faculty development staff have an opportunity to identify and respond to the specific challenge that a faculty member is facing (Kuhlenschmidt, 2010). Consultations regarding a technological challenge present unique opportunities, as the technical discussion often can serve as a platform for examining pedagogical practices and assumptions (Zhu, Kaplan, & Dershimer, 2011). Such consultations provide a unique way for faculty development staff to offer both instructional design assistance and technology support within the specific context of the faculty member's questions.

## Need for Evaluation of Consultations

It has long been argued and commonly accepted that evaluation is an important component for any successful professional development initiative (Gray & Shadle, 2009; Kirkpatrick, 1994; Levinson-Rose & Menges, 1981; Plank & Kalish, 2010). A comprehensive evaluation strategy yields numerous benefits to a faculty development center, including measuring achievement of mission, vision, and goals (Robertson, 2010); demonstrating impact on teaching and learning (Kucsera & Svinicki, 2010); and informing decision making and improving practices (Plank & Kalish, 2010). Centers commonly conduct evaluations to improve programs and services, document successes, and meet reporting mandates (Chism & Szabó, 1997).

Concerted efforts have been made to understand specifically how faculty development programs evaluate their services. Chism and Szabó (1997) conducted a national survey of centers for teaching and learning (CTLs) and noted that while evaluations of events were frequently performed (over 90 percent of the time), consultations were less frequently and less consistently assessed, due largely to the amount of time needed to record and evaluate them. As a result, they recommended regular efforts by institutions to assess user satisfaction in conjunction with more extensive formal studies as resources permit. They advised:

> Program staff . . . should be diligent in developing convenient systems for recording who their users are and for assessing satisfaction routinely. Such systems may involve only regular and standard record-keeping and survey research, which can be analyzed easily with simple database and spreadsheet applications. (p. 61)

Hines (2009) expanded on the comprehensive research by Chism and Szabó (1997) and investigated assessment practices of faculty developers to understand current assessment practices and offer recommendations for improvement. Hines found a consistent lack of evaluation of consultation services offered by faculty development centers. When asked about the lack of routine evaluation of consultation services, respondents noted that issues of confidentiality or service magnitude generally deterred evaluation. Consultation evaluation was believed to leave a paper trail, potentially exposing faculty inadequacies that could result in liability issues. Consultations were also seen as a small, low-impact service not justifying the need to be evaluated.

Hines (2010) extended her 2009 study and investigated assessment methods to measure outcomes of faculty development services at thirty-three established, centralized CTLs across the United States. While efforts at evaluating frequency and impact of many programs and services offered were common, a gap in program evaluation regarding consultation services was again identified. She reported:

> Consultation services were not routinely evaluated due to the desire to maintain confidentiality and also due to the perceived lack of time and resources. A small number believed consultation evaluation to be too difficult or the services were too irregular to justify assessing. Others chose not to since evaluations of consultations were not required. (p. 11)

In reality, consultation evaluation can be yet another method for program improvement, fostering the recognition of weaknesses, closing loops, and continual improvement. However, without an electronic system for capturing and analyzing this information, these telling data capable of yielding eye-opening insights that can help inform future strategic efforts are lost. As noted in the literature, the arduous mechanics for using a paper-based process to manually track consultations offered by numerous support staff has prevented the evaluation of consultation services. Implementing an easy-to-use electronic system for capturing these data and performing data analysis is the first step to incorporating consultation evaluation as part of a comprehensive assessment effort.

To evaluate better the breadth and scope of consultation services offered to faculty, teaching staff, administrators, and graduate teaching assistants at Northern Illinois University (NIU), the Faculty Development and Instructional Design Center (FDIDC) has implemented a comprehensive consultations tracking system for not only recording consultations but also conducting detailed analysis of consultation services offered, and it uses the results for continuous improvement purposes. The system, implemented as a Microsoft Access database, is one model for recording and analyzing faculty development consultations and can be customized to other universities.

## Consultations Data Management

Consultations are one of the many services FDIDC offers. After attending a particular program, many faculty, teaching staff, administrators, and graduate teaching assistants request individual consultations from center staff to receive more in-depth help on specific needs related to their teaching, technology integration into teaching, or other activities. For example, in 2011–2012, FDIDC offered 1,097 consultations to 398 unique individuals from 88 academic and support units at NIU and a few from outside NIU. The duration of consultations varies from a few minutes to several hours, and the mode of consultations can be face-to-face, phone, e-mail, or virtual. We recognized early on the value of information on our consultation services on our planning efforts and decided to operationalize the process for capturing and evaluating the increasing number of consultations offered.

### Challenges

As we initially set out to begin assessing our consultations services, we faced numerous challenges in the manual process for recording and analyzing consultations data, and that led us to implement a standardized consultation evaluation system. Due to the difficulty in distinguishing between various categories of consultations services, we developed formal definitions for each of these categories for the purpose of collecting data that continue to be used. After analyzing past consultations and discussing our data collection and analysis needs for consultations, we defined consultations to be at least thirty minutes in length and require back-and-forth conversation through various means, such as face-to-face meetings or a phone call. Requests (for information) and referrals (to other units on campus) are shorter (under thirty minutes) and conducted through the same means as consultations.

Once we agreed on the definitions for the types of consultation services, our staff began individually tracking and categorizing the consultations, requests, and referrals offered each month. In the absence of a formalized system, they selected whatever method for tracking they individually preferred. Some tried electronic spreadsheets for recording consultations data, while others resorted to keeping a note pad at their desk and writing down by hand the date, duration of the consultation, and name of faculty who received the service. The lack of one standardized approach resulted in a simple tally of the number of consultations, requests, and referrals offered. Each staff member compiled the total number of consultations, requests, and referrals offered each month and submitted them to the program coordinator for compiling and reporting. We documented in our annual reports numbers on total consultation services of the various types we offered, but little beyond reporting the frequency of total consultations was possible.

Without a centralized system, staff members were manually keeping track of their consultations individually and were not able to identify accurately the total number of unique consultees they served. For example, while a consultee might be considered "unique" for a particular staff member, that consultee might consult with other staff during the same or a different time period and would not be a truly "unique" consultee for those subsequent consultations. This required considerable time and effort at the end of the reporting period to identify truly new or unique consultees served by our center.

We recognized many obvious limitations to these early efforts at manual tracking of consultation services. Because the data we were attempting to collect were limited to the numbers of total consultations, we were not able to conduct a thorough analysis of our services. Beyond merely tracking the numbers of each type of consultation service, we wanted to collect data on consultation mode, topic, classification and affiliation of consultee, and other useful details. Envisioning the potential for analyzing the consultations offered and using the results to improve our consultation services as well as operational productivity, we realized the need to track various pieces of information associated with each consultation. In addition, we wanted our staff to be freed up from the time-consuming task of tallying and reporting their consultations each month but focus their efforts on offering programs and consultation services. Similarly, we wanted to simplify and speed up the consultation data analysis and assessment process.

## Characteristics of a Tracking System

In 2009, we conducted a needs analysis to review all aspects of our consultation services and came to the realization that we needed a centralized database system to track our consultation services and resolve the challenges we have been facing in the data collection and analysis process. We identified the following needs for such a consultation tracking system:

1. *Data definitions.* The system should allow defining and tracking consultation types (consultations, requests, and referrals), modes (face-to-face, e-mail, phone, virtual), consultation topics, consultees details, consulting staff, date and time of each consultation, and any additional open-ended details.

2. *Data entry.* The data entry process should be simple, consistent, menu driven, and easy for a nontechnical staff person to follow and use. The process should prevent manual look-up of data such as a consultee's department name or classification and allow easy verification that a consultee's information already exists in the system.

3. *Data extraction.* The data extraction process should be simple and guided by menus and prompts. It should allow a variety of queries for extracting data between date ranges, by particular values, data on a specific consultation or consultee or all consultations or consultees, and enable exporting data easily for analysis or report generation purposes.

4. *Data analysis.* The system should allow simple analysis of consultations data such as total number of consultations and number of unique consultees and consulting units during a particular period. It should also display required summary data in the form of charts and graphs for analysis purposes at any time by any of staff or the director.

5. *Centralized access.* The database system should be centrally located on a file server and accessed by all our staff from their work stations through our local area network.

6. *Flexibility.* The system should be simple and flexible to make changes in the future, and our staff or graduate assistants should be capable of maintaining the system on an ongoing basis.

7. *Backup and security.* The consultation data should allow easy backup by one person, and not all staff, on a regular basis, and the data stored in system should not be accessible by anyone outside our center.

8. *Affordability.* The database software cost should be minimal and not require special licenses, and the system design and development costs should be minimal because our center's budget is very limited.

These needs guided our consultations database system design, development, and implementation process. We recognized that these needs have to be met by the implemented system to be fully functional and usable for tracking our consultations and improving our consultation services.

## Consultations Database System Implementation

To meet the unique needs and requirements of our consultation data management, we internally designed and developed our consultations tracking database system. The design process included traditional systems analysis and design techniques (Kendall & Kendall, 2008) such as needs analysis, process modeling, and data modeling, as well as relational database system techniques (Silberschatz, Korth, & Sudarshan, 1999), such as preliminary database design (translation of the data model into an initial database design) and data normalization (elimination of insertion, deletion, and modification data anomalies in the database design) to arrive at a validated final design (Dutka & Hanson, 1989).

The final design had four tables—for consultee, consultations, staff, and units—that were related to each other through appropriate relationships between them and primary keys that uniquely identified records in each entity table. After considerable analysis of data to be queried or generated as reports from the consultations database system, we defined the necessary columns of each table to capture the data and the rules to enforce the range of acceptable values for those columns. Figure 12.1

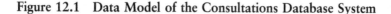

**Figure 12.1   Data Model of the Consultations Database System**

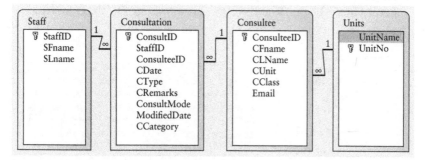

shows the relational data model with the tables, attributes, and relationships between the tables.

## System Implementation

For implementing the design, we chose Microsoft Access due to its affordability (Access is already available on all our staff work stations as part of the Microsoft Office package with no additional cost or licensing necessary), ease of use, and, most important, ease of development, implementation, and maintenance. One of the advantages of Microsoft Access is its graphical user interface, which makes designing queries, reports, and menus easy. Because no programming is required, any of our graduate assistants could also make changes to the system and maintain it in the long run.

Based on how our staff would use the consultations database system, we developed and implemented the user interface menus, data entry forms, queries, and reports using the built-in form, query, and report design features in Microsoft Access. The main menu includes the most used function: Enter Consultee/Consultations; other functions for adding or deleting consultees, consultations, staff, and consultee's units; and a second-level menu for queries and reports. The Queries and Reports menu offers fourteen query and report functions, and a third-level menu with queries for displaying consultation data in the form of nine different charts. Figure 12.2 shows the consultations database system's black-and-white versions of the main menu and the second-level menu for queries and reports.

---

Figure 12.2    Screen Captures of the Main Menu (Left) and the Second-Level Query Menu (Right) of the Consultations Database System

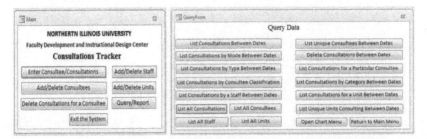

## System Features

When analyzing our staff needs for using the system easily, we recognized that some functions of the system had to be combined for ease of use but also needed the flexibility to be performed independently. For example, our staff wanted to create a new consultee as well as enter consultation data for that consultee on the same screen, but they also wanted the flexibility to create consultees separately as needed without having to enter consultations data. On the data entry screens, we included many drop-down boxes to easily select information such as consultee's employment classification and department, consultation type and mode, consulting staff's name, and date so that our staff do not have to remember such data or spend time looking up the information to enter it. On the data entry screens, our staff also wanted features for searching the database system to see if a consultee already exists in the system to prevent duplicate entries or to locate a consultee quickly to modify his or her information in the system. Figure 12.3 shows the black-and-white versions of the consultation and consultee data entry forms captured from the database system.

One of the important features of the system is the ability for several of our staff to enter their consultations data from their workstations into the same centralized database. For this purpose, the consultations database implemented in Microsoft Access was split into a back-end database containing data definitions and data and a front-end application system containing menus, data entry forms, queries, and reports. We installed the back-end database on a local file server connected to staff work stations

---

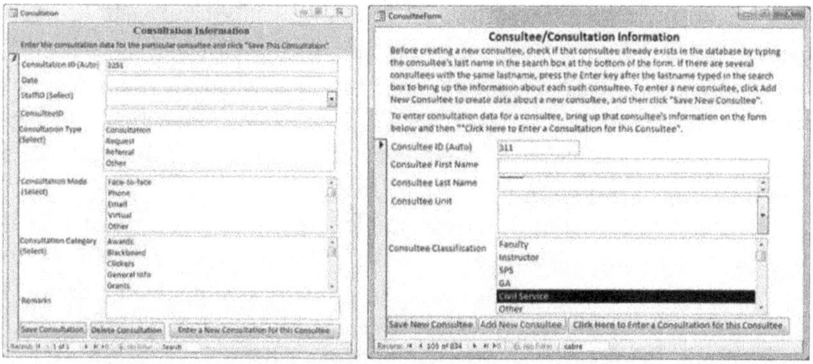

Figure 12.3     Screen Captures of Consultation Data Entry Form and Consultee/Consultation Data Entry Form

and installed the front-end database application on all staff work stations. This allowed our staff to use the application system on their work stations to access the back-end database independently and store, retrieve, or modify data on the centralized back-end database. Separating the back-end database containing the data has also made it easy for regularly backing up only the data instead of unnecessarily backing up the application system as well since it remains the same. Because the database resides on our local file server and not on a web server, the system is secure and cannot be accessed by anyone outside our center.

## Database System Use

The consultation database system has been in use since 2009 at our center, and all staff members use it for entering and querying consultations data. The director and program coordinator use the system for extracting and analyzing consultations data for assessment, planning, and reporting.

### Data Entry and Extraction

The data entry process in the consultation database system is straightforward, and the user interface menus and the data entry screens guide the process. After launching the front-end database application on their workstation, staff members can click the Enter Consultee/Consultations button on the main menu, which will display the Consultee/Consultation Information window, as shown in figure 12.3. In the search box at the bottom of the window, the first or last name of a consultee can be entered to check if the consultee already exists in the system; if the consultee is already in the system, his or her information is displayed on the window, and the staff member can click on Click Here to Enter a New Consultation for This Consultee. Otherwise the staff member can click the Add New Consultee button, enter the new consultee's information, and click the Save New Consultee button to save the data. Then the Click Here to Enter a New Consultation for This Consultee button can be clicked to enter consultations data for that consultee, which will bring up the Consultation Information data entry screen.

On the Consultation Information data entry screen, standardized response types are presented wherever possible as drop-down menu options to save time, prevent mistakes, and compile data in a uniform fashion to aid in data analysis. The data entry fields include the date of the consultation (which can be selected from the calendar displayed), ID of staff who offered the consultation, consultation type, consultation mode, consultation category, and remarks. A unique consultee ID is created automatically by the system when a new consultee's data are entered into the system, and, similarly, a unique consultation ID is created by the system when new consultation data are entered into the system and associated with that consultee. After entering consultation details, clicking the Save Consultation button saves the new entry, while the Enter a New Consultation for This Consultee button will save the new entry and display the consultation information screen for entering another consultation data entry for the same consultee. The Delete Consultation button will prevent entered consultation data from being saved.

Once data have been entered into the system, they can just as easily be extracted for analysis and reporting. Currently there are fourteen queries available within the system to view data for specified date range, consultation types, modes, categories, and consulting staff. The data, after being queried from the system, can easily be exported to another application for further analysis or reporting. Staff members can query the system at any time and check the consultations they offered, and the program coordinator can run the queries for assessment and analysis purposes. The chart menu allows the display of queried data in the form of bar or pie charts, which can be used for analysis.

## Data Analysis

The queries and charts available in the consultation system have been helpful for analyzing the consultation data and conduct formative as well as summative evaluation of our consultation services. The data analysis and evaluation efforts have benefited our center in numerous ways:

- ○ *Programming.* Data analysis on consultations services offered has frequently guided decisions on the need for new programs. If a number of faculty and teaching staff request consultations on the same topic, center staff develop and offer a new program or service to address the unique new needs expressed. For example, in 2010–2011, more faculty and teaching staff requested consultations than in other years due to a major upgrade of the Blackboard learning management system that year, which introduced many new features. As a result of the increasing number of consultations, center staff offered new programs on those topics, which has reduced the need for consultations on those same topics in 2011–2012.

- ○ *Staffing.* Analysis of consultation trends over a period of time has helped us to identify peak demand times during the year for consultations on particular topics and reassign staff responsibilities to address the demand during those times. Individual staff members have been able to query the system to extract data on their consultations for monthly reporting purposes, and the director has been able to query data on consultations offered by all staff, and use the information for balancing staff workload. Figure 12.4 shows a black-and-white sample of a consultations trend chart extracted from the system.

The consultation system has not only simplified data entry, extraction, analysis, assessment, and reporting but has also improved our staff productivity and consultation services. As a result of the center's assessment efforts, the center was recognized as Outstanding Practices in Assessment by Northern Illinois University's Assessment Panel in February 2012.

## Conclusion

Through our experience collecting, tracking, and analyzing consultations data now for several years, we have found that consultation evaluation can be yet another method for improving programs, recognizing limitations, closing feedback loops, and planning for continuous improvement. Tracking the number, type, mode, and frequency of consultations and consultees' data has provided valuable information for program planning, staffing, and improving support for faculty (see figure 12.5). We now collect, track, and analyze consultations data just as we do for all our other programs and services. Consultation services have become one of our measurable objectives and targets in promoting effective teaching.

Consultations have become a crucial component of services offered by our center and are needed to provide follow-up assistance to faculty after they attend programs or when they could not attend a program due to scheduling conflicts. We have found faculty are usually more enthusiastic about seeking consultations on technology integration, development grants, and career issues, and those consultations have helped our staff address the teaching-related needs of those faculty. As a result of using the consultations database system, our staff are able to provide customized consultation services and follow-up with individual consultees easily.

It is important to remember that any consultations tracking system is only as good as the data entry. Because the data entry cannot be completely automated and requires manual entry into the system by our staff, we continue to look for ways to clarify any questions staff might

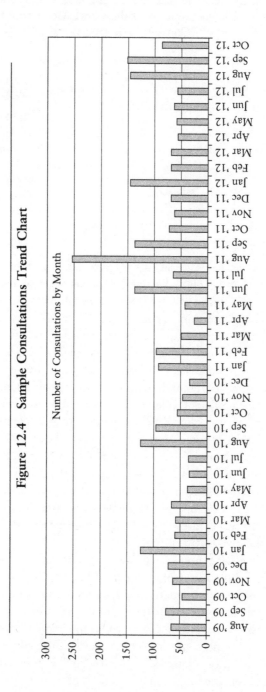

Figure 12.4    Sample Consultations Trend Chart

Figure 12.5    Screen Captures of the Chart Menu and a Pie Chart of
Consultee Classifications

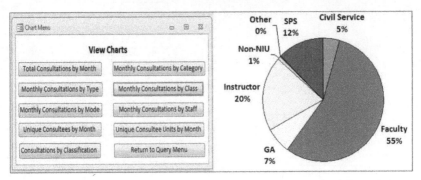

have and encourage best practices for accurate data entry. Staff members have noted that keeping the database open during the day on their computer work station allows quick entry of consultation information immediately after finishing a consultation session. The system has helped individual staff to analyze the consultations they offered, plan their workload, and improve their productivity. Before the consultation database system was implemented, center staff annually spent at least fifty hours to collect and compile manually the consultation data recorded on spreadsheets by eight individual staff and prepare annual reports on consultation services offered by the center. After implementing the consultations database system, this same process takes only a few minutes to generate not only numerical reports but also graphical summaries as needed by any of our staff. Considering that the center director, knowledgeable in database design and development, spent only about forty hours to design, develop, and implement the consultation database system, the system has already paid off within a year, thus justifying the return on the investment of time.

Because we have been using the consultation database system only since 2009, we plan to explore longitudinal data and trends over more extended time periods to analyze the long-term impact of our consultation services. Over time we will be able to look at multiyear time frames as well as cross-compare frequency, types, and modes with other institutional initiatives and conduct extensive statistical analyses.

Our consultation database system can be used by any faculty development or teaching and learning center and customized for its consultation tracking needs or related purposes. Interested faculty development centers can contact our center at facdev@niu.edu for a copy of our consultation database system.

## REFERENCES

Chism, N., & Szabó, B. (1997). How faculty development programs evaluate their services. *Journal of Staff, Program and Organizational Development, 15*(2), 55–62.

Dutka, A. F., & Hanson, H. H. (1989). *Fundamentals of data normalization.* Los Angeles, CA: Addison-Wesley.

Gray, T., & Shadle, S. E. (2009). Launching or revitalizing a teaching center: Principles and portraits of practice. *Journal of Faculty Development, 23*(2), 5–12.

Hines, S. (2009). Investigating faculty development program assessment practices: What's being done and how can it be improved? *Journal of Faculty Development, 23*(3), 5–19.

Hines, S. (2010). *An investigation of program assessment practices at established centralized teaching and learning centers: The findings report.* Unpublished manuscript, Saint Mary's University of Minnesota.

Kendall, K. E., & Kendall, J. E. (2008). *Systems analysis and design* (7th ed.). New York, NY: Prentice Hall.

Kirkpatrick, D. L. (1994). *Evaluating training programs: The four levels.* San Francisco, CA: Berrett-Koehler.

Kucsera, J. V., & Svinicki, M. (2010). Rigorous evaluations of faculty development programs. *Journal of Faculty Development, 24*(2), 5–18.

Kuhlenschmidt, S. (2010). Issues in technology and faculty development. In K. J. Gillespie & D. L. Robertson (Eds.), *A guide to faculty development* (2nd ed., pp. 259–274). San Francisco, CA: Jossey-Bass.

Levinson-Rose, J., & Menges, R. J. (1981). Improving college teaching: A critical review of research. *Review of Educational Research, 51*(3), 403–434.

Lewis, K. G. (2002). The process of individual consultation. In K. H. Gillespie, L. R. Hilsen, & E. C. Wadsworth (Eds.), *A guide to faculty development: Practical advice, examples, and resources* (pp. 53–73). Bolton, MA: Anker.

Plank, K. M., & Kalish, A. (2010). Program assessment for faculty development. In K. J. Gillespie & D. L. Robertson (Eds.), *A guide to faculty development* (2nd ed., pp. 135–149). San Francisco, CA: Jossey-Bass.

Robertson, D. L. (2010). Establishing an educational development program. In K. J. Gillespie & D. L. Robertson (Eds.), *A guide to faculty development* (2nd ed., pp. 35–52). San Francisco, CA: Jossey-Bass.

Silberschatz, A., Korth, H. F., & Sudarshan, S. (1999). *Database system concepts.* New York: McGraw-Hill.

Sorcinelli, M. D., Austin, A. E., Eddy, P. L., & Beach, A. L. (2006). *Creating the future of faculty development: Learning from the past, understanding the present.* Bolton, MA: Anker.

Zhu, E., Kaplan, M., & Dershimer, C. (2011). Engaging faculty in effective use of instructional technology. In C. E. Cook & M. Kaplan (Eds.), *Advancing the culture of teaching on campus: How a teaching center can make a difference* (pp. 151–166). Sterling, VA: Stylus.

# PART FIVE

# GRADUATE TEACHING ASSISTANTS: INNOVATIVE APPROACHES

# 13

# FROM OUTSIDERS TO INSIDERS

## GRADUATE ASSISTANT DEVELOPMENT AT STATE COMPREHENSIVE UNIVERSITIES

*Kathleen M. Brennan, Laura Cruz, Freya B. Kinner*
*Western Carolina University*

*We assess graduate assistant competency in key skills that employers in and outside of academia value and examine whether these skills are developed in the context of the graduate assistantship (GA) at a specific state comprehensive university. The GAs in our sample rate themselves as competent or very competent on all skills and report their GA experience somewhat influenced or influenced their skill competencies. Furthermore, perception of how one's graduate assistantship influenced skill competency was significantly associated with perceived skill competency level. Based on these findings, we discuss distinct gaps that could be addressed to facilitate GA development at state comprehensive universities.*

○

If you are a typical faculty member, odds are about fifty-fifty whether you received training as a graduate assistant (GA) outside of your disciplinary course work (Nyquist, Abbott, Wulff, & Sprague, 1991). Those odds are longer the further back you received your PhD. You are even less likely to have received such training if your highest degree is a master's degree and less likely still if you received your master's degree from a state comprehensive university (SCU). In many ways, graduate students at SCUs have been treated as outliers, even outsiders, by researchers and practitioners of graduate student development (Chen, 2003; Hagstrom et al., 2000).

## Background

The role and development of GAs has been overlooked at SCUs, at least in part because it has largely been overlooked everywhere else (Abbott, Wulff, & Szego, 1989; Wert, 1998). Graduate education as a whole has been one of the last frontiers for research and certainly one of the areas in which the least amount of reform has taken place. The reasons for this are complex, but one possibility is that the impetus for reform began in secondary education and then radiated out to neighboring areas, putting graduate education on the outlying fringe. Another possibility is that tradition has been more cloying in graduate education. Many faculty see graduate training as the last bastion that is truly the domain of the academic scholar, free from outside influences that may sully the purity of its imparting of knowledge.

The outsider or outlier status can also apply to SCUs. In his book, *Teaching at the People's University*, Bruce Henderson (2006) suggests that SCUs lack the clout and funding of research universities and the specific mission or traditions of community colleges or liberal arts colleges. Henderson argues that when SCUs, born as teachers' colleges, fail, it is because they try too hard to be like these other institutions and do not feel sufficiently comfortable to differentiate their own values and identity. The awkwardness is compounded when examining graduate programs at SCUs. By definition, comprehensive universities offer a variety of graduate programs at the master's level but few, if any, doctoral programs. While most graduate programs are patterned after their counterparts at research universities that do offer PhDs, little to no work has been done to find a distinctive identity for graduate programs in fulfilling the mission of SCUs (Freeman & Schmidt, 2000).

Graduate student development on the whole became a topic of conversation in the 1980s (Chism, 1998). By the 1990s, the National Survey of Teaching Assistant Training Programs and Services indicated that 71 percent of responding institutions had developed specific programs for graduate student development, but the majority of these were less than five years old (Lambert & Tice, 1993). Today the conversation has been extended to include GAs in broader conversations about the future of higher education and the raised profile of faculty and teacher professional development. When these efforts have been productive, they have been aimed largely at the doctoral and research universities. For example, Border and von Hoene (2010) have recently been working on a second national-level study designed to provide a taxonomy of best practices in graduate student certificate programs, but they have included a limited number of SCUs in their surveys. This is understandable, as these graduate programs are often considerably smaller and are generally limited to the master's level, but student enrollment in these programs is rising and is likely to continue rising at a faster rate than at other institutional types.

The challenge in looking at graduate development at SCUs comes from the diversity of goals and outcomes for graduate education. In the case of doctoral-granting institutions, the traditional, primary purpose of the PhD is to train future faculty for work in academia. While a study of career objectives for master's degree–seeking students has yet to be done on the national level, most evidence suggests that these programs must serve a variety of other outcomes for their students, including academia. Even at the PhD level, there are scholars who argue that graduate student development should include preparation for roles outside academia, especially given the stagnation in current academic job markets (Austin & Wulff, 2004; Conn, 2010). This need is even more acute for SCUs where academic careers are less of a common denominator. A graduate student survey at the University of Nebraska-Lincoln, for example, showed that doctoral students chose academic career goals across the board, but that master's-level students looked for careers in industry (22.9 percent), consulting (22.9 percent), and entrepreneurship (22.9 percent) (Bellows & Weissinger, 2005). According to the recent Pathways through Graduate School report, commissioned by the Council of Graduate Schools and ETS, approximately one-third of graduate students with master's degrees work in business and roughly one-fourth in teaching or faculty positions (Commission on Pathways, 2012).

A number of major studies in the 1990s demonstrated clear disconnects between the careers that graduate students eventually choose and the preparation they receive for them (Golde & Dore, 2001; Nerad, 2004). While 65 percent of the over four thousand survey respondents for the 2000 survey on doctoral education and career preparation indicated that their programs prepared them well for research and research-related activities, they were less confident in their preparation for various aspects of classroom teaching (National Association of Graduate-Professional Students, 2000). They expressed the least confidence in their training for participating in university citizenship (12.7 percent) and community outreach (13.8 percent). However, only 31.8 percent of the respondents said they participated in nonacademic job search opportunities.

Open-ended responses indicated that there were often disincentives for exploring nonacademic options.

The gap between preparation and careers that the survey indicated has led to concerted efforts in graduate student development, particularly in changing older models of training teaching assistants to more multifaceted preparing future faculty (PFF) initiatives (Gaff, 2002). Most PFF programs consist of a mix of formal and informal opportunities designed to address multiple aspects of academic work, and they provide this support in multiple formats, including voluntary, certificate, online, and credit-based programs (Lambert & Tice, 1993). The field also includes career development opportunities, incorporating training in teamwork, communication, conflict resolution, project management, and other job-related skills (Border, 2006). Even with expanding opportunities, graduate student development remains largely the domain of doctoral-granting institutions in spite of the fact that graduate students at SCUs also participate in all of these aspects of academic work, but usually with a shorter time frame for development.

Global assessment of the effectiveness of these strategic changes in graduate student development is in the beginning phases, though individual programs are usually well assessed and regularly evaluated. Broader discussions are currently focused on desired outcomes or objectives from which to form the basis of objective measurement across campuses, but under the leadership of the Professional and Organizational Development (POD) network, progress continues to be made (Bellows, 2008). A handful of studies suggest that institutions that offer graduate student development programs benefit in the areas of recruitment, retention, and job placement for their graduates (DeNeef, 1996; Lovitts & Nelson, 2000). In particular, measures of graduate student satisfaction tend to increase proportionately with the number of available graduate student development opportunities (Lovitts, 2004). At least on the surface, there seems to be no reason that institutions that do not confer doctoral degrees could not join in these benefits, but the graduate development programs would need to be adjusted to fit the career goals and expectations of students at SCUs and other master's-level universities.

At the SCU considered in this study, GAs work largely in two areas: teaching and research. A graduate development program exists, but like many other SCUs, the program is underdeveloped compared to those at research institutions where PFF initiatives are under way. For the purposes of a needs assessment, the Center for Teaching and Learning partnered with the Graduate School to survey GAs regarding their perceptions of career skills gained as part of their assistantships. The information was also intended to address gaps in the assistantship experience. As a case study, these data are not representative of the experience of GAs at all SCUs. However, its findings may be used to start the conversation. That being said, the purpose of this study is to begin to advance our understanding of graduate student development at SCUs.

## Method

### Data

In April 2010, an electronic survey was sent to all graduate students ($N = 302$) at an SCU in the southeastern United States who were employed as a GA at some point during the 2009–2010 academic school year. The survey asked the GAs to rate their competency in twenty-one transferable skills identified by the National Association of Colleges and Employers (NACE) Job Outlook Survey as important to a wide range of employers. (See table 13.1 for a listing of skills.) Each year, NACE surveys employers about employment-related issues in order to project the market for new graduates and to assess a variety of conditions that may influence that market (NACE, 2011). These versatile skills are the foundation of a variety of work, and students graduating with master's degrees from SCUs have a high likelihood of seeking employment in a wide range of jobs. Thus, it is crucial for SCUs to address these skills within the context of the graduate assistantship experience.

Respondents were also asked to rate and identify specific examples of how their GA experience influenced their competency level for each skill and comment on how effectively their mentor influenced the development of their transferable skills. GAs were also asked how well their GA duties fit their expectations of the position.

### Sample

A total of 114 GAs completed a questionnaire for a response rate of roughly 34 percent, adjusting for missing data. This response rate is quite respectable and surpasses that of many general population surveys (Cook, Heath, & Thompson, 2000). The majority (57 percent) of respondents reported they had been employed as a GA for two semesters, although 20 percent reported being employed as a GA for four semesters. Respondents were asked to select all GA job classifications that apply; most (57 percent) were employed as a research graduate assistant, while 32 percent, 28 percent, and 24 percent, respectively, were employed as a lab GA, administrative GA, or teaching GA (instructor of record). The characteristics of the sample resemble those in the institution's population of GAs for 2009–2010.

## Variables

For each of the twenty-one skills studied, respondents were asked to describe their level of competency on a four-point scale and the degree to which their experience as a GA influenced their competency in each skill. In addition to measuring the competencies individually, we also consider a twenty-one-item index measure of overall skill competency level (alpha = .859) and a twenty-one-item index measure of overall perceived influence of the graduate assistantship on skill competency level (alpha = .949).

GAs were asked how effectively their mentor, advisor, or supervisor influenced the development of their transferable skills (1 = Not Very Effectively, 2 = Somewhat Effectively, 3 = Moderately Effectively, 4 = Very Effectively). In addition, they were asked to comment on how effectively their mentor, advisor, or supervisor influenced the overall development of their transferable skills.

Respondents were asked how well their GA duties fit their expectations of the position (1 = Not at All, 2 = Somewhat Well, 3 = Moderately Well, and 4 = Very Well). They were also asked to provide an open-ended comment, if appropriate, about how well their GA duties fit their expectations of the position.

## Analysis

Our analyses focus on assessing how competent GAs are in transferable skills deemed valuable by a range of employers, as well as how their graduate assistantship at an SCU has influenced their competency. We offer a snapshot of our sample GAs' preparedness for employment outside academia and propose suggestions for improving training and development of GAs at SCUs.

## Results

Descriptive statistics for the twenty-one GA self-reported skill competencies are represented using medians and category percentages (see table 13.1). All self-reported skill competencies have median scores of 3 or 4, indicating that most GAs considered themselves competent (3) or very

Table 13.1  Descriptive Statistics for GA Self-Reported Skill Competencies

| Competency | Number | Median Score | Self-Reported Score | | | |
|---|---|---|---|---|---|---|
| | | | Not Competent | Somewhat Competent | Competent | Very Competent |
| Following instructions? | 103 | 4 | 0.0% | 1.9% | 35.9% | 62.1% |
| Listening to others? | 114 | 4 | 0.9 | 0.0 | 39.5 | 59.6 |
| Showing empathy to others? | 103 | 4 | 1.0 | 10.7 | 33.0 | 55.3 |
| Observing detail? | 107 | 3 | 0.0 | 8.4 | 43.0 | 48.6 |
| Communicating with others? | 103 | 3 | 0.0 | 4.9 | 46.6 | 48.5 |
| Using computers? | 103 | 3 | 0.0 | 8.7 | 43.7 | 47.6 |
| Writing? | 103 | 3 | 0.0 | 4.9 | 48.5 | 46.6 |
| Working on a team? | 103 | 3 | 1.0 | 5.8 | 46.6 | 46.6 |
| Scheduling? | 103 | 3 | 1.9 | 11.7 | 41.7 | 44.7 |
| Seeing patterns and connections? | 105 | 3 | 0.0 | 9.5 | 48.6 | 41.9 |
| Improvising solutions? | 106 | 3 | 0.0 | 10.4 | 49.1 | 40.6 |
| Asking others for ideas? | 106 | 3 | 0.9 | 10.4 | 48.1 | 40.6 |
| Coming up with new ideas? | 109 | 3 | 0.9 | 11.9 | 47.7 | 39.4 |
| Analyzing information? | 103 | 3 | 0.0 | 5.8 | 55.3 | 38.8 |
| Being precise? | 103 | 3 | 1.0 | 9.7 | 51.5 | 37.9 |
| Developing/mentoring others? | 111 | 3 | 0.0 | 5.4 | 60.4 | 34.2 |
| Seeing the big picture? | 103 | 3 | 0.0 | 11.7 | 54.4 | 34.0 |
| Evaluating options? | 105 | 3 | 1.0 | 7.6 | 60.0 | 31.4 |
| Planning detailed activity? | 103 | 3 | 1.0 | 20.4 | 50.5 | 28.2 |
| Designing things? | 103 | 3 | 1.0 | 27.2 | 48.5 | 23.3 |
| Living with ambiguity? | 103 | 3 | 1.9 | 32.0 | 44.7 | 21.4 |

competent (4) on each surveyed skill competency. This is also reflected in the percentages for each skill competency. GAs rate themselves most competent in following instructions and listening to others and least competent in living with ambiguity, designing things, and planning detailed activity.

Descriptive statistics for the influence of the GA experience on self-reported skill competencies are also represented using medians and category percentages (see table 13.2). Median results indicate that GAs reported their GA experience somewhat influenced (2) or influenced (3) their skill competencies. As indicated by the percentages, the skill competencies that were most influenced by the GA experience were communicating with others, developing/mentoring others, improvising solutions, analyzing information, coming up with new ideas, and scheduling. Those least influenced by the GA experience were writing, designing things, using computers, working in a team, and showing empathy to others.

Individual results from table 13.2 for the impact of the GA experience on skill competencies are consistent with GA responses to, "How effectively did your mentor, advisor, and/or supervisor influence the development of your transferable skills?" The median response indicates that GAs felt that their mentors were moderately effective in influencing their transferable skills (median = 3). Open-ended responses included common descriptions of mentors influencing GAs across an array of issues. One GA reported, "My mentor constantly addressed how my assistantship was creating and developing transferable skills. She also addressed how these skills may be desirable in the future in both academia and the workplace. She often offered and encouraged numerous helpful suggestions about future career paths and opportunities in both the professions of teaching and editing/publishing." Other GAs commented, "The mentor I observed taught me many things I still use, and I still ask her for advice even though I have a different mentor," and, "Truthfully, I would be lost without my advisor and his continued support."

In addition to these broad-based supports, students stated their mentors helped them communicate well with others. Examples include: "My two main mentors encouraged me to remain professional and dedicated, and they, along with my other mentors, helped me with skills to interact with people in order to complete my work as a GA," and, "I learned by my professors' example how best to communicate and tackle challenges." Often graduate students commented that communication skills developed during their GA experience were helpful for teaching: "I was given guidance in how to deal with students, how to give helpful feedback when grading papers, and how to best approach different course contents."

**Table 13.2  Descriptive Statistics for GA Self-Reported Influence of GA Experience on Skill Competencies**

| Competency | Number | Median Score | Self-Reported Score | | | |
| --- | --- | --- | --- | --- | --- | --- |
| | | | Did Not Influence | Somewhat Influenced | Influenced | Strongly Influenced |
| Developing/mentoring others? | 111 | 3 | 14.4% | 23.4% | 24.% | 37.% |
| Communicating with others? | 103 | 3 | 3.9 | 23.3 | 36.9 | 35.9 |
| Improvising solutions? | 106 | 3 | 8.5 | 30.2 | 29.2 | 32.1 |
| Analyzing information? | 103 | 3 | 10.7 | 31.1 | 28.2 | 30.1 |
| Coming up with new ideas? | 109 | 3 | 11.9 | 22.9 | 35.8 | 29.4 |
| Scheduling? | 103 | 3 | 13.6 | 28.2 | 29.1 | 29.1 |
| Working on a team? | 103 | 3 | 21.4 | 27.2 | 22.3 | 29.1 |
| Observing detail? | 107 | 3 | 11.2 | 29 | 33.6 | 26.2 |
| Asking others for ideas? | 106 | 3 | 11.3 | 31.1 | 32.1 | 25.5 |
| Following instructions? | 103 | 3 | 13.6 | 28.2 | 33.0 | 25.2 |
| Being precise? | 103 | 3 | 17.5 | 26.2 | 32.0 | 24.3 |
| Listening to others? | 114 | 3 | 13.2 | 25.4 | 41.2 | 20.2 |
| Evaluating options? | 105 | 3 | 12.4 | 28.6 | 40.0 | 19.0 |
| Seeing the big picture? | 103 | 3 | 16.5 | 33.0 | 36.9 | 13.6 |
| Writing? | 103 | 2 | 32.0 | 26.2 | 18.4 | 23.3 |
| Planning detailed activity? | 102 | 2 | 20.6 | 34.3 | 22.5 | 22.5 |
| Seeing patterns and connections? | 105 | 2 | 14.3 | 36.2 | 27.6 | 21.9 |
| Using computers? | 103 | 2 | 25.2 | 33.0 | 20.4 | 21.4 |
| Living with ambiguity? | 103 | 2 | 17.5 | 40.8 | 24.3 | 17.5 |
| Designing things? | 103 | 2 | 30.1 | 35.9 | 16.5 | 17.5 |
| Showing empathy to others? | 103 | 2 | 22.3 | 35.0 | 27.2 | 15.5 |

Regarding GA position fit to expectations, the median response indicates that GAs felt the position duties fit their expectations. Most indicated that the position met their expectations very well (median = 4). Likewise, open-ended responses reaffirmed that respondents found the job to be "challenging but not overwhelming" with "basic duties [that] were in line with my expectations."

Dependence between influence of the graduate assistantship and perceived skill competency variables is represented by gamma (see table 13.3). A statistically significant gamma value indicates how much we would reduce error in predicting the self-reported competency when we take the perceived influence of the graduate assistantship into account. The *t*-statistic and corresponding *p*-value indicate whether the relationship is statistically significant. The data in table 13.3 indicate statistically significant relationships for twelve of the twenty-one variables, based on a

Table 13.3   Gamma Values for Association between Influence of GA Experience on Skill Competencies and Self-Reported Skill Competencies

| Influence of GA Experience on Competency: Your Experience as a GA Influenced Your Competency in . . . | Number | Gamma Value | *t*-Value | *p*-Value |
|---|---|---|---|---|
| Coming up with new ideas? | 109 | 0.403 | 3.564 | 0.000 |
| Improvising solutions? | 106 | 0.501 | 4.099 | 0.000 |
| Designing things? | 103 | 0.479 | 4.212 | 0.000 |
| Developing/mentoring others? | 111 | 0.433 | 3.345 | 0.001 |
| Asking others for ideas? | 106 | 0.367 | 3.041 | 0.002 |
| Communicating with others? | 103 | 0.424 | 3.018 | 0.003 |
| Planning detailed activity? | 102 | 0.333 | 2.766 | 0.006 |
| Evaluating options? | 105 | 0.384 | 2.669 | 0.008 |
| Analyzing information? | 103 | 0.336 | 2.414 | 0.016 |
| Seeing patterns and connections? | 105 | 0.290 | 2.176 | 0.030 |
| Scheduling? | 103 | 0.272 | 2.166 | 0.030 |
| Working in a team? | 103 | 0.277 | 2.021 | 0.043 |
| Seeing the big picture? | 103 | 0.258 | 1.948 | 0.051 |
| Living with ambiguity? | 103 | 0.239 | 1.817 | 0.069 |
| Writing? | 103 | 0.207 | 1.561 | 0.119 |
| Showing empathy to others? | 103 | 0.206 | 1.487 | 0.137 |
| Following instructions? | 103 | 0.143 | 0.961 | 0.337 |
| Being precise? | 103 | 0.124 | 0.874 | 0.382 |
| Listening to others? | 114 | 0.057 | 0.399 | 0.690 |
| Using computers? | 103 | −0.026 | −0.199 | 0.843 |
| Observing detail? | 107 | 0.054 | 0.099 | 0.921 |

$p$-value of 0.05 or less. Eight of these twelve gamma values are significant at the $p < .01$ level and indicate a moderately strong, positive influence of the graduate assistantship on the skill competency level. The remaining four gamma values are significant at the $p < .05$ level and indicate a weak to moderate positive influence of the graduate assistantship on skill competency level.

The results in table 13.3 indicate that (1) GAs perceive themselves to be at least competent, if not very competent, in all skills, (2) they perceive that their GA experience at least somewhat influenced, if not influenced, their competency in all skills, and (3) a significant association exists between the influence of GA experience on skill competencies and self-reported skill competencies for more than half of the skills under consideration. Based on these findings, we consider the relationship between overall perceived influence of graduate assistantship experience on skill competencies and overall perceived skill competency as represented by two twenty-one item indices.

Table 13.4 presents descriptive statistics for each index. Results indicate GAs' average perception of overall skill competency is higher than their average overall perception of graduate assistantship influence on skill competency. However, results also indicate more diversity in scores for GAs' overall perception of graduate assistantship influence on skill competency.

Table 13.5. presents the results from linear regression analysis of overall skill competency on overall GA influence. Overall perceived influence of graduate assistantship on skill competency development has a significant, positive effect on overall perceived skill competency level. For every one unit increase in perceived overall influence of graduate assistantship on skill development, perceived overall skill competency level increased by .173 units ($p < .001$). Furthermore, perceived overall influence of graduate assistantship accounts for roughly 12.5 percent of the variance in perceived overall skill competency level.

---

Table 13.4  Descriptive Statistics for Twenty-One Item Indexes

| | Median | Mean | SD | Range | Minimum | Maximum |
|---|---|---|---|---|---|---|
| Overall GA influence on skill competency ($n = 102$) | 55.00 | 55.21 | 14.88 | 56.00 | 28.00 | 84.00 |
| Overall skill competency ($n = 103$) | 69.00 | 69.27 | 7.01 | 35.00 | 49.00 | 84.00 |

Table 13.5   Linear Regression of Overall Skill Competency on Overall
GA Influence ($N = 102$)

|  | B | SE | Beta |
|---|---|---|---|
| Overall GA Influence | .173*** | .044 | .366 |
| Constant | 59.697 | 2.515 | |
| Adjusted $R^2$ | .125 | | |

*$p$ <.05, **$p$ <.01, ***$p$ <.001.

## Discussion

The findings from this study suggest that the GA development experience at this SCU may not be uniform, which seems to be the case at other institutions as well (Anderson & Swazey, 1998; Redd, 2006). This is most likely due to the fact that graduate student development at the SCU in question mostly occurs in the context of individual graduate programs rather than an institutional graduate development program, many of which last only one day (Gray & Buerkel-Rothfuss, 1991). Most studies of graduate student socialization indicate the need to facilitate sustained development over time and across the major roles that graduate students typically inhabit (LaPidus, 1997), while at the same time taking institutional context into account. Weidman, Twale, and Stein (2001) suggest that institutional culture and peer climate are decisive factors in the graduate school experience. Graduate students at SCUs have shorter time frames in which to foster meaningful peer collaboration, as most programs last two years or less. In addition, they are more likely to interact with peers whose future plans do not include academia. Successful graduate development programs at SCUs need to take into account this distinctive contextual mixture.

The imperfect fit between the roles, context, and expectations of graduate students and their experiences at SCUs is evident in our survey results. One of the most noticeable gaps is between perception and reality of skill development. According to a recent comprehensive survey, undergraduate students, now more than ever before, rate their academic skills considerably higher than academic achievement indicators would suggest (Twenge, Campbell, & Gentile, 2011). Our findings indicate that a similar overconfidence may apply to graduate students, who ranked themselves competent or highly competent in all of the skills represented in our study. It is likely that this gap will only grow larger as current undergraduates transition into graduate study. This finding dovetails with other studies of self-reported abilities for graduate students, in which the majority of graduate student respondents ranked their teaching and other academic abilities at the highest levels prior to graduation (Meitl, 2008; Tompkins & Dimiduck, 2010). The phenomenon is sufficiently persistent that a minor field of study focused on managing overconfidence (at both the undergraduate and graduate levels) has emerged (Kruger & Dunning, 1999). In terms of building models for graduate student development, this gap between perception and reality represents a significant obstacle and potential point of resistance.

Our findings suggest a second notable gap in the communication of expectations, a factor that is often cited as significant in determining graduate student attrition rates (Golde & Dore, 2001). The majority of graduate students in this study come from undergraduate programs at SCUs within the same state. Many are the first in their families to attend graduate school, which may affect their expectations of the graduate experience. While many students found their GA experience consistent with expectations, as evidenced by a median score indicating GAs felt position duties fit their expectations "very well," others' experiences differed from what they anticipated. In open-ended responses, these students were frequently surprised by their GA duties, in both positive and negative ways. Regarding positive examples, GAs reported, "I was required to take more of a leadership position," and, "Working under [supervisor] has shown me the many sides of teaching . . . and [my field] better than I expected." Still other GAs stated their duties were worse than anticipated: "I was hoping to have more of a learning experience. I don't often feel challenged enough or a benefit to the department," and, "With the graduate research assistantship, I was disappointed with the limited interaction I had with my professor. I was eager to do research, but was not given as many tasks to complete or as much involvement with the research and writing as I had hoped."

At SCUs, perhaps more than at other institutional types, there is a need for foundational conversations about the nature of the graduate school experience. Part of the burden of responsibility for communicating these expectations rests on the faculty mentor or advisor. Many studies have emphasized the pivotal role of the mentor in graduate student development (Bair & Haworth, 1999; Boyle & Boice, 1998; Lovitts & Nelson, 2000; Park, 2004; Young & Bippus, 2008; Zhao, Golde, & McCormick, 2005), and graduate student satisfaction with mentor/advisor relationships tends to be higher at master's-level institutions (Conrad, Haworth, & Boulevard-Millers, 1993), a conclusion that is supported by previously discussed positive orientations towards advisors found in open-ended responses to our survey.

However, the importance of the mentoring relationship was also evident in responses that depicted mentors in a less-than-positive light. Some students struggled with lack of time with their mentor or lack of interaction: "[Supervisor] never ha[d] time for me, never interact[ed] with me, [taught] me, or allow[ed] me to help him with anything," and, "We didn't work together as often as I anticipated." These responses suggest the importance of faculty training for graduate student development. At SCUs, faculty members generally learn to mentor graduate students from their experience with their own mentors at doctoral-granting institutions, but that experience may be less applicable to the SCU environment. Few receive specific training in skills and experience needed in nonacademic job markets unless they had worked previously as practitioners in the field. This gap in faculty training is compounded by higher workload expectations that often characterize academic careers at SCUs, resulting in less time for faculty development and training, much less for their advisees (Henderson, 2006). Research on faculty expectations for graduate student work and learning outcomes might prove to be enlightening.

One of the strongest findings of our study is the clear disconnect between how students perceive or rate their transferable skills and how well they are able to identify, articulate, and use these skills. Most students identified teaching and research/scholarship/creative works as their primary responsibilities as GAs, but these experiences did not always translate into the transferable skills inventory. A handful mentioned help with career goals as a benefit to their experience, but largely in the context of teaching or research. For example, one respondent stated, "The teaching aspect . . . allowed me to experience firsthand the career I've chosen to pursue." This suggests a clear need for graduate development programs to include transferable skill education as an integral part of their offerings, a competency that traditional assistantships are not providing (Nettles & Millet, 2006).

## Conclusion

The self-reported competency in transferable skills found in our survey data provides important insight regarding GAs' perceived preparedness for future employment and perception of the degree of influence the assistantship had on level of preparedness. However, because our study looked at a cross-section of one cohort of graduate students at one SCU, it is limited in its applicability. Further research aimed at advancing understanding of graduate student development at SCUs should look at both broadening and deepening its scope. First and foremost, subsequent studies should include comparisons with other SCUs and other institutional types to reveal broader patterns of graduate experiences. Second, future studies should include longitudinal data to address generational issues suggested by the survey results, including information about pre- and postexperiences of the cohorts in question. Finally, more focused qualitative studies could be used to explore the lack of understanding regarding transferable skills revealed by our study. While our study provides a snapshot of how students view their current experiences, this does not immediately translate into appropriate practices for addressing future issues that arise. Further study is necessary to determine how to improve that experience for both current and future contexts.

This study represents a first step toward conceptualizing a model for graduate student development at SCUs. The results strongly suggest that there are distinct obstacles, cultural and social constructs, and gaps in communication and expectations in institutions that do not primarily train future faculty but are equally worthy of study, attention, and support. As we join broader movements to develop effective models for graduate student development at all levels, both PhD-granting institutions and master's-level institutions can learn much from one another in fostering viable, productive, and successful graduate students. This common commitment means turning outsiders into insiders.

REFERENCES

Abbott, R. D., Wulff, D. H., & Szego, C. K. (1989). Review of research on TA training. In J. Nyquist & R. Abbott (Eds.), *New directions for teaching and learning: No. 39. Teaching assistant training in the 1990s* (pp. 111–124). San Francisco, CA: Jossey-Bass.

Anderson, M. S., & Swazey, J. P. (1998). Reflections on the graduate student experience: An overview. In M. S. Anderson (Ed.), *New directions for higher education: No. 101. The experience of being in graduate school: An exploration* (pp. 3–13). San Francisco, CA: Jossey-Bass.

Austin, A. E., & Wulff, D. H. (2004). The challenge to prepare the next generation of faculty. In D. H. Wulff & A. E. Austin (Eds.), *Paths to the professoriate: Strategies for enriching the preparation of future faculty* (pp. 3–16). San Francisco, CA: Jossey-Bass.

Bair, C. R., & Haworth, J. G. (1999). *Doctoral student attrition and persistence: A meta-synthesis of research.* Paper presented at the annual meeting of the Association for the Study of Higher Education, San Antonio, TX.

Bellows, L. (2008). Graduate student professional development: Defining the field. *Studies in Graduate and Professional Student Development, 11*, 2–19.

Bellows, L.L.B., & Weissinger, E. (2005). Assessing the academic and professional development needs of graduate students. In S. Chadwick-Blossey & D. Reimondo Robertson (Eds.), *To improve the academy: Resources for faculty, instructional, and organizational development, Vol. 23* (pp. 267–83). Bolton, MA: Anker.

Border, L.L.B. (2006). Two inventories for best practice in graduate student development. *Journal on Excellence in College Teaching, 17*, 277–310.

Border, L.L.B., & von Hoene, L. M. (2010). Graduate and professional student development programs. In K. J. Gillespie, D. L. Robertson, & W. Bergquist (Eds.), *A guide to faculty development* (pp. 330–331). San Francisco, CA: Jossey-Bass.

Boyle, P., & Boice, B. (1998). Best practices for enculturation: Collegiality, mentoring, and structure. In M. S. Anderson (Ed.), *The experience of being in graduate school: An exploration* (pp. 87–94). San Francisco, CA: Jossey-Bass.

Chen, D. (2003). A classification system for metaphors about teaching. *Journal of Physical Education, Recreation, and Dance, 74*(2), 24–31.

Chism, N. (1998). Preparing graduate students to teach: Past, present and future. In M. Marinchovich, J. Prostko, & F. Stout (Eds.), *The professional development of graduate teaching assistant* (pp. 1–18). Bolton, MA: Anker.

Commission on Pathways through Graduate School and Careers. (2012), *Pathways through graduate school and careers*. Retrieved from http://www.ets.org/c/19574/19089_PathwaysReptqp.pdf

Conn, P. (2010, April 14). We need to acknowledge the realities of employment in the humanities. *Chronicle of Higher Education*. Retrieved from http://chronicle.com/article/We-Need-to-Acknowledge-the/64885/

Conrad, C. F., Haworth, J. C., & Boulevard-Millers, S. (1993). *A silent success: Master's education in the United States*. Baltimore, MD: Johns Hopkins University Press.

Cook, C., Heath, F., & Thompson, R. L. (2000). A meta-analysis of response rates in web- or Internet-based surveys. *Educational and Psychological Measurement, 60*(6), 821–836.

DeNeef, A. L. (1996). *The lessons of PFF concerning the job market*. Washington, DC: Association of American Colleges and Universities and Council of Graduate Schools.

Freeman, P. R., & Schmidt, J. C. (2000). An interdisciplinary teaching assistant training program at an MA institution. *Journal of Graduate Teaching Assistant Development, 7*(3), 126–141.

Gaff, J. G. (2002). Preparing future faculty and doctoral education. *Change*, *34*(6), 63–66.

Golde, C. M., & Dore, T. M. (2001). *At cross purposes: What the experiences of today's doctoral students reveal about doctoral education*. Retrieved from http://www.phd-survey.org

Gray, P. L., & Buerkel-Rothfuss, N. (1991). Teaching assistant training: A view from the trenches. In J. D. Nyquist, R. D. Abbott, D. H. Wulff, & J. Sprague (Eds.), *Preparing the professorate of tomorrow to teach* (pp. 40–51). Dubuque, IA: Kendall/Hunt.

Hagstrom, D., Hubbard, R., Hurtig, C., Mortola, P., Ostrow, J., & White, V. (2000). Teaching is like . . . ? *Educational Leadership*, *57*(8), 24–27.

Henderson, B. (2006). *Teaching at the people's university: An introduction to the state comprehensive university*. Bolton, MA: Anker.

Kruger, J., & Dunning, D. (1999). Unskilled and unaware of it: How difficulties in recognizing one's own incompetence lead to inflated self-assessments. *Journal of Personality and Social Psychology*, *77*, 1121–1134.

LaPidus, J. B. (1997). Doctoral education: Preparing for the future. *Journal of the American Physical Society*, *6*(11), 8.

Lambert, L. M., & Tice, S. L. (1993). *Preparing graduate students to teach: A guide to programs that improve undergraduate education and develop tomorrow's faculty*. Washington, DC: AAHE.

Lovitts, B. (2004). Research on the structure and process of graduate education: Retaining students. In D. H. Wulff & A. E. Austin (Eds.), *Paths to the professioriate: Strategies for enriching the preparation of future faculty* (pp. 115–136). San Francisco, CA: Jossey-Bass.

Lovitts, B. E., & Nelson, C. (2000). The hidden crisis in graduate education: Attrition from Ph.D. programs. *Academe*, *86*(6). Retrieved from http://www.aaup.org/AAUP/pubsres/academe/2000/ND/Feat/lovi.htm

Meitl, J. W. (2008). *Graduate teaching assistant (GTA) development*. Unpublished master's thesis, Oregon State University, Corvallis, Oregon.

National Association of Colleges and Employers. (2011). *Job outlook 2012*. Bethlehem, PA: Author.

National Association of Graduate-Professional Students. (2000). *The 2000 National Doctoral Program Survey*. Retrieved from http://www.nagps.org/survey2000

Nerad, M. (2004). The PhD in the US: Criticisms, facts, and remedies. *Higher Education Policy*, *17*(2), 183–199.

Nettles, M. T., & Millett, C. M. (2006). *Three magic letters: Getting to PhD*. Baltimore, MD: Johns Hopkins University Press.

Nyquist, J. D., Abbott, R. D., Wulff, D. H., & Sprague, J. (1991). *Preparing the professoriate of tomorrow to teach*. Dubuque, IA: Kendall/Hunt.

Park, C. (2004). The graduate teaching assistant: Lessons from a North American experience. *Teaching in Higher Education, 9*(3), 349–361.

Redd, K. E. (2006). Future shock! How immigration and demographic trends could affect financial aid and college enrollment. *Student Aid Transcript, 17*(2), 20–27.

Tompkins, L. J., & Dimiduck, K. (2010). *Confident or overconfident: Changes in the self-reported confidence levels of new teaching assistants pre- and post-training.* Paper presented to the annual ASEE (St. Lawrence Section) conference, Louisville, KY.

Twenge, J. M., Campbell, W. K., & Gentile, B. (2011). Generational increases in agentic self-evaluations among American college students, 1966–2009. *Self and Identity, 1*(1). doi:10.1080/15298868.2011.576820

Weidman, J., Twale, D., & Stein, E. (2001). *Socialization of graduate and professional students in higher education: A perilous passage?* San Francisco, CA: Jossey-Bass.

Wert, E. (1998). Foreword. In M. Marincovich, J. Prostko, & F. Stout (Eds.), *The professional development of graduate teaching assistants* (pp. xvii-xxii). Bolton, MA: Anker.

Young, S. L., & Bippus, A. M. (2008). Assessment of graduate teaching assistant (GTA) training: A case study of a training program and its impact on GTAs. *Communication Teacher, 22*(4), 116–129.

Zhao, C., Golde, C. M., & McCormick, A. C. (2005). *More than a signature: How advisor choice and advisor behavior affect doctoral student satisfaction.* Paper presented at American Educational Research Association Annual Meeting, Montreal, Canada.

# 14

# USING UNDERGRADUATES TO PREPARE INTERNATIONAL TEACHING ASSISTANTS FOR THE AMERICAN CLASSROOM

*Warren E. Christian, Brian J. Rybarczyk*
*University of North Carolina at Chapel Hill*

*This chapter describes how undergraduates may be used in the training of international teaching assistants (ITAs) in three ways: as conversation partners, classroom consultants, and guest instructors. Increasing the contact between undergraduates and international graduate students before they meet in the classroom as students and instructors can benefit each group. After a brief review of the literature that explores the challenges ITAs face in the American university classroom, we describe the roles that undergraduates may perform in training ITAs, explain the benefits to both ITAs and undergraduates, and provide a list of best practices for including undergraduates in ITA training.*

○

American universities continue to enroll a significant number of international graduate students. From 1980 to 1990, the number of doctoral degrees in the United States awarded to international students increased from 13 percent to 25 percent and has remained relatively stable since 1990 (National Center for Educational Statistics, 2012b).

While American universities continue to attract graduate students from around the world, the incorporation of international graduate students into American universities has not been seamless. One area where the discord is most evident is the relationship between American undergraduate students and international teaching assistants (ITAs).

Like many other graduate students, international graduate students are often called on to provide instruction to American undergraduates as teaching assistants, especially for larger, introductory courses where undergraduate students are less likely to have prior knowledge of basic discipline-specific concepts. Undergraduates commonly report that they cannot understand and cannot learn from their ITAs (Alberts, 2008; Bailey, 1983; Plakans, 1997; Williams, 2011). Those complaints of undergraduates have been heard outside the academy. In the 1980s and 1990s, more than fifteen states passed legislation mandating the English fluency of instructors in higher education in an effort to ensure that instruction is delivered in understandable English (Brown, Fishman, & Jones, 1990; King, 1998). Many universities have responded by designing programs to help ITAs acclimate to the expectations of the American university classroom and learn ways of communicating with American undergraduates. The training of ITAs has been a topic of academic research for over thirty years (Damarin & West, 1979; Kaplan, 1989; Kaufman & Brownworth, 2006; Kim & Kubota, 2012; Sarkisian, 1986; Smith & Ainsworth, 1987).

This chapter first gives a brief review of the literature that focuses on the sources and potential solutions to the challenges faced by ITAs in the American university classroom. Second, it discusses how the University of North Carolina (UNC) at Chapel Hill's Preparing International Teaching Assistants Program (PITAP) incorporates undergraduate volunteers into ITA preparation. Third, it identifies the benefits of the PITAP approach for both the international graduate students and undergraduate volunteers. A best practices section at the end shares advice on how to incorporate undergraduates incorporated into ITA training.

## ITA Literature

The ITA literature identifies three main actors in the communication difficulties between undergraduates and ITAs: ITAs, universities, and undergraduates. Most of this literature focuses on the role of ITAs. For example, ITAs sometimes do not have the English language proficiency skills, pedagogical skills, and cultural understanding necessary to be effective teachers in American classrooms. Some scholars explore the role that universities play in the sometimes strained relationships between ITAs and their undergraduate students. Other authors examine how undergraduate students' perspectives may contribute to the issues ITAs face.

Undergraduates, universities, and ITAs, however, are not monolithic groups. While most undergraduates in the United States are U.S. citizens and their first language is English, increasing numbers of undergraduates in the United States come from other countries and have a first language other than English.

ITAs come from all over the world and speak a variety of languages in their home countries, including English. In 2011, 63.9 percent of foreign students enrolled in American universities were from Asia (National Center for Educational Statistics, 2012c). The countries most represented were China (21.8 percent) and India (14.4 percent). In addition, foreign graduate students are not dispersed equally throughout all academic departments (National Center for Educational Statistics, 2012a). The fields with the highest percentages of doctoral degrees awarded to foreign students in 2011 were engineering (56 percent), computer and information sciences (50 percent), mathematics and statistics (47 percent), agriculture (41 percent), and physical sciences (41 percent).

## The Role of ITAs

There are many possible sources for undergraduates' complaints about ITAs. ITAs' English language skills are the most commonly given reason for communication breakdowns in the classroom. ITAs may not possess an extensive enough vocabulary in English needed to provide clear explanations (Alberts, 2008), and their nonstandard pronunciation patterns have been shown to promote miscommunication with undergraduate students (Anderson-Hsieh, 1990; Molholt, 1988; Morley, 1991). They sometimes place emphasis in the wrong areas—if they place emphasis at all (Hahn, 2004). Placing stress on certain words often marks new or contrasting information and aids listeners in understanding. ITAs may not make the correct tone choice needed to display empathy and involvement to American audiences. In addition, tone choice can change the connotative meaning of sentences (Pickering, 2001, 2004). ITAs may not make effective use of discourse markers that can be used to signal how ideas are related, draw attention to main points, transition between topics, and in general make speech more comprehensible (Tyler, 1992; Williams, 1992). While the literature points to ITAs' English language skills as the greatest potential source for miscommunication, it is not the only source.

ITAs' teaching skills and styles may not be appropriate for American undergraduate students. ITAs may not explain the connections between different pieces of course content and may fail to provide the necessary context, which impedes students' learning (Byrd & Constantinides, 1992). They do not always sufficiently elaborate their main points or direct students' attention to the most salient aspects of a lesson (Rounds, 1987; Williams, 1992). ITAs often do not express appropriate nonverbal actions to connect with students (Byrd & Constantinides, 1992; Jenkins & Parra, 2003). For instance, in the United States, making eye contact, smiling, and leaning forward may help signal involvement and listening.

The ITA literature indicates that many of the difficulties undergraduates encounter may be due to ITAs' different styles of teaching and English language use, but there is still at least one other possible source for miscommunication: cultural differences, which may also contribute to the strained relationships between ITAs and undergraduates. ITAs may come from an educational system where students are expected to be silent during class and not question their professors, and they may not deal well with American students who expect to participate actively and ask questions in the classroom (Sarkisian, 2006). ITAs and students may have different definitions about what constitutes appropriate classroom behavior and the roles that TAs or instructors in American university culture are expected to fill (Alberts, 2008; Ard, 1989; LeGros & Faez, 2012). ITAs are often unfamiliar with the secondary education experiences of American undergraduate students and thus have difficulty connecting new information with students' prior knowledge (Williams, 2011). Shiao-Yun Chiang and Han-Fu Mi (2008) point out that while ITAs' language may be understood, the meaning may still be lost due "partly to interactional procedures and partly to professional experiences that are both embedded deeply in one's sociocultural background" (p. 279). According to the literature related to ITAs' instruction of undergraduates, ITAs' language, teaching, and intercultural skills can cause perceived challenges for undergraduates. However, all of the onus for the relations between ITAs and undergraduates should not be placed on ITAs.

## The University's Role

While most of the literature describes how ITAs are responsible for the miscommunication in the classroom, some research emphasizes the university's role. Robert Kaplan (1989) argues that universities share some of the blame by thrusting international graduate students into teaching assistantships soon after they arrive in the country without adequate preparation. Michele Fisher (1985) urges universities to conduct self-studies in order to gauge how many international students they can adequately support. Others fault universities for not adequately testing international graduate students' English language skills prior to offering them admission or before assigning them instructional roles. These authors promote better language testing methods as an important response to the difficulties ITAs may face in American university classrooms (Halleck & Moder, 1995; Hoekje & Linnell, 1994; Xi, 2007; Yule & Hoffman, 1990).

Universities and ITAs each play a significant role in the sometimes tense interactions between undergraduates and ITAs, but the role of undergraduates should also be considered.

## The Undergraduates' Role

Commendably, some authors place a portion of the communicative burden on American undergraduates. Donald Rubin (1992) has conducted studies where American undergraduates are asked to evaluate a prerecorded lesson delivered by a native English speaker in standard American English. An image of a Caucasian woman meant to represent the instructor was shown to half of the students, and an image of an Asian woman was shown to the other half. Although all students heard the same recording, students shown the Asian woman performed worse in a test of listening comprehension and detected a nonexistent accent. Rubin concludes that no matter how well Asian ITAs are able to improve their spoken English and approximate American speech patterns, American undergraduates may still find fault with their teaching due to their Asianness.

When Fred Fitch and Susan Morgan (2003) examined undergraduates' stories about ITAs, they found a common narrative structure that viewed the ITA negatively, the undergraduate student as victim, and the university as the villain. They postulate that stories that portray ITAs negatively circulate throughout universities and account for much of undergraduates' apprehension toward ITAs. Donald Rubin and Kim Smith (1990) found that 40 percent of undergraduates actively avoided course sections taught by ITAs, and undergraduates who had more experience with ITAs were more likely to rate them favorably. According to some of the literature, undergraduates should share part of the blame for the challenges faced by ITAs in the American university classroom.

Realizing that undergraduates play a role in the strained classroom relationships between ITAs and undergraduates, Rubin (1992) advocates for programs that facilitate enjoyable gatherings between ITAs and American undergraduates. However, he laments, "such programs will require labor-intensive and time-intensive efforts, and will not be practical for the sort of large-scale sensitization needed on college campuses" (p. 528).

## The Solution

The most practical and widely used solution is training ITAs in the skills they need to develop to become effective instructors. These programs usually focus on a combination of English language skills, teaching skills, and intercultural communication. This generally occurs in one of four ways: orientations that take place a few days before the academic year begins; presession programs that last one to four weeks, usually before the semester begins; concurrent-term programs where ITAs enroll in a semester-long course as they engage in the roles of a TA; and preterm programs that last a full semester before students begin their TA responsibilities (Constantinides, 1989).

## Preparing International Teaching Assistants Program

PITAP was initiated in 2003 at UNC Chapel Hill, a large, research-intensive university, as a program to support the training of ITAs. The program consists of two semester-long courses: Communicating in the American University Classroom and Advanced Communicating in the American University Classroom. In line with the literature, the courses focus on improving international graduate students' English language skills, teaching skills, and intercultural communication skills. At UNC, the teaching and learning support unit for campus, the Center for Faculty Excellence, does not offer courses or programs targeted specifically to international graduate students. For this reason, PITAP courses are administered through the Graduate School. Each two-credit course is graded on a pass/fail basis. International graduate students enroll voluntarily in the courses, though sometimes at the behest of an advisor. The courses are designed for those who are currently providing instruction as a TA or who are likely to provide instruction as a TA in the future. PITAP currently serves approximately 15 international graduate students each semester. Since 2003, PITAP has served over 250 students.

Undergraduate student volunteers are recruited at the beginning of each academic year. The program seeks volunteers to serve in three ways: as conversation partners, classroom consultants, or guest instructors.

An advertisement is placed in the campus newspaper and e-mails are sent to listservs informing students of service-oriented opportunities. We have also had great success partnering with undergraduate courses that have a formal service-learning component and have a focus on teaching or international or cultural studies. These service-learning courses require thirty hours of volunteer service per semester that must relate to the topic of the course. The teaching and international aspects of PITAP have fit well with undergraduate service-learning courses in the fields of education and global studies. Some undergraduate volunteers accumulate hours to fulfill their commitment as university-recognized public service scholars.

We invite our volunteers to engage in as many service hours as they would like and invite student volunteers back each semester to continue accumulating service hours. Tapping into this resource of committed service-oriented undergraduate students has been effective, since the program continuously recruits undergraduate volunteers to support the needs of the program and since it is a mutually beneficial arrangement for both the undergraduates and PITAP. Each year, about ten undergraduates volunteer in varying ways.

Programs at other universities have used undergraduate volunteers as evaluators to help decide whether international graduate students are up to the task of being TAs, as guides in ITA workshops, and as commenters during ITA training (Civikly & Muchisky, 1991; Rubin, 1992; Schneider & Stevens, 1991).

## Conversation Partners

As part of the program's courses, international graduate students are required to keep a conversation log that provides space to reflect on their language development and progress over the course of the semester. Students must accumulate eight hours of conversations with at least three hours of conversation with American undergraduate students. On our course management website, we post e-mail addresses and short biographical paragraphs for each undergraduate volunteer. International graduate students contact undergraduate volunteers directly to set up a time and place to talk. Most meetings last between thirty minutes and one hour and take place on or near campus. When students or undergraduate volunteers ask what they should talk about during their conversations, we propose that they may be interested in discussing each other's cultures, similar nonacademic interests, and campus life, for example. We also advise students and volunteers to keep conversations informal. We remind students that undergraduate volunteers are experts in undergraduate culture and can provide insights into the lives of American undergraduate students in a way that instructors may not be able to provide.

The purpose of the conversation partners is two-fold. It gives ITAs a chance to practice their informal conversational skills and allows them to get to know undergraduate students. International graduate students are often much more comfortable when speaking in English about their field of study. They are already familiar with the field and often can predict where a conversation is headed. In informal conversation, however, the topic will likely not be in their field of expertise. Also, the topic of discussion can change at a moment's notice, and the course the conversation will take can be very difficult to predict. Our students often say that informal conversations are more difficult than their more formal discussions with peers and colleagues in their same field.

The required conversation partner interactions allow international graduate students to practice these more challenging, informal conversations. In addition, informal conversations allow international graduate students to practice their listening and speaking skills in a realistic setting. We encourage these students to seek feedback from their conversation partners about their English language skills. We also ask them to reflect on what aspects of their English language skills are improving and identify areas where they have room for growth.

Getting to know undergraduate students outside the classroom setting can be beneficial to ITAs as well. One important part of effective teaching is developing rapport with students. Although all graduate students are usually somewhat disconnected from undergraduates, international graduate students are often even more disconnected because of cultural differences, engagement in courses only with other graduate students, and a focus on their scholarship and research productivity. For American TAs, this separation from undergraduates is usually not a problem because they can draw on their own experiences as former undergraduates to help them relate to the undergraduate students they are teaching. International students do not have the same luxury. It will be more difficult for ITAs to develop rapport with American undergraduate students if their only contact with undergraduates comes while they are teaching. By meeting with undergraduate students in a relaxed atmosphere, ITAs can learn about ways to connect with undergraduates. The conversations also provide ITAs with insight into American undergraduate culture, what American undergraduates' value, and what their goals are. ITAs may then use this knowledge to help develop rapport with undergraduate students in their courses. Undergraduates may be able to give ITAs practical advice about different campus and local events, ways to get around town, and where to find different goods and services. When ITAs have already had some informal contact with American undergraduate students, a class full of American undergraduates will seem less foreign and less daunting.

Undergraduates who participate as conversation partners also benefit from the experience. They get firsthand experience interacting with students from different cultures. Many of our volunteers have academic interests related to international relations. Talking with international graduate students can help undergraduates contextualize some course content. Sometimes undergraduate volunteers have sought advice about class projects or writing assignments from international graduate students. In several instances, these volunteers have used the opportunity to learn more about a country that they have visited or may visit in the future. Some conversation partners have had a conversation in English and then had a conversation in the first language of the international graduate students when it is also a target language of the undergraduate volunteer. And questions from international students may provide undergraduate students with an opportunity to think critically about elements of American and university cultures.

## Classroom Consultants

Undergraduate volunteers may also be involved in PITAP as classroom consultants. International graduate students enrolled in PITAP courses perform a series of ten-minute microteachings where they teach material from their discipline to the class. During class days when these demonstrations are scheduled, we invite the undergraduate volunteers to join the class to provide feedback. During each microteaching, everyone present in the class (instructors, peers, and undergraduate volunteers) completes a rubric that asks for an evaluation of presentation skills, teaching skills, and task-specific skills. Undergraduate volunteers are instructed to act as if they are in a regular undergraduate class asking questions when they do not understand or need clarification. After each microteaching demonstration, undergraduates, along with international graduate students in the audience, are called on to deliver feedback and suggestions for teaching improvement.

Having undergraduates present during microteachings is beneficial to the international graduate students. Our students observe how undergraduates behave in a classroom setting, gain insight into undergraduates' learning needs and progress, and learn effective and ineffective teaching strategies from an undergraduate perspective. If at the end of an observed lesson, undergraduate volunteers report that they learned something new and achieved the desired learning goals of the lesson, then international graduate students know that they have been effective. This small success can help reduce the anxiety that they feel when confronting a classroom full of American undergraduates for the first time.

When giving feedback to international graduate students, undergraduate volunteers frequently validate what we have previously discussed in class. For example, we often urge our graduate students in mathematics and statistics to begin a lesson with an example or use real numbers rather than a complex formula with unfamiliar variables. Undergraduate students have offered similar advice when providing feedback. Hearing the same message from undergraduates is perhaps more salient than hearing it from instructors.

Undergraduates who participate as classroom consultants are asked to think reflectively about their own learning. This opportunity for reflection can help students take ownership of their learning and help them realize what aspects of different teaching styles they find beneficial for their learning. Some classroom consultants have said that the experience has helped them imagine the perspective of instructors and has informed their own presenting and teaching styles.

## Undergraduates as Instructors

On two occasions, we have had undergraduate volunteers develop and deliver lessons to ITAs. The volunteers created a lesson on undergraduate culture and another lesson on idioms and slang common among undergraduates. In both cases, undergraduates gave the graduate students direct insight regarding undergraduates that is inaccessible to us as instructors. For instance, undergraduates taught many contemporary slang terms that we were unaware of but that undergraduate students use frequently in their informal interactions with each other. Undergraduates are often in the best position to provide information about university culture.

A potential area of concern that arises when volunteers serve as conversation partners and classroom consultants is that undergraduates will see themselves in a superior role to international graduate students. Undergraduate volunteers may feel their role is to pass their knowledge on to the international graduate students. They may feel their responsibility is to serve and teach the international graduate students and not also to learn and benefit from their interaction with international graduate students. Yet, paradoxically, having undergraduate volunteers teach a lesson can increase the sense that they are learning from international graduate students. During the microteaching demonstrations, undergraduate volunteers who teach a lesson are not only providing feedback; they are also learning from the successes and miscues of international graduate students. As conversation partners, undergraduate volunteers who will go on to provide instruction can use the conversations as an opportunity to gather information that will help structure their planned lesson and make it more relevant and useful to the graduate students. Having the undergraduates teach a lesson helps to place international graduate students and undergraduate volunteers in a similar position where they both can learn from each other. Both can also commiserate about the anxiety that often accompanies teaching. When both international graduate students and undergraduate volunteers offer lessons, they are on a more equal footing.

Undergraduates who serve as guest instructors gain valuable teaching experience. They create learning goals, develop and then implement a lesson plan, and practice managing a classroom. They can gain confidence in their teaching abilities by instructing graduate students in an authentic teaching environment.

## Evaluation

On course evaluations, PITAP students have routinely rated undergraduate students' involvement as one of the most helpful aspects of the course. During the fall 2010 semester, the course incorporated extensive undergraduate involvement in two sections with fifteen international graduate students. Following the course, PITAP students rated feedback from undergraduates associated with microteaching demonstrations above all other aspects, including feedback from instructors, feedback from peers, and reviewing a video of their microteaching demonstration. Two-thirds of the PITAP students rated their interactions with undergraduate conversation partners as "very important and beneficial" or "extremely important and essential to the course." Two-thirds of the PITAP students also rated the session on undergraduate culture taught by undergraduate volunteers as "very important and beneficial" or "extremely important and essential to the course." PITAP students reported that their "confidence as a TA" improved from prior to taking the course to after taking the course. Half of the students rated their confidence as "below average" prior to the course and over two-thirds rated their confidence as "above average" after the course. PITAP students have expressed gratitude for the opportunity to get to know undergraduate students.

## Suggested Best Practices for Incorporating Undergraduates

We have organized the best practices that we have found in incorporating undergraduates in ITA training into four areas: recruitment and orientation of undergraduate volunteers, conversation partners, classroom consultants, and guest instructors.

### Recruitment and Orientation of Undergraduate Volunteers

- Recruit undergraduate volunteers through student newspapers, community-service-oriented listservs, and undergraduate courses and majors related to education and international relations.
- Encourage undergraduate volunteers to invite their friends to volunteer.
- Hold a brief orientation for interested undergraduate volunteers. Explain different ways to serve and allow undergraduates to choose how they would like to participate.
- Send e-mails to volunteers to let them know about upcoming microteaching dates, invite them to participate in any upcoming international events, and thank them for their service.

### Conversation Partners

- Post volunteers' contact information on a course management website so that ITAs have easy access to the information.
- Let volunteers know that they need not meet with every ITA who contacts them, but they should respond to every request.
- Encourage ITAs to start their conversation log early in the semester as everyone tends to get busy toward the end of the semester. Also, they should check with ITAs regularly about their progress in completing the log.
- Have a conversation log template that asks ITAs to record information about conversations including topics discussed, any new words or phrases encountered, what went well during the conversation, challenges, any feedback given, and linguistic areas they would like to improve.
- Collect conversation logs at the end of the semester and provide written feedback.

### Classroom Consultants

- At an orientation, have potential volunteers practice giving feedback after viewing a sample recorded microteaching demonstration.

○ Throughout the semester, ask classroom consultants to give general feedback to the class as a whole about where they see progress and where they see opportunities for improvement.

○ Ask volunteers to give constructive, actionable feedback that highlights both successful strategies and aspects to work on.

### Guest Instructors

○ Meet with undergraduate volunteers at the beginning of the semester to brainstorm potential topics. Encourage volunteers to look at the topics covered in the syllabus and pick one of those topics or propose a new topic.

○ Encourage volunteers to use the knowledge gained as a conversation partner and classroom consultant to inform their lesson.

○ Before the guest lecture, review a lesson plan with the undergraduate volunteers.

## Conclusion

Both international graduate students and undergraduate volunteers benefit from involvement with PITAP. While international graduate students learn about American undergraduate culture, undergraduates learn about different parts of the world in an informal, relaxed atmosphere. The relationships developed between ITAs and undergraduate volunteers help to reduce anxiety for each when they encounter other ITAs or undergraduates in a classroom setting. The contact with undergraduate volunteers helps to prepare PITAP students to be effective TAs, thereby benefiting all undergraduate students and the university as a whole.

PITAP allows both graduate and undergraduate students to practice their teaching and presenting skills while learning from one another. Through their interactions, ITAs and undergraduate volunteers recognize their differences and similarities. For both groups, being able to communicate effectively, teach, and learn from someone from another part of the world and a different culture will likely prove to be a very important skill.

REFERENCES

Alberts, H. C. (2008). The challenges and opportunities of foreign born-instructors in the classroom. *Journal of Geography in Higher Education*, *32*(2), 189–203.

Anderson-Hsieh, J. (1990). Teaching suprasegmentals to international teaching assistants using field-specific materials. *English for Specific Purposes, 9*(3), 195–214.

Ard, J. (1989). Grounding an ITA curriculum: Theoretical and practical concerns. *English for Specific Purposes, 8,* 125–138.

Bailey, K. (1983). Foreign teaching assistants at U.S. universities: Problems in interaction and communication. *TESOL Quarterly, 17*(2), 308–310.

Brown, K. A., Fishman, P. F., & Jones, N. L. (1990). Legal and policy issues in the language proficiency assessment of international teaching assistants. *IHELG Monograph, 90*(1).

Byrd, P., & Constantinides, J. C. (1992). The language of teaching mathematics: Implications for training ITAs. *TESOL Quarterly, 26*(1), 163–167.

Chiang, S. Y., & Mi, H. F. (2008). Reformulation as a strategy for managing "understanding uncertainty" in office hour interactions between international teaching assistants and American college students. *Intercultural Education, 19*(3), 269–281.

Civikly, J. M., & Muchisky, D. M. (1991). A collaborative approach to ITA training: The ITAs, faculty, TAs, undergraduate interns, and undergraduate students. In J. Nyquist, R. Abbott, D. Wulff, & J. Sprague (Eds.), *Preparing the professoriate of tomorrow to teach* (pp. 356–360). Dubuque, IA: Kendall-Hunt.

Constantinides, J. C. (1989). ITA training programs. In J. D. Nyquist & R. D. Abbott (Eds.), *New directions for teaching and learning: No. 39. Teaching assistants in the 1990s* (pp. 71–77). San Francisco, CA: Jossey-Bass.

Damarin, S., & West, G. (1979). Preparation of foreign graduate students to teach mathematics: An experimental course. *American Mathematical Monthly, 86*(6), 494–497.

Fisher, M. (1985). Rethinking the "foreign TA problem." In J.D.W. Andrews (Ed.), *New directions for teaching and learning: No. 22. Strengthening the teaching assistant faculty* (pp. 63–73).

Fitch, F. F., & Morgan, S. E. (2003). "Not a lick of English": Constructing the ITA identity through student narratives. *Communication Education, 52*(3), 297–310.

Hahn, L. D. (2004). Primary stress and intelligibility: Research to motivate the teaching of suprasegmentals. *TESOL Quarterly, 38*(2), 201–223.

Halleck, G. B., & Moder, C. L. (1995). Testing language and teaching skills of international teaching assistants: The limits of compensatory strategies. *TESOL Quarterly, 29*(4), 733–758.

Hoekje, B., & Linnell, K. (1994). "Authenticity" in language testing: Evaluating spoken language tests for international teaching assistants. *TESOL Quarterly, 28*(1), 103–126.

Jenkins, S., & Parra, I. (2003). Multiple layers of meaning in an oral proficiency test: The complementary roles of nonverbal, paralinguistic, and verbal behaviors in assessment decisions. *Modern Language Journal, 87*(1), 90–107.

Kaplan, R. B. (1989). The life and times of ITA programs. *English for Specific Purposes, 8*(2), 109–124.

Kaufman, D., & Brownworth, B. (Eds.). (2006). *Professional development of international teaching assistants.* Alexandria, VA: TESOL.

Kim, S., & Kubota, R. (2012). Supporting nonnative English-speaking instructors to maximize student learning in their courses: A message from the guest editors. *Journal on Excellence in College Teaching, 23*(3), 1–6.

King, K. (1998). Mandating English proficiency for college instructors: States' responses to the "TA problem." *Vanderbilt Journal of Transnational Law, 31*, 203–256.

LeGros, N., & Faez F. (2012). The intersection between intercultural competence and teaching behaviors: A case of international teaching assistants. *Journal on Excellence in College Teaching, 23*(3), 7–31.

Molholt, G. (1988). Computer-assisted instruction in pronunciation for Chinese speakers of American English. *TESOL Quarterly, 22*(1), 91–111.

Morley, J. (1991). The pronunciation component in teaching English to speakers of other languages. *TESOL Quarterly, 25*(3), 481–520.

National Center for Educational Statistics. (2012a). *Doctor's degrees conferred by degree-granting institutions, by race/ethnicity and field of study: 2009–10 and 2010–11* [Table]. Retrieved from http://nces.ed.gov/programs/digest /d12/tables/dt12_307.asp

National Center for Educational Statistics. (2012b). *Doctor's degrees conferred by degree-granting institutions, by race/ethnicity and sex of student: Selected years, 1976–77 through 2010–11* [Table]. Retrieved from http://nces.ed .gov/programs/digest/d12/tables/dt12_306.asp

National Center for Educational Statistics. (2012c). *Foreign students enrolled in institutions of higher education in the United States, by continent, region, and selected countries of origin: Selected years, 1980–81 through 2010–11* [Table]. Retrieved from http://nces.ed.gov/programs/digest/d12/tables /dt12_236.asp

Pickering, L. (2001). The role of tone choice in improving ITA communication in the classroom. *TESOL Quarterly, 35*(2), 233–255.

Pickering, L. (2004). The structure and function of intonational paragraphs in native and nonnative speaker instructional discourse. *English for Specific Purposes, 23*, 19–43.

Plakans, B. S. (1997). Undergraduates' experiences with and attitudes toward international teaching assistants. *TESOL Quarterly, 31*(1), 95–119.

Rounds, P. L. (1987). Characterizing successful classroom discourse for NNS teaching assistant training. *TESOL Quarterly, 21*(4), 643–671.

Rubin, D. L. (1992). Nonlanguage factors affecting undergraduates' judgments of nonnative English-speaking teaching assistants. *Research in Higher Education, 33*(4), 511–531.

Rubin, D. L., & Smith, K. A. (1990). Effects of accent, ethnicity, and lecture topic on undergraduates' perceptions of nonnative English-speaking teaching assistants. *International Journal of Intercultural Relations, 14*, 337–353.

Sarkisian, E. (1986). Learning to teach in an American classroom: Narrowing the culture and communication gap for foreign teaching assistants. In M. Svinicki, J. Kurfiss, & J. Stone (Eds.), *To improve the academy: Resources for faculty, instructional, and organizational development, Vol. 5* (pp. 120–131). Stillwater, OK: POD and New Forums Press.

Sarkisian, E. (2006). *Teaching American students: A guide for international faculty and teaching assistants in colleges and universities* (3rd ed.). Cambridge, MA: Harvard University Press.

Schneider, K., & Stevens, S. G. (1991). American undergraduate students as trainers in an international teaching assistant training program. In J. Nyquist, R. Abbott, D. Wulff, & J. Sprague (Eds.), *Preparing the professoriate of tomorrow to teach* (pp. 361–367). Dubuque, IA: Kendall-Hunt.

Smith, R. M., & Ainsworth, C. L. (1987). It's working: A training program for foreign teaching assistants. In J. Kurfiss, L. Hilsen, L. Mortensen, & E. Wadsworth (Eds.), *To improve the academy: Resources for faculty, instructional, and organizational development, Vol. 6* (pp. 157–167). Stillwater, OK: POD and New Forums Press.

Tyler, A. (1992). Discourse structure and the perception of incoherence in international teaching assistants' spoken discourse. *TESOL Quarterly, 26*(4), 713–729.

Williams, G. M. (2011). Examining classroom negotiation strategies of international teaching assistants. *International Journal for the Scholarship of Teaching and Learning, 5*(1), 1–16.

Williams, J. (1992). Planning, discourse marking, and the comprehensibility of international teaching assistants. *TESOL Quarterly, 26*(4), 693.

Xi, X. (2007). Validating TOEFL iBT speaking and setting score requirements for ITA screening. *Language Assessment Quarterly, 4*(4), 318–351.

Yule, G., & Hoffman, P. (1990). Predicting success for international teaching assistants in a U.S. university. *TESOL Quarterly, 24*(2), 227–243.

15

# TOMORROW'S PROFESSOR TODAY

TRACKING PERCEPTIONS OF PREPARATION FOR
FUTURE FACULTY COMPETENCIES

*Michael S. Palmer, Deandra Little*
*University of Virginia*

*The University of Virginia's Tomorrow's Professor Today (TPT) program is a broadly conceived graduate student professional development program designed to facilitate the transition from student to academic professional. Begun in 2005 in response to the recommendations of a number of national reform initiatives, TPT focuses on improving preparedness in three key areas: teaching, research, and service. We describe the key elements of the program and ongoing assessment efforts. Pre- and postprogram participant surveys from the first eight years show that TPT is improving perceptions of preparedness in twenty-one competencies tracked; follow-up studies support long-term impact.*

○

In 2005, the University of Virginia (UVa) Teaching Resource Center developed the Tomorrow's Professor Today (TPT) program, a graduate student professional development program designed to facilitate the transition from student to academic professional. Our program design was

We thank Tatiana Mathews and Ashley McHugh for help with data entry and Melissa Hurst, director of the University of Virginia Graduate Career Development, for statistical analysis of pre- and post-TPT survey data.

251

influenced by needs expressed locally by UVa graduate students, as well as research emerging from a number of national reform initiatives (Fagan & Suedkamp Wells, 2004; Gaff, 2002; Gaff, Pruitt-Logan, & Weibl, 2000; Goldsmith, Haviland, Daily, & Wiley, 2004; Nyquist & Woodford, 2000; Walker, 2004; Walker et al., 2008) and research focused on areas of mismatch between what junior faculty are expected to do and their doctoral training (Adams, 2002; Austin, 2002; Austin & Wulff, 2004; Berberet, 2008; Gaff, 2002; Wulff & Austin, 2004). Overall, these studies recommended increasing support for graduate students to better prepare them for a wide range of faculty roles and help them more clearly understand what an academic career entails. Specifically they recommend that teaching preparation be strengthened and that doctoral students be given more opportunities to explore innovative teaching techniques and fine-tune their teaching skills. Of the responsibilities new faculty take on, teaching often demands the most immediate attention and consumes the most time and energy. Finally, they advocate more robust and better-integrated professional development experiences for graduate students.

In response, we designed our program to improve doctoral student preparedness in three key areas—teaching, research, and service—and we divided program activities accordingly into three categories: for the classroom, for the profession, and at the university. Our goals were to design a program in which participants gain teaching abilities and credentials, are introduced to many of the responsibilities university faculty face, become better prepared for the challenges they will face in their future academic careers, and gain a broader understanding of how the various components of their graduate experience relate to one another in their current and future careers. When designing the program, we also considered a set of related oppositions:

o Providing structure through set program requirements while allowing flexibility and individual choice

o Balancing interdisciplinary networking outside individual departments with the need for specialized professional guidance best found within them

o Requiring a number of activities within a focused time frame while also encouraging reflection on the relative value of those experiences

o Creating a rigorous, effective program without being perceived as taking too much time away from participants' research and teaching responsibilities

In response to the challenges outlined by the reform initiatives and our program considerations, we incorporated into TPT many features common to existing graduate student professional development programs (Bellows, 2008; Border & von Hoene, 2010; Palmer, 2011) that address the full scope of faculty roles and responsibilities, including an emphasis on how these responsibilities differ with institutional contexts (Goldsmith et al., 2004). Generally TPT program activities include informational workshops, practical hands-on exercises, and reflection opportunities. Workshop topics range and fit into the three broad categories. For the Classroom workshops contribute to participants' understanding of student learning and teaching improvement. Ones that fit the For the Profession category focus on other topics that help prepare doctoral students for successful graduate careers, navigating the academic job market, and transitioning to an academic career afterward. Activities in the final category, At the University, focus on life as a faculty member, and include such topics as "What is service?" or "Lessons learned my first year as a professor." The hands-on exercises and reflection opportunities also fall into the three categories, and most are common to other future faculty programs (Border & von Hoene, 2010; Palmer, 2011). Participants, for example, must design course components including a syllabus, compose a reflective teaching statement, consult with teaching center staff on some aspect of teaching, and present research at a regional or national conference. Although we specify the type and number of activities they complete in each of these areas, such as twenty hours of workshop attendance, participants have the freedom to complete many of the activities in settings or on specific topics that fit their career goals.

Compared to similar programs, TPT is unique in several ways:

o During their first semester, participants take a six-week, noncredit seminar, Foundations of Scholarly Teaching.

o Regardless of their teaching status, participants are required to teach at least five hours, which requires those with research assistantships to seek outside opportunities to guest-lecture, lead a review session, teach at a local college, or facilitate teaching workshops.

o Participants conduct at least two informational interviews—one of a faculty member and one of a higher education administrator from UVa or a different type of institution.

o Participants are required to take on a service role in their department, at the university, or within an academic organization.

o As a capstone experience, participants write two short reflective essays exploring the most valuable things they learn during the program, placing them in the context of their own teaching or professional development. In these essays, participants might describe, analyze, and evaluate a teaching practice or discuss future changes they would make to a course after examining student learning or teaching practices.

Program design also strikes a balance between interdisciplinary and discipline-specific concerns. TPT participants are chosen to represent a wide range of disciplines within UVa's College of Arts and Sciences and several of its professional schools. This disciplinary diversity requires the program to be highly flexible to allow participants to complete the many program requirements in various ways. Although TPT is interdisciplinary, it is also designed to be discipline focused, delegating ultimate program advising responsibilities to participant-selected faculty advisors in their own or related disciplines. Participants choose an advisor who can offer professional advice, provide feedback on their program materials, and help the participant develop a plan to reach his or her future career goals. This aspect of TPT allows participants to tailor the program to meet their specific professional development needs and socialize them into the specific practice of their disciplinary communities (Golde, 2011). The participant and faculty advisor decide when the participant has sufficiently met the program requirements. Integrating both interdisciplinary and disciplinary components fosters community building among program participants and networking opportunities outside departmental silos, while also offering space for individualized, discipline-based professional development mentoring.

In sum, TPT participants engage in a wide range of activities sponsored by the teaching center and other university units to help them prepare for their future academic pursuits. Working closely with their faculty advisor, participants gain teaching abilities and credentials while being introduced to many of the responsibilities that university faculty and administrators face. As the assessment data we present show, participants complete the program with a more comprehensive understanding of how the various components of their graduate experience relate to one another and are better prepared for the challenges they will face in their future careers.

## Participant Selection and Completion

### Application Process

The TPT program attracts graduate students curious about or planning a career in academia. During the pilot year (2005), we invited applications from graduate students in five Arts and Sciences departments to apply and selected thirteen. In subsequent years, we opened the applicant pool to all UVa graduate students and began selecting approximately twenty-five new participants each year. As the program matured and developed a positive reputation, the number of applications has increased, and the acceptance rate has decreased from approximately 75 percent to 40 percent.

In addition to an abridged CV and a signed agreement that they understand the program requirements, applicants address three questions with short narratives explaining their motivations for, level of interest in, and individual goals for the program. The selection committee bases its decisions on applicants' responses to these prompts but also considers other factors, including balance among disciplines. This process has allowed us to form a highly diverse and interdisciplinary cohort each year.

## Participant Pool

To date, 192 graduate students, representing thirty-five distinct departments from the College of Arts and Sciences (CLAS) and three of UVa's professional schools (Curry School of Education, EDUC; School of Engineering and Applied Sciences, SEAS; and School of Nursing, NURS), have participated in TPT. The overall participant distribution across broad disciplinary groupings is shown in table 15.1. The majority of participants (68.2 percent) come from CLAS. Within CLAS, participants

Table 15.1    Overall and Gender-Separated Participant Distributions across Broad Disciplinary Groupings

|  | CLAS | | | Professional Schools | | | |
|---|---|---|---|---|---|---|---|
|  | Science and Math | Humanities | Social Science | SEAS | NURS | EDUC | Total |
| Total participants | 55(28.6) | 41(21.4) | 35(18.2) | 48(25.0) | 7(3.6) | 6(3.1) | 192 |
| Total female participants | 38(19.8) | 30(15.6) | 22(11.5) | 25(13.0) | 7(3.6) | 4(2.1) | 126(65.6) |
| Total male participants | 17(8.9) | 11(5.7) | 13(6.8) | 23(12.0) | 0(0.0) | 2(1.0) | 66(34.4) |

Note: Numbers in parentheses are percentages with respect to the total number of program participants ($N = 192$).

are more likely to come from science and math disciplines (42.0 percent) than humanities (32.3 percent) and social science ones (26.7 percent). Graduate students from SEAS account for 25.0 percent of participants. NURS and EDUC round out the TPT participant pool, accounting for 3.6 and 3.1 percent, respectively. These percentages are consistent with overall graduate enrollment figures at UVa. The combined current doctoral enrollments from these four schools is approximately 2,371 graduate students, comprising 70.6 percent from CLAS, 17.5 percent from SEAS, 1.9 percent from NUC, and 10.0 percent from EDUC (UVa Office of Institutional Assessment and Studies, 2012a). Comparing these enrollments figures with program participation, we see slight underrepresentation from CLAS and EDUC and overrepresentation from SEAS and NURS.

While tracking participation along disciplinary lines, we have noticed unexpected trends related to gender. Curiously, female graduate students make up 65.6 percent of the total TPT participant pool and are two to three times more likely to participate in the program than their male counterparts in almost every disciplinary grouping. In CLAS, where overall enrollments are nearly gender equal, we see a 69:31 split favoring female participation in TPT. In SEAS, where overall enrollments are consistently skewed toward male students (29:71), we see a gender-neutral distribution (52:48) in TPT. Although the female-to-male ratio here is essentially equal, TPT still oversamples the female population significantly when the overall enrollment numbers are considered. The reason for these imbalances is unclear, whether due to institutional or department cultures, some aspect of the application process, or even gender-related stereotyping or patterns of behavior on the part of applicants or their advisors. To the best of our knowledge, there is no reference in the literature to gendered participation trends in graduate student professional development programs, an area where additional research is warranted.

To make sure the selection process is not selectively biased toward female participants, we examined the gender composition of the entire applicant pool. We find that the gender distributions for the portion of the TPT applicant pool not accepted into the program are nearly identical to that of the participant pool; of those who applied but were not accepted, 60 percent were female and 40 percent were male. This suggests that the overall participant profile of TPT is representative of the applicant pool. The only notable exceptions are NURS and EDUC, where students in these disciplines make up 9.5 and 11.9 percent of the rejection pool, respectively, but only 3.6 and 3.1 percent of the participant pool.

*Program Completion*

To date, 83 of the 192 TPT participants (43.2 percent) have completed all program requirements. Of these, 59 are female (71.2 percent) and 24 are male (28.9 percent). On average, it takes participants 2.35 years to complete all program requirements, although 3 have completed it in as few as one year and 6 have taken as many as four to five years.

Forty-six participants (24.0 percent) left the program without finishing: 27 women (58.7 percent) and 19 men (41.3 percent). These participants typically leave in the first year of the program for a number of reasons, most commonly citing an immediate job offer. Other reasons are changes in career path, discontinuation of doctoral studies, and work/life balance issues.

Currently, 63 participants remain active in the program—40 women (63.5 percent) and 23 men (36.5 percent)—which mirrors the female-to-male ratio observed for the overall participant pool. One might expect that the completion and exit distributions would also mirror the makeup of the overall participant pool. We see, however, that female participants are slightly more likely to complete the program compared to male participants. Again, the reasons behind this observation are not clear and warrant additional research to tease out the underlying causes.

## Assessment

In 1999 the Survey on Doctoral Education and Career Preparation was prepared for the Pew Charitable Trust (Golde & Dore, 2001). Among other topics, the survey explored how effectively doctoral programs prepare students for various teaching, research, and service activities. Beginning with a subset of these questions, we created a TPT-specific survey to measure participants' perceptions about preparedness in twenty-one areas typically associated with junior faculty responsibilities. Participants complete the survey prior to entering our program and again after completing all requirements. We currently have preprogram surveys from 179 of the 192 TPT participants (93.2 percent response rate) and exit surveys from 62 of the 89 who have successfully completed the program (69.7 percent response rate).

We compare the TPT program assessment data to several baseline surveys:

- ○ 2008 UVa Graduate Student Survey (UVa Office of Institutional Assessment and Studies, 2012b). We administered our TPT survey to a random sample of graduate students across all schools at UVa;

611 students responded to the survey (43.3 percent response rate). At a 95 percent confidence level, the overall sampling error for the survey was ±2.6 percent. Results from this survey will henceforth be identified as UVaGrad.

o 1999 Survey on Doctoral Education and Career Preparation (Golde & Dore, 2001). Over four thousand third-year or later graduate students from twenty-seven universities in eleven arts and sciences disciplines participated in the survey (42.3 percent response rate). Results from this survey will henceforth be identified as PEW.

o 2007 Survey of Perceptions of Early Career Faculty (Berberet, 2008). A study sponsored by the TIAA-CREF Institute surveyed 450 junior faculty from Associated New American Colleges in their first five years (33.9 percent response rate) about their graduate preparation. Results from this survey will henceforth be identified as TIAA-CREF.

o The pre- and post-TPT surveys will henceforth be identified as pre-TPT and post-TPT, respectively.

Tables 15.2 to 15.4 show respondents' perceptions of preparedness in teaching-, research-, and service-related activities for each of the three baseline surveys—PEW, TIAA-CREF, and UVaGrad—as well as perceptions of TPT participants before and after program participation. (In order to determine statistically significant differences between the pre-TPT and post-TPT survey data, we conducted independent $t$-tests for each of the twenty-one survey items. This analysis revealed that students completing the TPT program are statistically significantly more able to navigate university or college administration at the conclusion of the program ($t(56)1.094$, $p = .031$). Although we found significant differences for only one item, due to the nature of the survey data (differing pre- and postsample sizes, anonymous survey data collection) and the qualitative nature of the study, we think that inferential statistical analysis is not the best method for displaying or communicating the findings of this survey. Only respondents reporting that they felt "very prepared" for the various competencies are shown in the tables. Competency areas not addressed in the PEW and TIAA-CREF surveys are noted with a dash.

## Teaching-Related Competencies

The survey data for the seven teaching-related competencies tracked are shown in table 15.2. In general, despite some variation, the baseline survey data show relatively comparable levels of preparedness across

Table 15.2   Percentage of Survey Respondents Indicating They Felt "Very Prepared" for Teaching-Related Competencies Associated with Typical Faculty Positions

|  | PEW ($n = 4,114$) | TIAA-CREF ($n = 450$) | UVaGrad ($n = 611$) | Pre-TPT ($n = 179$) | Post-TPT ($n = 62$) |
|---|---|---|---|---|---|
| Design an independent course | — | — | 23.2 | 12.8 | 62.9 |
| Teach an independent course | — | 31 | 29.7 | 21.2 | 74.2 |
| Teach a specialized graduate course | 23.3 | — | 15.3 | 5.0 | 46.8 |
| Integrate research and teaching |  |  | 17.0 | 5.0 | 46.8 |
| Incorporate technology in the classroom | 14.1 | 20 | 32.8 | 21.2 | 46.8 |
| Develop a teaching portfolio | 26.6 | 19 | 14.7 | 7.8 | 69.4 |
| Manage teaching assistants | — | — | 22.1 | 20.7 | 50.0 |

the competencies. A particularly interesting comparison is between the pre-TPT data and the UVaGrad data. In all competencies but one, the pre-TPT data are lower than the UVaGrad data, meaning that entering TPT participants feel less prepared than the average UVa graduate student to meet teaching expectations. This feeling of unpreparedness is consistent with program application data, which show the primary reason graduate students want to join TPT is to improve their teaching knowledge and capabilities.

The differences between pre- and post-TPT perceptions of preparation are striking and range from students feeling two to as many as nine times more prepared after participation in TPT. The most notable gains are in the areas of designing and teaching independent courses and developing a teaching portfolio. This finding seems logical, because these participants have repeated exposure to and practice in these three areas through multiple TPT activities, including the pedagogy seminar, syllabus and reflective teaching statement workshops, and the course development and classroom teaching components.

The large perceptual gains observed for the teaching-related competencies are consistent with the fact that the number and variety of teaching-related program activities far outnumber other professional development activities. The program places emphasis on teaching partly because TPT is offered through UVa's teaching center, but mostly because junior faculty consistently list this as the area they need most help with during their early-career years (Golde & Dore, 2001; Berberet, 2008). The gains are also likely related to participants' interest in the teaching aspects of the program, as indicated by their survey responses: 92.9 percent of participants claim their interest in a faculty position is due to their "enjoyment of teaching," while only 64.1 percent say "enjoyment of research" draws them to such a career.

## Research-Related Competencies

The survey data for the seven research-related competencies tracked are shown in table 15.3. Other than the PEW survey data showing a relatively high number of respondents who felt very prepared for conducting and

Table 15.3   Percentage of Survey Respondents Indicating They Felt "Very Prepared" for Research-Related Competencies Associated with Typical Faculty Positions

|  | PEW ($n$ = 4,114) | TIAA-CREF ($n$ = 450) | UVaGrad ($n$ = 611) | Pre-TPT ($n$ = 179) | Post-TPT ($n$ = 62) |
|---|---|---|---|---|---|
| Conduct research | 65.1 | 33.0 | 40.1 | 40.8 | 79.0 |
| Publish research | 42.9 | — | 24.1 | 22.3 | 56.5 |
| Present research | — | — | 37.9 | 47.5 | 85.5 |
| Collaborate in interdisciplinary research | 27.1 | 25.0 | 23.7 | 23.5 | 53.2 |
| Obtain research funding | — | 7.0 | 6.3 | 7.3 | 22.6 |
| Develop a writing habit | — | — | 22.8 | 14.0 | 50.0 |

publishing research, the results across the three baseline surveys are again roughly comparable. The UVaGrad survey data, in particular, are within a few percentage points of the pre-TPT data for most competencies, suggesting that the entering TPT participant pool is generally representative of the UVa graduate student population. Two notable exceptions are in the areas of presenting research and developing a writing habit. In the case of presenting research, TPT participants feel more prepared than other UVa graduate students. Because the UVaGrad survey included first-year graduate students and TPT is restricted to second-year students and up, it would make sense that TPT participants feel more prepared for presenting research than the general graduate student population simply because they have had more opportunities to do so. Year in program may also explain why respondents to the PEW survey—students in their third year and up—feel considerably better prepared to conduct and publish research than respondents of all the other surveys. If, however, academic level alone accounts for these differences, it is unclear why TPT participant responses do not align more closely with the PEW survey respondents. In the case of developing a writing habit, TPT participants feel less prepared than the UVaGrad respondents. Again, if academic level were to account for TPT participants' perceptions, one would expect the value to be higher, suggesting some other factor is at play. It may be that the UVaGrad and TPT respondents are inherently different in their preparation for these areas or that something about the TPT program is selecting out a unique population.

Though not as dramatic an increase as seen for teaching competencies, the post-TPT survey data show that graduate students who complete the TPT program are still roughly two to three times more likely to feel very prepared for each of the seven research-related competencies than when they entered the program. The question is whether these perceptual gains are developmental or a result of program participation. Since graduate programs traditionally emphasize research training (Golde & Dore, 2001), one could reasonably expect students, including those participating in TPT, to feel more prepared to do research as their studies progress. Though progress toward degree may be responsible for some of the gain, it does not appear to account for the magnitude of the shifts in most areas. If it did, one would expect a better correlation between the PEW respondents—composed of graduate students in their third year and beyond—and the post-TPT respondents—composed of students in their fourth year and up. In other words, it appears that aspects of the TPT program cause an increase in participants' perceptions of preparedness beyond developmental gains. This could stem from the minimal requirements of attending a conference and presenting research at a scholarly venue, from increased confidence produced by effective mentoring or the process of creating competitive job materials, or even from norming comparisons with peers in other disciplines. TPT participants report benefiting as well from occasional workshops on topics such as getting published and grant writing.

## Service-Related Competencies

Survey data for the seven service-related competencies tracked are shown in table 15.4. Except for the TIAA-CREF data, the baseline surveys compare reasonably well. Few TIAA-CREF respondents reported feeling very prepared for service on academic committees and advising undergraduate students. This may be due to the type of institution the Associated New American Colleges faculty come from (e.g., midsize private Carnegie Master's) or because the realities of committee work and advising are considerably more demanding than expected by graduate students.

Table 15.4   Percentage of Survey Respondents Indicating They Felt "Very Prepared" for Service-Related Competencies Associated with Typical Faculty Positions

|  | PEW ($n = 4{,}114$) | TIAA-CREF ($n = 450$) | UVaGrad ($n = 611$) | Pre-TPT ($n = 179$) | Post-TPT ($n = 62$) |
|---|---|---|---|---|---|
| Serve on university or departmental committees | — | 10 | 13.2 | 16.8 | 37.1 |
| Referee academic papers | — | — | 10.1 | 16.8 | 37.1 |
| Advise undergraduates | 26.8 | 8 | 30.2 | 22.3 | 61.3 |
| Advise graduate students | 16.5 | — | 10.1 | 9.5 | 30.6 |
| Navigate university or college administration | — | — | 7.4 | 3.4 | 25.8 |
| Understand tenure and promotion processes | — | — | 2.7 | 0.0 | 11.3 |
| Balance work and personal time | — | — | 19.7 | 10.1 | 40.3 |

Again, entering TPT participants report feeling less prepared for service-related activities than students in the other survey pools. In fact, nearly 10 percent fewer TPT participants feel very prepared for each of the competencies compared to UVaGrad respondents. The gains observed post-TPT are likely due to targeted programming in a number of service-related areas, typically through workshops or panel sessions, such as a biennial panel discussion on understanding tenure and promotion at a variety of institution types.

Among all the competency categories, students clearly feel least prepared to engage in service-related activities, even after completing TPT. Informed by this data, we added programming to address related competencies. In addition to existing workshops defining service roles, we recently included a new program requirement: TPT participants must serve on a committee within their department, the university, or a professional disciplinary organization. We expect perceptions of preparedness—and actual preparedness—to continue to increase.

## Career Interests

The TPT-specific surveys also ask participants about their career interests. When entering the program, 51.9 percent of participants are interested in positions at research-focused universities, 40.0 percent at teaching-focused institutions, and the remainder (8.1 percent) in a variety of nonfaculty positions in business, government, and nonprofits. After leaving the program, interest in positions at research-focused universities drops to 35.5 percent and interest in positions at teaching-focused institutions drops to 25.8 percent, while interest in nonfaculty positions increases to 38.7 percent. Nonfaculty positions identified include college administration and other alternative academic careers; research and management positions in private, nonprofit or government sectors; and independent consulting. A 2007 survey of graduate students at University of California (UC) campuses ($N = 8,400$) mirrors these shifts (Mason, Goulden, & Frasch, 2009). The UC investigators found that from the start of students' doctoral programs to the time of the survey, interest in research-focused faculty positions declined from 41.9 to 31.3 percent, interest in teaching-focused positions remained relatively unaffected at approximately 23.5 percent, and interest in nonfaculty positions increased from 32.5 to 41.9 percent. Notably, TPT participants' initial interests in research- and teaching-focused positions are considerably higher than the UC sample. This is likely due to TPT participants' self-selection into a program focused on preparing future faculty. As TPT

**Table 15.5    UVaGrad and Pre- and Post-TPT Survey Respondents'**
**Perceptions of Preparation for Applying Immediately to Faculty Positions**

|  | UVaGrad ($n = 611$) | Pre-TPT[a] ($n = 184$) | Post-TPT[a] ($n = 6 2$) |
|---|---|---|---|
| Very prepared | 9.3 | 2.2 | 48.4 |
| Somewhat prepared | 39.4 | 43.0 | 48.4 |
| Not prepared | 51.3 | 53.1 | 1.6 |

[a]Sum of percentages is less than 100 percent because some respondents skipped this question.

participants finish the program, however, their career interests are nearly identical to the UC sample, suggesting that factors beyond the scope of TPT are affecting career interests.

## Preparation for the Job Market

In the UVaGrad, pre-TPT, and post-TPT surveys, respondents were asked: "If you were to go on the job market today, how prepared are you to apply for faculty positions?" The response data are shown in table 15.5. Here again, we see that entering TPT participants' perceptions of preparedness mirror those of the general UVa graduate student population. On completion, however, over 98 percent of TPT participants feel very or somewhat prepared compared to fewer than 50 percent for the average UVa graduate student, suggesting that the program meets this immediate need of participants.

Although perceptions of preparedness for the job market are encouraging, these data do not clarify how successful TPT participants are in their search for faculty positions, for those who seek them, or their eventual success in such positions. Several researchers have suggested that graduate student activities that align well with competencies developed by successful junior faculty have the most positive impact on their professional development (Austin & McDaniels, 2006; Seldin, 2006; Bellows, 2008; Smith & Simpson, 1995; Schönwetter & Ellis, 2011; Walker et al., 2008), yet measures of long-term, causal impact from these sorts of broad professional development programs are relatively scarce in the literature (Border, 2006; DeNeef, 2002; Kalish et al., 2011; Marincovich, Prostko, & Stout, 1998; Taylor, Schönwetter, Ellis, & Roberts, 2008).

In spring 2011, we began investigating the long-term impact of TPT by extending our assessment of the program to include interviews from participants who had obtained faculty ($n = 14$) and postdoctoral ($n = 6$) positions (Little, Palmer, Hurst, & Maher, 2011). Initial analysis of the data in this IRB-approved study confirms long-term benefits of the program. For example, participants who are now teaching reported that mastering classroom instruction before they began their current position was invaluable. Representative comments included, "For me, it [TPT participation] was the only teaching preparation I had for my role . . . The knowledge and skills related to teaching that I gained from the workshops . . . were extremely beneficial" (nursing faculty); "I use the skills from the [teaching] workshops all the time" (biology faculty). We are finding comparable trends in other competency areas and are actively pursuing research to better measure long-term impact.

## Summary

Based on a recently published taxonomy of graduate professional development programs, UVa's Tomorrow's Professor Today program is defined as a professional and teaching development program with a broad scope that requires high participant commitment (Palmer, 2011). Through a variety of activities, participants prepare for a suite of responsibilities junior faculty face. Ongoing assessment of TPT shows sizable gains in participants' perceptions of preparedness in twenty-one teaching-, research-, and services-related competencies tracked throughout the first eight years of the program. These gains are observed even when only limited programming is offered in competency areas, which suggests that the structure of the program not only gives participants knowledge of how to address different competencies but also provides the flexibility necessary for each participant to meet specific professional development needs. On the strength of participants' perception data alone, one could conclude that the TPT program is having a significant effect on preparing future faculty. Through follow-up interviews with former participants who have since taken faculty positions, we are beginning to see evidence of positive, long-term effects.

REFERENCES

Adams, K. A. (2002). *What colleges and universities want in new faculty.* Washington, DC: Association of American Colleges and Universities. Retrieved from http://www.aacu.org/pff/pdfs/PFF_Adams.PDF
Austin, A. E. (2002). Preparing the next generation of faculty. *Journal of Higher Education, 73*(1), 94–122.

Austin, A. E., & McDaniels, M. (2006). Preparing the professoriate of the future: Graduate student socialization for faculty roles. In J. C. Smart (Ed.), *Higher education: Handbook of theory and research, Vol. 21* (pp. 397–456). Netherlands: Springer.

Austin, A. E., & Wulff, D. H. (2004). The challenge to prepare the next generation of faculty. In D. Wulff & A. Austin (Eds.), *Paths to the professoriate*. San Francisco, CA: Jossey-Bass.

Bellows, L. (2008). Graduate student professional development: Defining the field. In L.L.B. Border (Ed.), *Studies in graduate and professional student development: Vol. 11. Defining the field* (pp. 2–17). Stillwater, OK: New Forms Press.

Berberet, J. (2008). *Perceptions of early career faculty: Managing the transition from graduate school to professorial career*. TIAA-CREF Institute: Research Dialogue. Retrieved from http://www.tiaa-crefinstitute.org/institute /research/dialogue/rd_92.html

Border, L.L.B., & von Hoene, L. M. (2010). Graduate and professional student development programs. In K. J. Gillespie & D. L. Robertson (Eds.), *A guide to faculty development* (2nd ed.). San Francisco, CA: Jossey-Bass.

DeNeef, A. L. (2002). *The preparing future faculty program: What difference does it make?* Washington DC: American Association of Colleges and Universities.

Fagan, A., & Suedkamp Wells, K. M. (2004). The 2000 National Doctoral Program survey: An on-line study of students' voices. In D. H. Wulff & A. E. Austin (Eds.), *Paths to the professoriate*. San Francisco, CA: Jossey-Bass.

Gaff, J. G. (2002). The disconnect between graduate education and the realities of faculty work: A review of recent research. *Liberal Education, 88*(3), 6–13.

Gaff, J. G., Pruitt-Logan, A. S., & Weibl, R. A. (2000). *Building the faculty we need: Colleges and universities working together*. Washington, DC: Association of American Colleges and Universities and the Council of Graduate Studies.

Golde, C. (2011). Entering different worlds: Socialization into disciplinary communities. In S. K. Gardner & P. Mendoza (Eds.), *On becoming a scholar: Socialization and development in doctoral education* (pp. 79–95). Sterling, VA: Stylus.

Golde, C. M., & Dore, T. M. (2001). *At cross purposes: What the experiences of doctoral students reveal about doctoral education*. Retrieved from http:// www.phd-survey.org/reportpercent20final.pdf

Goldsmith, S., Haviland, D., Daily, K., & Wiley, A. (2004). *Preparing future faculty initiative: Final evaluation report*. Retrieved from http://www.aacu .org/pff/pdfs/PFF_Final_Report.pdf

Kalish, A., Robinson, S., Border, L.L.B., Chandler, E. O., Connolly, M., Eaton, L. J., . . . & von Hoeneer, L. (2011). Steps toward a framework for an intended curriculum for graduate and professional students: How we talk about what we do. *Studies in graduate and professional student development: Vol. 14. Mapping the range of graduate student professional development* (pp. 163–173). Stillwater, OK: New Forms Press.

Little, D., Palmer, M., Hurst, M., & Maher, M. A. (2011). *Investigating the long-term impact of a graduate student future faculty program.* Paper presented at the 2011 Conference on Higher Education Pedagogy, Blacksburg, VA.

Marincovich, M., Prostko, J., & Stout, F. (Eds.). (1998). *The professional development of graduate teaching assistants.* Bolton, MA: Anker.

Mason, M. A., Goulden, M., & Frasch, K. (2009). Why graduate students reject the fast track. *Academe, 95,* 11–16.

Nyquist, J., & Woodford. B. (2000). Re-envisioning the Ph.D. *What concerns do we have?* Seattle: University of Washington, Center for Instructional Development and Research. Retrieved from http://depts.washington.edu /envision/resources/ConcernsBrief.pdf

Palmer, M. S. (2011). Graduate Student Professional Development: A Decade after Calls for National Reform. In L.L.B. Border (Ed.), *Studies in graduate and professional student development: Vol. 14. Mapping the range of graduate student professional development* (pp. 1–17). Stillwater, OK: New Forms Press.

Schönwetter, D. J., & Ellis, D. E. (2011). Taking stock: Contemplating North American graduate student professional development programs and developers. In J. E. Miller & J. E. Groccia (Eds.), *To improve the academy: Resources for faculty, instructional, and organizational development, Vol. 29.* San Francisco: Jossey-Bass.

Seldin, P. (2006). Tailoring faculty development programs to faculty career stages. In S. Chadwick-Blossey & D. R. Robertson (Eds.), *To improve the academy: Resources for faculty, instructional, and organizational development, Vol. 24.* Bolton, MA: Anker.

Smith, K. S., & Simpson, R. D. (1995). Validating teaching competencies for faculty members in higher education: A national study using the Delphi method. *Innovation in Higher Education, 19,* 223–233.

Taylor, K. L., Schönwetter, D. J., Ellis, D. E., & Roberts, M. (2008). Profiling an approach to evaluating the impact of two certification in university teaching programs for graduate students. In L.L.B. Border (Ed.), *Studies in graduate and professional student development: Vol. 11. Defining the field* (pp. 45–75). Stillwater, OK: New Forms Press

University of Virginia, Office of Institutional Assessment and Studies. (2012a). *Data digest: Admission.* Retrieved from http://avillage.web.virginia.edu /iaas/instreports/studat/dd/adm_grad.htm

University of Virginia, Office of Institutional Assessment and Studies. (2012b). *Graduate professional development survey*. Retrieved from http://avillage .web.virginia.edu/iaas/survey/portal/2008–09/08graduatedev.shtm

Walker, G. E. (2004). The Carnegie initiative on the doctorate: Creating stewards of discipline. In D. H. Wulff & A. E. Austin (Eds.), *Paths to the professoriate*. San Francisco, CA: Jossey-Bass.

Walker, G. E., Golde, C. M., Jones, L., Bueschel, A. C., & Hutchings, P. (2008). *The formation of scholars: Rethinking doctoral education for the twenty-first century*. San Francisco, CA: Jossey-Bass.

Wulff, D. H., & Austin, A. E. (2004). *Paths to the professoriate*. San Francisco, CA: Jossey-Bass.

# PART SIX

# ENHANCING STUDENT LEARNING

16

# STUDENT CONSULTANTS OF COLOR AND FACULTY MEMBERS WORKING TOGETHER TOWARD CULTURALLY SUSTAINING PEDAGOGY

*Alison Cook-Sather, Praise Agu*
*Bryn Mawr College*

*Through positioning undergraduate students as pedagogical consultants to college faculty, Students as Learners and Teachers is a program that provides reconceptualized "counterspaces" for students and faculty members with whom they work. In our study of the experiences of consultants of color, we found that those students and their faculty partners used program counterspaces to explore links between their lived identities and pedagogical commitments and to share authority and responsibility in developing culturally sustaining pedagogy. In this chapter we report on participants' experiences in these collaborations and how they legitimate the knowledge of students of color in faculty learning.*

o

Thanks to Jody Cohen, James Groccia, Toni King, Elliott Shore, Steve Volk, Alicia Walker, and three anonymous reviewers for insights developed within and responses to drafts of this chapter.

Over twenty years ago, Allen (1992) asserted that "far-reaching, enduring change in higher education . . . will only come about when universities come to feel more keenly their responsibility for changing the system
of unequal societal relationships based on race" (p. 42). Working toward
that end, scholars have argued for the development of "culturally sustaining pedagogy" (Paris, 2012) that recognizes and values diverse
students (Colbert, 2010; Fasching-Varner & Seriki, 2012; Gay, 2002;
Pappamihiel & Moreno, 2011) "while simultaneously offering access to
dominant cultural competence" (Paris, 2012, p. 95). Such practices mitigate the need for students from underrepresented groups to seek or
create "counterspaces"—academic and social spaces on and off their
campuses "where deficit notions of people of color can be challenged and
where a positive collegiate racial climate can be established and maintained" (Solórzano, Ceja, & Yosso, 2000, p. 70).

The Students as Learners and Teachers (SaLT) program at Bryn Mawr
College redefines counterspaces, framing them as institutionally valued
forums that affirm students of color rather than alternative arenas necessary to counterbalance "the daily barrage of racial microaggressions
that [students] endure both in and outside of their classes" (Solórzano
et al., 2000, p. 70). The program creates opportunities for students of all
identities to share their perspectives and partner with faculty in
explorations of teaching and learning, but in this discussion, we focus on
how it provides spaces wherein students of color are recognized as
"holders and creators of knowledge" (Delgado-Bernal, 2002, p. 106) and
that knowledge becomes a resource for faculty learning.

We begin with a description of the SaLT program and its redefined
counterspaces. We then situate the program at the intersection of scholarship on student voice, faculty development that includes students as
partners, and critical race theory. Finally, drawing on the words of student consultants and their faculty partners, we describe the ways in which
student and faculty participants have used the counterspaces of the
program to share authority and responsibility for developing culturally
sustaining pedagogy. Their work models how new kinds of counterspaces
can change who participates in shaping educational practice and who
contributes to institutional change.

## The Students as Learners and Teachers Program as Counterspace

The SaLT program is part of the Teaching and Learning Institute at Bryn
Mawr College, supported by a grant from the Andrew W. Mellon

Foundation and the provosts at Bryn Mawr and Haverford Colleges. SaLT invites undergraduate students to take up the paid position of pedagogical consultant to college faculty who choose to participate in the program. Faculty and student pairs work in semester-long partnerships to analyze, affirm, and revise the faculty member's pedagogical approaches in a course as she or he teaches it.

Each week the consultant observes her faculty partner's classroom, shares her observation notes, and meets with her partner to discuss what is working well and what might be revised. Student consultants apply for this paid position (they must submit an explanation of why they want to assume this role, procure letters of recommendation from a faculty or staff member and a student, and sign a confidentiality agreement). They attend an orientation, receive a set of guidelines for developing partnerships with faculty members, and participate in weekly meetings with the first author of this chapter, Alison, in her role as coordinator of the program, and other consultants. In these meetings, they discuss how best to partner with faculty in the work of recognizing the diverse experiences and perspectives students bring to their studies and developing classrooms that are both welcoming and productively challenging.

Between 2006 and 2012, 150 faculty members participated in over 225 partnerships. Of the 90 students who assumed the role of pedagogical consultant in those years (many of them for more than one semester), 49 were students of color or international students. As part of an ongoing action research project Alison has maintained for six years, she, who self-identifies as a white woman, and Praise, the second author of this chapter and an experienced student consultant who self-identifies as African American, conducted a study during the spring 2012 semester through which we focused on the experiences of 16 students who self-identify as people of color and were able to complete a survey or participate in a focus group, or both. (This chapter does not address the experiences of international students.)

In contrast to the "spaces of marginality" (Huber, 2009, p. 710) in which many students of color must develop "cultural wealth" (Solórzano, Villalpando, & Oseguera, 2005), the SaLT program creates counter-spaces that are central to student empowerment and faculty learning. In these redefined counterspaces—the program itself and its weekly meetings of same- and cross-constituency participants—student consultants have, as one consultant explained, "a space to share [their] unique experience, a space to listen, and a space to engage," all of which, consultants find, "affirm who I am." Furthermore, because student consultants are "not responsible for the content [and] free of the grading," as one faculty member put it, they can, according to another faculty member, talk about their experiences as students of color "in a frank way that I appreciated." The culture and hierarchy of higher education do not generally encourage or support such exchanges; by making them the focus of faculty learning, the SaLT program helps the college realize its "responsibility for changing the system of unequal societal relationships based on race" (Allen, 1992, p. 42).

The notion of counterspaces as we use the term here is particularly important when understood as professional counterspace—an intersection of the personal and the academic that is more neutral and individual than either social spaces or academic spaces. Unlike social or residential spaces, the counterspaces of the SaLT program do not demand that students join a group or stay living there. Unlike classrooms, these counterspaces do not feel to students like places within which they must take a particular intellectual stance and stick with it. Bounded in terms of the temporal commitment they require, these spaces allow students to come and go, change and evolve, risk and change. Many of these same qualities support faculty development as well: they characterize the intersection of the personal and the academic in a confidential space and time set apart from the rest of faculty responsibilities in which learning and growth are invited, supported, and affirmed by the institution.

## The SaLT Program Situated in the Literature

The SaLT program as counterspace sits at the intersection of scholarship on student voice, faculty development that includes students as partners, and critical race theory.

Student voice, developed largely in the context of K–12 schools in Australia (Holdsworth, 2000), Canada (Levin 2000), and the United Kingdom (Fielding 2004, 2006; Rudduck 2007), embraces a students' rights perspective. The basic premises of this work are that young people have unique perspectives on learning and teaching, that their insights warrant not only the attention but also the responses of adults, and that they should be afforded opportunities to actively shape their education (Cook-Sather, 2006, 2009b). "Voice" can be understood as the actual practice of each person speaking as and for herself but also as the valuing of what is said collectively by students as a group as essential contributions to dialogue that informs action. Positive manifestations of voice include the presence of, active participation in, and influence of students within conversations about and reform of educational practice. But voice can also be problematic—reduced to tokenism and manipulation (Fielding, 2004; Lodge, 2005).

The amplification of student voices does not assert or imply the silencing or muting of faculty or other voices. Voice as metaphor suggests a resonance beyond the singular/individual speech act—the bringing of student voices and faculty voices into dialogue such that each is informed by as well as informs the other. Collaborative models of professional development that include students as partners (Bovill, Cook-Sather, & Felten, 2011; Cook-Sather, Bovill, & Felten, 2013) bring the fact and spirit of student voice work to the postsecondary context. Such models position students as pedagogical consultants (Cook-Sather, 2008, 2009a, 2010, 2011, forthcoming; Cook-Sather & Alter, 2011; Cox & Sorenson, 1999) and members of teams with faculty and staff who design or redesign course curricula (Bovill, 2013; Delpish et al., 2010). Through these and other programs, students are not only partners but also change agents, a term that "explicitly supports a view of the student as 'active collaborator' and 'co-producer,' with the potential for transformation" (Dunne & Zandstra, 2011, p. 4; see also Healey, 2012; Neary, 2010).

Recent work in the scholarship of teaching and learning (SoTL) has similarly begun to recognize students "not as objects of inquiry . . . but as co-inquirers, helping to shape key questions, gather and analyze data, and then push for change where it is needed" (Hutchings, Huber, & Ciccone, 2011, p. 79; see also Werder & Otis, 2010; Werder, Thibou, & Kaufer, 2012). As in the student voice literature, students within some SoTL projects are positioned as partners with faculty members in dialogue and in action.

In focusing on the experiences of students of color in partnership with faculty, we can link the realms of student voice and faculty development to critical race theory. As Yosso, Parker, Solórzano, and Lynn (2004) have argued, "To fully understand the ways in which race and racism shape educational institutions and maintain various forms of discrimination, we must look to the lived experiences of students of color . . . as valid, appropriate, and necessary forms of data" (p. 15), this program positions students of color as both informants on their experiences and analysts of the conditions that create those experiences. Solórzano et al. (2000) explain that the basic critical race theory model consists of "five elements focusing on: (a) the centrality of race and racism and their intersectionality with other forms of subordination, (b) the challenge to dominant ideology, (c) the commitment to social justice, (d) the centrality of experiential knowledge, and (e) the transdisciplinary perspective" (p. 63). They suggest that critical race theory offers insights, perspectives, methods, and pedagogies that guide our efforts to identify, analyze, and transform the structural and cultural aspects of education that maintain subordinate and dominant racial positions in and out of the classroom" (Solórzano et al., 2000, p. 63).

Creating pedagogical partnerships between faculty members and students of color at once raises awareness of and begins to enact changes in structural and cultural inequities. This work confirms findings that strong faculty-student relationships at once mitigate the effects of negative campus climate (Cress, 2008) and predict academic achievement among students of color (Allen, 1992; Baker & Griffin, 2010). Both student consultants and faculty members benefit from critical explorations of the ways in which what is considered "universal" in higher education is actually "quite limited"—is "just reflecting a particular experience" and is, "quite often, exclusionary" (Lee, 2004, p. 146).

The SaLT program supports partnerships between faculty of all backgrounds and student consultants of all backgrounds, but because our focus in this chapter is on the experiences of students of color, we do not include examples of white or international student consultants working with faculty. We focus on student consultants of color working with faculty of color and with white faculty, sharing authority and responsibility for creating more culturally sustaining pedagogy.

## Students of Color Sharing Authority and Responsibility

Our findings suggest that through their participation in the SaLT program, student consultants of color experience their identities and perspectives as legitimate and important, develop their voices within the forums of the SaLT program, build confidence in their capacities as students and consultants, and feel empowered within and beyond their partnerships (Cook-Sather & Agu, 2012). While these outcomes are consistent with outcomes for domestic and international student consultants across racial and cultural backgrounds, they are particularly significant in terms of challenging deficit notions of students of color, for those students themselves and for others.

Many students of color used the term *voice* to capture the experience of literally speaking more but also more metaphorically, of developing a sense of presence, power, and agency when they are positioned as consultants to faculty members. The SaLT program provides them with arenas within which voice itself can be examined, as well as developed, in a way that is unlikely in most classrooms. As one consultant explained:

> I feel like being a Student Consultant literally gave me a voice. I started being more vocal in and outside of class. As an African American

student, I used to let people tell me how I should think and act. I used to let them reprimand me for not being black in the way they'd like. Looking back on those times, I am embarrassed and vow to never let someone have that kind of power over me ever again. I attribute much of this sense of empowerment to my participation in the [SaLT program]. It made me feel like who I am is more than enough—that my identity, my thoughts, my ideas are significant and valuable.

In the context of the SaLT program, the lived experiences this student of color articulates become "significant and valuable" as part of her own process of empowerment and as "valid, appropriate, and necessary forms of data" (Yosso et al., 2004, p. 15) for faculty learning.

The sense of empowerment students of color experience leads them to see themselves as change agents: "I felt like I could create change or make an impact because I was working as a *partner* alongside those that are typically viewed as having the power [faculty]." Such experiences are rare for all students and particularly for underrepresented students: "A lot of times, my point of view was not considered throughout my educational experience since my demographics are underrepresented. Being a student consultant gave me a seat at the proverbial table and the courage to speak up for what I believed and wanted to see." Having a "seat at the proverbial table" means that students of color have power and legitimacy in conversations with faculty, and they model empowerment and agency for students. This is particularly important for other students of color who do not often see people of color in positions of authority. As one student consultant explained: "I think it might have been important for other students of color or underrepresented groups to have seen me in this new and 'high level' role with respect to the professor in that their perspective was welcomed, would be treated well and was valued as a driving force to change classroom dynamics." Another student consultant affirmed this conjecture: "It is empowering to see strong, passionate, intelligent and active women of color on campus be able to be in prestigious academic positions."

When students of color experience themselves and see other students of color in positions of authority, they develop confidence in contexts beyond the counterspaces of the SaLT program. As one student consultant explained: "Being a Student Consultant gave me voice as a person of color when I was not in the role of student consultant . . . by reinforcing that not only did my perspective, assessment skills and commitment to make spaces safer for underrepresented groups deeply matter—they could drive important transformation in classrooms and in the student-teacher relationship." Through their participation in the SaLT program, students of color develop both an individual and a more collective sense of capacity and influence with the potential for institutional change: "I think that generally we [students of color] felt like we were more a part of the larger school community. There was strength in numbers considering that our viewpoints about what we wanted to receive from our education deserved to be taken seriously and was useful not only to us, but to the professors and other students."

## Faculty Sharing Authority and Responsibility

Both faculty of color and white faculty members use the counterspaces of the SaLT program to explore links between their lived identities and pedagogical commitments and to share authority and responsibility in developing culturally sustaining pedagogy.

Faculty of color are still grossly underrepresented and inequitably treated in many higher education contexts (Cook & Córdova, 2006; Fries-Britt, Rowan-Kenyon, Perna, Milem, & Howard, 2011; Patitu & Hinton, 2003), despite efforts to recruit more faculty of color for reasons of equity and for their important contributions to undergraduate education (Umbach, 2006). Formerly students of color themselves and still in the minority in higher education, faculty of color also need redefined counterspaces within which to empower themselves and catalyze change. The SaLT program provides those by structuring forums for dialogue that are about sharing experiences and developing effective practices. The empowerment of students of color in the role of consultant and the collaborations with those students contribute to the empowerment and development of faculty.

One faculty member of color explained that "from the first moment we met," she and her consultant talked about questions of race and culturally sustaining pedagogy because they both "self-identified." One of her enduring questions was "how to make academia a better place" for students of color. This faculty member articulated the potential of real, deep, difficult conversation—the kind she had with her student consultant—to effect learning and growth: "Dealing with the uncomfortable places real conversations can take you allows you to reconstruct more productive approaches to the classroom." The counterspaces of the SaLT program provide a context and support for those conversations, positioning students of color as sources of knowledge and partners to faculty of color in extending and building on that knowledge as it intersects with their own.

Another faculty member of color commented on how the positioning of student consultants of color benefits the students enrolled in her courses and reshapes her sense of her own participation in the teaching and learning enterprise. Her courses enroll a majority of students of color, and, as she explained, "For them to see my consultants, who were both students of color, come in and to know that students of color can be authorities in the classroom, was incredibly transforming and powerful for the students who were actually participating in the class." As an experienced faculty member of color who confronts racial dynamics within and beyond her courses, this faculty member also commented on the effect of working with student consultants on her own practice. Speaking to the spirit of partnership she felt in working with her consultants and in the SaLT program overall, she voiced her relief at recognizing that she "can share the responsibility for what happens in the classroom with students . . . [and she need not] be the only voice speaking."

The kind of dialogue and sharing of responsibility these two faculty members describe extends beyond the faculty-student partnership within the SaLT program to inform pedagogical practice and student participation. This form of professional development is a kind of learning to speak with, learning to share the space of—and responsibility for—the classroom; it is work that has institutional impact as it carries beyond the classes on which faculty focus for this program and into their other courses and relationships.

For white faculty members, the SaLT program affords an opportunity to access and learn from the experiences and perspectives of students of color that they might not otherwise have. Developing ways of speaking—and listening—across differences is one important dimension of culturally sustaining pedagogy. One faculty member wrote that being in partnership with a student consultant of color gave her a space within which to develop strategies in her ongoing effort "to speak more openly and frankly about race." Her student consultant offered "suggestions for how to redirect the conversation, how to call out students, or how to support other students in the class to contest [racist] views." Another faculty member explained that "listening to and talking with [my consultant] after class widened my interpretations and often cleared the way for me to listen and see more sensitively and with expanded or adjusted context in subsequent classes." These examples highlight how, in conversation across their differences of identity and perspective, student consultants of color and white faculty together develop heightened awareness and concrete practices for pursuing culturally sustaining pedagogy.

These faculty members highlight the enduring influence of their work with student consultants of color. Another white faculty member who worked with three different student consultants of color commented that one of her student consultant's experiences "of some particular class activities and discussions—seen and responded to through her lens as a student of color—strongly influenced and continue to inform my understanding of what's going on in the classroom" (see Cook-Sather, Cohen, & Shumate, 2011). Like the other faculty members quoted here, this faculty member both comes to understand her own perception and practice differently and also develops a keener awareness of the opportunities she structures for diverse student affirmation and engagement.

In their positions as consultants, students of color change what faculty—and, in turn, students in those faculty members' courses—can see and envision. Through their insights developed within the redefined counterspaces of the SaLT program, faculty members, like student consultants, develop capacity and agency to create classrooms that welcome the experiences and perspectives of diverse students. These processes begin to effect change in higher education. When the identities, experiences, and knowledge of students of color are deemed legitimate resources rather than deficits as part of a humanizing effort that affords wide access, the need for counterspaces outside the classroom is reduced.

## Challenges and Drawbacks

The challenges and drawbacks of this work center around vulnerability (during the experience) and frustration (with other contexts and people who do not share the willingness to be vulnerable in this way).

Student consultants initially worry that they are vulnerable to faculty dismissal. One student consultant of color explained, "These profs have been doing this for quite some time, they have advanced degrees, you're a kid with some college. You are trying to come in and say, 'Do this better, do that.' You could easily be dismissed." Faculty vulnerability is the flip side of this fear. White faculty members talk about how it is "wonderful and also scary at times" to have students of color observe and analyze their teaching because while such students "have a certain legitimacy," they also make faculty "feel more exposed" because these students might be "able to see all the things that were problems" in the faculty member's classroom. For faculty of color, the need to reposition students in this way is a painful reminder of their "own, often marginalized experiences as students of color," of the vulnerability many still feel as people of color in the academy, and of the enduring need to change both higher education and the larger society.

The frustration both consultants and faculty feel focuses on the difficulty of accepting that one cannot always be in such open, honest partnerships. One consultant explained that in exploring issues of difference and otherness, "one of the strengths of being a student consultant is that you can challenge the professor to think about times in their lives when they have felt privileged." She lamented what a contrast that kind of engagement can be to "the real world": "Some people are really afraid of it in the real world, I've learned." A faculty member explained a related frustration, born of institutional hierarchy and expectations, of not yet having found a way to extend such open partnership to all students: "There are a lot of students who could have given me insight," but given the norms of higher education, "I haven't figured out how to make that part of the class."

## Conclusion: Moving toward Culturally Sustaining Pedagogy and Institutions

The work students of color and faculty do through the SaLT program redefines who has authority in regard to the development of culturally sustaining pedagogy. Student consultants' and faculty members' reflections highlight an increased sense of awareness and responsibility, fostered in a collaboration within which students of color are positioned as knowers—legitimate participants and authorities—and faculty are invited to develop more informed and culturally sustaining classroom practices. Particularly within the context of a faculty-student dynamic that counters the standard hierarchical arrangements that often reinforce white experiences and perspectives, the SaLT program invites faculty exploration and growth, guided by students of color as well as other diverse students.

As faculty and students, we should think about how to turn more of the spaces within which we interact with one another into such flexible and responsive spaces—spaces that invite not only difference but also change and growth. It is particularly important to create spaces and roles within which students of color can have strong and legitimate voices in dialogue with faculty, explore their own and others' identities, and develop a stronger sense of belonging and agency. Support more than training is key to such efforts: creating loosely structured, institutionally legitimate spaces within which faculty and students can engage in genuine dialogue is a small investment for the payoff of creating more culturally sustaining pedagogies and changing the system of unequal societal relationships based on race.

Higher education—and society at large—suffers when students and faculty of color drop out or leave because of the campus atmosphere. We need to work toward transforming counterspaces into community spaces that affirm the presence, insights, and participation of students of color in the professional development of faculty and the creation of classroom and associated arenas conducive to learning, challenge, and affirmation for all students and faculty. This work neither aims for nor can achieve resolution. Rather, it supports what must be ongoing processes of negotiation across differences toward greater equity.

REFERENCES

Allen, W. R. (1992). The color of success: African American academic student outcomes at Predo. *Harvard Educational Review, 62*(1), 26–44.

Baker, V. L., & Griffin, K. A., (2010, January/February). Beyond mentoring and advising: Toward understanding the role of "faculty developers" in student success. *About Campus,* 2–8.

Bovill, C. (2013). An investigation of co-created curricula within higher education in the UK, Ireland and the USA. *Innovations in Education and Teaching International.*

Bovill, C., Cook-Sather, A., & Felten, P. (2011). Students as co-creators of teaching approaches, course design and curricula: Implications for academic developers. *International Journal for Academic Development, 16*(2), 133–145. doi:http://dx.doi.org/10.1080/1360144X.2011.568690

Colbert, P. J. (2010). Developing a culturally responsive classroom collaborative of faculty, students, and institution. *Journal of College Teaching and Learning, 7*(11), 15–24.

Cook-Sather, A. (2006). Sound, presence, and power: Exploring "student voice" in educational research and reform. *Curriculum Inquiry, 36*(4), 359–390.

Cook-Sather, A. (2008). "What you get is looking in a mirror, only better": Inviting students to reflect (on) college teaching. *Reflective Practice, 9*(4), 473–483. doi:http://dx.doi.org/10.1080/14623940802431465

Cook-Sather, A. (2009a). From traditional accountability to shared responsibility: The benefits and challenges of student consultants gathering midcourse feedback in college classrooms. *Assessment and Evaluation in Higher Education, 34*(2), 231–241. doi:10.1080/02602930801956042

Cook-Sather, A. (2009b). *Learning from the student's perspective: A sourcebook for effective teaching.* Boulder, CO: Paradigm Publishers.

Cook-Sather, A. (2010). Students as learners and teachers: Taking responsibility, transforming education, and redefining accountability. *Curriculum Inquiry, 40*(4), 555–575.

Cook-Sather, A. (2011). Teaching and learning together: College faculty and undergraduates co-create a professional development model. In J. E. Miller & J. E. Groccia, (Eds.), *To improve the academy: Resources for faculty, instructional, and organizational development, Vol. 29* (pp. 219–232). San Francisco, CA: Jossey-Bass/Anker.

Cook-Sather, A. (forthcoming). Student-faculty partnership in explorations of pedagogical practice: A threshold concept in academic development. *International Journal for Academic Development.*

Cook-Sather, A., & Agu, P. (2012, October 27). *Students of color and faculty colleagues developing voice in the "counterspaces" of a professional development program.* Paper presented at the Annual Meeting of the Professional and Organizational Development Network. Seattle, WA.

Cook-Sather, A., & Alter, Z. (2011). What is and what can be: How a liminal position can change learning and teaching in higher education. *Anthropology and Education Quarterly, 42*(1), 37–53. doi:10.1111/j.1548-1492.2010.01109.x

Cook-Sather, A., Bovill, C., & Felten, P. (2013). *Engaging students as partners in teaching & learning: A guide for faculty.* San Francisco, CA: Jossey-Bass.

Cook-Sather, A., Cohen, J., & Shumate, T. (2011). Embracing productive disruptions: Excerpts from an ongoing story of developing more culturally responsive classrooms. *Teaching and Learning Together in Higher Education, 4.* Retrieved from http://teachingandlearningtogether.blogs.brynmawr.edu/archived-issues/current-issue/embracing-productive-disruptions-excerpts-from-an-ongoing-story-of-developing-more-culturally-responsive-classrooms

Cook, B. J., & Córdova, D. I. (2006). *Minorities in higher education: Twenty-second annual status report: 2007 Supplement.* Washington, DC: American Council on Education.

Cox, M. D., & Sorenson, D. L. (1999). Student collaboration in faculty development. In M. Kaplan (Ed.), *To improve the academy: Resources for faculty, instructional, and organizational development, Vol. 18* (pp. 97–106). San Francisco, CA: Jossey-Bass/Anker.

Cress, C. M. (2008). Creating inclusive learning communities: The role of student-faculty relationships in mitigating negative campus climate. *Learning Inquiry, 2*(2), 95–111. doi:10.1007/s11519-008-0028-2

Delgado-Bernal, D. (2002). Critical race theory, Latino critical theory, and critical raced-gendered epistemologies: Recognizing students of color as holders and creators of knowledge. *Qualitative Inquiry, 8*(1), 105–126. doi:10.1177/107780040200800107

Delpish, A., Holmes, A, Knight-McKenna, M., Mihans, R., Darby, A., King, K., & Felten, P. (2010). Equalizing voices: Student-faculty partnership in course design. In C. Werder & M. M. Otis (Eds.), *Engaging student voices in the study of teaching and learning* (pp. 96–114). Sterling, VA: Stylus.

Dunne, E., & Zandstra, R. (2011). *Students as change agents: New ways of engaging with learning and teaching in higher education.* Bristol: ESCalate Higher Education Academy Subject Centre for Education/University of Exeter.

Fasching-Varner, K. J., & Seriki, V. D. (2012). Moving beyond seeing with our eyes wide shut. A response to "there is no culturally responsive teaching spoken here." *Democracy and Education, 20*(1). Retrieved from http:// democracyeducationjournal.org/cgi/viewcontent.cgi?article=1049&context =home

Fielding, M. (2004). Transformative approaches to student voice: Theoretical underpinnings, recalcitrant realities. *British Educational Research Journal, 30*(2), 295–311. doi:10.1080/0141192042000195236

Fielding, M. (2006). Leadership, radical student engagement and the necessity of person-centred education. *International Journal of Leadership in Education, 9*(4), 299–314. doi:10.1080/13603120600895411

Fries-Britt, S. L., Rowan-Kenyon, H. T., Perna, L. W., Milem, J. F., & Howard, D. G. (2011). Underrepresentation in the academy and the institutional climate for faculty diversity. *Journal of the Professoriate, 5*(1), 1–34.

Gay, G. (2002). Preparing for culturally responsive teaching. *Journal of Teacher Education, 53*(2), 106–116.

Healey, M., (2012, October). *Students as producers and change agents.* Plenary session presented at the Meeting of the International Society for the Study of Teaching and Learning. Ontario, Canada.

Holdsworth, R. (2000). Taking young people seriously means giving them serious things to do. In J. Mason & M. Wilkinson (Eds.), *Taking children seriously.* Bankstown: University of Western Sydney.

Huber, L. P. (2009). Challenging racist nativist framing: Acknowledging the community cultural wealth of undocumented Chicana college students to reframe the immigration debate. *Harvard Educational Review, 79*(4), 704–730.

Hutchings, P., Huber, M. T., & Ciccone, A. (2011). *The scholarship of teaching and learning reconsidered: Institutional integration and impact.* San Francisco, CA: Jossey-Bass.

Lee, E. (2004). Taking multicultural, anti-racist education seriously. In K. D. Salas, R. Tenorio, S. Waters, & D. Weiss (Eds.), *The new teacher book: Finding purpose, balance, and hope during your first years in the classroom* (pp. 140–150). Milwaukee, WI: Rethinking Schools Press, 1994.

Levin, B. (2000). Putting students at the centre of education reform. *Journal of Educational Change, 1*(2), 155–172.

Lodge, C. (2005). From hearing voices to engaging in dialogue: Problematising student participation in school improvement. *Journal of Educational Change, 6*(2), 125–146. doi:10.1007/s10833–005–1299–3

Neary, M. (2010). Student as producer: A pedagogy for the avant-garde? *Learning Exchange, 1*(1). Retrieved from http://www.scribd.com/doc/48662051/Neary-Student-as-Producer

Pappamihiel, N. E., & Moreno, M. (2011). Retaining Latino students: Culturally responsive instruction in colleges and universities. *Journal of Hispanic Higher Education, 10*(4) 331–344.

Paris, D. (2012). Culturally sustaining pedagogy: A needed change in stance, terminology, and practice. *Educational Researcher, 41*(3), 93–97. doi:10.3102/0013189X12441244

Patitu, C. L., & Hinton, K. G. (2003). The experiences of African American women faculty and administrators in higher education: Has anything changed? In M. Howard-Hamilton (Ed.), *New directions for student services: No. 104. Meeting the needs of African women* (pp. 79–93). doi:10.1002/ss.109

Rudduck, J. (2007). Student voice, student engagement, and school reform. In D. Thiessen & A. Cook-Sather (Eds.), *International handbook of student experience in elementary and secondary school* (pp. 587–610). Dordrecht, Netherlands: Springer.

Solórzano, D., Ceja, M., & Yosso, T. (2000). Critical race theory, racial microaggressions, and campus racial climate: The experiences of African American college students. *Journal of Negro Education, 69*(1/2), 60–73. Retrieved from http://www.jstor.org/stable/2696265

Solórzano, D., Villalpando, O., & Oseguera, L. (2005). Educational inequities and Latina/o undergraduate students in the United States: A critical race analysis of their educational progress. *Journal of Hispanic Higher Education, 4*, 272–294. doi:10.1177/1538192705276550

Umbach, P. D. (2006). The contribution of faculty of color to undergraduate education. *Research in Higher Education, 47*(3), 317–345. doi:10.1007/s11162–005–9391–3

Werder, C., & Otis, M. M. (Eds.) (2010). *Engaging student voices in the study of teaching and learning.* Sterling, VA: Stylus Publishing.

Werder, C., Thibou, S., & Kaufer, B. (2012). Students as co-inquirers: A requisite threshold concept in educational development? *Journal of Faculty Development, 26*(3), 34–38.

Yosso, T. J., Parker, L., Solórzano, D. G., & Lynn, M. (2004). From Jim Crow to affirmative action and back again: A critical race discussion of racialized rationales and access to higher education. *Review of Research in Education, 28*, 1–25. Retrieved from http://www.jstor.org/stable/3568134

# 17

# MEASURING STUDENT LEARNING TO DOCUMENT FACULTY TEACHING EFFECTIVENESS

*Linda B. Nilson*
*Clemson University*

*Recent research has questioned the validity of student ratings as proxy measures for how much students learn, and this learning is a commonly accepted meaning of faculty teaching effectiveness. Student ratings capture student satisfaction more than anything else. Moreover, the overriding assessment criterion in accreditation and accountability—that applied to programs, schools, and institutions—is student learning, so it only makes sense to evaluate faculty by the same standard. This chapter explains and evaluates course-level measures of student learning based on data that are easy for faculty to collect and administrators to use.*

———o———

Student ratings are probably the most universally used indicator of teaching effectiveness in faculty reviews. It would be difficult to find an institution that does not place considerable importance on these ratings. Faculty developers have long urged bringing other measures into the equation (Arreola, 2007; Braskamp & Ory, 1994; Cashin, 1989, 2003; Stark-Wroblewski, Ahlering, & Brill, 2007), but many institutions still give predominant, if not exclusive, weight to these ratings. Recent research suggests that it is time to replace student ratings or counter-balance them with other indicators. Furthermore, no other academic entity except individual faculty is evaluated on student opinions. All the others must produce evidence of student learning. If teaching effectiveness is the ability to motivate and facilitate student learning, it only makes sense to assess faculty, at least primarily, on their students' learning in their courses.

## The Validity of Student Ratings

Over three decades ago, Cohen (1981) defined teaching effectiveness in terms of student learning/achievement and justified using student ratings as a proxy because of their moderately strong positive relationship to student learning: "It [teaching effectiveness] can be further operationalized as the amount students learn in a particular course . . . If student ratings are to have any utility in evaluating teaching, they must show at least a moderately strong relationship to this index" (p. 281). However, a great deal of recent evidence shows that this relationship has broken down. At best, it is now weak or nonexistent (Clayson, 2009; Marks, Fairris, & Beleche, 2010; Weinberg, Hashimoto, & Fleisher, 2009); at worst, it is negative (Carrell & West, 2010; Clayson, 2009; Johnson, 2003). Furthermore, student ratings on items most directly related to learning, such as the rigor of the course, the challenge of its content, and required student effort, vary negatively with instructor ratings (Steiner, Holley, Gerdes, & Campbell, 2006; Weinberg, Fleisher, & Hashimoto, 2007; others cited in Clayson, 2009).

Another problem with using student ratings to represent student learning is the increasing array of biases plaguing their validity—now over a dozen variables unconnected to learning and mostly outside faculty control, from the instructor's physical attractiveness to his or her public personality to the length of the class meeting (summarized in Nilson, 2012). In fact, students largely form their opinions about an instructor's teaching—the same ones that wind up on the student rating forms—before instruction even begins (Clayson, 2013). In addition, the correlation between expected course grade and student ratings has strengthened from a mild .10 to .30 (Cashin, 1995) to a substantial .45 to .50 (Clayson, 2011), making expected grade one of the best predictors of student ratings.

Finally, a few studies have found the factual accuracy and honesty of ratings to be wanting. In Sproule's (2002) and Stanfel's (1995) classroom research, between nearly half and nearly two-thirds of the students disagreed with the item on their instructor's promptness in returning graded work, even though both researchers returned all graded work at the very next class all semester long. The latter even asked his students to sign a document stating that they had received their graded work at the first possible opportunity every time he returned work, and they all signed it. In Clayson and Haley's (2011) survey of students, one-third admitted to "stretching the truth" and 20 percent to lying on their instructor rating forms.

All of the more recent findings on student ratings, those largely representing the responses of millennial undergraduates, back up faculty claims that their ratings suffer when they add rigor and challenge to their course, maintain high grading standards, or have personal characteristics that their students view as "alien." Faculty have also complained about factual misrepresentations in their ratings and student comments. More often than not, administrators and faculty developers have dismissed these grievances, citing decades-old studies that document the connection between student ratings and learning (Cohen, 1981; Feldman, 1989; Marsh, 1984). While calling ratings "a popularity contest" overstates the case, the global items best capture student affect toward and satisfaction with an instructor (Nuhfer, 2010). This explains why the instructor's public personality—specifically, his or her congeniality, self-confidence, enthusiasm, and optimism—explains half to three-quarters of the variance in student ratings (Clayson, 2011). Students strongly prefer energetic, expressive faculty who they believe care about and empathize with them (Clayson, 2011; La Lopa, 2011; Williams & Ceci, 1997).

## How Academic Units versus Faculty are Assessed

Accrediting agencies do not ask academic units for evidence of student satisfaction. They demand documentation of student learning, whether at the program, school, or institutional level. Similarly, legislators, government agencies, prospective employers of graduates, and the general public are concerned almost exclusively about student learning. Why should individual instructors be evaluated any differently from the units they make up? Given what students value, measures of their satisfaction may or may not belong in faculty reviews, but measures of student learning most definitely deserve a prominent place. After all, the job of an instructor is not to please students but to motivate and facilitate their learning, which corresponds to the mission of every college and university. In fact, learning can work against pleasing students. It often makes them uncomfortable and even dissatisfied for a time because it requires effort, focus, self-examination, acknowledgment of error, and changes in values, beliefs, attitudes, and behavior. Relying on measures of course-level student learning to evaluate the quality of faculty members' instruction would bring the indicators of the academic effectiveness into alignment across institutional levels.

## Measures of Student Learning on the Course Level

Few disciplines offer course-specific standardized tests, and those that do (e.g., economics and physics) offer only one or two tests at the introductory level. Student portfolios are cumbersome and time-consuming to evaluate. Members of accreditation teams may have the time to examine a representative sample, but administrators clearly do not. Therefore, these two instruments for measuring student learning—versions of which work on the institutional, school, and program levels—will not work for courses. Faculty need instruments that make data on their students' learning easy to collect and easy to reduce to a single number for each course. The latter is essential to facilitate administrative use in reviews. In addition, for the sake of efficiency, these instruments should do double-duty as learning enhancements or as major tests or assignments that the faculty would give anyway.

The options presented here meet these conditions. They all come from recent literature and have been used to measure learning, though not all for faculty review. The instruments fall into four classifications determined by when the instructor collects the data—only at the end of the course or at the beginning and the end in a pre- and posttest design—and whether these data are direct or indirect measures of student learning. Table 17.1 displays the instruments as classified. Of course, the most

---

Table 17.1   Course-Level Measures of Student Learning

|  | Indirect | Direct |
|---|---|---|
| End of course only | Perceived student learning gains instruments (self-regulated learning activity) | Integrative essay or journal entry (capstone paper or final exam)<br>Targeted essay (capstone paper or final exam) |
| Pre- and posttest | Knowledge surveys (self-regulated learning activity) | First writing (ungraded) and correction exercise (final exam)<br>First-week essays (ungraded) and "value-added" essay<br>Final exam<br>First-week final exam (ungraded) and final exam |

scientifically legitimate category measures learning directly in a pre- and posttest design. Only this type of indicator separates course-acquired knowledge and skills from those learned prior to the course.

## Indirect, End-of-Course-Only Measures

This category includes all instruments that ask students to assess their learning in a course at the end of it. They tap students' perceived learning, not their actual learning, which is why they are called "indirect." The two instruments described here can be used by instructors for free and have been validated or are in the process of validation. Student scores on the relevant items can be averaged to reduce the results to a single number.

The Student Assessment of Learning Gains (SALG) survey instrument (at http://www.salgsite.org) is the best known and most widely used of this type. Elaine Seymour, author of *Talking about Leaving: Why Undergraduates Leave the Sciences* (1997), developed it for chemistry courses in 1997. Ten years later, she and two colleagues revised it for use across the disciplines. The questions ask students to assess their learning gains in a course and the degree to which specific course components helped that learning. The items address different facets of learning: general, understanding concepts, acquiring skills, developing positive attitudes about the course or subject matter, and integrating information. The course components include class activities, assessments, specific learning methods, laboratories, and resources provided. Students respond on a five-point scale, from "no gains" to "great gains" or from "no help" to "great help." Instructors can easily customize the questions to their own courses. Some faculty have submitted their SALG results in their personnel review—a few in lieu of student ratings (Seymour, Wiese, Hunter, & Daddinrud, 2000).

In validity testing, student scores on the revised version correlated moderately but significantly ($r = .41$) with student scores on the final exam. In specific topic areas, the correlations between students' SALG scores and the corresponding subsection on the final exam ranged between .49 and zero.

A modest learning enhancement accompanies this instrument. Students examine and assess what they have learned, which is a self-regulated learning activity (Schraw, 1998; Zimmerman, 1998, 2002). As a one-time exercise, it will help them realize that they have indeed learned something, reducing the likelihood that they will complain on their student rating form that they did not learn anything.

The Transparency in Learning and Teaching (TLT) survey instrument (https://illinois.edu/sb/sec/1428) is so new that it is still two to three years into its pilot phase. As of mid-2012, this phase had surveyed about seventy-five hundred students in seventy-two courses at nine institutions in five countries. The instrument aims primarily to measure the learning impact, as perceived by students, of transparent teaching methods—that is, those that raise students' awareness of the processes by which they are learning. Such methods span a range of instructor actions that help students learn how they learn, including these: explaining in advance the learning goals, outcomes, benefits, and standards of success of the course activities and assignments; letting students help plan classes; telling them about upcoming topics and questions and inviting them to select related material they would like to learn about; gauging their understanding with in-class conceptual and application questions; teaching them brain-based learning principles; having them assess their own work using the instructor's grading criteria; asking them to correct their errors and strengthen the weak areas in their work; and having them record, analyze, and evaluate the process they use to prepare for exams and complete assignments.

The TLT starts out with three general questions about how well students understand course content, how accurately their submitted work reflects this understanding, and the extent to which course work and course activities benefited their learning. These and the other twenty-five perceived-learning items offer a choice of five Likert-type responses. The next nine questions ask students how much the course has helped them acquire or refine certain skills, such as writing effectively, learning how to learn, and applying concepts to practical problems or in new situations. Another nine questions begin with the stem, "As a result of taking this course," and ask students to assess their judgment about opinions different from their own, ideas in general, the reliability of sources, and the like; their confidence in their ability to succeed academically or in this field; and the likelihood of their discussing course-acquired ideas outside class and asking future instructors about the learning benefits of course components. The final four perceived-learning items address miscellaneous issues, such as whether students understand what successful work is in the course and how much the instructor valued them as students.

Most of the transparent teaching methods are standard activities and assignments for helping student develop self-regulated learning skills (Wirth, 2008; Zimmerman, 1998, 2002). Therefore, in a course that has these skills among its learning outcomes and uses these teaching methods, the TLT instrument can serve at least two purposes. First, it can help students assess their progress in developing these skills and the impact of these skills on their learning in the course. If a course incorporates enough of these teaching methods, it can indeed build self-regulated skills. Second, the TLT should be able to measure differences in students' perceived learning against baseline courses without such methods.

**Weaknesses.** Of course, perceived learning is not actual learning. In addition, students are not always good judges of their learning and abilities. The literature on student self-assessment, as meta-analyzed by Falchikov and Boud (1989), reports that students tend to rate their skills and the quality of their work higher than faculty rate the same student performances. Students' self-assessments are especially inflated among nonscience and introductory-level students. Others have found that students' perceived learning is unrelated to their actual learning but is related to the grade they expect to receive (Weinberg, Fleisher, & Hashimoto, 2007; Weinberg et al., 2009). Similarly, students in the Wabash study failed to perceive how much they had learned as measured by several standardized tests (Bowman, 2011; Porter, 2012). To explain the disjuncture between self-reported and actual learning, Porter proposed and found considerable evidence for the belief-sampling model of survey response, which hypothesizes that students base their self-reports on how many beliefs, feelings, and memories about learning related content they can easily access. The more recollections they have, the greater the learning gains reported, which accounts for why perceived learning correlates with students' academic ability, interest in the subject matter, and experiences in their major.

## Indirect, Pre- and Posttest Measures

Knowledge surveys, classic examples of this type of measure, are useful because their results vary with student learning (Nuhfer & Knipp, 2003; Wirth & Perkins, 2005, 2008). They ask students to rate how confident they are that they can answer questions or perform tasks covering the course content and skills. Students choose from three or four levels of confidence. (Examples of suitable geology questions and tasks, each labeled by the required cognitive operation, are at http://serc.carleton.edu /NAGTWorkshops/assess/knowledgesurvey/examples.html.) Knowledge surveys also claim the scientific legitimacy of pre- and posttest measures because the instructor administers the same survey at the beginning and end of the course. A course score representing student learning can be calculated by finding the average difference in pre- and posttest confidence ratings across items or by using the more refined methods in the section below on direct, pre- and posttest measures. Because knowledge surveys make students reflect on their learning, as do the indirect, end-of-course-only measures above, they also have some additional value as a self-regulated learning activity.

**Weaknesses.** As an indirect measure of student learning based on student perceptions, knowledge surveys have the same validity problem as the indirect, end-of-course-only measures. When students come into a course, most of them, especially nonscience introductory-level students, are overly confident about what they know and can do. At the end of the course, however, they may underestimate what they know and can do and perform better on the final exam than their knowledge survey results would predict. Wirth and Perkins (2008) recorded this pattern in at least one course. Either distortion will lead to underestimating the amount of student learning in a course.

## Direct, End-of-Course-Only Measures

One major advantage of direct, end-of-course measures of learning, whether end-of-course-only or pre- and posttest, is that they can double as a final exam or capstone assignment. Of course, they should reflect the ultimate (end-of-course) student learning outcomes of the course, if not some mediating outcomes as well. So if the ultimate outcomes of a management course on decision modeling are to diagnose a real-world managerial problem, devise multiple solutions, and evaluate them to select the best, this is exactly what the final assessment instrument should have students do, mostly likely for a given case study. Instructors can report their students' learning as the average numerical score (grade in percentage terms) of the final exam or capstone assignment.

The literature suggests two other approaches to measuring end-of-course learning. One is the integrative essay or journal entry in which students review all the course material and draw their own conclusions about the most important things they learned and the value of this material to them now and in the future (Atlas, 2007). A more concrete, applied alternative is to place students in a real-world situation they are likely to face soon and ask them how they would use the course material. For example, a job interviewer asks them to describe the most important things they learned in the course and to demonstrate their skills in applying these things (Weimer, 2007).

**Weaknesses.** As with any other end-of-course-only measure, it is impossible to identify and "remove" the course-related knowledge that students already had coming into the course. In addition, instructors can stack the grading and the results to ensure their students do well. Peer reviewers might want to see the questions that the students answered on the grading rubric and some sample essays.

## Direct, Pre- and Posttest Measures

From a scientific standpoint, these measures are the gold standard because they can remove students' precourse knowledge from the end-of-course assessment. They entail an assessment at the beginning of the course, the pretest, and the same or very similar assessment at the end, the posttest. Both of these presumably reflect the course's learning outcomes. In Griffiths's (2010) version, she gives her students in her Miscarriage of Justice course the pretest the first week of the semester in the form of an ungraded writing assignment. She asks them to define key concepts, cite important statistics, describe processes, and do other things that they generally will not be able to do accurately until they complete the course. Then for the final, she asks the students to think of themselves as professors of the course and to critique and grade their first-week assignments. Their specific task is to write a letter to their "preclass self" correcting errors, poor reasoning, and misconceptions and to supply accurate answers to the questions.

Anthropology professor John Coggeshall (personal correspondence, 2010–2011) gives his students a first-week, ungraded writing assignment that asks them to take a position, from strongly agree to strongly disagree, on seven statements—some true but most commonly believed myths—and to justify their stand in a sentence or two. For example, one statement claims that the arrival of the Europeans was responsible for Native Americans developing complex societies and another that agriculture and animal domestication radically improved most human lives. At the final exam, he returns these assignments and has his students critique and rewrite four of their original answers, drawing on the course material for supporting evidence and describing how and why their thinking has changed, if it has. He calls these second, much longer essays "value-added," and he scores them on the quality of the evidence students incorporate to justify their end-of-course position. This criterion reflects his most important ultimate learning outcome.

Another option, which may be more suitable for science, technology, engineering, and mathematics courses, is to give students the final exam in class the first week, calling it an ungraded diagnostic exam, and again as the regular final at the end of the course. During the first week, students need little time to complete the test. If an instructor informs them afterward that they just took the final exam, they will try to remember all they can and watch for relevant material during the course. Faculty who feel uncomfortable with this pre- and posttest arrangement can use a previous final exam as the pretest, although the pre- and posttest comparison will not be pure. The same is recommended for faculty who administer the pretest online and risk their students downloading the document.

For his faculty reviews, Coggeshall simply reports the percentage of his students who buttressed their positions on their value-added essay final with anthropological evidence, and all the reviewing parties honor this approach. In many institutions, the average score on the final exam may serve as adequate evidence of student learning. But to provide true pre- and posttest results, an instructor must score (though not grade) the pretests in order to determine students' learning gains during the course.

Two ways to calculate these gains are available. The first gives the percentage by which students increased their knowledge of the course subject matter during the course:

$$\text{Ideal types of social capital}\left(\frac{\text{Average posttest\%} - \text{Average pretest\%}}{\text{Average pretest\%}}\right) \times 100$$

Therefore, if the students' average score was 20 percent on the pretest and 75 percent on the final, students increased their knowledge and skills in the subject matter by 225 percent during the course:

$$\frac{75 - 20}{20} = 55 = 2.75 \times 100 = 225$$

Critics of this method view this result as meaningless (Hake, 1998). They argue that the relevant ratio is the actual average learning gain (posttest minus pretest) to the possible learning gain in the course (100 in the posttest minus the pretest)—that is, how much the students learned of all that they could have learned in the course. This ratio is represented by this equation, which Hake calls the "average normalized gain":

$$\frac{(\text{Average posttest\%} - \text{Average pretest\%}) \times 100}{(100\% - \text{Average pretest\%})}$$

Given the same average percentage scores as above, students learned 68.75 percent of the knowledge and skills that they *could* have learned in the course:

$$\frac{(75 - 20)}{(100 - 20)} = \frac{55}{80} = .6875 \times 100 = 68.75$$

Obviously it is important that instructors state the calculation they are using and interpret the results correctly for their reviewers.

## Conclusion

Institutions have good reason to shift from student ratings to measures of student learning to assess the teaching effectiveness of their faculty. Not only have student ratings lost their validity as proxy measures of learning, but programs, schools, and entire institutions gain or lose their accreditation and their legitimacy with their stakeholders on the basis of their students' learning. Shouldn't faculty be evaluated on the same criteria as the units they constitute?

None of the measures of course-level student learning examined here are perfect, though direct, pre- and posttest measures are probably the least flawed. Any of them can be slanted in the instructor's favor, but to an extent, so can the indicators of student learning used by programs, schools, and institutions; they can be set to increase the likelihood of meeting expectations. No measure of anything as complex as student learning will be perfect, but we can do better by our faculty than to assess their teaching effectiveness using a measure that is no longer related to student learning.

REFERENCES

Arreola, R. A. (2007). *Developing a comprehensive faculty evaluation system: A guide to designing, building, and operating large-scale faculty evaluation systems* (3rd ed.). San Francisco, CA: Jossey-Bass.

Atlas, J. L. (2007, June/July). The end of the course: Another perspective. *Teaching Professor*, 3.

Bowman, N. A. (2011, April 11). *The validity of college seniors' self-reported gains as a proxy for longitudinal growth*. Paper presented at the annual meetings of the American Educational Research Association, New Orleans, LA.

Braskamp, L. A., & Ory, J. C. (1994). *Assessing faculty work: Enhancing individual and institutional performance*. San Francisco, CA: Jossey-Bass.

Carrell, S. E., & West, J. E. (2010). Does professor quality matter? Evidence from random assignment of students to professors. *Journal of Political Economy, 118*(3), 409–432.

Cashin, W. E. (1989). *Defining and evaluating college teaching* (IDEA Paper No. 21). Manhattan: Center for Faculty Evaluation and Development, Kansas State University.

Cashin, W. E. (1995) *Student ratings of teaching: The research revisited* (IDEA Paper No. 32). Manhattan: Center for Faculty Development and Evaluation, Kansas State University.

Cashin, W. E. (2003). Evaluating college and university teaching: Reflections of a practitioner. In J. C. Smart (Ed.), *Higher education: Handbook of theory and research* (pp. 531–593). Dordrecht, Netherlands: Kluwer Academic.

Clayson, D. E. (2009). Student evaluations of teaching: Are they related to what students learn? A meta-analysis and review of the literature. *Journal of Marketing Education, 31*(1), 16–30. Retrieved from http://jmd.sagepub .com/content/31/1/16.full.pdf+html

Clayson, D. E. (2011). *A multi-disciplined review of the student teacher evaluation process.* Retrieved from http://business.uni.edu/clayson/Ext/SET Summary2011.doc

Clayson, D. E. (2013). Initial impressions and the student evaluation of teaching. *Journal of Education for Business, 88,* 26–35. doi:10.1080/08832323 .2011.633580

Clayson, D. E., & Haley, D. A. (2011, Summer). Are students telling us the truth? A critical look at the student evaluation of teaching. *Marketing Education Review, 21,* 101–112.

Cohen, P. A. (1981). Student ratings of instruction and student achievement: A meta-analysis of multisection validity studies. *Review of Educational Research, 51,* 281–309.

Falchikov, N., & Boud, D. (1989). Student self-assessment in higher education: A meta-analysis. *Review of Educational Research, 59*(4), 395–430.

Feldman, K. A. (1989). The association between student ratings of specific instructional dimensions and student achievement: Refining and extending the synthesis of data from multisection validity studies. *Research in Higher Education, 30,* 583–645.

Griffiths, E. (2010). Clearing the misty landscape: Teaching students what they didn't know then, but know now. *College Teaching, 58,* 32–37.

Hake, R. R. (1998). Interactive-engagement versus traditional methods: A six thousand-student survey of mechanics test data for introductory physics courses. *American Journal of Physics, 66*(1), 64–74.

Johnson, V. E. (2003). *Grade inflation: A crisis in higher education.* New York: Springer-Verlag.

La Lopa, J. M. (2011). Student reflection on quality teaching and how to assess it in higher education. *Journal of Culinary Science and Technology, 9*(4), 282–292.

Marks, M., Fairris, D., & Beleche, T. (2010, June 3). *Do course evaluations reflect student learning? Evidence from a pre-test/post-test setting.* Riverside:

Department of Economics, University of California, Riverside. Retrieved from http://faculty.ucr.edu/~mmarks/Papers/marks2010course.pdf

Marsh, H. W. (1984). Students' evaluations of university teaching: Dimensionality, reliability, validity, potential biases, and utility. *Journal of Educational Psychology, 76,* 707–754.

Nilson, L. B. (2012). Time to raise questions about student ratings. In J. E. Groccia & L. Cruz (Eds.), *To improve the academy: Resources for faculty, instructional, and organizational development, Vol. 31* (pp. 213–228). San Francisco, CA: Jossey-Bass.

Nuhfer, E. B. (2010). *A fractal thinker looks at student ratings.* Retrieved from http://profcamp.tripod.com/fractalevals10.pdf

Nuhfer, E. B., & Knipp, D. (2003). The knowledge survey: A tool for all reasons. In C. Wehlburg & S. Chadwick-Blossey (Eds.), *To improve the academy: Resources for faculty, instructional, and organizational development, Vol. 21* (pp. 59–78). Bolton, MA: Anker.

Porter, S. R. (2012). Self-reported learning gains: A theory and test of college student survey response. *Research in Higher Education, 54,* 201–226. doi:10.1007/s11162–012–9277–0

Schraw, G. (1998). Promoting general metacognitive awareness. *Instructional Science, 26,* 113–125. Retrieved from http://www.springerlink.com/content/w8840214g78445h/

Seymour, E. (1997). *Talking about leaving: Why undergraduates leave the sciences.* Boulder, CO: Westview Press.

Seymour, E., Wiese, D. J., Hunter, A., & Daddinrud, S. M. (2000, March 27). *Creating a better mousetrap: Online student assessment of their learning gains.* Paper presented at the national meetings of the American Chemical Society Symposium, Using Real-World Questions to Promote Active Learning, San Francisco, CA. Retrieved from http://www.salgsite.org/docs/SALGPaperPresentationAtACS.pdf

Sproule, R. (2002). The underdetermination of instructor performance by data from the student evaluation of teaching. *Economics of Education Review, 21,* 287–295.

Stanfel, L. E. (1995). Measuring the accuracy of student evaluations of teaching. *Journal of Instructional Psychology, 22*(2), 117–125.

Stark-Wroblewski, K., Ahlering, R. F., & Brill, F. M. (2007). Toward a more comprehensive approach to evaluating teaching effectiveness: Supplementing student evaluations of teaching with pre-post learning measures. *Assessment and Evaluation in Higher Education, 44*(5), 539–556. Retrieved from http://www.tandfonline.com/doi/pdf/10.1080/02602930600898536

Steiner, S., Holley, L. C., Gerdes, K., & Campbell, H. E. (2006). Evaluating teaching: Listening to students while acknowledging bias. *Journal of Social Work Education, 42,* 355–376.

*Student Assessment of Learning Gains (SALG) survey instrument.* (n.d.). Retrieved from http://www.salgsite.org

Transparency in Learning and Teaching survey instrument. (n.d.). Retrieved from https://illinois.edu/sb/sec/1428

Weinberg, B. A., Fleisher, B. M., & Hashimoto, M. (2007). *Evaluating methods of evaluating instruction: The case of higher education* (NBER Working Paper No. 12844.) Retrieved from http://www.nber.org/papers/w12844

Weinberg, B. A., Hashimoto, M., & Fleisher, B. M. (2009). Evaluating teaching in higher education. *Journal of Economic Education, 40*(3), 227–261. Retrieved from http://dx.doi.org/10.3200/JECE.40.3.227-261

Weimer, M. (2007, February). Helping students take stock of learning. *Teaching Professor,* 4.

Williams, W. M., & Ceci, S. J. (1997). How'm I doing? Problems with student ratings of instructors and courses. *Change, 29*(5), 13–23.

Wirth, K. R. (2008, November 19–21). *A metacurriculum on metacognition.* Keynote address presented at the National Association of Geoscience Teachers Workshops: The Role of Metacognition in Teaching Geoscience, Carleton College, Northfield, MN. Retrieved from http://serc.carleton.edu/NAGTWorkshops/metacognition/wirth.html

Wirth, K. R., & Perkins, D. (2005, April 2). Knowledge surveys: The ultimate course design and assessment tool for faculty and students. In *Proceedings of the Innovations in the Scholarship of Teaching and Learning Conference,* Northfield, MN. Retrieved from http://www.macalester.edu/geology/wirth/WirthPerkinsKS.pdf

Wirth, K. R., & Perkins, D. (2008, November 19–21). *Knowledge surveys.* Session presented at the National Association of Geoscience Teachers Workshops: The Role of Metacognition in Teaching Geoscience, Carleton College, Northfield, MN. Retrieved from http://serc.carleton.edu/NAGTWorkshops/assess/knowledgesurvey/

Zimmerman, B. J. (1998). Developing self-fulfilling cycles of academic regulation: An analysis of exemplary instructional models. In D. H. Schunk & B. J. Zimmerman (Eds.), *Self-regulated learning: From teaching to self-reflective practice* (pp. 1–19). New York: Guilford.

Zimmerman, B. J. (2002). Becoming a self-regulated learner: An overview. *Theory into Practice, 41*(2), 64–70.

# 18

# MOBILE APP LEARNING LOUNGE

## A SCALABLE AND SUSTAINABLE MODEL FOR
## TWENTY-FIRST-CENTURY LEARNING

*Michael H. Truong*
*Azusa Pacific Univeristy*

Education in the mobile age does not replace formal education, any more than the worldwide web replaces the textbook; rather it offers a way to extend the support of learning outside the classroom, to the conversations and interactions of everyday life.
(Sharples, Taylor, & Vavoula 2007, p. 243)

*Twenty-first-century learning is increasingly defined by the use of mobile devices and applications. Centers for teaching and learning can help faculty and students acquire greater familiarity and fluency with just-in-time learning using mobile apps by creating informal, inviting, and informative learning spaces on their campuses. This chapter features the Mobile App Learning Lounge (MALL), a low-cost, high-impact initiative of a center for teaching and learning at a California research university. Beyond sharing how MALL works, this chapter offers practical suggestions and strategies for replicating a similar initiative at other institutions.*

o

In the 2012 Horizon Report, mobile applications (or mobile apps) ranked as the most immediate technology that has "impacts on virtually every aspect of informal life, and increasingly, every discipline in the university" (Johnson, Adams, & Cummins, 2012, p. 6). Apps are the software that runs new mobile devices like smart phones and tablets, many of them equipped with always-on data network, cameras, accelerometer, and location-based technology. As of October 2012 there are close to 700,000 apps available for download within the Android marketplace and over 600,000 apps within the Apple marketplace. Moreover, smart phone and tablet users worldwide downloaded more than 45 billion apps in 2012, nearly twice as many as in 2011 (Reisinger, 2012).

Two key factors have facilitated the growth and popularity of mobile app use within the education sector. First is the plethora of the types of educational apps available. Given the thousands of educational apps, there is bound to be an "app for that" for whatever discipline, project, task, topic, or interest. There are many websites (e.g., appitic.com, iear.org, and teacherswithapps.com) dedicated to helping teachers and students find just the right app to accomplish a task. A second factor is the low cost of apps. Most educational apps cost a few dollars, and many ad-supported or limited-feature versions are free. Given the cheap price tag of most educational apps, students are more willing to pay for this kind of technology compared to purchasing software for their computers. The abundance and affordability of mobile apps have made it possible for students and teachers to customize their devices to suit their needs and interests easily and economically.

This chapter addresses two key questions: How is mobile technology affecting learning? and What role can centers for teaching and learning (CTLs) play in helping to foster the meaningful adoption of mobile technology at their campuses? I feature a nationally recognized initiative of the Center for Research on Teaching Excellence (CRTE Center) at the University of California, Merced (UCM): the Mobile App Learning Lounge (MALL). Beyond sharing how MALL supports undergraduate teaching and learning goals, this chapter offers practical tips and strategies for institutions interested in implementing (or enhancing already existing) mobile technology initiatives.

## Mobile Technology and Its Impact on Learning

According to the EDUCAUSE Center for Applied Research's (ECAR) Study of Undergraduate Students and Information Technology Report (Dahlstrom, 2012), laptop ownership among college students nationally is currently around 85 percent (a change of 83 percent since 2004), and the rate of smart phone ownership is around 62 percent (a whopping change of 5,545 percent since 2004). Experts predict that the rate of smart phones and tablets ownership among students will continue to increase in the next couple of years to a point equal to or greater than that of laptops. Given their cheaper price tag, lighter form factor, and the ever-growing app market, mobile devices are poised to become students' primary and preferred technology for communication (e.g., SMS, e-mail, phone), social networking (Facebook, Twitter), and course management (accessing course materials, checking grades, completing assessments) (Johnson, Adams, & Cummins, 2012).

Mobile learning has not just changed but dramatically challenged the traditional academic context (Brown & Diaz, 2010). For example, the high rate of ownership of smart phones and other mobile devices like laptops has made keeping mobile technology out of the classroom almost impossible. Course policies could mitigate the presence of cell phones, but perhaps a more fruitful approach to this technology would be to leverage them toward academic and classroom purposes, bridging the social and the academic worlds students straddle. As a result, teachers must learn how to channel and direct mobile technology use among their students to support the curriculum constructively. Otherwise the enormous potential of mobile technology to improve learning will go unrealized or, worse, disconnected from the daily realities of students.

## Redefining the Classroom

Mobile learning is not just challenging the traditional understanding of the classroom as the center of learning; it is also demystifying the way students learn (Sharples, Arnedillo-Sanchez, Milrad, & Vavoula, 2009). In the traditional classroom model, an illusion of centrality is supported by a fixed location, common resources, a single teacher, and a faculty-derived curriculum. In reality, learning (both formal and informal) has never been bounded by any particular location, time, topic, or technology. Rather, it occurs between and across these contexts, whereby what is learned in one domain influences and is informed by another. For example, much of what students learn in informal contexts (from friends and the media, say) can become a resource for more formal contexts like seminars, lecture halls, and exams. With the advent of always-on mobile devices, students can navigate between and across these contexts more easily, more quickly, and more seamlessly, learning to make meaning from the flow of everyday activities.

Students with mobile devices and constant communication do not fit the traditional educational model (Sharples et al., 2007). Traditional classroom learning is regulated by curriculum and mediated by a teacher, which contrasts significantly from the rich interaction of mobile learning with texts, Twitter, and Tumblr. Higher education is entering what Randy Bass (2012) refers to as the "postcourse era"—a time when the formal curriculum of bounded, self-contained courses is no longer the primary place where the most significant learning takes place. Mobile technology is unbundling the course and paving the way for ubiquitous learning, defined as true, authentic learning that takes place beyond the classroom walls, without a formal curriculum, and absent formal teacher figures (Cope & Kalantzis, 2009).

Mobile technology is ushering in what is being called just-in-time or on-demand learning—the concept that students with network-connected mobile devices can access relevant information in the immediate context they are in and at the exact time they need it. For example, in a class where all course materials (syllabus, readings, assignments, lectures, and so on) are available on a learning management system (LMS), students are able to access what they need, wherever they are, and whenever they need it. This learning model radically transforms the traditional learning environment, characterized as static, inefficient, and standardized, into a dynamic, interactive, and customized environment where students become active agents in their own learning (Hall, 2001). In this new environment, students, performing at varying levels with varying types of needs, in theory can get the appropriate information they seek at just the right time.

In short, instead of seeing mobile learning as a threat to formal education, teachers can identify and harness the potential benefits of mobile technology to transform the learning experience for their students. Here are four concrete examples of how mobile learning can radically redefine the classroom.

- *Interspersed learning.* Since mobile devices tend to be highly personal and portable, like a wallet, individuals typically take their devices wherever they go. As a result, learners can fit learning into their own schedule (as opposed to rigid, scheduled times), enabling them to learn during down time and in transit. For example, students using digital text/book apps like Kindle, Kno, Inkling, and CourseSmart can access their course readings at their convenience throughout the day with just one device compared to having to carry all of their course texts.

- *Social learning.* Mobile devices allow teachers and students to have greater access to and communication with one another, making mobile learning inherently more interactive and social. For example, text messaging and other messaging apps like Facebook Messenger,

Voxer, Skype, and Twitter facilitate direct and instantaneous communication between two individuals or a group of individuals. Teachers and students can send reminders and time-sensitive messages, providing just-in-time and just-enough information. (One caveat is the importance of setting boundaries, protecting intrusions into private lives. For example, teachers and students alike probably do not appreciate receiving text messages at midnight or other odd times. It is important to have policies establishing ground rules of using this form of communication.)

○ *Context-based learning.* Most mobile devices equipped with GPS and other context-awareness features bring a new dimension to learning in the field. For example, students doing fieldwork or on a field trip can use apps like Evernote and Catch to take pictures, write notes, and record audio and video files—all of which will have contextual data, such as the exact time, location, and condition of when and where the data were collected.

○ *Reflective learning.* Mobile devices can be used to record personal reflections and engagement with materials as learning happens. For example, students can use annotation apps like Adobe Reader, Notability, and iAnnotatePDF to highlight and mark up what they are reading. Moreover, study apps like StudyBlue and Quizlet allow students to create flash cards based on reading materials that they can use for reviewing and reinforcing key concepts and understanding.

## Improving Student Learning and Engagement

One of the key questions surrounding the efficacy of mobile learning in higher education is whether it improves learning. According to one of the earliest empirical studies, students' use of a mobile app in an introductory statistics class increased their motivation and improved their ability to obtain significantly higher final grades (Nihalani & Mayrath, 2010). The researchers cited the portability and interactive tools of the apps as the primary motivations for continued use, leading to improved student learning experiences. Moreover, students reported using the mobile app more often than they used their textbooks. Other studies involving the use of iPads have yielded similar positive results, including improved performance on course learning outcomes (Hoover & Valencia, 2011), increased content engagement (Marmarelli & Ringle, 2011), and enhanced academic experience (Walker, 2011). Mobile devices coupled with appropriate educational apps have increased students' engagement and interaction with course content, augmented face-to-face instruction, and ultimately led to improved performance.

According to Belshaw (2011) of JISC InfoNet, United Kingdom's leading advisory organization on information and learning technology for higher education, mobile learning works because it not only aligns well with many goals of educational institutions (e.g., curriculum redesign, digital literacies, reducing costs) but also reinforces established principles of learning (e.g., personalized learning, active learning, increased engagement). A case in point is our library's iPod Touch Tour—a virtual tour downloaded on an Apple iPod Touch designed to help students get acquainted with the library's services, space, and resources (Davidson & Mikkelson, 2009). After the virtual tour, students complete an assignment that assesses their understanding of the library's space, services, and resources. Based on two years' worth of data, the library found that students who did the iPod Touch Tour scored just as well as, if not better than, in-person instruction. Moreover, students noted a significant preference for learning about the library using the iPod Touch Tour compared to other synchronous in-person methods.

The power of mobile learning is being leveraged across many areas of higher education. Many institutions already use modern LMSs, such as Blackboard, Desire2Learn, and Canvas, that come with mobile access via native or web apps, allowing students to access their course resources, complete surveys, submit assignments, and communicate with instructors and peers. Moreover, many discipline-specific apps are helping students develop and deepen disciplinary knowledge in ways that learning with desktop and laptop computers cannot or is not as convenient. For example, in mathematics, apps such as Wolfram Alpha Course Assistant, Video Calculus, and Khan Academy help students learn and reinforce key mathematical concepts using audio and video files, question banks, and step-by-step problem-solving tutorials. For students majoring in life sciences, Biology Buddy, The Elements, and Science360, among other apps, are designed to inform, instruct, and inspire users to hone their skills in the discipline. Beyond anywhere, anytime availability, many educational apps leverage the audio, video, spatial, and interactive interfaces mobile devices afford, making learning deeper, richer, and longer compared to traditional approaches.

## The Role of CTLs in Fostering Mobile Learning

Mobile learning is not merely changing higher education; it is transforming it in profound ways. "Faculty benefit [from mobile learning] because students are more engaged. They [students] are more interested in the material, they operate at a more advanced level, and it has actually been the most rewarding teaching I've done in 25 years," says Bill Rankin, director of educational innovation at Abilene Christian University (2012). Mobile learning promises to help teachers and learners communicate more frequently, collaborate more closely, and converge around learning. In other words, CTLs can leverage mobile learning to enhance curriculum, reimagine pedagogy, and ultimately transform roles whereby students are seen as participants and agents in learning activities and teachers act as their guides and mentors. Moreover, the "classroom" is no longer defined by or confined to the physical space within four walls, but exists also in virtual space, including e-mails, discussion forums, chat, social media sites, and many other channels. The key question for CTLs is figuring out how to harness current and emerging trends in mobile learning into practical pedagogies and best practices that are helpful to advance teaching and learning.

Many universities have robust mobile learning initiatives. Arguably, the best publicized is Abilene Christian University's (ACU) Connected Initiative. Since 2007, ACU has been providing its four thousand students and seven hundred professors with iPhones and, more recently, with iPads, making them a one-to-one device campus. ACU's innovative mobile learning initiative has helped garner it national and international attention, making it a model school for how mobile learning can enhance and extend learning inside and outside the classroom. Similar initiatives at other universities, including MIT, Boise State University, and Northeastern University, have received less publicity, but they too have done innovative work to show how mobile learning is helping to improve student learning and engagement.

These mobile learning initiatives are hard to duplicate at other campuses because they require extensive resources in terms of funding, personnel, and expertise. As a result, schools that are resource strapped (and many are these days) may feel they are not able to embark on similar initiatives. Another issue is that most campuses are typically bigger and fiscally more challenged than ACU and other private institutions with campuswide mobile initiatives. To address these implementation challenges, our center has taken mobile learning to a social format, bridging the gap between traditional classrooms and learning in the twenty-first-century. The MALL project offers an alternative low-cost, high-impact model that requires significantly fewer resources and yields equally important results.

## Conceiving MALL

It is not uncommon to find students listening to their music on their portable device or tapping away at their phones or tablets on most college campuses. In fact, on my daily bus commute to campus, I see the majority of the riders, most of them students, with their eyes glued to their mobile device screens (as I am too). This scene is not restricted to the bus. As I get off the bus at the campus library stop and walk to my office building, I see most students carrying a mobile device in one hand and their backpacks or books in the other. Since owning a mobile device became affordable and mainstream, many students have found themselves increasingly reliant on their devices in the same way they have with their desktop and laptop computers to get them through the day. CTLs have an important role to play in helping campus communities use mobile technology appropriately and effectively. For example, mobile technology is ideal for certain kinds of learning experience (e.g., creating flash cards, reviewing recorded lectures, looking up facts and information) and not for others (composing their essays on their tablets, fostering teamwork). In short, CTLs can educate a campus about innovative and appropriate ways to leverage mobile technology without compromising the learning experience.

In summer 2010, the center acquired access to forty Apple first-generation iPads, purchased by the writing program through a federal grant. Our center partnered with the writing program to create a loaner system that allowed faculty to check out iPads on a short-term basis as a way to explore their potential uses. Starting in spring 2011, the center made these iPads available for small seminar classroom use, whereby a faculty member can check out up to twenty iPads for use during a class session. Initially faculty employing these iPads mostly used them like laptops, asking students to look things up on the Internet. As the Apple iTunes Apps Store matured and offered more educational apps, faculty employed iPads in more sophisticated ways, such as using mind-mapping (MindMeister) and note-taking apps (Evernote) to facilitate brainstorming and writing sessions.

In fall 2010, the center explored ways to extend and expand the use of the forty iPads by approaching the library and asking it to host a monthly event open to the entire campus. The librarians offered one of their instructional rooms that was equipped with an LCD projector and a smart board. Because we wanted to create an environment that was physically comfortable and technologically engaging, the room was not set up like a typical classroom with tables and chairs forward facing.

The CRTE and the library brought in comfortable couches and set up tables and chairs to encourage and foster collaboration. It is important to note that the room where MALL takes place did not compromise the library's instructional spaces. Because it is a heavily used room, the layout had to stay multifunctional with flexible furniture. Prior to each MALL event, the library would set up the room and revert the room back to a classroom setup after the event. In the end, we created a learning lounge— a fun, social, and educational playground for participants to gather, share, and learn from one another. With a learning lounge in place, the first MALL event took place in January 2012.

The key lesson for CTLs interested in starting a similar mobile initiative is to identify an ally, partner together, and collaboratively bring the initiative to life. Through sharing their mobile devices, the writing program served as the initial impetus. Instead of purchasing devices, CTLs can partner with academic units that have already purchased or plan to purchase devices for their mobile initiative. Moreover, the library has been an ideal partner because it has premium real estate on campus—one that is frequently occupied by students and faculty and conveniently located at the heart of the campus. Having events located in the library made it easier to attract participants because it was already a high-traffic, high-profile location. Moreover, the mission of the library, focused squarely on information literacy and technological fluency, aligned and reinforced the goals and outcomes of the MALL initiative. Besides the library, other potential allies exist in academic affairs (e.g., the Learning Center, the Office of Undergraduate Studies) and student affairs (the Office of Student Life, Residential Life). The strategy is to find an ally open to experimenting with learning spaces and leveraging mobile technology to advance teaching and learning.

## Learning Lounge Layout

The design of physical spaces has an impact on learning in profound ways. Researchers have noted that learning spaces are themselves agents of change, and changed spaces can produce a change in pedagogy and practice (Joint Information Systems Committee, 2006). In other words, there is a built-in pedagogy in most learning spaces, whether that is the traditional classroom or informal study halls (Oblinger, 2006). Many students today prefer to learn in active, participatory, experiential ways, as opposed to sitting and listening to their professors. To that end, well-designed learning spaces can encourage exploration, collaboration, and inspiration.

MALL is designed to be experience-centric and focused on the learner, as opposed to presentation-centric, which typically foregrounds the teacher. The learning lounge allows participants to come and freely explore at their own pace and based on their interests. Individuals who do not have their own device can check out a loaner iPad, loaded with featured educational apps. A few volunteer facilitators are always available, roaming the room, ready and willing to engage with participants. The environment is similar to what one would find at an Apple Store, a museum, or an art gallery.

MALL offers bite-sized resources that can be consumed quickly and easily. Instead of a formal lecture or presentation about the latest and greatest mobile apps, participants get many small tips and ideas that are easy to digest and quick to implement for a wide range of participants from instructional staff, to undergraduates, to faculty. At every event, we distribute a one-page handout filled with featured apps and their practical application. Many participants who do not have time to stay the entire session simply stop by and grab a handout (also available on our website). What participants learn at MALL is meant to whet their appetite, not make them full. The intention is similar to Ted Talks, movie trailers, and appetizers before the main course.

In addition to being experience-centric and bite-sized, MALL promotes group learning. Learning today happens in community and distributed networks (Siemens, 2005; Thomas & Brown, 2011). Instead of one expert and many learners, MALL events encourage all participants to connect, share, discuss, engage, and learn with and from one another. The expertise and content are crowd-sourced and come directly from the participants, not any one particular person. The creation of meaning and the spark of learning happen in the act of exchange among participants. It is the same principle employed by Wikipedia, discussion forums, and social network sites. Participants who are new to mobile technology observe others, ask questions, and experience firsthand how mobile apps might benefit them. Experienced participants get to showcase their favorite apps, talk about how they use them, and share personal tips, tweaks, and frustrations. Our center also employs and trains student assistants to serve as teacher models for their peers during the event.

To facilitate learning that is centered on experience, bite-sized content, and group learning, the room is divided into two primary spaces. The first is a show-and-tell area located around the LCD screen, where volunteer presenters give brief presentations (less than five minutes) about their favorite apps and how they use them to accomplish common tasks (e.g., annotating readings, taking notes, managing files). The majority of the presentations are typically done by students. Faculty and staff who attend MALL are interested in learning how to leverage mobile technology to better reach and engage their students. The rest of the lounge is a free exploration area where participants congregate around the couches and tables, asking questions, sharing tips, and troubleshooting problems. In short, MALL serves as a rich learning community, bringing together learners of all types around mobile technology. Often interactions that begin at MALL continue beyond the event through sharing contact information or connecting to each other's social network Facebook or Twitter accounts.

In addition to developing instructors, CTLs need to play a greater role in the design of learning spaces on college campuses. Through designing new spaces or reimagining existing ones, CTLs can foster twenty-first-century learning, characterized by mobility, flexibility, and interactivity. At our campus, we were able to change the built-in pedagogy of the library by converting a traditional classroom into a learning lounge for MALL events. We have created a new learning space that encourages participants to explore mobile learning and, we hope, inspires new pedagogy and practices.

## Scaling and Sustaining the Initiative

Designated as a Hispanic-serving institution (HSI), the University of California, Merced, enrolls six thousand students, with projected growth to ten thousand students by 2020. The diverse student demographic at our institution is distinctive, with a majority of our students of Hispanic background, Pell Grant recipients (low-income), and first-generation college goers. This population is particularly at risk not to finish a college degree.

MALL events serve as a small yet important intervention, providing our students opportunities to learn, experience, and develop fluency around mobile technology. The events help reinforce high-impact educational practices such as fostering faculty-student interactions, learning communities, collaborative learning, and experiential learning—practices that have been proven to improve student retention and persistence among students in general and minority students in particular (Kuh, 2008). MALL events also attempt to close the ever-widening digital divide that many of our at-risk students face. Mobile technology has become such an integral part of learning that a student without access to a mobile device is regarded as disadvantaged. While the ownership rate of mobile devices among college students is around 60 percent nationally, the rate at our campus is half that, around 30 percent, according to a recent campus IT survey. Through MALL events and our iPad loaner program, students have access to these devices. Our financial aid office has worked closely with students and their families to ensure they can afford to purchase the appropriate technology necessary to succeed during their tenure as students.

Given the popularity and success of MALL events, the CRTE and the library are well positioned to expand the initiative. However, like most other public universities in recent years, our institution is facing severe budget cuts and constraints, so scaling our mobile learning initiative must be done in a way that is strategic and sustainable. In particular, we have developed five principles that will guide the continued development and growth of our mobile learning initiative.

First and foremost, we will need to work with IT to ensure that the wireless network throughout the campus will be robust enough to support the proliferation of devices. Our campus wireless networks are aging and reaching their limits, especially in high-density areas like the library and the classroom buildings. For mobile learning to become more widespread at our campus, IT will need to bolster the wireless infrastructure, as well as prepare to support hardware problems, such as device malfunction and troubleshooting.

Second, we will continue to align MALL to contribute directly to campus mission and priorities: student success, teaching effectiveness, and technological stewardship. We have been collecting participant feedback from each MALL event, and it has provided us valuable insight into the initiative's effectiveness and impact. We plan to extend our assessment strategy by doing a campuswide survey regarding the use of mobile technology to improve teaching and learning. When a mobile learning initiative addresses campus concerns head-on and is supported by data, it invites attention, allies, and, we hope, administrative support and resources from the top.

Third, the MALL initiative will need to focus on added pedagogical and practical value for our campus community. In other words, stakeholders, especially teachers and students, need to see tangible benefits when employing mobile technology. For students, it might mean seeing their grades improved because of the use of a specific app. For faculty, it might mean reducing their workload because a particular app helps them do something more quickly or more easily. In short, the addition of technology alone is not enough; it must be deployed purposefully and meaningfully to achieve results. Participants take what they learn at

MALL and apply it to their respective contexts, with the goal of improved experiences, learning, and productivity.

Fourth, MALL will need to continue as a low-cost, high-impact initiative in order to be scalable in tough economic times. Currently one paid staff and two student assistants spend about five hours planning, publicizing, and organizing each MALL event. MALL will continue to rely on the many participants who volunteer at each event, giving presentations, facilitating discussion, and providing content. This is a crowd-sourced model for sustaining our mobile learning initiative.

Finally, to establish MALL and put it on a sustainable path, we need to strengthen our partnership with the library, while also inviting other campus units to join in. We hope to partner with the academic schools, the bookstore, and other units, striving for mutual benefits. The collective approach could lead to the pooling of resources to expand MALL and its impact on campus.

## An Invitation to Exploration and Inspiration

The potential benefit of mobile technology on teaching and learning is incalculable, and CTLs should not leave the important task of forging a mobile learning strategy on their respective campuses to others. Those most concerned about teaching and learning should work to realize some of the promises of anytime, anywhere learning by using mobile devices and apps. At the same time, we should also work to resolve some of the known barriers and bottlenecks, such as the lack of awareness and fluency with how to apply this technology appropriately and meaningfully to improve student learning.

Like most other disruptive innovations, mobile devices and their impact on learning will not be fully understood or valued until they become common practice. Rather than waiting for the dust to settle, campuses waiting on the sidelines should begin to take small steps and get involved immediately, perhaps by starting an initiative like MALL. CTLs should consider MALL as a first step—one that serves as a springboard to more ambitious projects, such as organizing small pilots or awarding mini-grants for faculty to experiment with mobile devices in their classrooms. The sooner a campus establishes a culture for mobile learning, the sooner it will be able to identify best practices and address some of the barriers and roadblocks. For campuses not engaged with mobile learning, MALL represents an invitation to come, explore, and be inspired.

## REFERENCES

Abilene Christian University. (2012, September 7). Rankin, mobile learning initiative featured on Icelandic television. *ACU News.* Retrieved from http://www.acu.edu/news/2012/120907-rankin-mobile-learning-featured-on -icelandic-tv.html

Bass, R. (2012). Disrupting ourselves: The problem of learning in higher education. *EDUCAUSE Review, 47*(2). Retrieved from http://www.educause.edu /ero/article/disrupting-ourselves-problem-learning-higher-education

Belshaw, D. (2011, August 31). *Why mobile learning.* Retrieved from https:// mobilelearninginfokit.pbworks.com/w/page/41751178/Why-mobile-learning

Brown, M., & Diaz, V. (2010). *Mobile learning: Context and prospects.* Retrieved from http://net.educause.edu/ir/library/pdf/ELI3022.pdf

Cope, B., & Kalantzis, M. (Eds.). (2009). *Ubiquitous learning.* Champaign: University of Illinois Press.

Dahlstrom, E. (2012). *ECAR study of undergraduate students and information technology, 2012* (Research Report). Retrieved from http://net.educause .edu/ir/library/pdf/ERS1208/ERS1208.pdf

Davidson, S., & Mikkelsen, S. (2009). Desk bound no more: Reference services at a new research university library. *Reference Librarian, 50*(4), 346–355. doi:10.1080/02763870903143591

Hall, L. (2001). Just-in-time learning: Web-based/Internet delivered instruction. In *Proceedings of the Seventh Americas Conferences on Information Systems 2001* (pp. 912–914). Boston, MA. Retrieved from http://frank.itlab.us /forgetting/just_in_time.pdf

Hoover, D., & Valencia, J. (2011). iPads in the classroom: Use, learning outcomes, and the future. Paper presented at the EDUCAUSE Annual Conference. Retrieved from http://www.educause.edu/sites/default/files/library /presentations/E11/SESS081/iPads+in+the+Classroom.pdf

Joint Information Systems Committee. (2006). *Designing space for effective learning: A guide to 21st century learning space design.* Retrieved from http://www.jisc.ac.uk/uploaded_documents/JISClearningspaces.pdf

Johnson, L., Adams, S., & Cummins, M. (2012). *The NMC Horizon Report: 2012 higher education edition.* Retrieved from http://www.nmc.org/pdf /2012-horizon-report-HE.pdf

Kuh, G. D. (2008). *High-impact educational practices: What they are, who has access to them, and why they matter.* Washington, DC: Association of American Colleges and Universities. Retrieved from http://www.neasc.org /downloads/aacu_high_impact_2008_final.pdf

Marmarelli, T., & Ringle, M. (2011). *The Reed College iPad study.* Retrieved from http://www.reed.edu/cis/about/ipad_pilot/Reed_ipad_report.pdf

Nihalani, P., & Mayrath, M. (2010). *Mobile learning: Evidence of increased learning and motivation from using an iPhone app.* Retrieved from http://gylo.com/WhitePaper_03302010_Stats1.pdf

Oblinger, D. G. (2006). Space as a change agent. In D. G. Oblinger (Ed.), *Learning spaces* (pp. 1.1–1.4). Louisville, CO: EDUCAUSE. Retrieved from http://www.educause.edu/research-and-publications/books/learning-spaces

Reisinger, D. (2012, September 27). *Can Apple's Apple's App Store maintain its lead over Google Play?* Retrieved from http://news.cnet.com /8301—1035_3—57521252—94/can-apples-app-store-maintain-its-lead-over -google-play/

Sharples, M., Arnedillo-Sanchez, I., Milrad, M., & Vavoula, G. (2009). Mobile learning: Small devices, big issues. In N. Balacheff, S. Ludvigsen, T. de Jong, A. Lazonder, & S. Barnes (Eds.), *Technology-enhanced learning* (pp. 233–249). Dordrecht, Netherlands: Springer. doi:10.1007/978–1–4020–9827–7

Sharples, M., Taylor, J., & Vavoula, G. (2007). A theory of learning in the mobile age. In R. Andrews & C. Haythornthwaite (Eds.), *The Sage handbook of elearning research* (pp. 221–247). London, UK: Sage. doi:10.4135 /9781848607859

Siemens, G. (2005). Connectivism—a learning theory for the digital age. *International Journal of Instructional Technology and Distance Learning*, 2(1), 3–10. Retrieved from http://itdl.org/journal/jan_05/article01.htm

Thomas, D., & Brown, J. S. (2011). *A new culture of learning: Cultivating the imagination for a world of constant change.* Lexington, KY: CreateSpace.

Walker, J. D. (2011). *The student experience: Student survey and focus group preliminary.* Retrieved from http://www.oit.umn.edu/prod/groups/oit/@pub /@oit/@web/@evaluationresearch/documents/article/oit_article_354354.pdf

# PART SEVEN

# NEW PEDAGOGICAL CONCEPTS

19

# DETERMINING OUR OWN TEMPOS

## EXPLORING SLOW PEDAGOGY, CURRICULUM, ASSESSMENT, AND PROFESSIONAL DEVELOPMENT

*Peter A. Shaw, Bob Cole*
*Monterey Institute of International Studies*

*Jennifer L. Russell*
*Academy of Art University, San Francisco*

Being Slow means that you control the rhythms of your own life. You decide how fast you have to go in any given context. If today I want to go fast, I go fast; if tomorrow I want to go slow, I go slow. What we are fighting for is the right to determine our own tempos.

Carlo Petrini

*Key concepts and values in the Slow Living movement speak to many questions and tensions arising around calls for change in higher education, porous work/life boundaries, rapid developments in technology, concerns about sustainability, and a desire to question assumptions and move beyond tips and tricks to more fundamental issues in curriculum and pedagogy. We propose a framework for Slow learning and teaching that incorporates various trends in curriculum, pedagogy, and assessment with implications for the role of technology and for professional development.*

---------○---------

The key to Slow Living (Honoré, 2004) is an emphasis on balance, reflection, and deliberation. The more time available for reflecting and assessing, the more fully we can commit to developing our ideas and practices. In Slow writings, terms such as *careful, reflective, mindful, considered,* and *attentive* are common. The Slow movement is a response to the speed and changeability of modern life; it involves wellness, meditation, simplicity, creativity, mindfulness, and complexity. It considers the best use of time, not as "a slow-motion version of postmodern life" but as "the negotiation of different temporalities, deriving from a commitment to occupy time more attentively" and "investing it with significance through attention and deliberation" (Parkins & Craig, 2006, p. 3).

The Slow movement advocates a cultural shift toward slowing down life's pace in the face of a "more, faster, better culture" and its negative consequences, including isolation, distraction, decreased satisfaction, and stress (Levy, 2006). Its beginning can be traced to the Slow Food movement, founded in 1984 by Carlo Petrini, who was disturbed by the effects of fast food on Italian culinary traditions. It has become an international movement, aiming to preserve the best of regional cuisines; encourage the farming of plants, seeds, and animals appropriate to the local ecosystem; and make eating a deliberate and pleasurable event (Petrini, 2001).

The movement has greatly diversified. It includes facets like Slow Art, Slow Travel, and Slow Money. The slow science movement (see http://www.slow-science.org) stresses the importance of having time to plan, fail, retry, and reflect as critical to effective learning. In broader terms, Berthelsen created the World Institute of Slowness, presenting a vision for an entire "Slow Planet" and a need to teach the world the way of Slow, including Slow Education. Meredith and Storm (2009) summarize slow living as follows: "Slow Living means structuring your life around meaning and fulfillment. Similar to 'voluntary simplicity' and 'downshifting,' it emphasizes a less-is-more approach, focusing on the quality of your life . . . Slow Living addresses the desire to lead a more balanced life and to pursue a more holistic sense of well-being in the fullest sense of the word."

Honoré (2004) chronicles the worldwide trend toward slowing life down, and his work has also laid the foundation for Slow Parenting

(Honoré, 2008), arguing that young people's lives are accelerated in many aspects (he refers to "academic hot-housing") and calling for giving children the time and space to explore the world on their own terms, including who they want to be. In short, "A growing body of evidence suggests that children learn better when they learn at a slower pace." Honoré cites Holt, author of a 2002 manifesto calling for "Slow Schooling": "At a stroke, the notion of the slow school destroys the idea that schooling is about cramming, testing, and standardizing experience" (Honoré, 2004, p. 255). Priesnitz (2000) summarizes Langer's (1998) work on mindfulness, sketching an outline of Slow learning to stress the importance of examining the world at the learner's own speed, relishing, questioning, and comprehending the experiences encountered, and reflecting on the outcomes. Slow, mindful learning is oriented away from rapid results or competitive features and toward inquiry, dialogue, and learner autonomy.

Developing attitudes to learning and instruction in the academy are sufficiently congruent with various aspects of the slow movement that we can justify the use of the term *Slow teaching*. A large cluster of concepts (including cooperative learning, project-based learning, service-learning, contemplative pedagogy, social constructivism, metacognitive learning strategies, student autonomy, and integrative learning) points in the direction of quality over quantity; of deeper processing of smaller amounts of material; of making multiple connections among new concepts, fresh data, the real world, and the individual learner. Slow teaching has things to say about the use of technology, curriculum, pedagogy, assessment, and faculty development; in each case, we offer a sketch of those implications.

## Slow Teaching and Technology

First, the role of technology must be clarified, but with some caveats. To further the analogy between Slow teaching and Slow Food: Some is useful, healthy, and underscores community, vitality, connectivity, and intentionality. In contrast, other foods and technologies are produced and consumed without much thought, as in replacing a five-course meal with a five-dollar burger deal. Both are filling but vary greatly in their production, quality, variety of ingredients, and effects on producers and consumers. If the pedagogical purpose behind technology integration drives its inclusion, then technology can magnify the collaborative features, inputs, and reach of student work. However, if unrelenting pressures on faculty to adopt technology are allowed to override a clear understanding of both benefits and costs, then it simply replaces one tired, unreflective pedagogical practice with another.

In other words, if the tools drive the teaching, then technology is an add-on, a distraction, or a gimmick. If, however, the teaching shifts to explore new possibilities for using the tools, then collaboration, empowerment, and efficiency will follow. For example, merely transcribing lecture notes onto PowerPoint slides posted online deploys the tool, but the curriculum, pedagogy, and level of engagement remain unchanged. Conversely, if a class uses Twitter to discuss readings outside class and talk to experts in the field, then several things have shifted: in-class time is freed up for workshop and peer critique, and students establish a link to the real world while discussing discipline-relevant topics. We recommend that technology integration decisions be carefully weighed, considering work/life balance, speed, intentionality, and informational and mental capacity. Efficient knowledge acquisition for the sake of speed is no match for deep engagement, regardless of the tools used. Figure 19.1 displays some of the technological tools and enhancements for the curricular and pedagogical issues we discuss in this chapter.

### Figure 19.1    A Possible Framework for Slow Teaching with Technological Enhancements

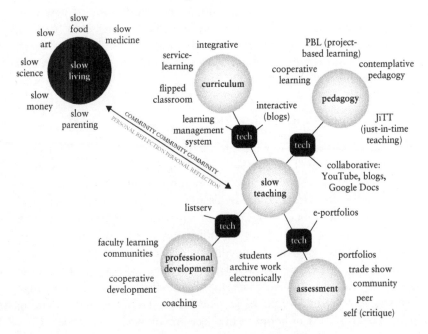

## Slow Teaching and the Curriculum

Significant shifts in accounts of effective learning will carry pedagogical implications but must also be considered in curricular terms. The movement from what Applebee (1996) calls "knowledge-out-of-context" to "knowledge-in-action" includes emphases on critical thinking, mindfulness and individual reflection, cooperative learning, and empowerment of lifelong, autonomous learners. This is summarized as *curriculum as conversation*; thus, for Applebee, planning a course syllabus has two crucial steps: selecting worthwhile content and facilitating relevant conversations about that content. Limiting content to a feasible amount is vital: "The essence of conversation is that it must allow interaction: among teacher and students, among students, among students and the texts they read or watch or listen to. If there is too much material to cover—and pressure for coverage is usually the villain here—dialogue is almost of necessity supplanted by monologue, in which the teacher reverts to telling students what they need to know" (p. 56).

This villainous urge to maximal coverage has also been diagnosed as *anupholsteryphobia*. It was Stanlee Brimberg (of the Bank Street School for Children in New York City) who coined this delicious term, defined as the fear of not covering all the material. Interviewed by learner.org about his own practice, Brimberg (n.d.) notes the diversity of students in terms of prior knowledge, skills, and learning styles. Content has to be made accessible in different formats and media, and time is a key element:

> One of the things that is really important to me is that kids have time to really digest a piece of content. I think what happens too often is that the pacing is driven by the content. The luxury at Bank Street—which shouldn't be a luxury; I think it really should be the way that it is—is that we will bite off a little bit less and we'll go over it in a number of different ways over a longer period of time. You need to have that information reinforced by reencountering it. So the more times you can go over it, the better—and of course—there's a limit. One of your most precious resources, maybe the most precious, is time.

The *anupholsteryphobia* concept is addressed in terms of college curricula by the St. John's University Center for Teaching and Learning (1999), heading its newsletter with this "not-very-funny joke": "Which condition most often afflicts university professors? Anupholsteryphobia—the dreaded fear of not covering the material. On the serious side of this issue is the fact that when faculty members begin to take student learning more seriously, they also begin to question some long held assumptions—like the importance of covering the material. This questioning of assumptions is likely to set off shock waves elsewhere in the curriculum" (p. 1).

We propose that there is a key link between this issue of coverage and that of signature pedagogies (SP) (Shulman, 2005)—instructional procedures that are deeply compatible with the core values of a particular discipline. SPs involve identifying each discipline's deep structure and following the path from there to the signature events that embody them. Shulman (2005, p. 52) defined SPs as "the types of teaching that organize the fundamental ways in which future practitioners are educated for their new professions . . . elements of instruction and of socialization that teach disciplinary novices to think, to perform, and to act with integrity to the discipline." Textbook examples of SP are hospital rounds in medical education, legal case studies, and the critique in the arts. Two recent collections (Chick, Haynie, & Gurung, 2012; Gurung, Chick, & Haynie, 2009) survey SPs across multiple disciplines. The commonality is that the traditional curriculum must make room for ways to overtly incorporate the core values, thinking, and behaviors of each discipline.

A clear example is the work of Calder (2006) in history. Encouraged by the shrinking of "the mystique of coverage," he identifies an increasing realization among history teachers that everything of significance can no longer be included; that effective history instruction is becoming oriented to "uncoverage" (Wiggins & McTighe, 1998): the design of classroom experiences to expose key ideas of historical inquiry that are neither readily observed nor easily mastered. In a survey course of American history from World War II, Calder includes a documentary film for each major topic. This in itself is not new; however, he is also determined that his students understand how a historian watches such films, processes the information and images, and reflects on the value (much as, perhaps, a medical student must learn to look at and interpret X rays or MRI images). This metacognitive dimension, crucial to "uncoverage," requires classroom time and thus reduces "coverage." In terms of syllabus design, then, SPs can provide important criteria for selecting material: Which topics will best facilitate the exposure of students to core values and discipline-specific behavioral and cognitive patterns?

In addition to the amount of material in a course syllabus, there is also the issue of pacing, which Timpson and Bendel-Simso (1996) identify as a key decision area for university instruction. They note:

> While everyone believes that students need to be challenged intellec-
> tually, it is surprising how often we teachers find ourselves faintly

apologetic for an ambitious class plan. Haven't almost all of us, at one time or another, assured our students that the material "really isn't all that difficult"? This sort of reassurance, however, can be misguided, since the message given is mixed. (p. 16)

In other words, calibration of the difficulty of learning tasks and materials, on the one hand, and of the time available for completion and mastery, on the other, is tricky. The importance of getting this right is neatly captured in Csikszentmihalyi's (1990) concept of flow, where optimal learning experiences are located in the flow channel and the levels of challenge and resources (particularly time) are suitably balanced. This dilemma is seen in Glasgow's (1997) case for student-centered, problem-based learning: "Teaching less content in a more relevant way can be scary. What must be left out? Educational inertia is at work here. Rigor should be defined not by the amount of information to memorize or the number of chapters covered, but by the complexity of solving a real problem" (p. 68).

Problem solving and introspection can be meaningfully related to experiential learning. A prominent example in recent years has been community service-learning, which has been identified as an aspect of signature pedagogies in disciplines such as psychology (Peden & Van Voorhis, 2009), women's studies (Hassel & Nelson, 2012), and physical therapy (Schaber, Marsh, & Wilcox, 2012). In all cases, class or online time again must be devoted to examining the menu of possible placements; going over the procedures for documenting the project; sharing stories, case studies, and insights; relating cognitive and affective responses; measuring their own effectiveness; and analyzing broader issues through critiques of individual experiences.

## Slow Teaching and Pedagogy

Slow teaching in curricular terms, then, means limiting the amount of material in order to incorporate various process elements. In pedagogical terms, the key point is this: the postponing of the instructor's direct participation to the best possible moment. Rather, the teacher provides a structure and facilitates the sequence of tasks. Using concepts and procedures from "the flipped classroom," JiTT (just-in-time teaching) (Millis, 2010) and naked teaching (Bowen, 2012), resources are provided in advance for students to access and organize relevant information. Coming to class, they engage in cooperative tasks, generating problem solving, critical thinking, brainstorming, and integrative processes that culminate in contemplative, reflective, and evaluative codas (see Millis, 2010, for specific cooperative tasks for use in JiTT). Slow teachers wait patiently for the appropriate timing, form, and content of their participation. Direct instruction is brief, relevant, and integrated for maximum impact. Learning is scaffolded, permitting students to develop their own understanding, rehearse and consolidate new strategies of language and thought, and apply them in fresh contexts.

One key to Slow pedagogy is cooperative learning and the use of such well-tested procedures as jigsaw reading (Kagan, 1992). Another valuable collaborative tool is a procedure provided by the Faculty Development team at the Academy of Art University (AAU) in San Francisco: the Gallery Walk Critique (http://faculty.academyart.edu/resource/PlanningClass4 .html), which combines a well-established cooperative learning technique, the gallery walk (Academy of Art University, 2009; Kagan, 1992), with a central signature pedagogical move in the arts, the critique. Klebesadel and Kornetsky (2009) describe the critique as "a means of understanding and evaluating the students' work . . . a formative mode of feedback . . . to reinforce technical skills, change behavior, or modify thinking to improve performance" (pp. 101–102). Students learn about creative processes and the subjective and objective aspects of assessment and confront the various value systems and criteria for excellence in their field. The critique enables students to learn simultaneously about their field and about their own creative process, developing successful artists who can apply their critical sensibility to their own work and development, as well as to that of others.

Discussing the critique in studio art education, Klebesadel and Kornetsky (2009) emphasize the importance of "the students and the teacher developing a collaborative or team-like relationship that influences all the projects in the class" (p. 112). They also underscore the value of peer critiques. However, no specific procedures are mentioned. Similarly, Sims and Shreve (2012) affirm that "a common aim of the crit [sic] is for students to become practiced in articulating their critical and contextual awareness and judgments, ideally with decreasing intervention from the teacher" (p. 61). Again, no specific procedure is offered. The AAU faculty development team provides a step-by-step guide for the gallery walk version: students prepare a critique form to post beside their work, introducing the piece and posing a focus question; everyone then circulates, writing their comments in the space provided; individuals summarize the feedback provided and write a summary, including the implications for their future work. The instructor may indicate trends noted across the class as well as consulting with individual students.

In other words, rather than taking student work one at a time and leading the critique, the teacher structures the processes of peer feedback and self-assessment and examines those outcomes before adding comments or indicating the insights of greatest value. The procedure permits students to work at their own pace, lingering at items of particular interest and carefully formulating their feedback, thus developing the personal and professional critical sensibility that is the key learning outcome.

The use of time is a common issue for debate in the cooperative learning literature. Lakey (2010) describes how teachers naturally worry about time when facilitating group learning and reports the common plaint: "There's not enough time to get everything done . . . !" The key, he suggests, is to recognize that there is always enough time to complete important tasks; we must let go of the less important. In a Slow teaching approach, such collaborative procedures are complemented by opportunities for individual reflection and contemplation. Barbezat and Pingree (2012) describe how contemplative exercises can sharpen attention, enrich comprehension, foster the integration of new material with personal experiences, and generate new insights. They show how simple exercises can be deployed across the curriculum to enrich learning, peer relationships, and self-knowledge. An example of classroom practice is provided by Palmer and Zajonc (2010). Patricia Owen-Smith (2010), of Emory University, reports positive outcomes (students more present, attentive, open, alert, creative) from playing meditative, soulful, and lyrical music for seven to nine minutes at the start of each class and urging students to practice contemplation and stillness. In short, Slow pedagogy replaces the direct transmission of knowledge with collaborative and individual procedures promoting critical thinking, reflection, and introspection.

## Slow Teaching and Assessment

If the Slow curriculum involves difficult decisions about limiting content to make room for conscious, deep, and deliberate processing and Slow pedagogy indicates postponing, limiting, and even eliminating direct instruction in favor of team tasks, experiential learning, and individual reflection, then Slow assessment in the academy means continuing the move from summative (terminal, relatively brief) to formative (continuous, time-consuming) procedures. Elements requiring critical reflection, peer, and self-assessment and catalogues of emerging skills and insights are incorporated at regular intervals, invoking the use of tools such as journals, blogs, wikis, and podcasts. This trend can be seen most clearly in courses that incorporate a significant project, such as a community service-learning requirement. The most compelling product of formative assessment is the portfolio, a rich, integrated blend of artifacts, reflection on the significance of those artifacts, and self-assessment. What the portfolio as an assessment instrument may lack in reliability, some argue, is more than compensated for by the variety and depth of its validity (Lynch & Shaw, 2005).

Thus, assessment becomes tightly woven into curriculum, which in turn becomes more explicit, with assessment procedures and criteria being discussed at the outset and regularly revisited. Discussing signature pedagogies in professional education for physical therapists, especially structured fieldwork, Schaber et al. (2012) note recent challenges to the implicit curriculum, resulting in more specific and concrete orientations to courses in terms of the modes and patterns of relating other participants in the learning experience: peers, fieldwork supervisors, clients, other professionals, and so on. Promoting such a multirelational approach means procedures and tools for students to document all of these interactions and reflect on learning outcomes from both the content and the form of their experiences, covering cognitive, performative, and affective domains.

Additional feedback may also come from beyond the class as community and online partners are invited to participate. For example, students in the master's program in language education at the Monterey Institute present their curriculum design projects in a trade fair format. Each team has worked with an existing language program and has interacted with administrators, teachers, students, and other stakeholders to establish needs and has then accordingly produced syllabus designs, lesson plans, and materials, which they display in booths. The event is open to all who contributed to the project as well as the MIIS campus community. Students divide their time between welcoming visitors, explaining the project and answering questions, and visiting other booths and exploring and critiquing the work of their peers. Students thus learn not just from their own efforts and outcomes but also from those of their colleagues, and a key learning outcome is the ability to present one's work to interested persons who are not versed in the terminology and conceptual frameworks of one's field.

The trade fair approach adds a further dimension to Slow assessment: the public. Drafts and final products are shared among students for multi-iterative processes like writing, art, and design projects such as the MIIS curriculum example and are increasingly shared with the world beyond through blogs, websites, videos, and the like. These public elements, we note, have the potential to engender accountability for learning beyond the teacher or campus.

In fields where the client is the final judge of a work's quality (such as translation, design, writing, and advertising), students who tackle an authentic assignment collaboratively under a teacher's management must develop positive interdependence in order to succeed. The faculty member steps back to the role of project manager and facilitator and serves as a resource to students where guidance and coaching is needed and as the quality control assurance to the client. The collaborative results can surpass what students and even professionals achieved working solo (Kiraly, 2000).

In short, the essence of Slow assessment might be captured in an analogy from Slow Food: the meal is subject to commentary and assessment dish by dish, course by course; time is allocated between courses for these conversations; after dessert has been discussed, no one leaves the table: everyone lingers to review the meal as a whole and make plans for preparing such feasts in the future.

## Slow Teaching and Professional Development

At the core of our own conversations around Slow teaching and collaborative professional development have been the questions and tensions arising around calls for change in higher education, porous work/life boundaries, coping with the rate of change in technology, concerns about sustainability, and a desire to question assumptions and move beyond tips and tricks. It is therefore of vital importance that the incorporation of Slow Living principles in the academy embrace professional development.

Faculty developers have long debated the breadth of the mandate in working with faculty members, especially newly appointed assistant professors. Riley (2009) summarizes the case for addressing a wide spectrum of issues, including three kinds of support: personal, relational, and professional. In terms of pace, she cites Brammer (1991), who argues that new faculty "need time and space to reflect and take hold of the new possibilities ahead" (p. 361). Here we note three approaches to faculty development—professional conversations, coaching, and faculty writing groups—which we believe honor this call for a measured, whole-person strategy and echo the themes of Slow Living.

Professional conversations (Shaw, & Cole, 2011) are based on the work of Edge (2002) in combining the themes of empowerment, respect, empathy, and mutuality with Rogerian listening techniques to produce a framework for a pair of colleagues to interact. One, the speaker, has a professional issue (often a challenge in instruction or assessment) to raise and explore; the other, the understander, is an active listener who seeks clarification and explication but may not make suggestions or give advice. The procedure fosters deep critical thinking about learning and teaching and promotes autonomy as participants develop confidence and skills in clearly identifying difficulties and laying out possible solutions and an action plan.

In our faculty development work at the Monterey Institute of International Studies, professional conversations are often witnessed by a collegial group, all familiar with the procedure. Discussion after the conversation both debriefs the two participants, finding new insights into the two roles, and continues to explore the topic, leaving all with a deeper understanding of and renewed commitment to personal and professional development.

The case for coaching in the development of educators (Joyce & Showers, 1982) demonstrates that simple exposure to and basic training in new techniques will not increase the active pedagogical repertoire of the great majority of teachers. Only a highly driven, self-motivated 5 percent can attend a workshop, return to their classroom, and successfully and regularly implement the new procedure. The rest of us need additional support in the form of a colleague, a peer coach, who will exchange observations, provide feedback, check perceptions and assumptions, and mutually reflect on successes and frustrations—all in an empathetic and confidential setting. The key to successful coaching is that the partner who is to teach and be observed is able to dictate those aspects of the lesson (and they must be few in number and specific) to be observed and later discussed. Coaching is not evaluative, and it is not a broad-spectrum opportunity to comment on many aspects of a colleague's teaching. It is focused, deliberate, and therefore slow.

These same practices and values are clearly being incorporated into faculty development in the academy. Boye and Meixner (2011) describe a peer observation model promoting self-reflection and fostering a community of reflective and collaborative practitioners. Little and Palmer (2011) also present a nonjudgmental model of individual consultations in which the coaching process provides descriptive rather than prescriptive feedback, thus stimulating the faculty member's own creativity and resources and leading to greater self-confidence, autonomy, and motivation to continue to improve.

The third example is the faculty writing group. Ambos, Wiley, and Allen (2009) describe in terms of time management an issue to be addressed in professional development in the academy: moving faculty members from "binge writing" (blocks of days in semester breaks devoted to frantic, continuous writing) to a more moderate (slow) approach, writing regularly for short periods of time. This transformation is approached through the Scholarly Writing Institute. Davis, Provost, and Major (2011) emphasize that faculty developers use writing groups not just to empower participants to fulfill scholarly and research expectations but also to meet key Slow Living goals: "establish equilibrium in work practices, and maintain work-life balance" (p. 31). In terms of the latter, one participant describes the writing group as "a place where colleagues can 'feed their souls' through creative writing . . . where you can breathe and share your creative work with your peers and discuss it in supportive and substantive ways" (p. 39). Davis et al. conclude, "Faculty writing groups create a safe space for members to take creative and intellectual risks and to be their authentic, full selves" (p. 41). The emphasis on holistic development at a measured pace by taking risks and being creative in a secure, supportive environment echoes many key facets of Slow Living.

## Conclusion

We close with the acknowledgment that the picture we have sketched of Slow learning and teaching is an idealized, utopian vision of the possible culmination of a variety of developments in the academy. From our own work, we are very much aware of the normal pace of faculty development: that the movement from "coverage" to "uncoverage," from teacher-centered to learner-centered procedures, from slide-supported lectures to experiential and contemplative procedures, while discernible, is generally not rapid. We also stress that students may not be ready for Slow learning experiences: they will need orientation, preparation, and support. Developments in curriculum, pedagogy, and assessment should be carefully brought together and integrated, and the role of technology should continue to be studied and clarified. In addition, behind the practice, we look forward to learning more about the neuroscience of Slow learning and teaching. How, for example, do social media and online resources influence how students learn, access and process new information, and reach new insights? How can mindfulness meditation practices have an impact on curriculum and pedagogy in the academy? What place might the sensible and person-centered notions of Slow Living find on college campuses? How much control might we have over the tempos of our life?

REFERENCES

Academy of Art University. Faculty Development Department. (2009). *The gallery walk critique.* Retrieved from http://faculty.academyart.edu/resource /Critique3GalleryWalk.html

Ambos, E., Wiley, M., & Allen, T. (2009). Romancing the muse: Faculty writing institutes as professional development. In L. Nilson & J. Miller (Eds.), *To improve the academy: Resources for faculty, instructional, and organizational development, Vol. 27* (pp. 135–155). San Francisco, CA: Jossey-Bass.

Applebee, A. N. (1996). *Curriculum as conversation.* Chicago, IL: University of Chicago Press.

Barbezat, D., & Pingree, A. (2012). Contemplative pedagogy: The special role of teaching and learning centers. In J. Groccia & L. Cruz (Eds.), *To improve the academy: Resources for faculty, instructional, and organizational development, Vol. 31* (pp. 177–194). San Francisco, CA: Jossey-Bass.

Bowen, J. A. (2012). *Teaching naked: How moving technology out of your college classroom will improve student learning.* San Francisco, CA: Jossey-Bass.

Boye, A., & Meixner, M. (2011). Growing a new generation: Promoting self-reflection through peer observation. In J. Miller & J. Groccia (Eds.), *To improve the academy: Resources for faculty, instructional, and organizational development, Vol. 29* (pp. 18–31). San Francisco, CA: Jossey-Bass.

Brammer, L. M. (1991). *How to cope with life transitions: The challenge of personal change.* New York, NY: Hemisphere.

Brimberg, S. (n.d.) *Commentary.* Retrieved from http://www.learner.org /workshops/tml/workshop6/commentary.html

Calder, L. (2006). Uncoverage: Toward a signature pedagogy for the history survey. *Journal of American History, 92*(4), 1358–1370.

Chick, N., Haynie, A., & Gurung, R. (Eds.). (2012). *Exploring more signature pedagogies.* Sterling, VA: Stylus.

Csikszentmihalyi, M. (1990). *Flow: The psychology of optimal experience.* New York: HarperPerennial.

Davis, D. J., Provost, K., & Major, A. E. (2011). Writing groups for work-life balance: Faculty writing group leaders share their stories. In J. Miller & J. Groccia (Eds.), *To improve the academy: Resources for faculty, instructional, and organizational development, Vol. 31* (pp. 31–42). San Francisco, CA: Jossey-Bass.

Edge, J. (2002). *Continuing cooperative development.* Ann Arbor: University of Michigan Press.

Glasgow, N. (1997). *New curriculum for new times: A guide to student-centered, problem-based learning.* Thousand Oaks, CA: Corwin Press.

Gurung, R., Chick, N., & Haynie, A. (Eds.). (2009). *Exploring signature pedagogies*. Sterling, VA: Stylus.

Hassel, H., & Nelson, N. (2012). A signature feminist pedagogy: Connection and transformation in women's studies. In N. Chick, A. Haynie, & R. Gurung (Eds.), *Exploring more signature pedagogies: Approaches to teaching disciplinary habits of mind* (pp. 143–155). Sterling. VA: Stylus.

Honoré, C. (2004). *The power of slow: Finding balance and fulfillment beyond the cult of speed*. New York, NY: HarperCollins.

Honoré, C. (2008). *Under pressure: Rescuing our children from the culture of hyper-parenting*. New York, NY: HarperCollins.

Joyce, B., & Showers, B. (1982). The coaching of teaching. *Educational Leadership, 40*(1), 4–8, 10.

Kagan, S. (1992). *Cooperative learning*. San Juan Capistrano, CA: Resources for Teachers.

Kiraly, D. (2000). *A social constructivist approach to translator education: Empowerment from theory to practice*. Manchester, UK: St. Jerome.

Klebesadel, H., & Karnetsky, L. (2009). Critique as signature pedagogy in the arts. In R. Gurung, N. Chick, & A. Haynie (Eds.), *Exploring signature pedagogies: Approaches to disciplinary habits of mind* (pp. 99–120). Sterling, VA: Stylus.

Lakey, G. (2010). *Facilitating group learning*. San Francisco, CA: Jossey-Bass.

Langer, E. J. (1998). *The power of mindful learning*. New York, NY: Perseus Books.

Levy, D. M. (2006). More, faster, better: Governance in an age of overload, busyness and speed. *First Monday, 7*. Retrieved from http://www.firstmonday.org/issues/special11_9/

Little, D., & Palmer, M. (2011). A coaching based-framework for individual consultations. In J. Miller & J. Groccia (Eds.), *To improve the academy: Resources for faculty, instructional, and organizational development, Vol. 29* (pp. 102–115). San Francisco, CA: Jossey-Bass.

Lynch, B., & Shaw, P. (2005). Portfolios, power, and ethics. *TESOL Quarterly, 39*(2), 263–297.

Meredith, B., & Storm, E. (2009). *Slow living: Learning to savor and fully engage with life*. Retrieved from http://www.create-the-good-life.com/slow_living.html

Millis, B. J. (2010). *Cooperative learning in higher education*. Sterling, VA: Stylus.

Owen-Smith, P. (2010). Appendix A: In the classroom: Knitting through the hallellujah. In P. Palmer, A. Zajonc, & M. Scribner (Eds.), *The heart of higher education: A call to renewal. Transforming the academy through collegial conversations* (pp. 157–161). San Francisco, CA: Jossey-Bass.

Palmer, P. J., & Zajonc, A. (2010). *The heart of higher education: Transforming the academy through collegial conversations.* San Francisco, CA: Jossey-Bass.

Parkins, W., & Craig, G. (2006). *Slow living.* New York: Berg.

Peden, B., & Van Voorhis, C. (2009). Developing habits of the mind, hand and heart in psychology undergraduates. In R. Gurung, N. Chick, & A. Haynie (Eds.), *Exploring signature pedagogies: Approaches to disciplinary habits of mind* (pp. 161–182). Sterling, VA: Stylus.

Petrini, C. (2001). *Slow food.* White River Junction, VT: Chelsea Green Publishing Company.

Priesnitz, W. (2000). *Challenging assumptions in education.* Toronto, CAN: Alternate Press.

Riley, A. (2009). Meeting new faculty at the intersection: Personal and professional support points the way. In L. Nilson & J. Miller (Eds.), *To improve the academy: Resources for faculty, instructional, and organizational development, Vol. 27* (pp. 351–364). San Francisco, CA: Jossey-Bass.

St. John's University Center for Teaching and Learning. (1999). Taking learning seriously. *News, 5*(6), 1–2.

Schaber, P., Marsh, L., & Wilcox, K. (2012). Relational learning and active engagement in occupational therapy professional education. In N. Chick, A. Haynie, & R. Gurung (Eds.), *Exploring more signature pedagogies: Approaches to teaching disciplinary habits of mind* (pp. 188–202). Sterling, VA: Stylus.

Shaw, P., & Cole, B. (2011). Professional conversations: A reflective framework for collaborative development. In J. Miller & J. Groccia (Eds.), *To improve the academy: Resources for faculty, instructional, and organizational development, Vol. 29* (pp. 116–131). San Francisco, CA: Jossey-Bass.

Shulman, L. (2005). Signature pedagogies in the professions. *Daedalus, 134*(3), 52–59.

Sims, E., & Shreve, A. (2012). Signature pedagogies in art and design. In N. Chick, A. Haynie, & R. Gurung (Eds.), *Exploring more signature pedagogies: Approaches to teaching disciplinary habits of mind* (pp. 55–67). Sterling, VA: Stylus.

Timpson, W. M., & Bendel-Simso, P. (1996). *Concepts and choices: Meeting the challenges in higher education.* Madison, WI: Magna Publications.

Wiggins, G., & McTighe, J. (1998). *Understanding by design.* San Francisco, CA: Association for Supervision and Curriculum Development.

20

# PEDAGOGICAL GAMIFICATION

## PRINCIPLES OF VIDEO GAMES THAT CAN ENHANCE TEACHING

---

*Kevin Yee*
*University of South Florida*

*Edutainment products have long tried to harness the "fun" quotient of games and video games for education, but the principles of gamification have only recently begun to be better understood and operationalized for business and education. The concepts that underpin successful games can be put to use in online as well as face-to-face classes, resulting in educational experiences that have the best of both worlds: a game-based overlay without becoming too technical. This chapter explains the concepts involved in successful games and provides ideas for translating those principles into practice in the classroom (or online) environment.*

---
o
---

The term *gamification* has become increasingly popular, chiefly among businesses that are using the concept with their products. Defined simply, gamification refers to transforming a boring or mundane task into a fun one by applying the principles that make games engaging. By adding elements such as competition between various users, an otherwise-boring process can become interesting, sometimes even addictive. An often-cited example of gamification is the mobile phone application Foursquare, which allows users to "check in" electronically wherever they are. The

335

resulting data are a bounty for advertisers who buy banners within the Foursquare app to target their messages with much greater precision. After all, by definition they know exactly where their potential customers are at that moment. Users are willing to forfeit their privacy in large part because of the gamelike elements of the application. Whoever checks in to a given location the most often across repeated visits earns the badge of "mayor" of that place, in the process "ousting" the previous mayor. Simple competitiveness drives heavy use, particularly when participants are vying with their real-life friends who use the same app.

As more companies turn to gamification to increase consumer awareness and use of their products, the principles of successful conversion to game-based processes are becoming increasingly well understood. This chapter examines how higher education might benefit from those principles and isolate best practices in gamification that translate well to classroom instruction.

## Brief History of Gamification

It has not escaped the attention of educational theorists and instructional designers that consumers like to play games. Some of the earliest types of software in the 1980s were specifically meant to combine education and entertainment holistically (Gustavo, Fung, Mallet, Posel, & Fleiszer, 2008; Whitton, 2011), but "edutainment" products failed to generate as many sales as more traditional games, and the category waned as CD-ROM products were phased out. Software was difficult and expensive to build, and the high barriers to entry kept the playing field relatively lightly populated.

In more recent years, technology has begun to catch up. The rise of social networks and the concomitant explosion in mobile computing coincided with a surge in smaller games. Best-sellers like Angry Birds were not as graphics intensive or as complicated as most PC-based or console-based games, so it was all but inevitable that app-based games proliferated quickly in the smart phone and tablet era. Such games are not as expensive to build as the edutainment titles that were attempted two decades prior, and the tools used to construct games became faster and ever simpler to use, adding yet more incentive for others to build games and saturate the market.

The potent combination of mobile computing and social networks gave rise to a particular kind of social gaming, injecting a new dimension into the gaming experience. Most games of the previous twenty years offered a single-player game at the core of the primary experience: the player competed against the game itself rather than against other people. That balance shifted with social networks, as can be seen in the success of Facebook games such as FarmVille and Mafia Wars, which rely on the use of other players in cooperative contexts. The console-based video game industry also turned to social gaming, increasingly relying on multiplayer options using the Internet, such as Xbox Live and PlayStation Network.

Ninety-seven percent of American teenagers now play games at least once a week (Lenhart et al., 2008). When examined on a planetary scale, we spend 3 billion hours every week playing games (McGonigal, 2011). Given the groundwork laid by gaming in other facets of life, it is little surprise that augmented reality and game-based learning is poised to increase dramatically in education in the coming years (Johnson, Smith, Willis, Levine, & Haywood, 2011). Indeed, the expectation of many leading theorists is that video games will be, or in some cases should already have been, adopted as a primary learning tool in formal education (Gee, 2003; Kirkley & Kirkley, 2004; Prensky, 2001). It seems likely that students entering college now and in the future will increasingly expect elements of game-based learning to be integrated into the curriculum, rendering gamification a subject of primary relevance for faculty developers.

## Five Principles of Gamification

To establish the concepts of gamification means to examine what makes games fun. This is no small task, and there is little agreement among scholars or game creators. Ralph Koster (2004) identifies the brain's unquenchable search for patterns and constant process of selection as the main drivers determining the enjoyability of a given activity, while Rick Raymer (2011) points to rewards as the primer driver of fun.

The lack of agreement makes it difficult to identify with certainty the best practices for using the underlying principles of successful games, with the result that various scales proliferate. McDaniel and Telep (2009) attempt to isolate ten guidelines: use existing resources, ask students to produce, avoid being overly prescriptive, be aware of nonelectronic options, focus on learning rather than technology, provide lead-up and debriefing, embrace interdisciplinarity, use games seriously in other contexts, use virtual worlds, and playtest often. Sarah Smith-Robbins (2011) points to a goal, obstacles, and collaboration or competition as the main ingredients of a game. Michele Dickey (2005) identifies clear tasks, constant feedback, and advancing levels of challenge as crucial to gamification. However, many of the categories that scholars have created can be combined, giving rise to fewer overall principles. This study narrows the field to five principles of gamification:

- Display progress.
- Maximize competition.
- Calibrate difficulty carefully.
- Provide diversions.
- Employ narrative elements.

## Display Progress

Games of all stripes share a common core of progression toward a task, from leveling up to simply advancing through different stages. Without progress, an activity would be monotonous, the very opposite of fun. As Gee (2009) points out, players who have a personal stake in the goal are more motivated to complete it. Thus, progress must be displayed prominently (Dickey, 2005; Young, 2010). Some games imply progress through the collection of tokens or badges, relying on people's natural inclination to collect and hoard. Such badges should be displayed in a global, highly visible spot.

Badges and progress bars ultimately point to visible rewards. Game designer Rick Raymer (2011) identified two categories of rewards: momentary and persistent. Persistent awards are the progress bar or badge list. Momentary awards may be flashed across the screen only at the moment of success, such as a quick pop-up to congratulate the player on a victory. Rewards can come not only for success but also to acknowledge effort, the better to provide encouragement to players that the game itself is fun to play (Raymer, 2011; Salter, 2011). Finally, rewards can come at regular intervals (after finishing a level, for instance, or collecting five tokens), but can also come randomly so as to keep the gameplay just unpredictable enough that it provides the right level of challenge.

## Maximize Competition

Humans may be hard-wired to compete with each other to varying degrees (Smith-Robbins, 2011), and many games rely on that as the bedrock principle. Single-player games certainly exist, but sales figures alone demonstrate that video games with an active multiplayer (or, better yet, online multiplayer) option perform better than single-player games

(Douglas, 2012). If competition is the key to a game's appeal, then players must know how they stack up against other players. Thus, the progress bars and badge lists need to be displayed publicly so that other players can see the progress. In an advanced (automated) system, this is sometimes accomplished with a progress bar that displays a single bar chart graphic. When multiple players compete at the same game, the progress bar concept can be exchanged for a leaderboard that displays names and summary (cumulative) scores.

## Calibrate Difficulty Carefully

All games must maintain a delicate balance when it comes to level of complexity and difficulty. A game that is too simple quickly becomes boring. A game that is too difficult leads to player frustration; only the perfect balance, akin to a Goldilocks zone (Gee, 2003; Raymer, 2011), that is, "not too cold and not too hot," will be perceived as rewarding and fun for players.

Difficulty needs to be added in stages. Successful games begin with easy wins and add expectations of developing player skill sets incrementally (Raymer, 2011). The major principle undergirding this gradual ratcheting up of challenges is that of cognitive load. A typical video game might ask players to move three-dimensionally through a particular room, switching armaments and defenses while jumping to avoid enemy fire. The newest task in the list (say, switching to a different sword) becomes reasonable to demand of players only if the other requirements have been previously practiced and honed over time and now can be performed by muscle memory—an application of scaffolding from Vygotsky's (1978) well-known zone of proximal development, which stipulates that each new challenge has to be within reach based on the skills already mastered.

Good games also make use of spaced repetition, a well-understood educational practice in which concepts are introduced early and retested at several intervals over time, each instance deepening the learning and increasing the likelihood of student recall (Allen, Mahler, & Estes, 1969). For example, spaced repetition is the fundamental principle behind the use of flash cards to memorize foreign language terms. Often the employment of incremental increases in difficulty and spaced repetition together manifests itself in the form of "boss levels" that add extra challenge, make use of the most recently added skill, and provide a measure of closure to a chapter in the longer story of the game. Seen in that light, the overall narrative should rightfully be understood as a series of climaxes rather than one large arc with a single crescendo.

## Provide Diversions

Popular video games such as the Legend of Zelda series or any Super Mario Brothers title have long understood that players prefer to switch their attention every so often away from the main goal or quest, the same human tendency that leads educational theorists to urge that teachers chunk lectures into smaller segments and provide breaks between them, perhaps to test student comprehension using interactive techniques (Sousa, 2011). In games, this is realized in secondary games (often called mini-games) that have nothing to do with the larger purpose at that moment but may require learning a minor new skill (Sanchez, 2009). Players in a Zelda game, for example, may be asked to master throwing items at targets akin to a carnival midway game, even though the larger Zelda game never again asks the players to repeat that skill. The mini-game provides a break in the action and resets player attention, allowing better focus on the main task. Many companies, including Cisco Systems and Miller Brewing Company (Aldrich, 2007), have started to use mini-games for training purposes.

A similar desire for diversion can make the discovery of hidden items fun. These hidden items (commonly called Easter eggs) are sometimes intentionally planted for players to locate, but usually in out-of-the way places. Knowing to expect Easter eggs, some players venture further afield than strictly required by the normal gameplay, and are rewarded when they discover the hidden items. In this fashion, Easter eggs can be used to reward exploration. Chris Taylor (2000) notes that Easter eggs extend the life of a product, since players want to explore everything. Taken to its furthest extreme, exploration can mean creating multiple pathways to successful completion of the tasks, or even nonlinear elements, which allow players to complete tasks in any order or skip some altogether.

## Employ Narrative Elements

While board games usually do not rely on a highly evolved storyline, most video games do (Jensen, 2012), in recognition that human beings react well to narratives, possibly as an evolved trait learned from generations of communication that was necessarily oral in nature. Whatever the origin, research demonstrates that listeners—including college students—recall material better when it is packaged as part of a story (Heath & Heath, 2007).

Any story added to a gamified experience will likely be helpful, but not all stories are equally interesting. Drama is driven primarily by conflict, so a narrative with a clearly defined central conflict stands the best chance of being perceived as organically interesting to an audience. It may also be worthwhile to think less about a plot than about a mystery—when there are gaps in knowledge and a puzzle to unravel, players become more emotionally engaged. It can be useful to imagine as many details as possible for characters, back stories, and settings before laying out the specifics of the plot.

## Caveat to the Five Principles

Note that it is not required to use elements from every category in order to gamify a process or to build a successful game. For instance, there are no narrative elements in older video games such as Pac-Man or newer gamified apps such as Foursquare. Conversely, some successful games eschew competition entirely in favor almost exclusively of narrative, such as the best-selling computer game hit of 1993, Myst, which allowed players to explore a deserted tropical island to uncover a mystery—one presented to the players with no ticking clock and no other players to compete against. The five principles of gamification can be favorably compared to ingredients for cooking that might be assembled in various combinations, in one attempt stressing a single element over all others, and other times omitting one or more ingredients completely. There is no single recipe for successful gamification.

## Gamification in Classroom Instruction

There is little agreement about what successful gamification looks like inside a college classroom, and in any event success is likely to be varied by discipline, context, and individual faculty member. To some extent, games have always been an instructional option available to professors. Low-stakes activities that are short term rather than those that persist throughout the term are especially popular choices for serving as ice-breakers for new material or when reviewing before a test (Angelo & Cross, 1993). Television game show formats such as *Jeopardy* and *Super-Password* seem to lend themselves particularly well to this format. Yet the principles of gamification outlined above seem likely to offer the greatest benefit with a sustained game or simulation that extends across several weeks or perhaps the entire term.

Although the principles of gamification have become better understood, technology has not yet advanced far enough for simple digital games to be built by amateurs for "short" purposes such as a course

(Raymer, 2011; Smith-Robbins, 2011). Constructing even a rudimentary game as an app or a browser-based activity, such as a Flash game, requires many hours of programming in advanced computer languages and remains an expensive proposition not commonly undertaken for individual courses. Nor do learning management software (LMS) solutions like Blackboard or Desire2Learn come with built-in functionality to construct games. A more recent LMS, Canvas by Instructure, does promise easier integration with outside companies, applications, and websites using Learning Tool Integration (allowing one-click linking of courses with external games). While such integrations may make it easier to create and link to diversions such as mini-games, there is no comprehensive solution to contextualize whole modules or an entire course under a single game structure.

The lack of easy gamification solutions does not have to translate to abandoning the idea until technology catches up. Many attempts at gamification of college instruction can make use of workarounds and low-tech solutions to provide a game-based framework. It is feasible to include game elements on a purely face-to-face basis inside the physical classroom and to record progress with low-tech methods such as paper and pencil, but to realize maximum gains from a semester-long game simulation, instructors are likely to harness the tools of an LMS to serve as the repository of game elements, including both the activities and the long-term tracking of student progress. A gamified class might look like a regular LMS presence plus a few external garnishes such as lists of badges or a leaderboard on the home page. Many of the game elements would be integrated into the fabric of the assignments and readings themselves. In other words, many tasks might remain the same, but the contexts around them, as well as the students' motivation for completing them, would be altered. It is perhaps most accurate to conceptualize pedagogical gamification as a process rather than a product. It provides a means of thinking about organizing the various activities and rewards of the class (many of them already present in the curriculum) into a coherent schema of rewards first promised and then delivered.

The first principle of gamification, the need to track progress, offers an example of how gamification leverages existing tools and functionality to new purposes. Progress is acknowledged in ways both momentary and persistent. Momentary rewards are an easy match for the LMS in the form of self-grading quizzes, perhaps set so that students can retake the assessment as often as necessary until they obtain a perfect score. Similarly, embedded games (such as Flash games created locally, online, or using third-party software) promise autonomous feedback to students immediately. Persistent tracking of progress is much harder to automate. It is here that tech-savvy instructors with knowledge of programming sometimes attempt to craft applications that will automatically record, tally, and display progress such as badges earned by individual students. For everyone else, the lack of automation seems daunting and all but insurmountable. Would most professors want to add to their workloads by attempting to track badges manually and spend time placing each one individually on a digital leaderboard? Yet employing a few tried-and-true pedagogical methods brings the workload to a more manageable level. Just as representative student work can sometimes replace the need to read and grade every last student submission, so too can badges by individual students stand in for a wider group. If students are organized into groups, only one of them needs to perform the task to earn the badge for the entire group, and the instructor's workload is reduced significantly.

The second principle of gamification, competition, has been around in many educational contexts for decades. When college classes are small enough and the topic of discussion warrants it, many faculty reach for a competitive activity as an outgrowth of the regular curriculum (Angelo & Cross, 1993), which can be as simple as dividing the class in half and using the whiteboard for quick quizzes, drawing games, or practice solving problems. But a semester-long competition calls for a more robust tracking system than tally marks on the whiteboard. The heart of competition is public approbation and the reward or shame that accompanies one's performance displayed to the world (Young, 2010), so a leaderboard of some sort is normally indicated. However, many countries limit the release of student educational records, including grades. Due to these privacy laws (an example is the Family Educational Rights and Privacy Act in the United States), the leaderboard cannot display the results of material that was required of students and counts for a grade. That leaves optional assignments as the only source material for the publicly visible badges. In this case, the assignments to earn badges are likely to be value-added types of activities that deepen learning rather than provide the initial instruction. Examples could include discussion board posts about TED videos, performing online research about a related but ancillary topic, or creating a video using an online tool such as Animoto or Xtranormal.

An alternative method could be to keep the tracking of badges private and visible only to each student using an online grade book. While this has the advantage that regular (required) course content could then be included in the items that earn a badge, it has the disadvantage that students lack the spark of competition. In fact, there is no functional difference between a privacy-enabled leaderboard and the existing LMS grade book in a course otherwise lacking gamification elements.

No matter the reporting mechanisms, it is crucial to have some visible reward structure in place because students are likely to react with maximal enthusiasm if there is something at stake beyond simple bragging rights in winning the competition (Gee, 2009). Due to privacy laws, awarding points toward the semester total seems contraindicated if the leaderboard is public, but a college instructor has other rewards available. Perhaps students in the winning group might be permitted to drop their lowest (individual) test grades or could be allowed to skip the final exam and use their chapter test average as a replacement.

Putting together these elements—badges for optional assignments, a nongrade reward for the winning group, and the need for a leaderboard—implies some manual processes that the faculty member will have to perform. Although strategies can be employed to minimize the number of badges awarded each week, absent an advanced program or app to automate the process, the instructor will have to manually update the leaderboard on the LMS with the newest scores or badges. Careful choices in the construction of groups and numbers of available badges can limit the additional workload on the faculty member.

The advice to ratchet up the difficulty in careful, measured ways corresponds with good pedagogical practice for any course, even without gamification (McClarty, Orr, Frey, Dolan, Vassileva, & McVay, 2012). Students always realize a psychological boost when they notch an early win that promotes positive associations with the course material and their potential mastery of it (Salter, 2011), but the logic in providing an early assessment designed to be easy, even rewarding, is more compelling still when the course has been gamified and students are expected to engage more than usual. Similarly, the directive to add skills only one at a time is well known to educational theory in the form of scaffolding, since learners require a context around new concepts and a foundation on which to build (Ambrose, Bridges, DiPietro, Lovett, & Norman, 2010). Yet it may not been enough to simply trust in the process of typical course design; more can be done to ensure success by mapping the skills and activities across the semester onto individual game elements and decisions, so that the rollout of skills and tests is more deliberate. In his discussion of brain-based learning, Sousa (2011) noted that educators should strive for an optimal level of anxiety in a classroom—neither so simple that it is boring nor so difficult that it induces anxiety, and the same is true of balance in game elements.

What qualifies as an appropriate diversion for a gamified class is subject to considerable debate (Taylor, 2000). At a simple level, strategies designed to encourage and reward exploration satisfy the basic definition of diversion toward gamification, such as links to optional content that support and deepen the main learning objectives (TED talks or other videos are common in this regard) or Easter eggs in the form of humorous floating captions (contained in the ALT text of the HTML code) for images embedded with the reading. Small, targeted activities, often Flash-based games and widgets, offer a close analogy to mini-games that are used to great effect in video games. Some large individual institutions keep a team of programmers on staff to create such games, either customized by course or easily populated with course-specific material by the instructor. Similar games can be found in off-the-shelf software developed for this purpose (Wondershare, Hot Potatoes), as well as many websites (Quizboxes.com, Quizlet.com, Purposegames.com). Experience suggests that students are less likely to engage in optional activities if they must click a link to access them, so whenever practical, it is better to embed mini-games directly amid the required content. At the high end of the range of diversions is the concept of nonlinear progress toward course goals, in which participants have a number of possible pathways toward the same outcome, or sometimes toward one of several possible outcomes, similar to Choose Your Own Adventure books (McDaniel, Fiore, & Nicholson, 2010). Configuring a nonlinear game scenario increases the complexity of the instructor's task considerably and may be best implemented when a custom game interface and automated tracking can be programmed for the course so that manual processes are kept to a minimum.

In the hands of an experienced storyteller, narrative-based instruction increases both listener attention and later ability to recall details (Heath & Heath, 2007; Sanchez, 2009). To some extent, all instruction can include narratives to draw learner interest, but the benefit is magnified when introduced in a course with other elements of gamification. Rather than separate narratives with no apparent connection to each other, a single narrative that spans a longer block of time, perhaps even the entire term, provides the greatest benefit to a gamified class. All other elements, from mini-games and badges, to leaderboards and Easter eggs, achieve integration only when placed in the larger frame narrative that provides both context and structure.

At the heart of a narrative is a central conflict, but instructors looking to introduce a central story to their classes might profitably think first about a high-concept description, as if provided in an elevator pitch.

A memorable hook will increase retention of the narrative (Heath & Heath, 2007). One effective way to craft the story line could be to explore alternate time lines, such as starting in the middle of the action to generate interest in both backstories and future outcomes. When inventing a narrative, faculty members might consider the basic Aristotelian structure of setup, buildup, and payoff. The individual diction choices within the course, such as introducing assignments and tasks, might also serve the narrative, such as referring to objectives as "quests" or whatever is appropriate to the chosen context.

## Role of Faculty Development Centers

Faculty developers interested in introducing gamification to their faculty audiences might start with workshops explaining the principles of gamification and providing model courses that have been gamified. Faculty developers serve many roles (Lewis, 1996), but one of the most urgent functions they fulfill is to provide solutions to instructional problems, often by employing creative workarounds (Wager, 2006). Faculty members may well wish to cultivate strategies that convert high-tech game concepts into low-tech solutions.

Teaching centers may also play a part in helping faculty with improving the overall appearance and production values of the gamified course, so that students experience more than mere words in the game. The principles behind gamification could theoretically be applied to a purely text-based environment. Indeed, early computer games were strictly text based. However, there are no more text-only games for sale today, for the simple reason that consumers prefer a rich visual interface when that is an option. Accordingly, gamified college courses should do what is feasible to provide visual reinforcement. Games and game elements do not need to feature rich (and expensive) custom graphics, but neither should they be strictly text based. A simple shift to image-heavy presentation would help, and teaching centers can provide support for faculty needing to make such a shift, such as pointing faculty to royalty-free images from Creative-Commons websites and the means using HTML to embed images natively.

## Next Steps

While gamification offers significant promise for enhancing the educational experience, it is not yet an experimentally proven strategy, and research is needed to ascertain its basic efficacy. In particular, it would be useful to identify which specific variables separate success from failure. Are all five principles of gamification equally central to success, or are some indispensable, while others merely add to the richness of the experience without being fundamental to it? For instance, if narrative elements are not crucial to the success of gamification, do they nonetheless intensify the experience to a sufficient degree that students learn better, as measured by the class assessments, when compared to a class that contains the other gamified elements but lacks the narrative component?

It will also be necessary to expand the vision for possible gamified operations, such as developing alternate methods to deploy competition and leaderboard tracking within an LMS. As technology advances, it seems likely that software will someday soon make the granting and tracking of badges into a fully automated process. At that point the texture of the gameplay will change, possibly throwing into sharp relief which of the principles of gamification are most vital to success and lead to new questions about how best to structure them into a course design.

An approach that privileges technology, however, misses the point that the principles of gamification can be made more or less electronic, depending on instructor time and preference. Gaming theory appears to be optimized for digital delivery, and indeed this is how it is most commonly consumed by today's students, yet it actually comprises well-established best practices in teaching merely imported into a digital context. The degree to which those practices remain digital or are recaptured for an analog (face-to-face) delivery is subject to each instructor's design preferences, and certainly further study is warranted to determine if an optimal mixture can be ascertained.

REFERENCES

Aldrich, C. (2007). Engaging mini-games find niche in training. *T+D, 61*(7), 22–24.

Allen, G. A., Mahler, W. A., & Estes, W. K. (1969). Effects of recall tests on long-term retention of paired associates. *Journal of Verbal Learning and Verbal Behavior, 8*(4), 463–470.

Ambrose, S., Bridges, M., DiPietro, M., Lovett, M., & Norman, M. (2010). *How learning works: Seven research-based principles for smart teaching.* San Francisco, CA: Jossey-Bass.

Angelo, T., & Cross, K. (1993). *Classroom assessment techniques: A handbook for college teachers* (2nd ed.). San Francisco, CA: Jossey-Bass.

Dickey, M. D. (2005). Engaging by design: How engagement strategies in popular computer and video games can inform instructional design. *Educational Technology Research and Development, 53*(2), 67–83.

Douglas, A. (2012). *Here are the 10 highest grossing video games ever.* Retrieved from http://www.businessinsider.com/here-are-the-top-10-highest-grossing -video-games-of-all-time-2012–6?op=1

Gee, J. P. (2003). What video games have to teach us about learning and literacy. *ACM Computers in Entertainment, 1*(1), 1–4.

Gee, J. P. (2009). Deep learning properties of good digital games: How far can they go? In U. Ritterfeld, M. Cody, & P. Vorderer (Eds.), *Serious games: Mechanisms and effects* (pp. 67–82). New York, NY: Routledge.

Gustavo, D., Fung, S., Mallet, L., Posel, N., & Fleiszer, D. (2008). Learning while having fun: The use of video gaming to teach geriatric house calls to medical students. *Journal of the American Geriatrics Society, 56*(7), 1328–1332.

Heath, C., & Heath, D. (2007). *Made to stick: Why some ideas survive and others die.* New York, NY: Random House.

Jensen, M. (2012). Engaging the learner: Gamification strives to keep the user's interest. *T+D, 66*(1), 40–44.

Johnson, L., Smith, R., Willis, H., Levine, A., & Haywood, K. (2011). *The 2011 Horizon Report.* Retrieved from http://net.educause.edu/ir/library/pdf /HR2011.pdf

Kirkley, S. E., & Kirkley, J. R. (2004). Creating next generation blended learning environments using mixed reality, video games, and simulation. *TechTrends, 49*(3), 42–89.

Koster, R. (2004). *A theory of fun for game design.* Phoenix, AZ: Paraglyph.

Lenhart, A., Kahne, J., Middaugh, E., Macgill, A. R., Evans, C., & Vitak, J. (2008, September). *Teens, video games, and civics.* Retrieved from http:// www.pewinternet.org/Reports/2008/Teens-Video-Games-and-Civics.aspx

Lewis, K. G. (1996). A brief history and overview of faculty development in the United States. *International Journal for Academic Development, 1*(2), 26–33.

McClarty, K., Orr, A., Frey, P., Dolan, R., Vassileva, V., & McVay, A. (2012). *A literature review of gaming in education* (Pearson research report). Retrieved from http://education.pearsonassessments.com/hai/Images/tmrs /Lit_Review_of_Gaming_in_Education.pdf

McDaniel, R., Fiore, S. M., & Nicholson, D. (2010). Serious storytelling: Narrative considerations for serious games researchers and developers. In J. A. Cannon-Bowers & C. A. Bowers (Eds.), *Serious game design and development: Technologies for training and learning* (pp. 13–30). Hershey, PA: Information.

McDaniel, R., & Telep, P. (2009). Best practices for integrating game-based learning into online teaching. *Journal of Online Learning and Teaching, 5*(2), 424–438.

McGonigal, J. (2011). *Reality is broken: Why games make us better and how they can change the world.* New York, NY: Penguin.

Prensky, M. (2001). *Digital game-based learning.* New York, NY: McGraw-Hill.

Raymer, R. (2011). *Gamification: Using game mechanics to enhance eLearning.* Retrieved from http://elearnmag.acm.org/featured.cfm?aid=2031772

Salter, A. (2011, September 30). Games in the classroom (part 3). *Chronicle of Higher Education.* Retrieved from http://chronicle.com/blogs/profhacker/games-in-the-classroom-part-3/36217

Sanchez, A. (2009). Games for good—How DAU is using games to enhance learning: Games and simulations at DAU. *Defense AR Journal, 16*(3), 342.

Smith-Robbins, S. (2011). "This game sucks": How to improve the gamification of education. *Educause Review, 46*(1), 58–59.

Sousa, D. (2011). *How the brain learns* (4th ed.). Thousand Oaks, CA: Corwin.

Taylor, C. (2000). The yolk's on us. *Time, 155*(14), 148.

Vygotsky, L. S. (1978). *Mind and society: The development of higher psychological processes.* Cambridge, MA: Harvard University Press.

Wager, W. (2006). *Faculty development at 15 universities: A sabbatical report.* Retrieved from mailer.fsu.edu/~wwager/sabreport.doc

Whitton, N. (2011). Game engagement theory and adult learning. *Simulation and Gaming 42*(5), 596–609.

Young, J. (2010, January). *Five teaching tips for professors—from video games.* Retrieved from http://chronicle.com/article/5-Lessons-Professors-Can-Learn/63708/

21

# THE REACTING TO THE PAST PEDAGOGY AND ENGAGING THE FIRST-YEAR STUDENT

*Paula Kay Lazrus*
*St. John's University*

*Gretchen Kreahling McKay*
*McDaniel College*

*This chapter investigates the value of the Reacting to the Past pedagogy with regard to engaging first-year students. In recent years, calls to improve student engagement and active learning techniques have grown, and few have been as successful in producing the desired results as*

We extend our thanks to Mark Carnes, Ann Whitney (Olin Professor of History at Barnard College), Dana Johnson, and the Reacting Advisory Board for the work they do for Reacting to the Past. We offer this chapter in support of professors using the pedagogy and to encourage faculty members who have not taught with Reacting to do so. Special thanks to Judith Shapiro, professor of anthropology and president Emerita of Barnard College, for helping us organize the panel (March 2009) at the Conference for Academic Renewal sponsored by the Association of American Colleges and Universities that led to this chapter. In addition, P. Lazrus thanks the Center for Teaching and Learning and the Writing across the Curriculum programs at St. John's for organizing helpful and successful faculty writing retreats.

*Reacting to the Past. This chapter investigates why Reacting is so successful in meeting the goals of high-impact practices that increase student engagement and learning. We also examine how the Reacting pedagogy and first-year seminars encourage problem solving, critical thinking, and writing among students.*

---
o
---

One of the most prominent concerns for institutions working to strengthen their general education curricula, and especially their first-year programs, has been the drive to improve student engagement while also assessing student learning. Whether the focus is incorporating active learning techniques, improving critical thinking, or addressing ways to improve students' abilities to connect classroom learning to the real world, professors and administrators have been exploring all manner of high-impact methodologies that promote students' engagement in their education. But what do we mean when we use terms such as *engagement, active learning,* and *critical thinking?* In this chapter, we propose that engagement is best understood as an aspect of active learning. That is, engagement is not simply the involvement in school activities, an issue that was recently highlighted in the study and book *Academically Adrift* (Arum & Roksa, 2011). Among the findings in Arum and Roksa's study is the administrative push for retention that often leads campuses to focus on student activities in residence halls, student organizations, and other cocurricular programming rather than the role academics might play in keeping students engaged. We argue in this chapter that the Reacting to the Past (Reacting) pedagogy engages students deeply in their classrooms, putting the focus of student engagement on learning, and can be particularly effective when paired with first-year seminars.

With all of the emphasis placed on engagement outside the classroom, many have wondered if it can happen *in* the academic classroom. We are convinced that it can, if students participate directly in the act of learning through research, writing, reasoning, oral presentation, and teamwork. The Reacting pedagogy gives students a chance to embrace all of these elements of active engagement, which are the foundations of learning in a liberal arts education and the skills that all citizens must have to be active members of their communities. Active learning of this type contrasts with the simple acquisition of content delivered to students by professors, or the passive response systems like clickers that are often promoted as active learning techniques. Active learning involves the acquisition of knowledge by the student while building skills that most employers require of their employees, and make for strong scholars and citizens.

For active engagement to work well, students and professors must agree to be partners in the learning process. Simplistic debate that reduces college learning to content versus skills overlooks the fact that if you cannot reason or question what you are reading or being taught, then all the memorization in the world will not make you more learned or productive (Berrett, 2011; Bok, 2006). Simulations and role playing have long been used in the classroom. The National Model UN programs have a forty-year record of teaching through hands-on learning, and business and management classes have adopted similar exercises. Role playing of this sort heightens the experiential nature of learning which studies have shown to be among the most effective ways of retaining information ("Welcome to National Model United Nations," n.d.; Gorton & Havercroft, 2012; Lane, 1995).

Among the many excellent teaching methods and curricular programs developed in this context, the Reacting pedagogy is among the most innovative and creative. Both of us have used Reacting with our first-year students. Here we discuss why Reacting is so successful at meeting the goals set by the Association of American Colleges and Universities 2007 report on Liberal Education and America's Promise-LEAP (Kuh, 2008), the ideals of student engagement in academic pursuits, and the outcomes set by many first-year programs.

## The Reacting Pedagogy

Reacting consists of elaborate, tightly structured role-playing activities that integrate high-impact teaching practices in a seamless manner that simultaneously allows students to explore pivotal moments in the human experience. According to Liberal Education and America's Promise (LEAP), high-impact practices such as First-Year Seminars, shared intellectual experiences, collaborative learning, intensive writing and research, and global learning (among others) have been repeatedly tested and proven to be beneficial to student learning (Association of American Colleges and Universities & National Leadership Council, 2007). Combining the Reacting pedagogy with the first-year seminar (FYS) experience, which itself has been shown to be an effective practice for student engagement and learning, returns impressive results (Higbee, 2008; Lightcap, 2008). This is also noticeable when Reacting is used as part of core or general curriculum classes that are often required of first-year students in subjects ranging from theology and philosophy to history and science.

Developed in the late 1990s by Mark C. Carnes, professor of history at Barnard College, Reacting won the 2004 Theodore Hesburgh Award for innovative pedagogy (TIAA-CREFF Institute, n.d.; Carnes, 2004). Reacting consists of units referred to as "games." As increasing numbers of professors use the pedagogy, it continues to be strengthened and improved by those teaching with Reacting as well as by those writing new games, and all those who participate in the yearly Reacting Institute at Barnard. This results in a form of constant peer review and improvements to the pedagogy. Students purchase the gamebook as they would a text, and this contains background information, schedules, instructions, and primary documents. As each game unfolds, students are immersed for extended periods (typically nine to twelve twice-weekly classroom sessions) in the contextual world in which the topical events take place. In the initial, or setup, phase, which typically lasts three class sessions, the professor leads discussions and lectures on the background and context of the historical period in which the game is set. During this phase, students complete primary and secondary source reading and begin additional research as necessary. At the end of this phase, students are assigned roles or characters from within the historical context and a set of victory objectives to achieve before the game ends. In some cases, they begin working with other characters/students to develop partners and build coalitions to support their ongoing objectives.

The second phase of every Reacting game unfolds as the students begin to apply and use the knowledge they have learned in the setup phase by interacting with one another, debating intrinsic ideas and issues from the period, all while using primary texts and documents as evidence for their arguments. In addition, the students take on increasing responsibility for the organization of class time. It is this feature of the Reacting pedagogy that provides students the chance to apply the knowledge to real-world problems. The discussions and debates at the center of the Reacting pedagogy provide students with problem-solving challenges that require both individual and team efforts. Developing students' ability to apply knowledge to new situations is a learning goal for many higher education institutions, and Reacting offers a key exercise for students to develop and demonstrate those skills. Each student is challenged to work individually but also to come together with classmates to solve important issues at hand; for instance, in the Athens game, students consider whether Socrates should be put to death or exiled, and in the India game, students untangle issues surrounding that country's emergence from colonialism in a way that will satisfy the needs of its many diverse citizens. Like case studies used in law and business classes, students must respond to unexpected ideas, strategies and news supplied by their peers or by faculty members thus reinforcing their critical thinking capacities.

Faculty members are provided with separate detailed materials (available through a free online collaborative forum), developed with great care, that include all the roles, texts, and other contextual information they need to manage the game. Students are expected to do additional research so as to understand how their character would think and to flesh out the topics they will have to address, pushing them to take more initiative in their own learning. In the first-year seminar or other introductory general education classes, students may not be comfortable with the research process. Thus, professors often take some additional time to build in basic research and referencing instructions, which might include how to find appropriate texts and cite them.

Every Reacting game emphasizes oral communication. Students give speeches on their assigned or chosen topics and respond to questions from fellow students in the give-and-take of the discussions. All game activities require students to move beyond simply looking up information. Papers are written in the first person (from the point of view of their role) and must be consistent with their character's knowledge during the time frame of the game. Such a scenario pushes students to engage actively in their own learning in order to complete additional research to prepare for the questions posed by their classmates and helps them focus on applying the information gleaned from their reading to the actual issues being addressed in the class forum. Plagiarism is reduced because of the first-person nature of the writing. Students are required to think critically about the problems and concerns they are addressing in a contextual manner and must analyze information rather than simply memorize it. Students must think on their feet when answering questions after giving their speeches. They use the information they have gathered in their formal speeches and papers, but also in response to unscripted, and perhaps unexpected, questions from their fellow students in opposing factions. Because there is both a written and oral component to class work, students begin to move from the notion of writing a paper for their teacher to conceiving of writing as a method of sharing and transmitting ideas.

But Reacting is not a scripted debate. In fact, although the games are carefully crafted to produce outcomes that are similar to those that occurred historically, they are not fixed, and thus it is possible for the class result to be ahistorical, which has been a concern of many faculty members. In defense of potentially anomalous outcomes, they provide excellent teaching opportunities for the final phase of the experience when the professor once again takes the reins of the class and explains not only what actually happened in the context explored (regardless of the actual class outcome), but clarifies specific events and instances that need more in-depth discussion. It also provides a moment to reflect on the contingencies of historical events and can be used to illustrate how many factors converge to produce any particular incident in history and its potential relevance to current events. Through Reacting, students learn that despite what may appear at a distance to be a predetermined outcome historical events are not, in fact, preordained.

Faculty who are reticent regarding the adoption of Reacting often express concern about carving out several weeks of class to investigate a particular topic in such detail, but there are always choices we make in class regarding what to cover. The interdisciplinary nature of the games and their intense skill building in areas important in the first-year curriculum usually convince even the most skeptical of faculty (Higbee, 2008). Reacting can be stressful for some students due to peer expectations of preparedness or because of the oral requirements, but no pedagogy serves all students. In traditional lectures there will be those who are bored, for example, or cannot keep up with the pace. It has been our experience and that of colleagues that a far greater percentage of students remain engaged in the class and turn in higher-level work than with a more traditional lecture format (Carnes, 2005; Higbee, 2008)

## Discussion

In today's world, student interaction and cooperation can be difficult to cultivate. Since nearly all Reacting games include several different factions (or teams) that need to work together to achieve broad goals and persuade others to support their objectives and views, faculty can address this obstacle by offering students guidance in group work situations, including how to develop workload distribution, communication plans, and conflict resolution. Attempts to engage students directly in their own learning and to work with others is sometimes stymied by their immersion in the world of technology, which often cuts them off from one another despite claims to the contrary by online social networking sites. Reacting requires teamwork, and instructors may need to take time to explain the basics of working in groups.

The emphasis on factions results in multiple perspectives and encourages students in the development of persuasive arguments providing an excellent structure from which to learn positive ways of engaging with the material and each other. Reacting pushes students to teach one another and engage in informal forms of peer review while honing their critical thinking skills. All of this—the teamwork, persuasion, and critical thinking—requires students to be active participants in their own learning. The professor's role is to guide students to appropriate resources and provide coaching to fully understand the material, and regarding writing, reasoned argument and oral presentation skills. The students, however, take the lead and drive the activity. While professors are responsible for assessments (written comments and grading) on speeches and papers, the students lead the class as actors in this unscripted play. Some students may struggle with the relative freedom of choosing topics to speak or write about or having to make that decision on short notice in response to debates in the classroom. Although this format is challenging for some students, they benefit from learning how to make decisions, that what they have to say or write matters, and that they must be prepared and respect due dates.

The Reacting library of games offers a wide array of topics that are commonly found in core curricula and first-year seminars and extend beyond use in history classes. They range chronologically from the classical period to contemporary times, and in geographical extension from Puritan New England to Imperial China (Carnes & Winship, 2005; Carnes & Gardner, 2005). In terms of subject matter, they vary from examining the politics of nation building to the development of scientific advances and from Confucian ideals to the issues surrounding the call for the right of women to vote, whether in Athens or New York City, making them ideal for many liberal arts and sciences classes. Although they often have historical settings, they are by no means adopted primarily by history classes (Higbee, 2008). Reacting games use classical texts and materials on a globally diverse array of topics and thus provide a strong foundation for both teaching and learning in terms of interdisciplinarity and critical thinking.

Reacting can be offered in different ways. One method is to offer a stand-alone first-year seminar, which is usually composed of three different games or topics that can be linked by geography, chronology, or thematic focus. A number of institutions have chosen to use Reacting for first-year seminars including Trinity (Hartford, Connecticut), Smith, McDaniel, and Barnard Colleges. The combinations chosen will reflect the focus of the faculty member teaching the class, the size of the class, or the curricular focus in the course as defined more generally. The many choices available show the flexibility of Reacting, but the true importance of the pedagogy is the focus on critical thinking, reading, writing and speaking that any game brings to the classroom.

At McDaniel College, a four-year, private college in central Maryland, Reacting has been promoted by the school's Center for Faculty Excellence and has been used in connection with the *first-year seminar* program since 2006, when the Athens game was first used in a seminar on critical thinking. Reacting promotes critical thinking in several ways. Students must read primary texts to figure out why they hold the beliefs that they do and how to argue for their ideas persuasively. Because there are always characters in each game with strong beliefs on one or two ideas (and not all), there are moments when persuasive speaking will be successful. Critical evaluation of texts and ideas is promoted through the preparation of speeches on various topics that emerge in the game. Each student must write at least two papers that require in-depth research, but since they are writing in the first person and must use only materials that are time appropriate, it is possible for the professor to gauge just how well they have understood the fundamental nature of the argument they are making, and so will their classmates who need to respond to their ideas.

At McDaniel, McKay typically chooses three games for her first-year seminar. These games are chosen thematically. Usually the Athens game is paired with two games currently in development, Constantine and the Council of Nicaea: 325 CE and The Second Crusade: The War Council of Acre, 1148 (Gaudette, in development; Henderson, in development). At St. John's University in Queens, New York, some individual faculty members have inserted a single Reacting game into the required first-year course entitled Discover New York. This course is designed to give students a foundation in the types of learning objectives outlined in the AACU's LEAP initiative such as critical thinking, research, writing, oral presentation. and information literacy, which are also the foundational curricular objectives of this class (Kuh, 2008). In Lazrus's classes, the game Patriots, Loyalists, and Revolution in New York City, 1775–1776 (Offutt, 2011) provides an opportunity to integrate the benefits of Reacting within the course's larger curricular objectives just outlined through her disciplinary perspective (archaeology, history, and anthropology). Having students read John Locke and Thomas Paine (among others) and use their ideas to guide the decisions New Yorkers made during the year leading up to the signing of the Declaration of Independence is challenging, but students learn to make reasoned arguments and support their ideas with textual and factual information, and that is the heart of critical thinking.

McDaniel has created its own assessment of the pedagogy's effectiveness in the first-year seminar program through a survey that was distributed to students with Reacting as their first-year seminar. Approximately seventy students responded to this survey. The findings indicate that students engage deeply with texts and ideas in these Reacting first-year seminar classes. Students are asked what skills they have learned in the course and are not offered a list from which to choose; McDaniel wants them to assess their own learning. Sixty-one percent noted that they developed their abilities in public speaking and oral communication. In terms of student engagement, 91 percent of the respondents indicated that they would recommend Reacting to a fellow student. In McKay's most recent first-year seminar (2011), when polled for the required extra class hour, the students unanimously requested to meet in the library to research and prepare for the next day's speeches. This result indicates that students understand that to be engaged requires work—research, analysis, critical thinking— and that learning occurs through active research and the use of information. Similar surveys at Eastern Michigan University (where Reacting was inserted into a US History survey) also point to increased student engagement and learning. There, 82 percent of students across three sections reported learning more through the games and 78 percent said they had worked harder in the class than they would have otherwise (Higbee, 2008). They also reported staying after class more frequently to discuss topics and to have met more often with their professor (Higbee, 2008).

Reacting is now used by over 250 institutions of higher education in the United States and abroad (Powers, Burney, & Carnes, 2009). The Reacting approach has been shown to promote the following learning outcomes, all of them LEAP objectives: inquiry and analysis; oral communication; critical thinking; integrative learning; and teamwork. In a survey conducted by the Reacting Advisory Board in 2009, faculty who had used Reacting in at least one class were asked to assess the pedagogy's potential to meet the student learning outcomes identified in the LEAP study. Specifically, faculty noted that Reacting to the Past was "very effective" or "effective" in producing student learning or skill development in the following areas: inquiry and analysis (96.2 percent), oral communication (96.1 percent), critical thinking (96.1 percent), integrative learning (92.4 percent), and teamwork (90.6 percent). Faculty also gave Reacting high marks in developing effective learning outcomes for written communication (86.75), knowledge of human cultures (88.7 percent), civic knowledge of democracy (86.5 percent), and ethical reasoning (75.5 percent) (Higbee, 2008; Stroessner, Beckerman, & Whittaker, 2009).

## Conclusion

It is difficult to transmit the excitement and energy of participation or the depth of critical thinking and analytical skills that students develop without experiencing this method of teaching first hand. Students find the Reacting pedagogy empowering. While intellectually challenging, this method opens new avenues for students to safely explore different points of view (Stroessner et al., 2009). Sometimes the experience can be unnerving, but most students rise to the occasion and appreciate the opportunity to take control of their learning process. Shy students often blossom and occasionally become leaders; strong students learn new organizational and collaborative skills. Students who never knew they were leaders suddenly discover they have that capacity. The following quotations are but two examples of student comments that may illuminate the value of Reacting as a powerful teaching method from the student perspective: "Reacting was completely unique in my college experience. In playing those games, the words of Gandhi, Socrates, and other historical figures became mine, transcending the academic distance to which I had grown accustomed and tapping into a very personal, intimate realm. Their thoughts, their histories, their biographies are real and alive in my mind" (Houle, 2006). Another student said, "Before this game I would think of the Revolution the way that the textbook describes. I never thought of the people and what problems they faced, why they made certain decisions, how this all was affecting them, how they were living, or small details that occurred during that period of time. Throughout the game I began thinking of how much this truly affected the people of that time. They had to worry about their homes, themselves, their families, jobs, property, everything" (Voula Gavalas, St. John's University, class reflections, March 31, 2009). The changes that professors observe in their students after they have had a Reacting class have led many early adopters of the pedagogy to reach out to their colleagues and help them see how powerful a teaching and learning tool this can be. We both believe it provides a strong method for delivering content, as well as for engaging students directly in their own learning.

Faculty interested in adopting RTTP usually attend the annual Barnard Reacting Institute held in June in New York City or regional workshops as preparation. Centers for teaching and learning are also instrumental in this process: they often offer short workshops run by faculty who have used RTTP or sponsor faculty to go the larger events. RTTP has proven to be an effective way to integrate experiential learning and role playing into the curriculum and as a method of reinforcing critical thinking, group work, and oral presentation in the classroom. It can provide a model for addressing the challenges and opportunities inherent in such pedagogical strategies across other disciplines.

RTTP is a pedagogy that brings students face-to-face with a historical moment. Students are forced to engage in texts, debates, and issues from these times. The surveys and other assessments that have been done (Stroessner et al., 2009) testify to Reacting to the Past's power to engage students. Pairing Reacting with other high-impact practices, for instance, the first-year seminar, makes for an even more powerful experience. Reacting corresponds well with AACU's LEAP learning objectives and goals for students and is an example of a high-impact practice that we hope will be used at more institutions of higher learning in the future.

In terms of assessment, Reacting provides multiple opportunities to evaluate students' abilities and knowledge across diverse skill sets and the application of knowledge in problem solving, writing, and critical thinking. If professors also include a reflective component (written, online, portfolio, or in class), it can be used to gauge the depth and breadth of student learning not only in terms of content, but also in terms of their personal growth and understanding of the world in which they live. This is particularly true if reflective exercises ask students to use what they have learned to connect to current events. For instance, after discussing the merits of "just war" in the Second Crusade game, McKay asks her first-year students on the final exam to think about the wars in Iraq and Afghanistan through the lens of the ideas of "just war." Administrators who visit Reacting classes often are astonished by the level of interaction among students, the depth and intensity of discussion, and the overall engagement with the subject matter demonstrated by the students. This is truly active and engaged learning at its best.

## REFERENCES

Arum, R., & Roksa, J. (2011). *Academically adrift: limited learning on college campuses.* Chicago, IL: University of Chicago Press.

Association of American Colleges and Universities, & National Leadership Council (US). (2007). *College learning for the new global century: A report from the National Leadership Council for Liberal Education and America's Promise.* Washington, DC: Association of American Colleges and Universities.

Berrett, D. (2011, September 25). Which core matters more? Differences in definitions of quality lead to new debates over the importance of teaching practical skills versus specific knowledge. *Chronicle of Higher Education.*

Retrieved from http://chronicle.com/article/In-Improving-Higher-Education /129134/

Bok, D. C. (2006). *Our underachieving colleges: A candid look at how much students learn and why they should be learning more.* Princeton, NJ: Princeton University Press.

Carnes, M. C. (2004). The liminal classroom. *Chronicle of Higher Education,* 51(7), B7.

Carnes, M. C. (2005). Inciting Speech. *Change,* 32(2), 6–11.

Carnes, M., & Gardner, D. K. (2005). *Confucianism and the succession crisis of the Wanli emperor* (3rd ed.). New York, NY: Pearson Longman.

Carnes, M. C., & Winship, M. P. (2005). *The trial of Anne Hutchinson: Liberty, law, and intolerance in Puritan New England: Reacting to the Past.* Upper Saddle River, NJ: Pearson.

Gaudette, H. (in development). *The Second Crusade: The War Council of Acre, 1148.* Retrieved from http://reacting.barnard.edu/second-crusade-war -council-acre-1148

Gorton, W., & Havercroft, J. (2012). Using historical simulations to teach political theory. *Journal of Political Science Education,* 8(1), 50–68. doi:10.1080/15512169.2012.641399

Henderson, D. (in development). *Constantine and the Council of Nicaea: Defining orthodoxy and heresy in Christianity, 325 CE.* Retrieved from http://reacting.barnard.edu/constantine-and-council-nicaea-defining-orthodoxy -and-heresy-christianity-325-ce

Higbee, M. D. (2008). How Reacting to the Past games "made me want to come to class and learn": An assessment of the Reacting Pedagogy at EMU, 2007–08. In J. L. Bernstein (Ed.), *Making learning visible: The scholarship of teaching and learning at EMU.* Ypsilanti: EMU. Retrieved from http:// commons.emich.edu/sotl

Houle, A. (2006). Reacting to "Reacting." *Change,* 38(4), 52.

Kuh, G. (2008). *High-impact educational practices: What they are, who has access to them, and why they matter.* Washington DC: Association of American Colleges and Universities.

Lane, D. C. (1995). On a resurgence of management simulations and games. *Journal of the Operational Research Society,* 46(5), 604–625.

Lightcap, T. (2008). *Reacting to the Past: Extended simulations and the learning experience in political science.* Paper presented at the American Political Science Association Teaching and Learning Conference, San Jose, CA.

Offutt, W. (2011). *Patriots, loyalists, and revolution in New York City, 1775– 1776.* Boston, MA: Longman.

Powers, R. G., Burney, J. M., & Carnes, M. C. (2009). *Reacting to the Past: A new approach to student engagement and to enhancing general education* (White Paper). New York, NY: Teagle Foundation.

Stroessner, S. J., Beckerman, L. S., & Whittaker, A. (2009). All the world's a stage? Consequences of a role-playing pedagogy on psychological factors and writing and rhetorical skill in college undergraduates. *Journal of Educational Psychology, 101,* 605–620.

TIAA-CREFF Institute. (n.d.). TIAA-CREF Institute—TIAA-CREF Theodore M. Hesburgh Award Winner—2004. Retrieved from http://www.tiaa -crefinstitute.org/awards/hesburgh/2004/2004.html

Welcome to National Model United Nations. (n.d.). Retrieved from http://www .nmun.org/ncca.html